NEW PERSPECTIVES ON THE SOUTH

Charles P. Roland, General Editor

Daughters of Canaan

A Saga of
Southern Women

MARGARET RIPLEY WOLFE

THE UNIVERSITY PRESS OF KENTUCKY

Scholarly publisher for the Commonwealth,
serving Bellarmine College, Berea College, Centre
College of Kentucky, Eastern Kentucky University,
The Filson Club, Georgetown College, Kentucky
Historical Society, Kentucky State University,
Morehead State University, Murray State University,
Northern Kentucky University, Transylvania University,
University of Kentucky, University of Louisville,
and Western Kentucky University.

Editorial and Sales Offices: Lexington, Kentucky 40508-4008

Library of Congress Cataloging-in-Publication Data

Wolfe, Margaret Ripley, 1947-
   Daughters of Canaan : a saga of southern women / Margaret Ripley
Wolfe.
      p.   cm.—(New perspectives on the South)
   Includes bibliographical references and index.
   ISBN 0-8131-1902-2 (cloth : acid-free paper).—ISBN
0-8131-0837-3 (paper : acid-free paper)
   1. Women—Southern States—History. 2. Sex role—Southern States—
History. I. Title. II. Series.
HQ1438.S63W65   1995
305.4'0975—dc20   94-30150

for my daughter
Stephanie Ripley Wolfe
and the future of southern women
that she and her generation represent

Contents

Illustrations follow page 84

Editor's Preface

No tenet in the southern mythology has been more pervasive or persistent than that of the existence of the distinctive southern woman. The famed northern abolitionist traveler and observer Frederick Law Olmsted found little to praise about the pre-Civil War South, yet he was moved to say that the region's women were "unexcelled in the world for every quality which commands respect, admiration, and love." A distinguished modern historian of nonsouthern origin, Professor Richard N. Current, whose studies lead him to conclude that in its basic values the South at last agrees with the rest of the nation, utters a "Vive la différence!" on southern women, along with two other institutions that are frequently associated with southern womanhood: southern speech and southern cuisine.

The image of the mythological southern woman has run the gamut from that of the honeyed and helpless "southern beauty" through that of the devoted and gracious "southern lady" (the eternal Melanie Wilkes) and the vain, headstrong, and manipulative "southern belle" (the eternal Scarlett O'Hara) to that of the resourceful and resolute southern "iron [or steel] magnolia." Margaret Ripley Wolfe draws upon two decades of serious study and reflection, and a lifetime of experience and observation as a southern woman, to produce an insightful and vivid, frequently startling, and sometimes shocking work of revisionist feminine history. Affirming parts of the myth, challenging others, and modifying still others, she evokes a picture of a flesh-and-blood woman who has emerged from the historically patriarchal society of the region to become her own person in the truest sense of the expression.

Because southern women have traditionally been both ultra-southern and ultra-feminine, the present study is essential to "New Perspectives on the South," a series intended to give a fresh and comprehensive view of the region's history. Each volume is designed to comprise a synthesis of the outstanding scholarship on the subject, reinforced by the author's research in the sources and shaped by her or his interpretation.

Charles P. Roland

Acknowledgments

Since the early 1970s I have witnessed the emergence and development of women's history as a specialty, and I have become acquainted with many of its finest practitioners. Along the way I have enjoyed the company of first-rate women historians. The manner in which they have acquitted themselves, their presentations at professional meetings, and their publications have contributed immensely to my own career. Knowing them has enriched my life. Jo Ann Carrigan of the University of Nebraska at Omaha has often provided advice and encouragement; she has been a mentor and a friend for two decades. Martha H. Swain, Texas Woman's University, gave the manuscript on which this book is based a thorough reading and meticulously analyzed its content. Her insights and recommendations significantly improved my work. I deeply appreciate her keen intellect, her objectivity, and perhaps above all the down-to-earth balance and sense of humor that she brings to the study of history and to life. I also want to thank four others for taking time to discuss with me their respective opinions of the proposed title of this work: Julia Kirk Blackwelder, professor and department chair, Texas A & M University; Catherine Clinton of Riverside, Connecticut, a former professor at Harvard and Brown Universities, now an independent scholar and freelance writer; Jacquelyn Dowd Hall, professor of history and director of the Oral History Program, University of North Carolina, Chapel Hill; and Marjorie Spruill Wheeler, a professor at the University of Southern Mississippi.

Historians cannot function without the keepers of books, documents, and photographs and the caretakers of manuscripts and artifacts. Ever mindful of my heavy dependence and continual reliance on librarians and archivists as a class, I would like to mention four among them who have contributed immensely to my work on this project as well as many others: Edith Keys, longtime reference librarian at East Tennessee State University's Sherrod Library, now retired; Beth Hogan, a natural-born detective, who presently is in charge of interlibrary loan there; and Helen Whittaker, librarian, and Julana C. Croy, library assistant, at ETSU/UT at Kingsport. Helen and Julana have routinely responded to my myriad and frequent requests, some of which must have seemed more than a little peculiar to them. In any event they have cheerfully indulged me. Likewise I recognize the staffs of these federal agencies and governmental units for their photographic assistance: the Library of Congress, the National Archives and Records Administration, the National Aeronautical and Space Administration, and the United States Department of Justice. I also appreciate the services rendered by Nancy Disher Baird, Kentucky Library, Western Kentucky University, and Stephen D. Cox, Tennessee State Museum. Tony Marion of Blountville, Tennessee, an indefatigable collector of published and unpublished materials pertaining to the American South, has graciously shared items from his private holdings.

Although I have enjoyed the support of females and males alike, this book, which deals with *southern women*, owes its existence largely to *southern men*. My dear friend and former classmate Thomas H. Appleton, Jr., managing editor of the Kentucky Historical Society, recommended me for this project; he has never been too busy to lend moral support and advice throughout my career. On occasions too numerous to mention he has called my attention to bibliography that I might otherwise have overlooked. The editorial skills that he exercised on an earlier version of this manuscript rendered it a far better product than it would otherwise have been. One of my colleagues at East Tennessee State University, Dr. Alvin Tirman of the Mathematics Department, a New Yorker by birth but a southerner by choice, employed his proofreading skills to my considerable advantage. I value both his friendship and his intellect more than mere words could ever say. I have been especially blessed by the unflagging encouragement of Charles P. Roland, editor of the New Perspectives on the South series. Apparently he never lost interest in this topic or faith in me; at times I must have taxed him sorely. Likewise I fully acknowledge the assistance of Dr. Ronnie M. Day, who as chairman of the Department of History at East Tennessee State University since 1991 has worked diligently to create and foster an environment conducive to collegiality and scholarship; it was his advocacy that secured for me a noninstructional assignment so that I could complete this book. Finally, for almost three decades my husband, David E. Wolfe, whose own employment and professional interests rest with private industry and engineering, has tolerated my personal eccentricities—and I, his—while I have pursued a career as a professional historian. Together through it all we seem to have produced a relatively normal daughter, Stephanie, and brought her, our only child, almost to adulthood.

Prologue

For thousands of years the eyes of women have watched the sun rise over the misty South, but the southern woman of myth and legend was born almost four centuries ago when the English planted the first permanent colonies in North America, and she survives as the twentieth century nears its end. I am privileged to chronicle her story. It is one of hardships, endurance, fortitude, triumphs, and, above all, survival—a testament to the extraordinary lives of ordinary people. I write of real warm-blooded women, untainted and unaffected by scholarly digressions, females who have had no truck with passing interpretive schemes and would have found them amusing if they had taken the time to consider them.[1] In mythology, southern women appear vapid or frivolous; in reality, they epitomize strength. By my definition they are females indigenous to states in which the practice of slavery persisted until the Civil War or nonindigenous females who have spent significant portions of their lives in the South, often making lasting contributions to the region.

The poet James Dickey and the painter Hubert Shuptrine chose the first city of Canaan that fell to Joshua as the emblematic title of their artistic panorama *Jericho: The South Beheld.* In another time and place the biblical King David had offered up "a new song" of praise for his Lord "*that* our daughters *may be* as corner stones, polished *after* the similitude of a palace" (Psalm 144). In a manner not unlike that of the ancient Hebrew psalmist, the contemporary southern bard lifted his voice in a paean to women. "We love women here," Dickey wrote; "they give us hope, and above all they give us grace."[2] Dickey and Shuptrine were hardly the first and surely will not be the last to liken the American South to the promised land of the Hebrews. Biblical analogies have come naturally to Dixie, and just as the scriptures are divided into two parts, so is the history of the South. Whether Old or New, the patriarchy has been as omnipresent in the culture below the Mason-Dixon line as in the sacred writings of the Jews and the Christians.

I, too, have been intrigued by the imagery as well as the irony of biblical stories and southern history. This work therefore bears the title *Daughters of Canaan: A Saga of Southern Women*. Patriarchy, so intrinsic to the Judeo-Christian tradition, has had a long-running heyday in the American South; but historic forces have gradually undermined its overriding influence on feminine lives in the region. In a figurative sense, it seems not inappropriate to suggest that southern women, by design or by default, have often found themselves shackled to pedestals just as surely as Jehovah's chosen people had been enslaved by the pharaohs. Likewise, historical southern women, not unlike the biblical Hebrews, have spent considerable time wandering in the proverbial wilderness and looking for the promised land. If in the late twentieth century they have actually glimpsed that "land of milk and honey," it has been both overwhelming and exhilarating. I tend to view the sexes in history as men and women in tandem, with men more often in the lead, but not always. This seems to me a truism, not that it reflects the world as I personally would have it. I prefer cooperative teams, working alongside each other, full well realizing that this is rarely the case. Those who are satisfied with circumstances turn to yesteryear, while the *repressed* and *oppressed* await tomorrow. "Canaan" symbolizes promise, and for activist women in particular, the South has been as much promise as fulfillment. Presumably the South has a future as well as a past.

The eminent historian Gerda Lerner, a pioneer in women's studies, draws a distinction between "patriarchy" and "paternalism." Writing in *The Creation of Patriarchy*, she declares, "*Patriarchy* in its wider definition means the manifestation and institutionalization of male dominance over women and children in the family and the extension of male dominance over women in society in general." She contends that although "*Patriarchy . . .* implies that men hold power in all the important institutions of society and women are deprived of access to power, . . . it does *not* imply that women are either totally powerless or totally deprived of rights, influence, and resources." Lerner identifies "*Paternalism*" as "a subset of patriarchal relations." "*Paternalism*, or more accurately *Paternalistic Dominance*," she maintains, "describes the relationship of a dominant group, considered superior, to a subordinate group, considered inferior, in which the dominance is mitigated by mutual obligations and reciprocal rights." Although a father might hold "absolute power over all the members of his household," they could expect him to honor "the obligation of economic support and protection."[3] Dictionaries offer less precise delineations between the terms. "Patriarchy" and "Paternalism" have coexisted in the South, and I have chosen to employ the terms interchangeably.

Vestiges of the patriarchy that was established during the colonial era, reinforced during the antebellum era, and eroded but not eradicated by the

Civil War and Reconstruction have survived even into the twentieth century. During the 1930s, the historian Julia Cherry Spruill observed that "the situation of gentlemen in the southern colonies more nearly resembled the Old Testament characters than did that of fathers of families in England, for they were lords and masters, not only of wives, children, and servants, but likewise of bond servants and slaves." The patriarch ruled over them all, and his word was absolute.[4] That inveterate colonial penman William Byrd II used the biblical analogy to describe his own circumstances: "Like one of the Patriarchs, I have my flocks and my herds, my bondsmen & bond women and every sort of trade amongst my own servants so that I live in a kind of Independence of every one but Providence."[5]

Elaborate public social rituals and the genuine affection that existed in many private male-female relationships took the edge off some of the harsher aspects of what in the more extreme instances amounted to masculine tyranny. The historian Arthur M. Schlesinger, Sr., in an analysis of seventeenth-century English manuals of etiquette, found that "for the Southern aristocracy this literature provided a fairly consistent chart of behavior—something to aspire to if not always to attain." Emulating "the ancient ideals of Christian chivalry," the gentleman strove for "valor, probity, justice, piety and courtesy" and expected the ladies to be modest, chaste, godly, and compassionate. "A gentlewoman should refer all offers of marriage to her parents and after wedlock tender her husband unquestioning obedience." If her husband strayed, she was to pretend ignorance of his infidelities; if he was ill-tempered, she was not to provoke him; and if he drank to excess, she should view this as a balance to her own inadequacies.[6]

Given this masculine-contrived mind-set, the behavior of the southern woman who deviated from expectations reflected adversely on her male relatives. The historian Bertram Wyatt-Brown in his highly acclaimed study of southern honor suggests that southern men feared women. "Women *were* dangerous," he argued; "they could present a husband, father, or brother with an illegitimate child and thereby cast doubt on the legitimacy of the line and desecrate the inmost temple of male self-regard."[7] Such views were not peculiar to the Old South. In his landmark analysis *The Mind of the South*, Wilbur J. Cash argued forcefully that male notions of southern honor had not been vanquished by military defeat in the Civil War and that they persisted in the New South; indeed they may have been sanctified by the spilled blood of thousands of rebel soldiers.[8]

Southern patriarchs, then, like their Old Testament forebears, set exceedingly high standards to which their women should aspire; and the unsung women of the South most assuredly served as their region's cornerstones. More of them than not have been on a first-name basis with hardships and suffering, but their lives have often possessed a day-to-day richness infused with measures of joy and happiness. Women's strength and labor have provided the superstructure for the family and, in turn, the region. This is a fact conspicuously absent in many, if not most, of the historical treatments of the South. It is likewise distorted and obscured by such slick, superficial, and commercially successful volumes as Florence King's *Southern Ladies and Gentlemen* or Sharon McKern's tape-recorded tour of southern womanhood, *Redneck Mothers, Good Ol' Girls, and Other Southern Belles.* Add to them *A Southern Belle Primer: Or, Why Princess Margaret Will Never Be a Kappa Kappa Gamma* by Marlyn Schwartz and her more recent *New Times in the Old South: Or Why Scarlett's in Therapy and Tara's Going Condo.*[9]

Such titles continue to attract media attention and lend sustenance to stereotypes that characterize the region's women as charming and captivating yet weak and vaporous creatures. Meanwhile, on another front, scholars have been systematically disassembling the mythological "southern lady" and her adolescent soul mate the "southern belle." Their findings indicate clearly that females in Dixie have often been charming but rarely weak and vaporous. The year 1970 marked an especially important watershed in the professional study of southern women. On the very cusp of a segment of the American women's movement popularly designated Women's Liberation, Anne Firor Scott's *The Southern Lady: From Pedestal to Politics, 1830-1930* appeared.[10] Although such individuals as Julia Cherry Spruill and A. Elizabeth Taylor had previously made valuable contributions, Scott's timely and seminal work heralded a new era.[11] It signified a reawakening of interest in southern women as historical figures, and it inspired graduate students as well as veteran scholars to undertake major projects. The last two decades or so have witnessed a veritable avalanche of scholarship either directly or indirectly relevant to southern women's history.

For approximately twenty years I have seriously studied and researched women's history.[12] *Daughters of Canaan: A Saga of Southern Women* is the fruit of that labor. Of necessity this book relies on the impressive work of others as well as my own efforts. That such an undertaking was possible is a testimonial to the variety and richness of existing scholarship. The fine quality of much of the historiography pertaining to the South and southern women served as an inspiration. Dame Cicely Veronica Wedgwood, a prominent student of seventeenth-century English history, once commented on a dilemma that routinely plagues the historical profession. Confronted by ignorance and the inability to interpret data with absolute accuracy, the historian, Wedgwood maintained, should be overwhelmed by humility. She added that to a greater degree than any other writer the historian is "in bondage to [the] material" that is being scrutinized.[13] That goes doubly for one who is engaged in synthesis and interpretation. Therefore I can only hope that the historians on whom I have relied have been correct and that I have understood their work and presented it faithfully.

This book will certainly not be the last word on southern women, but it marks the first serious attempt by a professional historian to synthesize existing scholarship and interpret the experience of southern women across the centuries. In a sense it is historical pentimento, the peeling away of layers of the past to allow the images and contours of southern women's history to emerge on the canvas of time. I fancy it to be somewhat in the vein of two landmark treatments of American women that I admire a great deal—Nancy Woloch's *Women and the American Experience* and Sara M. Evans's *Born for Liberty: A History of Women in America*.[14]

Throughout the region's and their history, the majority of southern women have held firmly to tradition while a small but vigorous minority, capable of envisaging a brave new tomorrow, have challenged the status quo. The mantle of *victimization* falls all too readily on the majority, for they apparently have neither been able nor willing to extricate themselves from circumstances in order to shape their own destiny or to influence their region. Furthermore, paternalism may indeed have been more firmly entrenched in the American South than anywhere else in the country. Although it has at times been fashionable among some feminists, it is too simple, too easy, to write southern women off as victims or pawns. Even worse, it is probably incorrect, for women have often been knowing and agreeable accessories to men in history. Truly they have been acted upon, but they have also been actresses. Another stratagem widely employed in women's studies, *empowerment*, has a tendency to assign females too much autonomy, to overestimate potential autonomy, or to exaggerate the influence of activists; it seems to have had slight impact on the scholarly treatment of southern women.[15]

The understanding of southern women will permit neither blind devotion to New England models of feminism—indeed to no other existing models of feminism—nor fastidious commitment to only the grand historical schemes of war, diplomacy, and politics.[16] Coming to terms with females below the Mason-Dixon line demands attention to the subtleties and nuances of women's private worlds of life and work in addition to the dynamics of the public arenas of their eras. The females and their history are products of both time and place. Any tendency toward the typecasting of southern women is treacherous business for a historian. They are, after all, human; and underneath that mien of piety—natural in some and affected in others—a goodly number of them have possessed a raucous sense of humor, which has served them well in coping with southern men. Being pious, proper, and pretty in public has sometimes given way to remarkable frankness, ribaldry, and earthiness in private. Southerners, both men and women, count among themselves large numbers of passionate and sensual people, and it poses no historiographical risk to point out that southern men and women generally find each other appealing. With geography as a backdrop and having a story line interwoven with strands of time and place, this study examines critical eras, outstanding personalities and groups, and prevailing trends and themes in women's history of the American South. It unveils a collage of diversity rent with shared experiences within a heterogeneous but common national setting.

Researching the topic of southern women has been a personal, rewarding, and sometimes painful journey, for I am one of those venerable creatures by virtue of ancestry, birth, education, and long residence on southern soil. It is the heritage bestowed by my mother, Gertrude Blessing Ripley, and all the grands- and greats- that preceded her; it is the same heritage that I share with my sister, Pamela Dawn Ripley; and it is this legacy that I bequeath to my daughter, Stephanie Ripley Wolfe, to whom this book is dedicated.

The third of January 1993 was the last day of mortal existence for Hester Cordelia Davidson Blessing, my eighty-five-year-old maternal grandmother, the last of my surviving grandparents. Having outlived her husband by almost seventeen years, she presided as the ruling matriarch of the clan. Nine children, nineteen grandchildren, and twenty-five great-grandchildren survived her. During the weeks immediately preceding her death my grandmother disposed of her chickens. She had raised them her whole life, never underestimating the importance of butter-and-egg money; for it had helped to sustain her family in more-difficult years. She reportedly played the piano and sang hymns at a daughter's home during her last month. She distributed gifts, as was her annual custom, to all the members of her large family who came to pay homage to her on Christmas Day. Around New Year's she visited her ninety-two-year-old sister, confined to a nursing home, one last time, asking another daughter and granddaughter to return her yet again to the room—after she had already said her good-byes—to embrace her sister. With all of these obligations satisfied, she died quickly of a massive heart attack; and she was laid to rest in the family cemetery within a few hundred yards of the house that she had occupied for most of her adult life. Clinch Mountain, in her native Scott County, Virginia, located in the southwestern corner of the state, stands as a sentinel over her grave.

My grandmother's life was unique in the sense that any life is, but it is also symbolic of the lives of many southern women. Hers was hard in some respects, but one marked by enormous strength and quiet dignity. She was rooted in a strong rural tradition, and she was sustained by her abiding sense of family and a deep religious faith derived from evangelical Protestantism. Her father died in a logging accident approximately three months before she was born; she married young and gave birth to the first of her nine children when she was seventeen; this and the subsequent eight births occurred at home where she was attended by a physician. She took an avid interest in the full range of her family's activities, whether inspecting newborns; greeting the soldiers returning from Vietnam, Saudi Arabia, or some other foreign land; rushing to the hospital when calamities struck a relative; or attending the burials of three sons-in-law who preceded her in death. Although never employed away from her home and farm and never receiving a paycheck, she worked slavishly alongside her husband to make a living. It would never have occurred to either of them to do otherwise; "welfare" simply did not exist in their personal lexicon and was anathema to them when they heard of it from others.

Although from the highlands of the Upper South and hardly to the manor born, both my maternal grandmother and my paternal one, Eva Parker Ripley, were southern ladies in the truest sense. Southwestern Virginia and northeastern Tennessee are far removed from the Mississippi Delta, which the historian James C. Cobb has labeled "the most southern place on earth."[17] Nonetheless, this mountainous section, too, is the South; and the image of the "southern lady" has permeated even Appalachia, for that image was not and is not necessarily restricted to the gentry or to the cotton belt. Ideals and imagery have affected the lives of women—north, south, east, and west—and routinely enter into scholarly discourse. Such phrases as the "cult of domesticity," the "cult of true womanhood," the concept of the "gentle tamer," "the new American woman," "the feminine mystique," "the total woman," "superwoman," *and* "the southern lady" are dress forms to which the women in history are matched. It is wise to challenge these models—these intellectual constructs that we use in attempting to come to grips with the past. Whatever resemblance they have to reality, they are sometimes merely historical conveniences; once established, however, they can become traps.

Southern women seem especially susceptible to mythmaking, for the American South itself has too frequently been regarded as a wasteland waiting to be redefined by such wide-ranging individuals as abolitionists, travelers, soldiers, carpetbaggers, suffragists, civil-rights workers, journalists, and literary figures. The South possesses comforting strains of continuity, but it is also a swirling array of kaleidoscopic images. Few would deny that today the contemporary South is generally a more humane place than it was a century or even half a century ago, but perverse aberrations still occur. Whether the victims of cruelty or the beneficiaries of chivalry, southern women—as well as their sisters elsewhere in the United States—have been and remain second-class citizens. Still, southern women have shared in such feminist gains at the national level as suffrage, affirmative action, and reproductive freedom.

The myriad pieces of the mosaic of the *South* and the *southerner* have produced such a distorted image that we native-born southerners are sometimes confused about who we are and what the South is. The South has often been depicted as the domicile of good ol' boys and good ol' girls. In his 1974 presidential address before the Southern Historical Association, George B. Tindall suggested that the South is "the biggest single WASP nest this side of the Atlantic."[18] Its trademark has been red necks, white socks, and Blue Ribbon beer, if not white bed sheets, pointed hats, and burning crosses. The film actors Peter Fonda, Jack Nicholson, and Dennis Hopper in *Easy Rider* and Burt Reynolds and Jon Voight in *Deliverance* have fictionalized its bloody and perverted violence and splashed it across the silver screen; journalists have not lacked for realistic examples. The result is, in the words of the historians Edward D.C. Campbell, Jr., and Jack Temple Kirby respectively, "the celluloid South" and "media-made Dixie."[19]

The quintessential symbol of the southern lady remains firmly fixed in the southern mind and in American popular culture. Even as the twentieth century nears its end, she still impedes the development of southern women. When necessary, conservatives, reactionaries, and bigots have escorted her into the public arena to censure female troublemakers. Southern women activists have abused her, used her, and been occasionally amused by her. Still, through the centuries the southern lady, ageless and omnipresent, stands watch over her homeland. Like the apparitions of long-lost Indian braves, displaced Cavaliers, and the Confederate dead, the souls of hellfire-and-damnation evangelists, and the eerie skeletons of venomous demagogues and enchained Negroes, she belongs to Dixie's pantheon. While southerners have erected statues evidentiary to the physical existence of distinguished men, their fallen warriors, and the Lost Cause, the ephemeral southern lady occupies an elusive but equally real spiritual dimension in the southern mind. Suspended above the sin and shame of both the Old South and the New South, she endures, safe in her goodness, steeled by her suffering, and sedated by the ever-present fragrance of the magnolia blossoms.

Meanwhile the historical southern woman has possessed a triple handicap beginning with the stigma sometimes associated with being southern—that is, the full weight of southern history, mythology, and legends. This in turn is exacerbated by the limitations of being female and by the perpetual constraining images of the belle and the lady. Finally she is hamstrung by the racial question, applicable directly to the experience of African-American and Native-American women and somewhat less directly but just as relevantly to white females. Gender is a common denominator, but it does not transcend race, class, point of view, and a host of other factors. Regionalism in a sense has made women distinctive as southern belles and ladies, but the challenges of their everyday lives have almost guaranteed versatility. Shirley Abbott recalled in *Womenfolks: Growing Up down South* that her mother and the other females she knew as a child were farm women. "They were not innocent or submissive or delicately constituted," she wrote, "nor afraid of balky cows or chicken hawks. It took them approximately two hours to transform a live rooster into Sunday dinner. They could reason with a mule and shoot a gun." "But they also knew how to take hold of a baby and what to say to a weeping two-year-old."[20]

Much of the tenor of women's history and the region's has been derived from slavery and the rural lifestyles of the South, a legacy that has carried over into the twentieth century. Three-fourths of the families of the antebellum South owned no slaves, and the majority of slave owners possessed fewer than twenty chattels. Nonetheless the minority at the top of the heap determined to a considerable extent the nature of southern culture. Plantation mistresses constituted an intricate component of the productive and reproductive units of slave society, those island communities in the great expanse of the southern landscape. Isolation and economic bondage made homes, as these women knew them, dramatically different from those of their northern counterparts. Male heads of the plantation households dominated extended families of wives, children, and slaves and exercised a paternalism more far-reaching than that north of the Mason-Dixon line.[21] The degree of this paternalism and the pattern that it established intensified the subordination of women, making it all the more difficult for southern females to escape from positions of inferiority.

Yet with all of this, southern women have not been completely unlike their northern sisters; they share the commonality of a life cycle that encompasses the reproductive years from menarche to menopause, and they are all Americans. It defies both logic and reality, however, to attempt to force the historical southern woman into developmental lockstep with her northern counterpart. But just as females north of the Mason-Dixon line knew the constraints of privatism almost from the beginning of the American experience and throughout most of the nineteenth century, so did their southern sisters—to an even greater degree and for a longer period of time. The persistence of the frontier and, in its wake, long-lived rural traditions, the extensive kinship networks with their deference to paternalism, and the impact of evangelical Protestantism in sustaining the patriarchy effectively denied southern women the possibility of significant access to public life prior to the twentieth century. Whatever tenuous flexibility a few may have enjoyed hardly altered that fundamental fact.

Still, southerners, both male and female—black, red, and white—seem to have possessed a profound sense of place, deep attachment to the land, and loyalty to their region. Leaving their homeland has proved a wrenching experience for Native Americans, forcibly dislodged and dispatched on the "trail of tears," as well as for many white and black migrants of the great southern diaspora, which has not received the attention that it merits. The South is a region of breathtaking beauty characterized by such diverse geography as the rugged mountains of the Southern Appalachian chain and the bayou country of the Gulf Coastal Plain. It is confronted in the twentieth century with the consequences of progress, including the debilitating impact of industrial pollution and urban sprawl. Just as the varying strains of Negro spirituals, Appalachian ballads, the blues, jazz, rock-'n'-roll, Cajun, country-and-western, bluegrass, and protest songs resonate from the region, so, too, does a cacophony of female voices. Under the rubric of "southern," which suggests homogeneity, there has been considerable pluralism. It encompasses Native Americans, traditional white Anglo-Saxon Protestants, blacks, the old Spanish and French elements, "new" immigrants and their descendants as well as other ethnic groups, and the "boat people" of Asia and the Caribbean. They are plopped down in cities, on farms, and in the suburbs where they engage in varied economic pursuits; class striates their ranks. All of this and more is, in fact, southern women's sphere. What follows is their history.

ONE

❧

In the Beginning

During the seventeenth and early eighteenth centuries the American South witnessed a fundamental social, political, economic, and environmental transformation. European white males in the Chesapeake area and elsewhere in the southern colonies began the process of subduing the Native-American cultures that they encountered and imposing their will on this new land and its people.[1] The dominant English as well as other ethnic groups carried with them to North America considerable cultural baggage which formed the basis of the New World that they subsequently created. As a creole society took shape on land that Europeans considered virgin, old familiar ideas about gender relations proved amazingly resilient.

Although transplanted Englishmen found it possible to adjust their views temporarily as circumstances warranted, they rarely deviated over the long haul from what they considered the tried and true. In the southern colonies, they relegated women—red, white, and black—to perhaps even more pronounced positions of inferiority. For Indian females, this meant a devaluation of the status they had enjoyed in their traditional societies; for whites the continuation and, in some instances, the exacerbation of circumstances that had affected them in Europe; and for blacks, transplanted to America against their will, seemingly endless servitude and degradation. Elaborate philosophical arguments buttressed these emerging circumstances and, perhaps for white women, ameliorated the harsher aspects of a patriarchal order, because opportunities abounded in the Chesapeake and also in the other southern colonies for white women as well as men to better themselves socially and economically. For these females the measure of their success usually rested on either the accidents of their births and who their fathers were or on the matrimonial arrangements they made or had made for them and the status of their husbands. This, however, was hardly the case for Native-American and African-American women.

What historians know of initial encounters between European men and Native-American women is almost all from the perspective of the conquerors. If some of their accounts are taken literally, notes the historian Theda Perdue even as she challenges them, then Spaniards subjected the women at their mercy to rape as well as other forms of violence and abuse, whereas the English found themselves beseiged by native women and almost overwhelmed by their uninvited attentions. According to popular legend, the venerable Pocahontas rescued John Smith, married John Rolfe, and saved Jamestown; and if Smith is to be believed, on one occasion thirty naked young women, covered only partially by a few green leaves in front and behind, set upon him in his house. "These Nymphes more tormented him [than] ever," he complained in third person, "with crowding, pressing, and hanging about him, most tediously crying, Love you not me? Love you not me?"[2]

The combination of forwardness and nakedness hardly rendered the native women physically unattractive. More than one European thought to mention not only their pretty bodies but also the fact that Indian women seemed to do all of the work. The historian Edmund S. Morgan has written: "Nearly any activity that could be designated as work at all was left to the women. They were the principal means of production in Indian Virginia." When a man took a wife, which meant the exchange of goods, he expected her to support him. "He could make canoes, weapons, and weirs without losing his dignity," Morgan explains, "but the only other labor he ordinarily engaged in was clearing fields for planting, and the method employed [girdling the trees and burning brush] made this less than arduous." When the next growing season came, however, "the women worked the ground between the trees, using a crooked stick as a hoe and planting corn, beans, squash, and melons all together in little hills."[3] Superficially accurate though this statement may be, it fails to take into account the carefully defined gender roles and the relatively separate but nonetheless significant status of women in Native-American societies. It is true that women performed most of the labor, but they also had acknowledged title to the land they tilled, the houses they occupied, and the children they bore.

Captain Arthur Barlow[e], a participant in Sir Walter Raleigh's first expedition of 1584, had commented extensively and favorably on the wife of the Indian "king's" brother and the women around her, describing her as "very well favored, of mean stature, and very bashful." As for her dress, "she had on her back a long cloak of leather, with the fur side next to her body, and before her a piece of the same. About her forehead she had a band of white coral. . . . In her ears she had bracelets of pearl hanging down on her middle . . . and those were of the bigness of good peas." The "rest of her women of the better sort" wore copper pendants in their ears.[4]

Barlow also reported that the Indians were "of color yellowish, and their hair black for the most part, and yet we saw children that had very fine auburn and chestnut colored hair." The latter may have been the issue of native women and European sailors who had been shipwrecked on the coast several years earlier.[5]

The females Barlow described appeared to be thoroughly clad, but such was not always the case. European men generally linked the absence of clothing with licentiousness, and the Christians found nakedness uncommonly arousing. The bare breasts and sometimes uncovered pudenda proved disconcerting enough; that Indian women plucked their pubic hair distracted white males even more. Native-American women as well as men sometimes also wore tattoos, and whites considered this an effort to enhance sexuality. The Europeans also scrutinized the relative sexual freedom and overall conduct of Indian women, condemning it on one hand but maximizing it to their advantage on the other and rarely if ever viewing native mores within their own social context. The bawdy sense of humor that some Indian women displayed, their directness in sexual matters, their seeming lack of modesty, as well as the occurrence of premarital relations, easy divorce, and the practice of sororal polygamy, contradicted European male notions of appropriate feminine conduct. The eighteenth-century English trader-author James Adair, a visitor among the Cherokees, remarked with disgust that they "have been a considerable while under petticoat-government, and allow their women full liberty to plant their brows with horns as oft as they please, without fear of punishment."[6]

In some respects, however, the Indians were even more proscribed in their sexual conduct than were Europeans. Standards existed among the southeastern Indians relative to when, where, and with whom one might engage in sexual intercourse. Indeed, warriors preparing for or returning from battle, ball players readying for games, men on the winter hunts, and pregnant and menstruating women had to forgo pleasures of the flesh. Natives in the South, then, denied themselves for a greater portion of their lives than did their European counterparts. Taboos also existed against coupling in the agricultural fields, and rules regarding incest severely limited such possibilities. Among the Cherokees with their seven clans, for example, no one could marry into the clan of either parent, which meant that approximately one-third of all Cherokees were forbidden as partners.[7]

What the European men found especially peculiar and grievous, however, in the American South, given the fact that they regarded women as property, was the relative independence of Indian women and the seeming lack of concern or control on the part of their male counterparts. From the European perspective it was the responsibility of an honorable man to protect the chastity of his wife and daughters. Native males sometimes not only tolerated but even encouraged sexual activity between visitors and women who "belonged" to the native men. Matrilocal residence patterns and matrilineal kinship proved equally baffling to the English as well as other Western Europeans. When marriage occurred among southern Indians, the male took up residence among his wife's relatives because all buildings, garden plots, and sections of the common fields belonged to her lineage. Children traced kinship through their female relatives, and when and if divorce occurred, children remained with their mothers. Thus, men had no claim to the property they occupied or the offspring they fathered.[8]

By the early nineteenth century, southern Indians came to be known as the Five Civilized Tribes, in recognition of the alacrity with which they had adapted to transplanted European culture. Among other things, this meant a redefinition of gender roles. In the meantime the Spanish and French as well as the English accommodated themselves with Native-American women, sometimes even taking them as lifetime partners or "wives." "Sex," Theda Perdue has written, "was a kind of commodity to Europeans: they purchased it from prostitutes with money and from respectable women with marriage."[9] Consequently, the fact that some Indian women bartered their favors could hardly have been too surprising to the Europeans.

All the same, colonials and traveling foreign dignitaries took time to comment on such conduct. Colonel William Byrd, hardly one to be squeamish about human sexuality given the innermost thoughts that he recorded in his secret diary, wrote in his "History of the Dividing Line" that the "Young Ladies" of the Sappony Nation "had more the Air of cleanliness than any copper-Colour'd Beauties I had ever seen; Yet we resisted all their Charms." Still he considered "the Price they sat upon their Charms" reasonable. "A Princess for a Pair of Red Stockings can't, surely, be thought buying Repentance much too dear."[10] When another wayfarer took an Indian woman as a "wife" for a night, he awakened the next morning to find both his companion and his boots gone. As late as 1797, when the duc d'Orleans, later King Louis Philippe of France, traveled through the Tennessee country during his exile, he recorded that "all Cherokee women are public women in the full meaning of the phrase: dollars never fail to melt their hearts." He carefully noted that "some of these Indian women are quite lovely . . . and no Frenchwoman could teach them a thing."[11]

In practice, Englishmen during the age of exploration and colonization wasted little chivalry on women of any race, nor were their relations with the opposite sex particularly harmonious. In February 1585, for instance, Sir Francis Drake appeared off Cartagena, in South America, subsequently capturing it, burning the galleys that defended it, and liberating the slaves. When he finally left Cartagena in ashes on 10 April, he took with him three hundred Indians, most of them women, and two hundred Negroes,

Turks, and Moors. It is doubtful that Drake took time to pay deference to the wishes of the native or Negro women. He then headed for the Florida channel and attacked the Spanish fort at St. Augustine; local Indians meanwhile began to burn the town. The Spanish women and children who had been evacuated to the interior to escape the English then faced the danger of an Indian attack. Apparently Drake's moves at Cartagena and in Florida were intended to solidify Anglo-Indian relations at the expense of the Spanish and additionally to reduce the threat that St. Augustine might pose to any future English settlement.[12]

Later, in 1611, after Jamestown had been established but was still struggling against great odds, Sir Thomas Dale, its governor, sent George Percy to exact revenge on the Indians nearest Jamestown because he believed that Powhatan was harboring some runaway Englishmen. Percy and his men attacked the town, killed fifteen or sixteen Indians, and captured the "queen" of the tribe and her children. Percy took them back to the boats and embarked for Jamestown. His men began to grumble because the woman and her children had been spared. Percy obligingly threw the children into the brink, "shoteinge owtt their Braynes in the water." Back in Jamestown, Percy learned that Dale was displeased that the woman had been spared. One suggestion was to burn her, but Percy, already "haveinge seene so mutche Bloodshedd that day," rejected the more heinous fiery method in favor of the sword. She was led away and stabbed.[13] By the same token the Indians could hardly be described as lacking in grisly imagination. In one instance, native women used mussel shells to flay a live English captive.[14]

If white women fared better at the hands of Englishmen in the Chesapeake than did the native women, it was only because they were so desperately needed to nurture and sustain the struggling Virginia colony. Proper Christian Englishmen, for the most part, could hardly expect to find suitable mates among heathens, a fact that virtually dictated the early presence of white women in the colonial South. Seagoing vessels during the colonial era sometimes carried in their holds crudely fashioned cheap iron as ballast, which a few centuries later would prove extremely valuable as architectural ornamentation. Almost from the beginning of colonization they likewise carried women—equally practical "iron lace," as the ballast came to be called in English-speaking Australia—to undergird households and support families. More to the point, Englishmen in Virginia placed intrinsic economic value on women as breeders and servants.

Although there were no females among the earliest arrivals at Jamestown in 1607, seventeen women had come to Roanoke Island, the ill-fated colony off the coast of North Carolina, in 1587 and ultimately had disappeared. Out of that experience, Virginia Dare, reputedly the first white

English Christian child born in North America, won her place in American history. Governor John White recorded in his narrative that on "the 13th, Elenor, daughter of the Governor [the narrator's own daughter], and wife of Ananias Dare, one of the Assistants, was delivered of a daughter in Roanoke, and the same was christened there the Sunday following, and because this child was the first Christian born in Virginia, she was named Virginia."[15]

With the initial failures of English colonial ventures, promoters seemed all the more determined to achieve success; and white women figured prominently in their plans. A member of His Majesty's Council of Virginia wrote: "When the Plantation grows to strength, then it is time to plant with women as well as with men; that the plantation may spread into generations, and not be ever pieced from without." It was his perspective and the masculine viewpoint in general that women had a dual role: to reproduce and to see to the comforts of men so that "their minds might be faster tyed to Virginia."[16]

Even before 1619, when the Virginia Company of London became actively engaged in sending women to the new colony, females had made their way to Jamestown. The wife of Thomas Forrest and her maid, Anne Burras, arrived during the fall of 1608 in what was called the Second Supply. Some twenty women and children arrived the following August. In 1609 there were approximately one hundred women and four to five hundred men in Jamestown. These first women, just as the men, fell victims to sickness, hunger, and Indian massacres.[17] Around 1610, when only about sixty men, women, and children remained, cannibalism entered the picture. An account exists of a man who ate his wife during the "Starving Time." The truth, according to a pamphlet published by the Council of Virginia, was that he hated his wife and had taken advantage of circumstances to kill her, attempting to conceal his crime by claiming that she had died of natural causes and that he had eaten parts of her body to sustain himself. A modern chronicler, Arthur Frederick Ide, quoting from colonial records, reports that the starving denizens of Jamestown devoured "those Hogges, Dogges & Horses that were then in the Collony, together with Rates, mice, snakes . . . [and] the flesh . . . of man, as well of our owne nation as of an Indian, digged by some out of his grave after he had laien buried three daies & wholly devoured." Preference was given to female flesh, however, because it was deemed "in the better state of bodie" than that of a male "which proves toughe and sinewy."[18]

Those involved with the colony's development agreed that masculine comfort required the presence of women, which would serve to prevent men from returning to England. Sir Edwin Sandys, the company's treasurer, employed this justification when he recommended the sending of a hundred women to Virginia, with the shareholders to be reimbursed by planters who married them. In the spring of 1620 the company dispatched ninety maidens and fifty or so more in 1621-22. Apparently all of these had found husbands by 1622. A planter who married one of them incurred an obligation to the company of 120 pounds of his best tobacco. All the same, these early females had plenty of male attention. Some of them even stirred controversy by becoming engaged to several men at the same time, which forced the House of Burgesses to pass a law forbidding such practices. One disgruntled bachelor complained in 1623 of being unable to afford a woman servant and therefore being forced to pay an exorbitant price to have his washing done. Furthermore, because not enough women were available to attend to men who were sick, he claimed, many of the ailing departed the world in an unduly nasty condition. Nonetheless, even as he lamented the absence of enough females to make him and other males comfortable, he disparaged those already present, saying: "For all that I can find that the multitude of women doe is nothing but to devoure the food of the land without dooing any dayes deed whereby any benefitt may arise either to the Company or countrey."[19]

Despite the initial feeble efforts of the Virginia Company and the various forms that the importation of women took after Virginia became a royal colony, more males than females immigrated. This, coupled with natural attrition, so profoundly affected the colonists that women remained a scarcity throughout the seventeenth century. The company went to considerable lengths to cast the women whom they dispatched in the best possible light as suitable brides for male colonists. According to the historian David R. Ransome, writing in 1991, "fifty-seven young women . . . went out to Virginia in 1621 to become wives for the settlers." Daughters of artisans and gentry, two of whom were nieces of knights, they sailed aboard the *Marmaduke*, the *Warwick*, and the *Tiger*. Documents now available "testify to the women's social respectability and domestic skills." Just before departing for Virginia, most of these women had resided in London or nearby—this in keeping with circumstances of subsequent migration to America when that great English city served as a catch basin through which human elements of the British Isles drained.[20]

These women may have departed for America willingly enough, but others were misled or in some other manner were sent on their way to Virginia and elsewhere under duress. Even the willing incurred obligations. According to the historian Suzanne Lebsock, the vast majority of women colonists were bound laborers. During the seventeenth century a relatively small number of black women from Africa or from Africa by way of the West Indies may also have fallen into this category of temporary servitude. According to some accounts, about 80 percent of all English colonists, females among them, came as indentured servants, owing four to seven years of labor to those who paid their passages.[21]

How these individuals came to be procured and transported to Virginia and elsewhere has not been highlighted in the pages of American history. Expected to bring a "bride" price of 120 pounds of tobacco each and to become wives of planters, the 140 or more women of 1620-22, "tobacco maids" as they have sometimes been called, were not felons. Nonetheless, female convicts, most of whose offenses were relatively minor, were subsequently introduced into the Old Dominion and other colonies as well. During the 1650s, soldiers of the London garrison had reportedly even raided brothels, capturing more than four hundred women and dispatching them to Barbados as "breeders." In 1925, the historian Harold U. Faulkner wrote: "Probably more liberties have been taken with the truth as regards the history of Virginia than with that of any other of the colonies . . . The white population of Virginia instead of being composed of the best elements of English society, was composed to a considerable extent of the worst."[22] Phrased differently, more colonists represented the lower social and economic strata of English society than the privileged upper echelon.

Later in the colonial era, during the eighteenth century, Sir Alexander Grant hit upon a scheme to populate proposed English settlements in East Florida; he turned to the Magdalen House in London. Sir Alexander served as vice-president of that charitable establishment, which was intended to rescue from disease and degradation the several thousand prostitutes who walked the streets of that great city. "'Tis true," he had to admit, they "are not virgins." All the same, he declared them "comly, good tempered, reformed penitents, whose youth & inadvertency plunged into misfortunes which brought them into sad sufferings." Around 1768, four of the redeemed made their way to Florida and then disappeared from the historical record.[23]

English empire builders looked not only to the reproductive capacities of less fortunate white females but also to the work that might be squeezed from the inferior ranks of both sexes. For most of the seventeenth century in Maryland and Virginia, black slavery had not yet replaced demands for cheap white labor. As extensions of the English economy whose investors sought quick profits, Virginia and Maryland discovered a market for tobacco; and its production diminished the need for or interest in other mercantile activities. The two colonies quickly became a refuge or a dumping ground, depending on one's perspective, for the downtrodden men and women of the Old Country whom the privileged classes there considered dangerous and best disposed of elsewhere. They filled the void for what seemed at times to be the insatiable demands of the tobacco culture. The practice existed of "spiriting" or kidnapping young waifs, both male and female, and dispatching them to America. Some early planters in Virginia also ransomed white captives from the Indians in order to exact service from them.[24]

The historian Edmund S. Morgan has documented early instances of the physical abuse of male and female servants in Virginia. Elizabeth Abbott, for example, died after a series of beatings at the hands of her masters and their other servants. "Whether physically abused or not," declared Morgan, "Englishmen [and English women] found servitude in Virginia more degrading than servitude in England . . . [where] the hiring of workers was dignified by laws and customs that gave a servant some control over his [or her] own life." A servant could not only be sold to another master against her will but might also be gambled away. "Virginians," according to Morgan, "dealt in servants the way Englishmen dealt in land or chattels."[25]

Nonetheless, the historians Lois Green Carr and Lorena S. Walsh have pointed to the opportunities that existed for women in the raw environment of the Chesapeake even as they acknowledge the difficulties and pitfalls that awaited white female indentured servants. Untimely death, field work, sexual abuse, and bearing a bastard were definite possibilities, perhaps even likelihoods, in seventeenth-century Virginia and Maryland. All the same, according to Carr and Walsh, "until the 1660s, the expanding economy of Maryland and Virginia offered opportunities well beyond those available in England to men without capital and to the women who became their wives." If finding husbands were their objective, as indeed it was for many women, their chances were excellent. Carr and Walsh argue that "the woman who immigrated to Maryland, survived seasoning and service, and gained her freedom became a planter's wife." Because men so dramatically outnumbered women and because a female did not have to take into account the viewpoints of a father or brothers, "she had considerable liberty in making her choice," even though she might have longed for the presence of a male protector.[26]

Despite the glowing accounts floated by promoters, women who survived the seasoning process of the seventeenth century had hardly happened upon a New-World version of the Garden of Eden. Theirs was a beleaguered existence, for they performed hard physical labor just to carry out "all the day-to-day, never-done tasks" that made life possible. In reconstructing the life of a typical white woman of the period in Virginia, Suzanne Lebsock found that this female was about twenty years old when she arrived as an indentured servant. If she survived servitude, she married almost immediately, bore a child every year or two, and probably buried at least two of her offspring as children. She herself might not live to see her children reach maturity. Probably her husband, older than she, succumbed seven years into the marriage; and her demise followed in a few years. Untimely deaths disrupted Virginia families: only one marriage in three lasted as long as ten years; half of the children who reached the age of nine had lost one or both of their parents. The first successful English colony in

North America was "a land of widows, widowers, bachelors, and, above all, orphans."[27]

Lorena S. Walsh, in her work focusing heavily on the early English experience in Maryland, points out that because "the typical former [white] servant woman" had not entered into marriage until after her indenture ended, probably in her mid-twenties, she bore a relatively small number of children, perhaps three or four on average. Relieving the debt of passage used up several years of her childbearing cycle. The next generation of females, however, daughters of women who formerly had been servants, tended to marry younger and give birth to more children. Whatever the vicissitudes that accompanied the marital state, matrimony seemed a prerequisite for an adult female who wanted to enhance her social and economic status and acquire a modicum of security. Otherwise she probably remained a servant or perhaps an unwelcome dependent in another woman's household.[28]

"The prevailing legal and societal restrictions," according to Walsh, "did mean, however, that the nearly inevitable decision to marry had graver consequences for women than for men." Under common law the male exercised authority over his spouse and offspring; this extended to physical punishment for corrective purposes. A married woman, a feme covert, could not enter into contracts or retain control of property that she brought into the marriage unless she or a protective male relative had thought to negotiate a prenuptial agreement. Furthermore, she could not bestow gifts or execute her own will without her husband's consent. Assuming that no legal document existed to protect and enhance her economic position, she was expected to comply with her husband's judgment in the disposition of her property or any wealth they might accumulate together. An unfortunate choice of a mate therefore had profound consequences for a woman. Absolute divorces were unobtainable in either early Maryland or Virginia, and legal separations, not easily accomplished, hardly worked to the advantage of the female since the husband retained flexibility in his personal behavior and probably still had control of her property. If she resorted to desertion, she usually faced social ostracism.[29]

Although it was possible through equity law and the chancery in England for married women to circumvent the common-law disabilities of coverture, women in early Maryland and Virginia seem not to have benefited. Male relatives rarely maneuvered to execute premarital contracts and thereby to protect the interests of their female charges. They either placed too much reliance on dower rights or considered premarital contracts insulting to suitors, an affront to gentlemen's honor. In Maryland "the low level of economic development, which inhibited the creation of large and complex estates, certainly placed a further damper on the establishment of equitable trusts for daughters," writes the legal scholar Gwen Victor Gampel. Furthermore, unmarried female indentured servants of the Chesapeake who came from the lower classes of British society may have been ignorant of possibilities. The Maryland Chancery provided no leadership in the matter because it failed to set the precedent of requiring a husband to settle a separate estate on his wife before acquiring possession of land that was held in trust for her. After marriage, Gampel observes, "the planter's wife rarely sought an independent contractual capacity through *feme sole* [single female] trader activity or by postnuptial agreement." Widows, however, who possessed and controlled wealth and property were more likely to insist on premarital agreements before making the trek to the altar again, willingly sacrificing sentimentality to protect their vested interests. Even in the founding stages of English North America, however, the seeds were being sown for what the historian Joan Hoff calls "the masculinity of U.S. Constitutionalism." Male chauvinism joined with limited legal understanding, women's unabashed ignorance of the law, and a relatively simple economy to undermine female interests.[30]

All the same, there was a reality that transcended coverture and legal maneuvering. Only the extraordinarily wealthy could dismiss the critical role that the wife played in the domestic economy. Furthermore, selecting a mate and building a marriage involved matters of the heart; and in the colonial Chesapeake the emotional and the practical were not mutually exclusive. Husbands and the community as a whole recognized women's ability to supervise children, preside over households, and manage property. Most husbands named their mates as executors of their wills, and if no will existed, courts tended to designate widows as administrators. Even the most domineering would-be patriarchs surely realized, whether they accepted it or not, that a harmonious relationship counted mutual respect as a key ingredient.[31]

"Virginians may have believed in patriarchal authority with all their hearts, but conditions in the New World at times made enforcement difficult," Suzanne Lebsock notes. "The patriarchs simply did not live long enough."[32] The chaos that death visited upon Chesapeake families may indeed have been an impediment, but ultimately it did not prevent the development of a well-entrenched patriarchy. Middling and gentry families had become "increasingly patriarchal in seventeenth-century England," and some English law bearing on this matter made its way to the American colonies. The historian Allan Kulikoff, in his unvarnished and masterful study of the tobacco culture of the Chesapeake, minces no words about the flux in which the colonists found themselves even as he carefully outlines the rise of the patriarchal family in this section of the American South: "No Chesapeake family could possibly attain the harmony and complete separation of tasks that the domestic patriarchal ideal demanded. Husbands and wives bickered, argued, and occasionally even separated . . . [and] from time to time . . . brought their difficulties to local or provincial courts."[33] "Disagreements about the management or disposition of dower property were a major cause of legal separations and must have troubled many marriages that remained intact," Walsh notes.[34]

Kulikoff is of the opinion that the circumstances of the times did not dictate the development of domestic patriarchies, a strong class system, or a slave society. "Chesapeake planters did not *have* to choose to form domestic patriarchies," he writes; such alternatives existed as "the relatively egalitarian family system of the seventeenth century." He assumes that the planters adopted this arrangement because they harbored preconceived notions about how best to organize domestic life.[35] Peculiarities of the colonial Chesapeake experience certainly encouraged the fruition of these ideas. Not least among these characteristics were the climate and the fertility of the soil, which permitted and fostered the development of labor-intensive single-crop agriculture to which bound servitude and then the institution of slavery grafted easily.

Three factors hastened the development of the patriarchal order in the Chesapeake. First, the slave trade accelerated, which resolved the labor shortage and essentially eliminated the need for the white wives of slaveholders to work in the tobacco fields. Second, white immigration declined and natural increase kicked in to reduce the inequitable male-female sex ratio and the concomitant demand for teenaged brides. Finally, adult life expectancy increased and with that the longevity of marriages, which allowed clear patterns of authority within the household to emerge. By the early eighteenth century, Kulikoff observes, "tidewater gentlemen and their yeoman allies constructed a stable, conservative social order, characterized by interlocking class, racial, and gender relations." "White women," he explains, "usually acquiesced in patriarchal family government because of the rights and privileges they enjoyed as planters' wives." Reciprocity was the order of the day as long as each free partner in the contractual arrangement lived up to obligations, and gentlemen generally acquitted themselves in a manner that permitted them to tolerate and accommodate their "perceived inferiors," be they women, black slaves, or white males of the lower classes. The development of slavery, of course, became the most critical element in the social formula of the Chesapeake. Slaves, whether females or males, had little say in the matter although "the ordinary tensions embedded within Chesapeake society provided subservient groups like slaves and women with means to challenge domination without seeking to overthrow the system itself."[36]

The first black bond servants appeared in Virginia in 1619, but most of the seventeenth century seems to have passed before slavery became an intrinsic and rigidly fixed aspect of colonial life. Not until the late seventeenth or early eighteenth century did the demand for black slave labor replace the earlier reliance on indentured white servants. The circumstances under which blacks first labored in the seventeenth century remain somewhat nebulous. The historian Winthrop D. Jordan takes the position that "there is only one major historical certainty, and unfortunately it is the sort which historians find hardest to bear. There is simply not enough evidence to indicate with any certainty whether Negroes were treated like white servants or not." It is apparent that by about 1640 "*some* Negroes in both Virginia and Maryland were serving for life and some Negro children inheriting the same obligation."[37]

During the seventeenth century there was a discernible pattern in the Chesapeake of free blacks owning land, holding servants, using the court system, and occasionally attaining office. The early eighteenth century brought increasing reliance on slave labor and seems to have undermined the status of free blacks. Elsewhere, in the low-country environment of early colonial Carolina and Georgia, some blacks possessed a "sawbuck equality" with their white masters who worked alongside them. Furthermore, owners may have relied on blacks for "their superior knowledge of subtropical environments, cattle raising, and rice cultivation."[38] The challenges of clearing the land and mutual defense could have fostered a leveling influence. Nonetheless, the subsequent development of staple crops for export, the importation of increasing numbers of slaves, and the gravitation of the creole population toward the urban amenities of Charleston undermined any tendency toward a less structured give-and-take relationship that may have existed previously.

That "Mary a Negro Woman" arrived in Virginia around 1621 or 1622 is a matter of record. She managed to gain her freedom in some manner, and she married a free Negro man, Anthony, who worked with her on the same plantation. The family of Mary and Anthony, who appropriated the surname Johnson, included four children and eventually grandchildren as well. Whatever the explanation, they fared well economically; and the fluidity that initially characterized race relations seems to have worked to their advantage. Between 1662 and 1705, however, the House of Burgesses enacted a series of laws that defined slavery and delineated race relations in the colony. Although blacks themselves were not totally powerless to influence their masters and their circumstances, as the historian Eugene D. Genovese in *Roll, Jordan, Roll: The World the Slaves Made* has amply demonstrated, severe and fairly rigid proscriptions were put into place. "The typical black Virginia woman" by 1700, according to Lebsock, was "'chattel'—property—and as such she could be bought, sold, mortgaged, or swapped, or even gambled away in a card game." She would remain property for the duration of her natural life; so, too, her children for theirs—and they could be stripped from her any time, any place, at the pleasure of her master.[39]

African-born slave women of the seventeenth century had fewer marriage possibilities than white indentured female servants of the Chesapeake. Among blacks as well as whites, males outnumbered females throughout the first century. Nonetheless, initially the black women may have been owned by masters who possessed few other blacks; and later, in the early eighteenth century, slavery came to be concentrated on the large, relatively isolated estates where blacks—men, women, and children—may not have numbered more than twenty to thirty. Restricted in their movement from one plantation to another, some first-generation females quite probably found no mates who were acceptable to them. They seem to have been slow to enter into "marriages" and have children; they averaged about three offspring, usually losing one in its infancy. Lorena S. Walsh identifies such causative factors as "isolation, a diversity of tribal origins and languages, chronic ill health, and extreme alienation" for these patterns. Creole black women, the daughters of the African-born, not unlike the white females, married earlier and produced more children—six to eight, perhaps half of whom did not live to maturity. On large estates it was easier for black women to find mates among the local slave population; women who were owned by smaller planters and farmers often had both to look elsewhere for a husband and to face the consequences of living alone and rearing children with only occasional visits from the husband and father. Walsh concedes that by the late eighteenth century, slave women tended to reside among their kinfolks, and most of them had found mates and produced children. The conjugal pair and the nuclear family emerged. Still, the decisions or whims of their masters might disrupt family relationships.[40]

In retrospect it seems that slavery as it evolved in Virginia affected black females somewhat differently from males. Women were only about half as likely as men to be exported from Africa to America. In their native cultures, black women had farmed, their roles in agriculture resembling those of Indian counterparts in the American South. It may be that the Africans who acted as procurers for slave traders possessed some reluctance about upsetting this arrangement by which their societies subsisted. Women who were snatched from the land of their birth and dispatched to the New World experienced the horrible middle passage, which exacted a heavy toll of lives. They also faced the prospect of sexual exploitation while on board ship and in America as well. In Virginia the females labored in the fields just as the males did. The whip could be brought to bear on both sexes. Black females soon learned also that no legal protection existed for slave families. Although runaways included males and females, only about one in ten was a woman. Strong maternal bonds may have led women to express their resistance to slavery by more commonly resorting to such other means as slowing their pace of labor, destroying tools, feigning illness, setting fires, or, in the most extreme instances, attempting to poison their masters.[41]

During most of the seventeenth and early eighteenth centuries, Tidewater Virginia and Maryland hardly represented an orderly, pristine English society. Instead the reality was a raw, chaotic society, convulsed by tensions associated with class, gender, and race. All the common human frailties manifested themselves. Female culprits slandered their own kind, gossiped about their neighbors, and fornicated with willing partners. Some unfortunate souls came in for charges of witchcraft in seventeenth-century Virginia, but apparently no one was executed. Premarital sex excited little attention; a third of the brides were already pregnant on their wedding day. Nonmarital sex that might produce a child to burden the community required public censure. Authorities meted out punishments of public whippings and fines; sometimes they forced offenders to appear before church congregations draped in white sheets and clutching white wands.[42]

In a setting like seventeenth-century Virginia, where three races collided and interacted, miscegenation raised its head almost by default. For a while and in some instances, interracial fornicators simply faced the same types of punishments as any other couple. Even a 1662 act declaring that a child should be slave or free according to the status of its mother may not have been dictated entirely by racism. Mixed marriages also occurred, but in 1691 the assembly outlawed miscegenation in or out of wedlock. It called "for prevention of that abominable mixture and spurious issue which hereafter may encrease in this dominion, as well by negroes, mulattoes, and Indians intermarrying with English, or other white women, as by their unlawfull accompanying with one another." This act and the 1705 revision of it revealed more concern about illicit relations between white women and black men than intermarriage per se.[43]

The relative scarcity of white women placed their affections at a premium, and white men fervently expected to be the recipients of their attentions. Given the existence of documented cases of mulatto children born to white women during the late seventeenth and early eighteenth centuries, black men surely succeeded sometimes in the quest for their sexual favors. As for black slave women who gave birth to mulatto children, it hardly mattered. Their offspring were neither legitimate nor illegitimate, and the variations in skin tones had no bearing on their enslavement. Apparently this legislation did not cast a pall over the earlier and much-vaunted relationship between Pocahontas and John Rolfe or their descendants. But she was an Indian woman, not a white one, and he was an English man. Similar laws also appeared in Maryland.

Female sexuality concerned colonial officialdom, for they valued the reproductive capacities of their women. In the case of black slaves, fecundity enhanced wealth; and how fertilization transpired concerned the owners very little as long as it generated healthy offspring. Patriarchs of the Old Dominion and her sister southern colonies, however, fixated on the chastity of unmarried white women and the fidelity of wives. Their code of honor permitted not a scintilla of doubt as to the paternity of their heirs, which they zealously set about getting. Notwithstanding the strict standards of virtue to which they held the females of their families, predatory males roamed the highways and byways, partaking of sexual favors freely given or forcibly taken where they found them. The wives, sisters, and daughters of their peers were not necessarily off-limits, and Indian and black women, as well as whites whom they considered their social inferiors, often represented easy prey.[44]

"Virginians," writes the historian David Hackett Fischer, "had a way of thinking about fertility which set them apart from New England Puritans." The latter concerned themselves with "the biblical commandment to increase and multiply and replenish the earth," but Virginians, thinking "more of breeding stocks and bloodlines," prided themselves on "the fertility of their women and their animals—sometimes in the same breath."[45] Careful that no hint of scandal touched the mothers of their legitimate heirs or besmirched the family name, some of the gentry as well as nonelite men casually littered the countryside with various shades of misbegotten offspring.

Ladies meanwhile did not always conform to male-prescribed ideals, and the circumstances of colonial life hardly shielded them from prurient curiosity. Little girls, conditioned from birth to anticipate motherhood, sometimes pretended pregnancy at play. A visitor reported seeing gentlewomen in Virginia purchase male slaves after carefully inspecting their genitalia. Another observer, at the time of the Revolution, witnessed "young negroes and negresses running about or basking in the court-yard as they came into the world, with well characterized marks of perfect puberty." Young but mature male slaves, dressed only in loose shirts that fell half-way between their gonads and their knees, served white women "without any apparent embarrassment on one side, or the slightest attempt at concealment on the other."[46]

Some gentlewomen proved as lusty and sensual as their male counterparts. Whether creatures of passion or unenthusiastic but dutiful wives, the ladies of their class as well as those lower in the social order lived up to their obligations as "breeders" or died trying. "Large families . . . were the rule and the boast of rich and poor," writes Julia Cherry Spruill. "A large part of the time, strength, and attention of women went into the bearing and rearing of large families." Colonists, more than English kinsmen in the mother country, considered numerous children a material advantage and therefore assets. Virginians, who definitely earned their reputation as "great breeders," did not have sole claim to the title. In 1708, for example, a traveler remarked that most of the 250 families in South Carolina's Charles Town had ten or twelve children. A North Carolina promoter credited that colony with fostering fecundity even for women who moved there after many years of barrenness. It was not unusual for a couple to count in double digits the children of their union alone; in second marriages, his and hers plus theirs raised the ante. The risks of such profligacy ran high for women, and when a widower replaced the wife he had buried, who may have succumbed to the rigors of pregnancy and childbirth, his record of successful fertilization sometimes reached astonishingly high levels of twenty or more.[47]

Despite the dictum that a lady's name should appear in print only at her birth, marriage, and death, colonial newspapers occasionally reported the pregnancies of the elite. Lying-in took on the trappings of a ceremony as female friends and family gathered for extended visits and to attend the birth. Among the elite, expectant fathers sometimes subscribed to the superstition that pregnant women might miscarry if their wishes were not fulfilled. Anxious for healthy male heirs, the men yielded to frivolous requests. The great majority of enceinte females went to term without so much fanfare but with equal or greater risk. Usually attended by midwives of sorts, occasionally by physicians, but sometimes all alone, they faced the rigors and dangers of childbirth.[48]

Examples of the vapid helpless female, so much a part of the media-made mythology associated with the "lady," could probably be found in the colonial South, but strong, spirited women of all social ranks outnumbered them. Patriarchy in its most extreme forms depended on uncompromising acquiescence, and not enough women complied to allow the most dictatorial men unqualified rein on all fronts. Mary Horsmanden Filmer Byrd represented a durable female and a classic case of the far-ranging ties of kinship and influence that an elite colonial woman might promulgate. She married her cousin, Samuel Filmer, and moved to Virginia, where he died in the "seasoning" process. The widow Mary quickly married William Byrd and gave birth to William Byrd II. Robert Beverley and James Duke were her sons-in-law; Thomas Chamberlayne, Charles and Landon Carter, and John Page were her grandsons. Over the course of three generations, most of Virginia's first families claimed Mary Horsmanden Filmer Byrd as an ancestress. Nor were her familial connections confined to the Old Dominion. Frances Culpeper, Mary's first cousin, successively married three colonial governors. Frances also counted William Penn and Nathaniel Bacon among her cousins; the latter led a rebellion in 1676 against her third husband, Sir William

Berkeley. Similar convoluted genealogies existed in Virginia and other colonies, cutting across class lines and giving rise to the kinship ties that came to lace southern society.[49]

Highborn women enjoyed influence by birth, and others who recognized feminine scarcity for the powerful bargaining chip that it was throughout much of the colonial era sometimes demonstrated a strong sense of self. In Maryland, Margaret Brent acted as executrix for a governor, averted a mutiny, and requested the right to vote, making her in all likelihood the first woman to do so in the English colonies. When the Maryland assembly refused her request (actually for two votes—one as executrix and one as her own person), she protested, but to no avail. She moved to Virginia during the early 1650s and spent the remainder of her life more quietly at a Westmoreland plantation aptly named Peace. Sarah Harrison of Surry County, Virginia, refused to take the vow of obedience when she and James Blair were married in 1687. After making three futile attempts, the minister gave up on "obey," acceded to her wishes, and went on with the ceremony. Women participated in Bacon's Rebellion, and one, Anne Cotton, may have written a history of it. This occurred at a time in the South when correspondence, labeled the "gentlest Art in Seventeenth-Century Virginia" by the eminent scholar Richard Beale Davis, afforded women virtually their only literary outlet. Lady Frances Berkeley, the wife of the governor, rallied support in England and returned to Virginia with a thousand regulars and the authorization to crush those who challenged her husband's authority. After he died, she married her third governor, who served North Carolina but took up residence at Green Spring, her home in Virginia. Because men generally deemed females inferior, they ranked women like these who participated actively or made their wishes and opinions known in public life as exceptional—honorary men of sorts, or "deputy husbands."[50]

There seems little doubt that the railings of women occurred more frequently within the confines of private relationships than in public displays. Lucy Parke Byrd and William Byrd II rode out an outwardly successful but stormy marriage that terminated in 1716 with her death from smallpox. According to him they enjoyed a healthy sex life that was mutually satisfying. Lucy's sister Frances Parke Custis, on the other hand, consistently engaged in marital warfare with her spouse, Colonel John Custis of Arlington. Despite an elaborate premarital contract intended to safeguard her interests, his management of the property that she brought into the marriage did not meet with her approval. The besieged Colonel Custis ordered that a record of his sufferings be permanently inscribed on his tombstone. Apparently they found each other mutually repugnant and matched tit for tat. When he drove the carriage they both were occupying into Chesapeake Bay, she thought to ask where he was headed as the horses commenced swimming. "To hell, Madam," he retorted. "Drive on," she commanded, "any place is better than Arlington."[51]

Husbands' extramarital liaisons, physical violence and verbal abuse that they heaped on wives, and contradictory expectations for women also gave rise to inharmonious relationships. All but the wealthiest of women carried the burden of farm work and labor in the fields in addition to routine household chores.[52] Such brutal realities surely taxed their ability to affect and sustain femininity, refinement, virtue, modesty, delicacy, and graciousness. "We can be sure," notes the historian Stephanie Grauman Wolf, that "the fifty or more people who stayed with William Byrd each month, either on his plantation or at his home in Williamsburg, were not cared for by him in anything but the figurative sense; their bed linens, their wash, their food, and any incidental sewing was done or prepared by the women of the house." Responsibility for overseeing such "household tasks" usually fell to the "planter's wife, whose real job was to make polite conversation and manage the slaves." Yet "the plantation owner frequently economized on the household servants, providing his wife with too few helpers who were also too young, too old, or too untrained to allow her to devote her full time and attention to charming her guests."[53]

It remains customary to wax nostalgic about the quaint housewifery skills of colonial women and their powers of procreation. Without wallowing in all of it, it must be recognized that the exigencies of existence required that their lot include a steady regimen of cooking, gardening, and food preservation as well as nursing the sick, manufacturing clothing, and tending animals—all of this intermixed with seemingly incessant childbearing. If they were still emotionally inclined and physically able to "kick up their heels" at social gatherings or express themselves artistically in their needlework, all the more credit is due them.

"Women's sphere was not a subject of controversy or reflection in pioneer America," Elisabeth Anthony Dexter observes in *Career Women of America, 1776-1840*. "Men ruled in church and state, and they furnished the great majority of workers in practically all callings outside the home." Still, during the colonial and early national eras in the South and indeed throughout the English-influenced North, females pursued "a surprising number of occupations" and met the challenges with which their times and circumstances confronted them.[54] Women teachers, planters, tavern operators and innkeepers, printers, actors, and even preaching Quakeresses intermittently graced the social milieu of the colonial South.[55] Serving as helpmates to their husbands or carrying on as determined widows most often occasioned activities beyond the bounds of housewifery. Other feminine lives followed the course of quiet reflection as recorded in their diaries and letters, a few manifested themselves in somewhat more flamboyant and public fashion, but the great majority spent themselves in silent anonymity.

On the periphery of the English-speaking settlements in what would become the southern United States, other Europeans could be found at the French and Spanish outposts. French women, in particular, their numbers comparatively small, seem to have enjoyed a superior legal status to their English counterparts. At the French settlement of Ste. Genevieve, about sixty miles south of St. Louis on the west bank of the Mississippi River, which had been established about mid-eighteenth century, one traveler reported that the women "by no means" considered "themselves in the light of goods and chattels of their liege-lords"; another said, "The women have more influence over their husbands than is common in most other countries."[56]

The sexual imbalance at Ste. Genevieve because of its greater number of males placed females at a premium, but aspects of the French legal system that existed there throughout the eighteenth century proved equally important to the circumstances of women. The *coutume de Paris* governed the French colonies in North America, and the *coutume* followed the traditional practice of western regions of France. Property devolved equally among heirs of both sexes. The community of Ste. Genevieve showed great interest in protecting a bride's property, and a wife had the possibility of renouncing community wealth if debt burdened their joint estate at the time of the husband's death. In such cases, widows received their dowers and their personal effects, leaving the creditors to battle over any other tangible assets. Married women, but widows especially, proved knowledgeable about the region's economic and legal system.[57]

The legal status of women had gnawed away at French men on the Continent even during the seventeenth century; it may have affected life-styles in America as well. Although there has been some tendency to exaggerate interracial concubinage in French- and Spanish-held Louisiana, such an arrangement did, in fact, afford an alternative to matrimony with a white woman. Free black women resided in New Orleans as early as the 1720s, supporting themselves as maids and cooks in the households of families that had brought them from France to the city as part of their estates. The Crescent City soon became a great slave port and witnessed the auctioning of thousands of African women. The historian Thomas N. Ingersoll suggests that in colonial New Orleans, where "some men remained unmarried and lived openly with a black mate and children," their motivation may have been "absolute patriarchy." Blacks "had no secure inheritance rights according to the law," and "a white man who entered into unsanctified marriage with a black woman in the colonies would have absolute power to dispose of his estate and maintain a household of dependents who were especially motivated to obey his will."[58]

The Vieux Carré, wrapped in the curve of the mighty Mississippi River, reached out for European women. The first of them as well as their antecedents left no written history. Therefore "we can imagine how hard life was for the early French women who kept house and raised families in the fetid swamp, the Indian women who brought their wares to market there or the African women sold on the slave blocks to serve local wealthy families or work on plantations upriver," observes Mary Gehman, a New Orleans journalist and teacher. Long before the French Canadian Sieur de Bienville and his three hundred men founded Nouvelle Orleans in 1718, Indian women from the Choctaw, Natchez, and other tribes had graced this site, for it had been a center of trading activity for many centuries. Only twenty-eight of Bienville's men were married; presumably some of the others paid court to the Indian women. Native women cohabitated with French men within the city limits and raised families. Around 1730 the governor of Louisiana ordered the fiery execution of one unfortunate Natchez Indian princess on the site of what became Jackson Square. Her crime may have been conspiring with her own people to attack the French settlement.[59]

In his earliest missive to his king, Bienville besought his majesty to send a shipment of marriageable women. Unfortunates from the streets of Paris and the prisons of France, malnourished, unhealthy, and often enchained, represented the response to Bienville's request. Those who survived the voyage arrived at the Louisiana settlement of Mobile. Known as "correction girls," some of them ended their journey in New Orleans. In 1753 L'Abbé Prévost of France wrote a novel, *Manon Lescaut*, about one such woman; it subsequently became the basis for operas by Giacomo Puccini and Jules Massenet and a three-act ballet by Fromental Halévy.[60]

The Ursuline nuns, the first organized group of women to appear in New Orleans, stand in stark contrast to the unfortunate "correction girls." Responding to Bienville's petition for them to operate a military hospital in New Orleans, the Ursulines arrived during 1727. Not only did they operate the hospital for forty years, but they also established the city's first orphanage and one of the first, if not the first, schools for girls of European parentage in what would be the United States. They also pioneered in the education of Indian and black girls. They have denied any connection with the *filles de cassette* or *casquette*, the "casket girls," reputedly women of virtue from the French countryside who, anticipating marriage in America, carried with them to the New World their dowries or hope chests in long rectangular boxes. Indeed the "casket girls"—ascertaining their virtue taxes the skills of the historian—seem to have arrived in New Orleans at least ten years ahead of the Ursulines.[61]

Although the French, Spanish, African, and Native-American women, as well as those of other ethnic groups, represented pieces of the human patchwork that was the colonial South, denizens of the British Isles and their progeny had the most influence on its development. No offense to the high-strung colonial gentry in the other southern colonies and the scattered non-English transplants, but Albion's privileged white male Protestants established the foundations of the Old South in the Chesapeake during the seventeenth and early eighteenth centuries, this notwithstanding the early influence of the Catholic Calverts in Maryland. The world that the dominant newcomers fashioned included racism, as reflected in the subjugation of the Indians and the enslavement of Africans; a carefully defined but not inflexible class system; and the subordination of females. Patriarchy came to rest on the triad of racism, classism, and sexism, and this arrangement as conceived and implemented in the colonial South shaped the historical experience of southern women.

A specific Anglo-Saxon male elite set the parameters of southern society and, in as much as they could do so, on the backs of others. The demands of carving a new society in the wilderness deprived these men of absolute authority, and the expanse of western land that awaited acquisitive newcomers denied them unlimited control. Non-English groups among them included the French Huguenots of South Carolina, the Germans in Georgia, the Swedes in early Delaware (where Quakery and slavery subsequently coexisted), and the fiery Scotch-Irish Presbyterians of the back country; all of these and more were interwoven into the English social fabric, rendering it a hybrid and strengthening it in the process. Still, the presence of other ethnic and racial groups, though real enough, posed no serious threat to English influence in the colonial South.[62] With the patriarchy in place, the other Europeans who joined the English showed no serious inclinations toward abolishing black slavery, dismantling the class system, or elevating the status of women.

❧

And Another Generation Cometh

During the last half of the eighteenth century and into the opening decades of the new one, revolutionary turmoil and the expanding frontier provided the grist for American myths and legends. Masculine events played out in the public arena commanded center stage and obscured the more ordinary personal aspects and inner concerns of feminine existence. Dramatic though the circumstances surrounding warfare, treaty negotiations, and nation making were, they brought few fundamental changes in the status of most women; and the relatively minor transformations that occurred may have been more stylistic than substantive, more temporary than permanent. Still, the radicalism of the revolutionary era encouraged questions about all inequality, including that implicit in male-female relationships. In turn, some women, southerners among them, began to demonstrate an interest in politics, not previously considered a feminine province, and to assume a more assertive air. When in 1776, for instance, the husband of Sara Cantwell of South Carolina published what hitherto had been a routine announcement that disclaimed responsibility for her debts, she scathingly countered: "John Cantwell has the Impudence to advertise me in the Papers, cautioning all Persons against crediting me; he never had any Credit till he married me: As for his Bed and Board he mentioned, he had neither Bed nor Board when he married me; I never eloped, I went away before his Face when he Beat me."[1]

In revolutionary America the subordinate position of women that had been characteristic of the colonial North and South remained largely intact, but political and military upheaval most assuredly convulsed their lives. Variables of class, race, and political persuasions—theirs as well as those of their men—shaped the revolutionary experience of southern women. Furthermore, whether they lived in more settled rural areas, on the frontier, or in urban environments made a difference, as did their proximity to the movement of troops and the line of fire. "In addition to carrying small-pox," observes the historian Mary Beth Norton, "the armies brought a specific terror to American women: the fear of rape." The systematic exploitation of women "could occur only in areas where troops were stationed for long periods of time. . . . This was what saved the women of New England and, to a certain extent, southern women as well from the fate visited upon their counterparts in the middle states."[2] The extent of individual violations perpetrated in a random fashion, however, will never be known.

As men answered the call to arms, they left women alone to manage farms, businesses, and households. Faced with real deprivation and want, beset by hostile troops, and sometimes widowed, the "lesser sex" went on attending to such private matters as birthing babies and rearing children. Females also became involved as boycotters, camp followers, petitioners, fund raisers, loyalists, or patriots; but the question of their political viability remained unresolved. Men hardly considered women to be citizens even as they praised them for their patriotism, and the newly created states continued the practice of regarding married women as femes coverts. Neither the Declaration of Independence nor the Constitution of the United States recognized the *specific civil existence of women*.

Political exercises represented only one dimension of human experience in eighteenth-century English-speaking North America. Men and women who lived during those chaotic but invigorating times experienced spiritual as well as temporal upheavals. The religious revivalism that had swept through the American colonies during the 1730s and 1740s unleashed whirlwinds of salvation. Harvesting the souls of females as well as males, the Great Awakening, according to the historian Sara M. Evans, "provided further fuel to the gathering debate on woman's place." Be that as it may, the evangelical route to the hereafter certainly suggested egalitarianism. Eternal life—available to all regardless of class, color, or circumstance—seemed to undermine the prevailing lines of earthly authority.[3]

According to some standard historical interpretations, evangelical religion of the eighteenth and early nineteenth centuries possessed the strange and wonderful capacity not only to lift female converts to new heights but also to plummet them into an abyss. While such scholars as Evans have found evangelicalism of the eighteenth century a positive factor in expanding possibilities for women, Jean E. Friedman places great emphasis on its constraining influences in the nineteenth-century South. Nonetheless, both Friedman and Anne Firor Scott have acknowledged that the churches afforded southern women an entree into reform and public life during the latter part of that century.[4] In any event, the hearts and minds of eighteenth-century converts of both genders had the capacity to conceive and nurture visions of a better world and may have likewise proved receptive to more expansive possibilities on earth as well as in heaven.

Republicanism—a secular relative of eighteenth-century evangelicalism—also inspired utopian notions of liberty and true equality among all ranks and for both genders, but when American independence had replaced British rule, political rhetoric notwithstanding, class differentiations remained. Political, social, and economic realignments that occurred during the late eighteenth and early nineteenth centuries likewise reaffirmed the inferior status of females. For the most part, women of the colonial era had possessed limited social and economic opportunities but broad responsibilities. The variety of work experiences and the range of proprietorships, characteristic of a society still in flux, may even have declined for women after the American Revolution as institutional and political circumstances solidified.

The political conflagration of the eighteenth century did not herald a new "golden age" for women. Nor did it signal the collapse of an American Eden inhabited by New-World Eves.[5] In the American experience, improvements in women's overall status have tended to occur in minor incremental steps. Usually spawned by major feminist crusades within recurring cyles of reformism, such gains seem to depend on the relative economic prosperity of the nation. The improvements that were fostered by the new era of republicanism tended to center on access to education and property rights within marriage. They meant little to any except the economically privileged, but they generally defined all as wives and mothers, according to the historian Stephanie Coontz.[6] Marylynn Salmon, who has studied women and property law of the period, concludes that "despite the promise of republicanism, American independence had little direct effect on the legal status of women."[7] Rhys Isaac points out that as the men who subscribed to the Virginia Declaration of Rights grappled with the incongruous existence of slavery and republicanism, they "confined" contract to "men . . . when they enter into a state of society." "Slaves, like women," Isaac notes, "were not parties to the contract—they were the captives of the free men who had formed the association."[8] One might infer that "the free men" also regarded women either as their own personal possessions or as the belongings of other men. "To focus . . . on what the Revolution did not accomplish—highlighting and lamenting its failure to abolish slavery and change fundamentally the lot of women—is to miss the great significance of what it did accomplish," cautions Gordon S. Wood, who maintains that the Revolution "made possible the anti-slavery and women's rights movements of the nineteenth century and in fact all our current egalitarian thinking."[9] Still, frustration born of inordinate delay is fundamental to all human nature, even to some females in the American South.

At a time when the pursuit of a livelihood remained essentially home-based, the colonial courts in both the North and the South had routinely upheld the authority of male heads of households. Generally men did not leave the premises—that is, their residences, farms, or plantations—to go "out to work"; "long hunters" represented a notable exception. Women therefore "had no sphere for retreat nor any domain in which to exercise special authority." Whether acting as "deputy husbands" in a quasi-public realm or as keepers of hearth and home in an exclusively private domain, "woman's place was an explicitly subordinate and dependent one in every arena." Families provided "the very bedrock of state authority," which in turn rested on "a corporate, hierarchical community of households that subordinated family independence to the authority of household and community heads."[10]

Patriarchy—intrinsic to that hierarchy and particularly pronounced in the South—encouraged a general social acceptance of inequality and rank and the deference of lesser men to greater ones and servants to masters. The historian Stephanie Coontz maintains that "the subordination of women and the dominance of men" was "based less on ideas about gender than on ideas about the need for hierarchy in all relations" that characterized the times.[11] Still, this intricate arrangement permitted only males to be patriarchs, with widows sometimes legally recognized as heads of households. Therefore, patriarchy seems to have been gender-determined, which in turn meant that women occupied an inferior status. Class distinctions came into play, but white women deferred to white men; and in the European-influenced culture of colonial and revolutionary America, women of color acquiesced to white women and to all shades of men. In Coontz's words, southern colonial society possessed "some special characteristics," but "southern society, like northern, was still based on an organic interdependence of households in a tangle of hierarchy, deference, and obligation."[12]

When the colonies severed their ties with the British Empire, the historian Carl Bridenbaugh declares, "there was no South." Instead, he identifies at least three "modes of existence": "the old Chesapeake," a "youthful Carolina society," and "the lusty Back Country."[13] Out of this era developed the regional entity that John Richard Alden calls the First South. Its appearance, dating from 1775 to 1789, coincided with the creation of the American nation.[14] Diversity characterized the southern colonies when they broke with England, but semantics aside, men of the South figured prominently in the American Revolution and in the political restructuring that dominated public life during much of the eighteenth century.

The historian Marylynn Salmon claims that in at least one area involving females, men in the southern colonies had taken the lead. Courts in the region during the seventeenth and eighteenth centuries defended the property rights of women, even married ones, more aggressively than did the northern courts. Salmon writes that "statutes in Maryland and Virginia included guidelines for protecting the property rights of women from the beginning of the colonial period." Similar procedures existed in the Carolinas, and soon after South Carolina became a separate colony, it moved to reaffirm them. "Courts in all three colonies enforced the statutory requirements to the letter," Salmon observes. "Northerners, however, even after establishing rules for the recording of deeds, did not have the same degree of commitment to following common law rules on women's participation."[15]

Why southerners placed particular statutory emphasis on the private examinations of married women by courts to determine their state of mind on property conveyances is less certain. On the one hand, they may have "behaved in an overprotective, patriarchal fashion because they placed so much emphasis on female helplessness," Salmon explains. On the other, "Because courts in Maryland, Virginia, and South Carolina accepted the existence of coercion, they acted consistently in demanding both female acknowledgments and private examinations."[16] Another possible scenario is that southern men perceived the mishandling of property that a woman carried into marriage as an adverse reflection on her family and an affront to her male relatives. This in turn may have spurred their attentiveness to legal niceties involving females and property. All the same, mere compliance with common-law procedures relative to women's property rights in the public courts hardly negated the private paternalistic influences and the social conditioning that shaped or predetermined female responses.

In the new nation, both northern and southern women remained in a political netherworld that affected all other dimensions of their lives. Economic independence remained impossible for the great majority of American women, and access to any kind of formal education continued to elude many of them during the 1700s. As many as half probably could not write their names on wills, and a greater proportion could not compose and draft a coherent letter.[17] Illiteracy among females may have been even greater in the South during this era. In some respects the acceptance of a marriage proposal represented about the only significant decision to which an eighteenth-century female would ever contribute, and even in this she may not have acted entirely alone.

According to a deposition given before the clerk and master in equity for the Washington district in Tennessee on 9 February 1799, Peter Williams claimed to have witnessed Agnes Tarbet in various stages of dress and undress and in compromising positions with men other than her spouse. Once Williams had "observed the said Witt and Agnes both together sitting on the ground about twenty yards from a small path . . . the said Witt

and said Agnes lay on the ground and the said Witt got on top of said
Agnes—her clothes being up so as her skin was naked nearly as far as her
hips and remained in that position for some minutes." The witness, who
seems to have taken an extraordinary interest in Agnes's activities, claimed
that on one occasion he had "asked her why she had married Alexander
Tarbet seeing she did not live with him. She answered she never wanted to
marry him nor never wanted to live with him, and that her parents induced
her to marry him as she believed for the purpose of getting what he had."[18]

Along with the repressive circumstances common to almost all women
of the period, domestic violence visited itself on an unfortunate few. In
1806, for instance, a justice of the peace for Carter County, Tennessee, submitted a petition for divorce to the Tennessee Superior Court of Law and
Equity, then sitting in neighboring Washington County, on behalf of the
illiterate Elizabeth Crawley, who managed only to affix her mark to the
document. After her marriage in 1800, Elizabeth had lived with her husband, William, for a few months in North Carolina before moving to northeast Tennessee. She swore that her spouse "frequently beat and abused her
in a cruel and outragious manner, that compelled her to leave him and seek
shelter with a brother of hers without any cause or provocation; and kept
her in great dread and alarm by threatening to blow up the house with gun
powder and destroy her." This situation stemmed from his "habitual intox-
ication." On 13 April 1803

the said William Crawley abused her, and burned and distroyed all her wearing
apparel except that which she had on at the time, and threatening to burn her also
if she came in the house, and on the same day wilfully and maliciously abandoned
her. On the 23rd day of the said month the property of William Crawley was sold
by execution for his debts since which time, [the] petitioner has supported herself
by her own industry, without any aid or assistance from her husband, or benifit of
any of his property.

More than three years had elapsed since she had last cohabited with him.
Although Elizabeth Crawley lacked the rudiments of formal education, she
had the good sense to attempt to sever her legal connections with an abusive partner.[19]

The inferiority of women, upon which American society rested, contradicted eighteenth-century egalitarian ideals. Such unusual men as Thomas Paine and Benjamin Franklin recognized sexual discrimination for the
anomaly that it was, and Franklin specifically lent support to the idea of
educating females. During the last quarter of the 1700s, as schools for
young ladies proliferated in the new nation, the Moravians established
some of the best. One of these, Salem Female Academy in North Carolina,
opened in 1772 as a day school for very young girls. Thirty years later it
was catering to older boarders, and it welcomed females who were not

members of the denomination. The curriculum included a fairly rigorous academic program along with the expected ornamental work, drawing, and music.[20]

The academy attracted girls from great distances. Escorted by male relatives, usually their fathers, they rode hundreds of miles on horseback to enroll. "When Salem was reached," according to one source, "the horses were sold and the saddles hung in the saddle-room to remain four years. At the end of the course of study the fathers returned to Salem, purchased horses, the saddles were taken down, and the company bade farewell to the schoolhome." Two of its alumnae presided at the White House, and several of them graced southern governors' mansions. A few became the wives of high-ranking officers, among them Mrs. Thomas J. ("Stonewall") Jackson.[21]

Primitive though laudable in their beginnings, such female academies as the one at Salem represented the most modest of milestones toward elevating the status of women. From the vantage of the early nineteenth century, the British traveler Harriet Martineau charged that "the Americans have, in their treatment of women, fallen below, not only their own democratic principles, but the practise of some parts of the Old World." At the same time, "there is no country . . . where there is so much boasting of the 'chivalrous' treatment she enjoys." Martineau scornfully elaborated:

That is to say—she has the best place in the stage-coaches; where there are not chairs enough for everybody, the gentlemen stand; she hears oratorical flourishes on public occasions about wives and home, and apostrophes to women; her husband's hair stands on end at the idea of her working, and he toils to indulge her with money; she has the liberty to get her brain turned by religious excitements, that her attention may be diverted from morals, politics, and philosophy; and especially, her morals are guarded by the strictest observance of propriety in her presence. In short, indulgence is given her as a substitute for justice.[22]

Just as chivalry represented one extreme in male-female relations, misogyny provided the other. Landon Carter of Virginia's Sabine Hall, having become disenchanted with his son, Robert Wormeley Carter, attempted to explain his offspring's ingratitude, disrespect, and fondness for gambling. The cause, the elder Carter concluded, rested with Winifred Travers Beale, the son's wife. In his old age, Landon Carter assumed that "most women were Eve figures who had, as he remarked in August 1772, 'nothing in the general in view, but the breeding contests at home.'" Some five years later, when he learned that a few Philadelphia women had tampered with American guns and lent assistance to the British, he declared, "I don't think there can be a more treacherous, interprising, Perverse, and hellish Genius than is to be met with in A Woman." He continued: "Madam Eve we see at the very hazard of Paradise suffered the devil to tempt her; and of such a tendency has her sex been."[23]

Studying the commonplace books of William Byrd II and Thomas Jefferson, the historian Kenneth A. Lockridge discerned intense manifestations of misogyny in the private musings of two other elite representatives of eighteenth-century Virginia. Given the contents of Byrd's secret diary, with which the historical profession has long been familiar, Lockridge's revelations about him are hardly shocking; but with Jefferson's wide-ranging political influence, the complex and complicated author of the Declaration of Independence is more problematic; his subtle but undisguised misogyny is more troublesome. Along with entries of anecdotes, quotations, and material from other sources, keepers of commonplace books sometimes included commentaries, original essays, or other personal information. Both Byrd and Jefferson clearly lamented their sex's having to rely on women in order to reproduce themselves and that in this dimension of the human experience men had to place themselves at the less-than-tender mercies of females. Unwilling to risk the censure that venting their frustrations about women in public might bring, Byrd and Jefferson spilled their inky venom onto private pages.[24]

Lockridge further contends that during the eighteenth century "new public arguments had to be constructed" to disqualify women politically. Therefore, "modes of partial but confined participation for women" developed. "The mythologies of the 'republican wife' and the 'republican mother'" provided the vehicles that kept women "nicely confined to the home." In this manner, women citizens "functioned chiefly as symbols for affective values and for social solidarity that were being abandoned by a masculinized liberalism." "The subtle and perverse misogyny of the new democratic age," he writes, gave rise to "the republican wife and mother" who "like the Southern Belle . . . were traps for women still seeking liberation."[25]

Without succumbing to less-than-persuasive psychological ruminations, it bears mentioning that two of the greatest American revolutionaries—both Virginians, George Washington, one of republicanism's ablest practitioners, and Thomas Jefferson, probably its greatest philosopher—seem to have had strained relationships with their mothers; both of them also married widows, a tried-and-true course for Virginia gentlemen seeking to enlarge their patrimony. According to the historian Julia Cherry Spruill, Washington's mother "appears to have been a rather strong-willed person, uncultured and with little regard for appearances, and, in her latter days, she was obsessed with a fear of want." Washington did not wish to have her live at Mount Vernon, where he ensconced his wife, the widow Martha Dandridge Custis, but he visited his mother when he happened through Fredericksburg. Although he had bought her a house and garden that she selected and although he routinely responded to her requests for money, she seemed intent on embarrassing him. In fact, she complained so bitterly of her circumstances that a project was commenced in the Virginia Assembly to provide her with a pension. Washington, "mortified and indignant," arranged to halt the proceedings.[26]

Jefferson's mother, the widow Jane Randolph Jefferson, unlike Washington's, proved to be neither a whiner nor a public embarrassment. Mrs. Jefferson, in accordance with her dead husband's wishes, assumed full authority at Shadwell, the home built during Peter Jefferson's lifetime. She also managed the plantation and effectively controlled her five daughters and two sons, including Thomas, the eldest. Lockridge writes that "the rash of quotations on power, rebellion, and hateful women" in Jefferson's commonplace book seem to have dated from the time of Peter Jefferson's death until the younger Jefferson attained his majority. The entries include "references to the fatally ignorant decisions of men who marry, to a father's doom, to a vain wish to lay one's head in a mother's lap yet an inability to trust, to being misunderstood, to whipped boys, to struggles over money, to a desperate need to assert manhood and independence."[27]

Married but subsequently widowed, Jefferson avoided matrimony a second time. Almost obsessed with feminine cleanliness, he counseled fastidiousness in his daughter and cautioned her to avoid being a slut. Even the design of Monticello, his physical creation and nothing less than a masculine forum, placed no significance on the space assigned to women or family.[28] Robert Wernick, writing for the *Smithsonian*, observes that "life could not have been comfortable" on the mountain "before the building was completed in 1809, and it is painful to think of young, pretty Martha Jefferson arriving to start her honeymoon in an unlit, unheated house surrounded by three feet of snow and then living there, with her husband away most of the time governing Virginia or writing revolutionary prose." Mrs. Jefferson occupied "a house of never-quite-finished walls and a never-quite-finished roof, breathing brick and plaster dust, being buffeted by savage winds, bearing six children in ten years and losing four of them, till she died in 1782, not yet 34."[29] Dumas Malone, one of Jefferson's principal biographers, called the marriage a "genuine love match" and "the happiest period" of Jefferson's life.[30] Still, virtually nothing is known of Mrs. Jefferson's innermost thoughts. Adding the passages from Jefferson's commonplace book to other matters bearing on his private life and acknowledging the denials by all of Jefferson's principal biographers, one can still almost discern the echoing footsteps of his alleged mulatto paramour, Sally Hemings, glimpse the intimate Jefferson, and find plausible the inner emotions described by the historian Fawn M. Brodie. Whether Jefferson engaged in sexual relations with a black woman or not, there were mulattoes at Monticello, which indicates a white male presence in his slave quarter.[31]

Bounded by the extremes of misogyny and chivalry, republicanism—

the masculine-contrived political philosophy of the American Enlightenment—inadvertently encouraged feminine yearnings for alternative status if not outright independence. A woman "was no longer liable to be viewed as a loud-mouthed shrew, a meddling interloper, or a devil's accomplice," observes the historian Nancy Woloch. "Rather, she might now be considered a rational individual and even a quasi-autonomous one—within the family circle." Republican motherhood recognized women as "value transmitters" but limited them to "familial roles." Assuming that women had the capacity to make patriotic men of their sons, some citizens dared suggest that women needed to be prepared to do so. Headmasters of academies seized upon this argument to promote female education and to recruit students. In Georgia the founder of one such establishment declared that its goal was "to nurture and fix the principle of virtue."[32] Likewise, in some quarters, republicanism and the Enlightenment "shifted perspectives on family authority from a patriarchal view linking father, king, and God to a republican emphasis on contract, duty, and consent." Literate women expressed their enthusiasm for romantic love and companionate marriages instead of economic-driven male-dominated unions.[33] Such notions stood a better chance in settings where men proved more willing to eradicate human bondage.

The southern gentry carefully prepared girls for domesticity and a life of subordination to men. In a 1773 letter addressed to George Washington, Benedict Calvert wrote of his own daughter, Nelly, who was about to become engaged to Washington's stepson, John Parke Custis: "It has ever been the Endeavour of her Mother and me, to bring her up in such a manner, as to ensure the happiness of her future Husband, in which, I think, we have not been unsuccessfull." If that should prove not to be the case, "we shall be greatly disappointed."[34] Washington's letters to a niece during this era offer some insight into his attitudes regarding appropriate feminine conduct. He cautioned her to "remember that as she was being stamped with a character which would last a lifetime she should be careful of her company, and accept the advice of the cousins with whom she was living." Because she lacked wealth, "she should supply her want of fortune by cultivating submissiveness, industry, usefulness and frugality, traits of benefit not only to her but to the man she might marry."[35] Martha Washington, on the other hand, counseled an aggressive defense when, with less than perfect spelling, she communicated with a newly widowed niece: "If you doe not no one else will. . . . A dependance is I think a wrached state and you will have enogh if you will mannage it right."[36]

The venerable Jefferson encouraged his daughters to develop their minds at least to the point of being well read, but he also intended for them in due time to enter into marriages and assume their proper domestic roles. In 1790 he wrote to his daughter, the newly wed Martha Randolph: "The happiness of your life depends now on the continuing to please a single person; to this all other objects must be secondary."[37] In February 1791 he advised her that of all of her letters, the last two had given him the greatest satisfaction: "The one announced that you were become a notable house-wife, the other a mother."[38]

Both the high and the low anticipated matrimony and motherhood. Be-cause "the double standard was firmly in force," writes the historian Mary Beth Norton, "many genteel young women adhered . . . to strict standards of behavior." Those "who engaged in premarital sex, or who were merely suspected of having done so, had greatly lessened their chances for a good marriage." Even strict adherence to prescribed codes of conduct "could not guarantee that a girl would find a worthy husband, but careless behavior on her part would almost certainly lead to an unfavorable result." Poorer girls, too, understood the ground rules and sometimes valiantly resisted attempts on their virtue. "Let not your chiefest glory be immurd in the nice casket of a Madenhead withhold not what thou shoul[d]est communicate," an over-heated swain wrote to a North Carolina farmer's daughter. Another de-clared that her "coldness" led him to fear that he might "run Crasey."[39]

It may be assumed, however, that passion prevailed in more than a few instances. Rachel, a girl from a prominent Virginia family, for example, suc-cumbed to the charms of a French officer who served at Yorktown. He impregnated her but refused to marry her. When she gave birth to an ille-gitimate son, her friends recognized that she had doomed herself in polite society. Rachel's indiscretion also tainted her younger sister's chances for a worthy match. Ultimately Rachel married "an obscure man in her neigh-borhood" and gave birth to his two offspring.[40]

Although a double standard for the two sexes clearly existed, liberty and equality—those twin contagions of the American revolutionary exper-ience—spread among the enslaved and the free, giving rise to independent thoughts among blacks and whites, women as well as men. In 1769 two whites in East Florida bickered over the ownership of a black slave, but Miss Charlotte, as she was known, lived with neither of them and went about as she pleased, claiming her freedom.[41] Mary Beth Norton has written, "The war brought a chance—a slim one, admittedly, but still a chance—for freedom."[42]

On large plantations by the late eighteenth century, specialization in work assignments had developed. Nonetheless most black females probably had an intimate acquaintance with field work and similar forms of heavy labor. The lord of Mount Vernon, George Washington, for example, re-corded the following in his diaries:

October 27, 1787, "At the Ferry set 3 plows to Work—put the girl Eby to one of them."

May 5, 1787, "The Women Preparing, and hoeing the New grd. in front of the House."

April 11, 1787, "The Women . . . were hoeing the Wet part of the grd. between the Meadows which the plows could not touch. Ordered them as soon as this was done to go to the Ferry, and Assist in getting the grd. in the New Meadow in order for Oats and Timothy."

January 21, 1788, " . . . two Men were cutting Trunnels for Fences, and the Women were carrying Rails from the swamp side to the Division fence."[43]

In the course of a lifetime a black female in the eighteenth-century South could have performed a variety of tasks ranging from field work to minding children and serving in the big house; she might also have been called upon to fulfill the duties of nurse and midwife to both races. Whatever the demands and expectations, slave women by the mid 1700s generally lived in extended families and worked alongside sisters and brothers, mothers and fathers, sons and daughters, and an assortment of other relatives.[44]

The American Revolution touched the lives of slaves in at least two discernible ways. When southern planters found themselves deprived of British goods and services, they encouraged their black servants to develop skills. Trade restrictions and the war left the planters without manufactured cloth, so they fostered the development of spinning and weaving among their slaves. From the owners' perspective, chattels with skills possessed greater material value; in the slave quarters they may also have enjoyed a social status above the common run of field hands, garnering a measure of respect from other blacks and an enhanced sense of their own self-worth. More significantly and certainly more tangibly, British policy encouraged runaways. In November 1775 Virginia's last royal governor, Lord Dunmore, offered freedom to all indentured servants and black slaves who would join forces to suppress the rebellion. Some eight hundred slaves immediately answered the call. Wherever the British army made an appearance in the South, blacks fled from their American masters. Male runaways outnumbered female ones, but the war swelled the numbers for both genders. The fact that the South came out of the Revolution more devastated than the northern and middle states partially helps to explain the reluctance of southern white males to emancipate their slaves, educate their women, and institute egalitarian theory. Instead they occupied themselves with recreating what they themselves had lost, not with building a new society that would provide opportunities for others.[45]

No lesser revolutionaries or republicans than their northern brothers, southerners generously, if somewhat less substantively, employed the political rhetoric of the era and paid customary homage to the republican wife and mother. Indeed, no better example existed than Eliza Lucas Pinckney of South Carolina. So esteemed was she for having successfully inculcated civic virtue, piety, reason, and moderation in her sons—Thomas and Charles Cotesworth, who seemed destined for brilliant careers in federal service—that the national patriarch, President George Washington, paid her a special visit at Hampton, her daughter's plantation on the Santee River, in 1791. When she died two years later in Philadelphia, after a widowhood that spanned more than three decades, the president volunteered to serve as a pallbearer at her funeral.[46]

Some ten years later, on 10 June 1811, in Charleston, another noteworthy South Carolina woman, Martha Laurens Ramsay, expired, leaving a husband who was very much alive. Just three days earlier she had told her spouse, David Ramsay, about a diary that she had maintained for fourteen years of their marriage and instructed him to keep the manuscripts "as a common book of the family." Instead, David hurriedly arranged to publish and disseminate the diary. He supposedly believed that her *Memoirs* "would generate virtue wherever they were read" and "reasoned that a print memorial to an exemplary woman could encourage social harmony and civic duty" at a time when party strife and sectional divisions seemed to threaten the nation's integrity. David Ramsay epitomized the "lay patriot-preaching" citizen of the era, but much of poor Martha's diary actually dealt with her severe mental depression of 1795, which she called her "Dark Night of the Soul." Employing religious rhetoric, she revealed the very real and devastating circumstances that plummeted her into an emotional abyss.[47]

Of prominent Huguenot ancestry and accustomed to material comforts, having enjoyed the benefits of travel and residence in England and France, and sensitive to family honor, Martha appropriately deferred to males, first her father and uncle and then her husband. She had married David Ramsay, a physician already twice widowed, in 1787, a love match somewhat beneath her station. The enthusiasm with which the couple set about producing offspring led one female friend to write, "The act of getting them from the sweet Dr. must be very delightful for when you hear people talk of such things, you can't help bringing to your mind that situation."[48]

Martha's "profound depression" commenced in 1795 and lasted into the early months of the next year. It grew out of "the combined blows of economic distress, anxieties about social standing and reputation, and helplessness in her religious domain." Martha remained devoted to her husband although he bore personal responsibility for a substantial share of the couple's troubles. David's medical practice languished, and he demonstrated poor business acumen. As a consequence, the family found itself without necessities and even faced bankruptcy. The Ramsays mortgaged their home and underwent the legalities of dower renunciation, by which Martha gave up all properties she had brought into the marriage. In the midst of these calamities an orphaned niece eloped and made a disastrous marriage.[49]

"For readers who idealized the self-sacrificing virtue recently and classically exemplified by Revolutionary War heroes like George Washington or Nathanael Greene," writes the historian Joanna Bowen Gillespie, "David's insertion of a Good Wife into the pantheon of national heroes was audacious and timely." On another level, Martha's *Memoirs* provides access to the inner turmoil of a woman whose eighteenth-century professional family found itself under severe economic pressure in the aftermath of the American Revolution. Financial problems—even litigation over debts—declining social circumstances, and deteriorating health dogged her for the remainder of her life. In spite of all of this, the private musings of this proud southern woman remained "free of conventional feminine rhetoric—expressions of modesty, humility, dependence. Whatever her public impression, her private view of femininity was anything but self-effacing. . . . Her language does not differ essentially from that of any pious male diarist."[50] Details from the life of Martha Laurens Ramsay, on the one hand, and the publication of her *Memoirs* by David Ramsay, on the other, serve as reminders that a considerable chasm existed between the rhetoric associated with women's lives of the revolutionary era and the reality of their day-to-day existence.

Still, elite eighteenth-century South Carolinians like the Ramsays enjoyed the benefits of a fairly urbane existence. "Social and cultural barrenness" may have characterized plantation existence along the swampy Carolina coast, but "a mobile gentry overcame the twin blights of ruralness and isolation" in the town of Charleston. And "if the Chesapeake Society was noted for its men, the glory of the Carolina was its women," according to the historian Carl Bridenbaugh, who writes: "Rice-field butterflies made excellent wives and mothers." David Ramsay, a disciple of republicanism and a purveyor of the "republican wife" and "republican mother," in keeping with the spirit of the age, had observed that "the name of the family always depends on the sons; but its respectability, comfort, and domestic happiness, often on the daughters."[51]

As they graced polite society, the low-country women, revered for their beauty and charm, also won accolades for their strength of character. Charlestonians, too, had a strong claim to being the least provincial of the colonials. The economically advantaged among them enthusiastically embraced travel, theatricals, and genteel dancing. Originating as early as 1762, one long-lived purveyor of old southern social traditions, the St. Cecilia Society, represented patrons of music and assumed the sponsorship of an annual ball open only to the crème de la crème, a tradition that has endured into the late twentieth century. One sardonic commentator has mentioned that "even in the 1990s, a woman will be asked to leave the St. Cecilia's Ball in

Charleston if she arrives wearing a gown that shows her ankles." Whatever cultural discipline colonial Charleston may have lacked, it surmounted with its enthusiasm for the beaux arts, which gave rise to a "dilettante culture."[52]

What may have been the first women's club in America originated in Charleston. During 1707, "shortly after 170 male Dissenters had organized a political club, and while the town's only accused witch was still in prison," writes Bridenbaugh, the females followed suit. A disconcerted minister of that place and time declared, "What is most singular, the women of the town are turned politicians also and here have a club where they meet weekly among themselves, but not without falling out with one another."[53] The low country also claimed Henrietta Deering Johnston, perhaps the earliest American woman artist. She had come to Charleston in 1707 with her husband, the Reverend Gideon Johnston, and lived there until her death around 1728 or 1729; some of her pastel portraits survive.[54]

Even with such significant albeit incidental achievements, Josiah Quincy, who visited South Carolina in 1773, claimed that the ladies there lacked the vivaciousness of their northern counterparts. He also noted that it was customary in the polite society of Charleston for females to participate only in the first round of toasts at dinner and then to withdraw for the evening. Quincy thought to record two of the fairer sex's utterings on such occasions: "Delicate pleasures to susceptable minds" and "When passions rise may reason be the guide."[55] Janet Schaw, a British traveler who visited in North Carolina during the American Revolution, found that the women of Wilmington lacked fashionable clothes but observed that they "would make a good figure in any part of the world"; the men were less accomplished and cultivated.[56]

Superficial as certain aspects of eighteenth-century southern colonial society may have been and trite as the republican rhetoric applied to females, still some women below the Mason-Dixon line entered the fray, embracing the spirit of republicanism with great daring and personal bravery. Of these, Ann Bailey, born around 1742 and known as "the white squaw of the Kanawha," came to America from Liverpool, England, with her husband when she was about nineteen. When he was killed in 1774, she donned male garb and became a scout and messenger on the Virginia frontier. Adept with a gun and a horse and well versed in the lore of the woods, she counted among her exploits that she had ridden alone one hundred miles to secure gunpowder for the relief of Indian-besieged Fort Lee in 1791. When asked, "And what would the General say to you, when you used to get safe to camp with your ammunition?" she answered, "Why he'd say, you're a brave soldier, Ann, and tell the men to give me a dram." Reportedly fond of a dram, she no doubt took it. Ann Bailey spent her last days in Ohio, to which she had moved with a son. Denied a pension, she eked out an existence by raising fowl, which she carried some seven miles to market on her back.[57]

During this era the leisured political philosophers along the eastern seaboard expressed themselves eloquently in public discourse, sometimes fretting in private about the biological power of women and about men's dependence on females to continue the species; Jefferson, among them, dispatched magnificent missives from his mountaintop vigil. Meanwhile, land-hungry, independent-spirited common practitioners of republicanism marched steadily westward, procreating with abandon along the way. The likes of Ann Bailey epitomized the rough-and-rowdy denizens of that nebulous divide between civilization and barbarism, lending flesh and blood to frontier stereotypes.

The historian Daniel J. Boorstin has observed that all men and women of the backwoods were soldiers during the sporadic engagements of colonial warfare "because all lived on the battlefield." During 1766, when two families attempted to make their way to the protection of a fort in Shenandoah County, Virginia, five Indians attacked and killed both men. According to an account that Boorstin quotes, "the women, instead of swooning at the sight of their bleeding, expiring husbands, seized their axes, and with Amazonian firmness, and strength almost superhuman, defended themselves and children." A few years later, Mrs. Experience Bozarth "brained two Indians and disembowelled a third" with her trusty axe. "The backwoods was no place for the squeamish," writes Boorstin. "Anyone who waited for the arrival of 'troops' did not last long."[58]

Other women also confronted the challenges of the southern frontier in a less grandiose fashion; theirs, too, was a harsh lot. During the early 1700s while surveying the dividing line between Virginia and North Carolina, William Byrd II had come upon "a very civil woman." She displayed "nothing of ruggedness or immodesty in her carriage, yet she will carry a gun in the woods and kill deer, turkeys, etc., and shoot down wild cattle, catch and tye hogs, knock down beeves with an axe and perform the most manful exercises as well as most men in these parts."[59] The Reverend Charles Woodmason, an Anglican divine turned itinerant preacher, proved a sympathetic mid-eighteenth-century observer of the women of the Carolina backwoods. "In many places they have naught but a Gourd to drink out off Not a Plate, Knife or Spoon, a Glass, Cup or anything—It is well if they can get some Body Linen, and some have not even that. They are so burthen'd with Young Children, that the Woman cannot attend both House and Field—and many live by Hunting, and Killing of Deer—There's not a Cabbin but has 10 or 12 Young Children in it."[60] Commenting on frontier women of revolutionary Virginia, Nicholas Cresswell, a young English traveler, mentioned a notable housewife's inattention to cleanliness, a landlady's unattractiveness, and another woman's inebriation. He also attested to the custom among some white men of taking temporary Indian "wives."[61]

Native-American women and the white European wretches of the backwoods described by the Reverend Woodmason contrasted sharply with the privileged ladies of the low country; but the inhabitants of the upcountry, both native and white, who were engaged in the very struggle for survival, wasted little time or energy on self-pity. A durable and resilient breed, the Scotch-Irish, for example, had begun to migrate through such ports as Philadelphia and Charleston during the early eighteenth century. In the South these independent-spirited newcomers possessed neither the resources nor the desire to settle down among Englishmen and become the planters of rice and indigo. As they made their way into the wilderness, they left in their wake the established residents along the coast who were happy enough to send the newcomers on their way.[62]

That ever-advancing line of settlement and the seemingly insatiable appetite for western land had already served as catalysts for the French and Indian War. In 1756, two years after that conflict had begun, provincial troops from South Carolina, along with a lesser number of British, established the westernmost English outpost in America. Fort Loudoun, on the Little Tennessee River some five hundred miles from Charleston, shielded the Overhill Cherokee towns from attacks by French-inspired Indians. It also protected Cherokee women and children while their men absented themselves to campaign with the English. Garrisoned by his majesty's regulars, Fort Loudoun itself eventually came under siege from former allies, Cherokee warriors. For a variety of reasons, relations between the Cherokees and the English had deteriorated until these one-time friends were engaged in mortal combat with each other.[63]

Unable to take the fort directly, the belligerent Indians attempted to starve the garrison into submission, but Cherokee women temporarily foiled that plan. Some of them had white "husbands" at the fort to whom they managed to smuggle food. Their efforts notwithstanding, provisions reached such abysmal levels that the garrison in its last days subsisted principally on horseflesh. Along with providing sexual pleasures and companionship, the native women had gathered much-needed intelligence, which the commander, Raymond Demere, claimed was "amongst the Indians . . . always best." Defying the war chief who tried to stop their comings and goings, the women laughingly advised him that their relatives would kill him to atone for their deaths if he were to follow through with his threats. Nonetheless the almost inevitable surrender of Fort Loudoun occurred on 7 August 1760. Granted safe passage out of the back country, the English entourage began the trek toward South Carolina. After one day's march their escort vanished, and Cherokee warriors ambushed the soldiers and the women and children who accompanied them. Although accounts vary, at least three women seem to have perished during the attack, with one source placing the total number of dead as high as two to three hundred. Whether the victims included Indian women is not clear, for some soldiers had brought their white wives and families with them.[64]

Of Native-American women who lent sustenance to white settlers, no name has inspired greater reverence than that of Nancy Ward, "War Woman of the Cherokee." Born about 1738, Nanye'hi of the Wolf clan at Chota in present-day Tennessee, the principal town of the Overhill Cherokee, subsequently married Kingfisher of the Deer clan and gave birth to two children, Fivekiller and Catherine. In 1755 Nanye'hi accompanied her husband on an expedition against the Creeks. When he fell in battle, she seized the dead man's gun and assumed his place. That she took on a warrior's identity, a role usually reserved for males, had not heretofore been unknown among the Cherokees. Such women, though rare, enjoyed the adulation of their people as well as prestigious political and ceremonial status.[65]

Considerable discretionary authority also reposed with "war women." Lieutenant Henry Timberlake, who was stationed at Fort Loudoun during the 1750s, claimed that their power was "so great, that they can, by the wave of a swan's wing, deliver a wretch condemned by the council, and already tied to the stake." Nanye'hi had married Bryant Ward, a white trader, and had become known as Nancy Ward. In 1776 she intervened to save the life of Mrs. William Bean, who had been taken captive from one of the illegal settlements in northeast Tennessee. Nancy Ward, however, did not lift a finger to save a boy taken at the same time, so he was burned at the stake. On another occasion, in 1781, she chose to act surreptitiously when she and some other Cherokee women assisted in the escape of five white traders. Nancy Ward sided with the newly created United States during the American Revolution. Most of her own people supported the British because the Cherokees harbored resentments against the acquisitive colonials who had encroached on their lands. Nancy's second husband, Bryant Ward, the father of her daughter, Elizabeth, had returned to his South Carolina family after a few years of residence in and around Chota. Both Elizabeth and Elizabeth's daughter married white men. In 1822 Nancy Ward, who had become an innkeeper along the federal road that ran from Georgia to Nashville, Tennessee, died in the valley of the Ocoee River. She had moved there after the Cherokees ceded tracts of land that included her birthplace of Chota.[66]

In the wake of the French and Indian War, the breach between the mother country and the colonies widened. Politics placed men in America and those in the British Isles at political odds, but they formed a relatively united front along gender lines to keep women within their traditional roles and in their assigned places. On both sides of the Atlantic the male sex dismissed or trivialized the patriotic outpourings of females. When fifty-one women in Edenton, North Carolina, endorsed the Nonimportation Association's resolves of 1774 and offered a petition stating their inability to remain "indifferent on any occasion that appears nearly to affect the peace and happiness of our country," a cartoonist back in the mother country ridiculed the gathering. Arthur Iredell, another Englishman, expressed mock fear not only of the "Male Congress" but also of "a Female Congress at Edenton," for "the Ladies . . . have ever, since the Amazonian Era, been esteemed the most formidable Enemies."[67]

Discouraged but undaunted, women continued to organize. Inspired by the leadership of the Ladies Association of Philadelphia, American women in various locations (including Maryland and Virginia) raised money for the troops through door-to-door solicitation. Martha Wayles Jefferson, the wife of Virginia's Governor Thomas Jefferson, received a copy of the plan put forth by the Philadelphians. In poor health and unable to participate directly, she took limited action, sanctioned, she believed, by Martha Washington's suggestion that the Pennsylvania effort might be imitated. What seems to be Mrs. Jefferson's only surviving piece of correspondence, a letter to a friend, related to this matter. When the Philadelphia group stipulated that the money should go directly to the soldiers, General Washington refused it, suggesting alternatives but finally insisting that the money be spent for shirts and that the women make the shirts themselves to save the expense of seamstresses.[68] Washington's own wife, who spent every winter from 1776 until the end of the war with the general and the troops, "directed the officers' wives in knitting, sewing, patching, and the making of new garments whenever materials could be secured."[69]

Mary Beth Norton notes the irony of Washington's insistence on shirts. The Philadelphia women "had embarked on a very unfeminine enterprise, [but] were ultimately deflected into a traditional domestic role. The general's encomium made this explicit by its references to 'female patriotism' and 'those softer domestic virtues,' which presumably included the ability to sew." These particular females, "who had tried to chart an independent course for themselves and to establish an unprecedented nationwide female organization, ended up as what one amused historian has termed 'General Washington's Sewing Circle.'" The general enjoyed somewhat less success in dispatching the hundreds of women who refused to be separated from their husbands or from paid work in the camps; their persistence and his inability to dislodge them left him to acknowledge what he, in frustration, called the "Women of the Army."[70]

Lady Washington, as the soldiers sometimes addressed their commander's wife, the most famous camp follower of the lot (apparently with her husband's acquiescence, since he officially claimed expenses for her), "drove up from Virginia, her coach completely filled with cooked foods from Mount Vernon," to spend winters. The "role of republican queen" ill suited Martha. Needlework represented about the only accomplishment for which she had been trained, which may explain her husband's fixation on sewing as a proper feminine endeavor. "She had not read widely, she had slight interest in politics, and she could not make sparkling conversation," according to one standard source. Nearly sixty years of age when her husband assumed the presidency, "she had never been to Europe, much less to court. She was plump and had for years not attempted even the Virginia reel, which was the usual dance for Chesapeake people in the days of her youth." Never having attended dancing school, she sat out the minuets and quadrilles and watched her husband preen with other partners. Compared to Abigail Adams, her successor as first lady, she seems dull. All the same, "how much Washington got with the widow" may have blinded him to any faults and frailties. According to James Horrell, a businessman turned historian, Martha was worth about $6 million in modern terms, not including seventeen thousand acres of plantation land.[71]

Men of all stations harbored definite notions about the appropriate venue for women. When the war separated Oliver Hart, a South Carolinian, from his wife, he fantasized to relieve his loneliness: "On my farm, busying yourself with your Poultry, traveling the Fields, admiring the Flocks and herds, or within, managing the Dairy."[72] Although not the heady stuff of romance novels, Hart's daydreams about his own wife probably reflected the more normal circumstances of the life and labor of rural southern white women of the revolutionary era. Only the very well-to-do escaped the rigors of agricultural cultivation. Most women combined work in the fields and in their vegetable gardens with tending livestock and caring for their houses and children. A tutor, Philip Vickers Fithian, observed white women putting out corn in Virginia; and a female loyalist, Janet Russell of Georgia, claimed to have regularly milked thirty-two cows.[73] The mythological southern lady, surrounded by scores of slaves to attend her and wallowing in indolence, has ensnared even a few contemporary scholars, which sometimes renders them inattentive to matters of class and the wide-ranging life experiences of southern women. These scholars have been known to assume that white females below the Mason-Dixon line did not labor in the fields; others have seemed startled when their research indicates the contrary.

Sensitive to the criticism of women that was being bantered about and to the restrictions placed upon them, Eliza Wilkinson, a young widow who ran one of her parents' sea-island plantations during the American War for

Independence, declared: "I won't have it thought, that because we are the weaker sex as to *bodily* strength . . . we are capable of nothing more than minding the dairy, visiting the poultry-house, and all such domestic concerns; our thoughts can soar aloft, [and] we can form conceptions of things of higher nature; and have as just a sense of honor, glory, and great actions, as these 'Lords of the Creation.'" Wilkinson boasted in 1779 that there "never were greater politicians than the several knots of ladies, who met together. All trifling discourse of fashions, and such low little chat was thrown by, and we commenced perfect statesmen."[74] Three years later she was still ruminating about her status as a "female patriot": "I do not love to meddle with political matters; the men say we have no business with them, it is not in our sphere! . . . but surely we may have sense enough to give our opinions . . . without being reminded of our spinning and household affairs."[75]

Although Wilkinson wrote passionately about her patriotism and women's claims to citizenship, she expressed herself passively and privately. Other women actively engaged themselves in the public conduct of war. The camp followers, nurses, and Molly Pitcher types have occasionally attracted historical interest. "Molly Pitcher" may have been Mary Ludwig Hays Mc-Cauley in real life, but she became a heroine who carried water to cool the cannons in American mythology. Both Margaret Corbin and Mary Hays possessed some claim to having served as models for the image. Corbin assumed her spouse's position at a cannon when he went down defending Fort Washington, New York, in November 1776; Hays fought beside her husband, a gunner, at the Battle of Monmouth, New Jersey, in June 1778. In any event the historian Sandra Gioia Treadway observes, "the Molly Pitcher legend took deep root in American folklore . . . because it reflected the battlefield experiences of scores of anonymous civilian women who cared for the sick, carried water for the swabbing of cannons, and filled the fighting ranks when soldiers fell."[76]

Almost all of these women have remained historically unidentified, but on 6 February 1808 the Virginia General Assembly lifted one of them from obscurity when it enacted legislation that extended the state pension list; among the additional names was that of Anna Maria Lane, a native of New England, who with her husband, also a veteran of the Revolution, had settled in the Old Dominion after the peace. Treadway says that Lane, who had engaged the enemy on southern as well as northern soil, was "the only known female veteran of the American Revolution living in Virginia." Lane was awarded $100 annually for the remainder of her life, an amount two and one-half times that extended to the other new pensioners; the reason given was that she "in the revolutionary war, in the garb, and with the courage of a soldier, performed extraordinary military services, and received a severe wound at the battle of Germantown."[77]

Although the Virginia Assembly did not provide specifics, Anna Maria Lane had apparently performed in an exceptional manner. Throughout the South, women had routinely fed and sheltered the bands of patriots who hounded the British. A few among them also stretched the boundaries of traditional feminine conduct. On Powder Branch in the Watauga settlement of what would become northeast Tennessee, Mary Patton made the gunpowder that sustained the Overmountain Men at the Battle of King's Mountain in 1780; the museum at Rocky Mount Historic Site displays the kettle that she supposedly used. Females also labored at the Westham forage and foundry near Richmond and the gunnery at Fredericksburg, Virginia. When Indians had raided back-country stations, striking out at Fort Caswell in July 1776, Ann Robertson, a sister of the prominent frontiersman James Robertson, rallied the "fairer sex." The women armed themselves with kettles of boiling water and doused the hostiles as they attempted to scale the walls of the fort. In the Carolinas the likes of Emily Geiger, Anne Kennedy, and Betsy Dowdy carried messages between revolutionary forces, and they alerted citizens of impending dangers from the enemy. They traveled overland by horseback under perilous circumstances for distances of sixty to one hundred miles to aid the cause. Nancy Hart braved the waters of the Savannah River on a raft made of grapevine-secured logs to gather information for Georgia troops about enemy positions in South Carolina.[78]

For sheer determination the women and children along with the aged who followed Colonels Elijah Clark and William Candler from the Georgia and South Carolina frontier in 1780 to the relative safety of the Tennessee back country deserve recognition. Faced with retaliation from the British and the Indians against whom their men were engaged in guerrilla warfare, they began their eleven-day trek to the north. Hungry, ill clothed, and with sickness among them, through mountainous terrain where roving bands of Indians prowled, some four hundred of them traveled approximately two hundred miles to reach the Nolichucky and Watauga settlements.[79]

The South lay desolate in the wake of the Revolution, and the sorry circumstances occasioned by the war profoundly affected its women. The fact that the region had experienced a loss of fifty-five thousand or more slaves caused a severe labor shortage, further complicating an already grim situation. Betsy Ambler Brent, a patriot and a Virginian, observed in 1809 that the revolutionary era had brought "poverty and perplexity of every kind to her family." Eliza Lucas Pinckney described her own state of South Carolina in 1782 as "greatly impoverished" from having lost so many slaves.[80] Events of these years served to remind loyalist women as well as supporters of the American cause that their legal identity derived from their husbands. During the British occupation of Charleston, for instance,

Anne Hart worried that she might be driven from her home because her husband had openly and actively supported the Revolution; only with reluctance did she leave South Carolina to live with him in New Jersey when the war was over. Female patriots endured great hardship, but the wives of loyalists probably suffered more.[81]

After the war, women continued to claim the right to petition, which they had enjoyed during the colonial period; but the outcome of their pleas still depended on the exclusively male legislative and judicial systems. More traditional petitions for which precedents existed and with which established governmental machinery had experience usually received favorable responses. A mother seeking to save some property from her inheritance to provide for her children or well-to-do women trying to hang on to family lands or dwellings might meet with sympathetic responses. In 1788, however, when sixty-six seamstresses in Charleston, thirty-four of whom were able only to make their marks, asked the South Carolina General Assembly to place higher duties on imported ready-made clothing that was putting them out of business, the legislators showed no enthusiasm.[82] The Lanes in Virginia came out of the war in such desperate straits that they had to remain in the state guard and in sundry public positions for the rest of their lives. Haunted by poverty, Anna Maria Lane's life epitomized the plight of poor women who took up the American cause and who had almost no recourse except to follow their husbands.[83]

Women's prospects for gainful and legitimate employment may have declined by the late eighteenth century, and warfare is often blamed for a loosening of morals. In any event, some women turned to prostitution out of desperation or because it appealed to them more than other types of work available to them; "houses" could be found in most American cities by the end of the century. Newly constructed theaters sometimes featured a "special gallery . . . reserved for 'loose women' and their clients." White females filled the ranks of the "sex trade" in both the North and the South during that era when "ruined women" sometimes took up prostitution to avoid starvation.[84] In the aftermath of the war, even some respectable females below the Mason-Dixon line apparently renounced modesty, one of the requisites of the southern lady, for the frivolity of fashion. In 1801 a Georgia newspaper in jest offered a prize "to the lady . . . who shall so arrange her few garments as to appear nearest to naked." The writer undoubtedly was referring to the classical revival that was sweeping European fashion, then having some effect in America. To achieve the desired result, women bared more skin than had previously been the custom and arranged "diaphanous white muslin" about themselves "in the manner of classical sculpture."[85]

Such superficialities hardly portended more substantive prospects for women. In spite of tremendous wartime sacrifices, according to Mary Beth Norton, "the specific dimensions of the southern woman's role . . . and the peculiarly rigid nature of the social hierarchy established by aristocratic white southern males . . . seem to have stemmed directly from the Revolution and its devastating aftermath." The North, less adversely affected, entered a postwar interlude of "experimentation with new ideas and social forms." In the South, with its well-entrenched patriarchy and heavy reliance on slave labor, "the difficult post-revolutionary years confirmed and solidified prewar patterns." In the North the republican wife and mother provided the activist imagery to which women should aspire in the new nation, albeit within the usual domestic constraints, but southern men of this generation seemed to have preferred their women all the more demure and delicate.[86]

Still, as the historian Glenna Matthews has observed, "there are scattered accounts of southern women, principally of the upper class, taking an interest in public affairs of the eighteenth century and even participating in the boisterous electioneering." At Warrenton, North Carolina, in 1786 the visiting Elkanah Watson reported "the most obese woman" he had ever laid eyes on, who also "appeared to be an active leader at the polls." Watson subsequently dined with her and her son and learned that "she had more political influence, and exerted it with greater effect, than any man in the county."[87]

In a Fourth of July oration delivered in 1789, Charles Cotesworth Pinckney, the son of the extraordinary Eliza Lucas Pinckney, employed passive imagery in a paean to southern women. He likened them to "a number of slender Columns, the most beauteous models of elegance & taste, erect & unimpaired notwithstanding the violence that occasioned the desolation which surrounds them." Pinckney's phrasing could be dismissed as mere oratorical flourish did it not bear such striking similarity to the imagery surrounding the mythological southern lady. In keeping with southern eccentricities, it is fitting that Charles Cotesworth Pinckney's South Carolina also spawned the female reformer Sarah Moore Grimké, born in 1792, one of the greatest opponents of both slavery and the subordination of women in nineteenth-century America.[88]

Over the span of two centuries the transplanted Europeans along the eastern seaboard of North America had transformed themselves from colonials to nationals and had developed regional identities. Concurrently the roles of white women in the South experienced a metamorphosis. During the early seventeenth century, male colonizers had valued females as "breeders" and "servants"; by the end of the eighteenth century the dual image of "republican wives" and "southern ladies" hung over them. The first half of the nineteenth century resolved rather thoroughly any ambivalence about the ideals to which they should aspire and eliminated any doubt that may have existed concerning the status of women below the Mason-Dixon line. The advent of the new century did not bode particularly well for southern females, whether white, black, or red. That is not to suggest, however, that their lives were uniformly bland or without meaning and hope.

❧

THREE

A Garden Enclosed
Is My Sister, My Spouse

Moving from the colonial and revolutionary periods into the modern era required the American people to negotiate the nineteenth century. During that passage they attempted to address on their own terms the disparity between the ideals to which the nation aspired and the realities that it ultimately came to accept. Below the Mason-Dixon line the frontier process continued even as a beleaguered society became increasingly rigid. Although stigmatizing the South has soothed the nation's conscience, Dixie has never been able to claim a monopoly on inequality and injustice; it has, however, played host to peculiar regional manifestations of both. During the first half of the nineteenth century, a united nation continued for the time being to sanction the enslavement of blacks, the systematic persecution of Native Americans, and the repression of women. Racism, classism, and sexism flourished in the new settlements, just as in the old, and figured into the panoply that was antebellum America.

For the most part, both the North and the South assigned politics and public life to the masculine realm; and on the surface the status of white women hardly mattered in the plethora of differences that alienated the two American regions.[1] These disagreements had to do with the continuing practice of slavery, the single most important characteristic that distinguished the regions. During the first half of the century, white women of all classes and those of color, enslaved and free, in the American South existed under the auspices of a well-entrenched self-conscious but ultimately threatened patriarchy. The historian Stephanie McCurry, in a study of low-country yeomen, for example, has found that "the gulf between high and low culture was just not that great; evangelical values played a central role in both." "Low-country farmers," she writes, "may never have read a sermon by Thornwell or a tract by Harper, but they almost certainly heard a sermon at their local Baptist church by the likes of

Reverend Iveson Brookes or a speech at a July Fourth barbecue by a prominent politician such as Robert Barnwell Rhett." Like their planter-class counterparts but in a more "piecemeal" fashion, "male yeomen demonstrated an unequivocal commitment to hierarchical social order and to conservative Christian republicanism."[2] During the antebellum period, as the South came under increasing attacks from antislavery forces and other critics, it closed ranks, rejecting, in the words of Nancy Woloch, "all forms of change that tended to erode paternal power."[3]

As tempting as absolutes are, a historian is obliged to avoid their treachery. Even generalizations can be problematic in dealing with the antebellum South and one of its most sacred icons, the "southern lady." "American historians have . . . known for at least half a century that the plantation legend 'is one of great inaccuracy'—false to the character of Southern society, to the diversity of Southern whites, and to the realities of black life," the historian Edward Pessen wrote in 1980. One of the great advantages of myths is that they simplify the complex and explain the unknown. For that reason if no other, Americans, southerners among them, cling steadfastly to their symbols and icons. "The enduring popularity of *Gone with the Wind*," according to Pessen, serves as a reminder that "the popular mind continues to believe that the Old South was a land of large plantations populated by masters both honorable and courtly, cruel and sinful, by Southern belles 'beautiful, graceful . . . , bewitching in coquetry, yet strangely steadfast,' by loyal, lovable, comic, but sometimes surly Negroes, and by white trash or 'po' buckra.'"[4]

Even those who have the best of intentions may have difficulty separating myth from reality in southern history. With its rich storytelling tradition, the South yields up enough enigmatic examples to lend some credence to the stereotypes. When, for example, a fund raiser traveled through Georgia during the 1830s seeking contributions to establish a female college in that state, he sometimes met with less-than-enthusiastic receptions. One man whom he solicited declared, "No, I will not give you a dollar; all that a woman needs to know is how to read the New Testament, and to spin and weave clothing for her family." To make himself absolutely clear, he added, "I would not have one of your graduates for a wife, and I will not give you a cent for any such project."[5]

Not all southern males shared this man's opinion or his vehemence on the issue. Georgia Female College, established in 1839 at Macon, represented the first institution that purported to be a college for females in the United States. Its inception occurred in "a small town that still exhibited frontier characteristics, a Southern town committed to slavery secured by a conservative view of southern womanhood."[6] Nonetheless, southern society, dominated as it was by men, generally regarded woman "as merely an adjunct to the real human being, man, and it was not considered desirable to give her any other education than what sufficed to make her a good housewife and an agreeable, but not too critical, companion for her husband."[7]

Yet the South during the first half of the nineteenth century was not absolutely devoid of interesting women who left a perceptible historical record and commanded some public attention in their own day. Merely mentioning such women as Margaret O'Neal Eaton, whose marriage to John Eaton disrupted President Andrew Jackson's official cabinet, and Scotswoman Frances Wright of the Nashoba experiment in West Tennessee may be unduly titillating. A North Carolina-born Quakeress, Dolley Madison, made it to the White House. Something of a social butterfly and a clotheshorse, she still had enough presence of mind to save certain national treasures as she fled the British who occupied the national capital during the War of 1812. As a child, Rachel Donelson was with the flotilla that braved the treacheries of back-country rivers to establish the Cumberland settlements. While still a young woman and officially but unknowingly wed to Lewis Robards, she made the infamous trip to Natchez to marry Andrew Jackson. Her inattentiveness to detail detracted not a whit from the reverence in which "Old Hickory" held his pipe-smoking spouse.[8]

No overwhelming evidence suggests that even those who led anonymous, private, and ordinary lives spent themselves in a totally meaningless or joyless existence or that those in bonded servitude knew nothing of human dignity. When Sojourner Truth, a former slave whose servitude had been spent in New York, rose to address a women's-rights convention at Akron, Ohio, in 1851, she not only defended her womanhood but also delivered a stirring indictment of slavery, racism, and sexual discrimination:

Dat man ober dar say dat woman needs to be lifted ober ditches, and to have de best place every whar. Nobody eber helped me into carriages, or ober mud puddles, or gives me any best place and ain't I a woman? Look at me! Look at my arm! I have plowed, and planted, and gathered into barns, and no man could head me—and ain't I a woman? I could work as much and eat as much as a man (when I could get it), and bear de lash as well—and ain't I a woman? I have borne thirteen chilern and seen em mos' all sold off into slavery, and when I cried out with a mother's grief, none but Jesus heard—and ain't I a woman?[9]

Conventional wisdom, as well as a fair amount of what once passed for serious historical writing, suggests that the antebellum era was the great age of the "southern lady."[10] Nonetheless, this label, like so many others that have been categorically applied to women, takes on an ideological existence quite apart from the realities of human experience. Ridiculing the notion of indolent planter women, the historian Guion Griffis Johnson observed that "in any successful family whose fortune was built largely on agriculture, regardless of the number of slaves at their command, 'the feeble wife' was no less industrious or economical than her husband." As for women of the yeomanry, Johnson asserted, they performed the usual household tasks and also labored in the fields, "dropping seeds, chopping cotton, hoeing corn, setting, worming, and curing tobacco, picking cotton. They even helped with the more strenuous work of plowing, clearing fields, and pulling fodder."[11]

Eugene D. Genovese also has noted the inherent contradiction between the historical southern woman and the mythical southern lady when he wrote in *Roll, Jordan, Roll: The World the Slaves Made* that the mistresses of plantations, "however much they conformed to the image of the 'southern lady' in important respects, worked too hard under too many limitations to live up to their reputation as ethereal beings who wallowed in leisure." Indeed, that "they earned their reputation for graciousness and ladylike accomplishments while having to perform the grubbiest of chores speaks well for their character, but then, only prigs think that graciousness and dirty hands are incompatible."[12] Although another authority claims that "wealthy southern women were directly responsible for even fewer household tasks than northerners with comparable means," they did, in fact, supervise "the largest households on the North American continent."[13] In turn, they faced the not-inconsiderable challenge of exercising managerial skills to produce a smooth-running domestic operation.

Historians in pursuit of written sources from the past have often found themselves at the mercy of propaganda intended for public consumption, which probably inadequately reflects the private world of home and marriage; but it is possible to acknowledge the disparity between the idealized and the realized and still recognize the inferior predicament of antebellum southern women. Writing of "separate spheres" and the "cult of true womanhood" contemporaneous to the "southern lady," Carl N. Degler maintains that their "lineaments and content have been derived by historians from what publicists and writers of advice books at the time said the roles of wives and husbands ought to be." This involves "image, not necessarily the behavior of people."[14] Sally G. McMillen agrees that "women who lived in the Old South remain victims of myth or exaggeration . . . [which] for too long have prevented an accurate assessment of southern women's contributions, sacrifices, hardships, joys, and most important, their individuality." On the one hand, "slave and free black women have been portrayed as matriarchal or profligate"; on the other, "white women as delicate, submissive, and idle." Finally, the common run of rural women "have been ignored because their records are so few."[15]

Still, "like her northern counterpart, the southern woman was expected to be a model of virtue, a guardian of youth, and 'a restraint on man's natural vice and immorality,'" according to Nancy Woloch. "During the antebellum period, however, while northern women made new claims to influence and authority," she adds, their southern counterparts languished under the patriarchy.[16] Another historian, Jean E. Friedman, has attempted to explain how "southern traditional society inhibited female autonomy." Identifying sex segregation as a precondition for the formation of independent women's groups, she maintains that "neighborhood kinship groups and the family-centered evangelical church structure and discipline established the model of sexually integrated association" in Dixie. Opportunities for "consistent, stable patterns of association [among women] that held the potential for a reform network" did not materialize from such "socially marginal" activities as quilting parties or "ephemeral meetings" on the road to the market.[17] The rural landscape also loomed as a significant impediment to feminine social consciousness and women's organizations in the nineteenth-century South.

Inadequate education, confinement to the home, farm, or plantation, the burden of child rearing, and strictures on private and public conduct severely proscribed southern women's development. That is not to say, however, that theirs was a static world. Sound and sufficient research suggests the contrary. Although there was no southern counterpart to the women's-rights convention at Seneca Falls, New York, in 1848, southern women made contributions not only within the privacy of their families and households but also to the larger world of the communities in which they lived. Their influence, albeit limited, was no less real. In a 1928 article published in *South Atlantic Quarterly*, the historian Virginia Gearhart Gray described wide-ranging public activities of southern women between 1840 and 1860.[18] Elisabeth Anthony Dexter's *Career Women of America, 1776-1840*, which first appeared in 1950, documented a substantial array of female employment outside the home, which included numerous examples from the South.[19]

More recently a new generation of scholars has expanded and built upon the earlier work. In Suzanne Lebsock's study of women in Petersburg, Virginia, she observes that "positive change in the status of women can occur when no organized feminism is present. In Petersburg, there was considerable change . . . and much of it was change for the better . . . Women of both races made substantial gains in the acquisition and disposition of property; they formed organizations and built churches; they took up work in factories. White women made progress in education, and both white and black women displayed new varieties of personal assertiveness."[20]

Notwithstanding all of this, the dual nature ascribed to antebellum southern women proved problematic. Southern spokesmen considered white women superior to blacks but inferior to men of their own race, which required female deference to Caucasian males; concurrently, women supposedly possessed moral equality or perhaps even superiority to men yet needed their guidance. "This fragmented identity constituted the major and most troublesome weakness in the pro-slavery argument," according to the historian Nancy Ann White, because "the ambivalent, anomalous, and contradictory depiction of a white female identity generated uncertainty, anxiety and guilt regarding a white male identity and the entire system of white male mastery." Masculine unwillingness to recognize and guarantee "a free and independent womanhood evidence [white men's] anxious and guilt-ridden acknowledgement of the possibility that morality was a function of the individual will and that in this regard all people, men and women, black and white, were the same." [21]

In the South, prevailing views that were aired publicly about woman's proper sphere probably became all the more extreme, exaggerated, and magnified during the antebellum period. Because the temptation is so great to draw strict categorical distinctions between northern and southern women of the early nineteenth century—and enough historians have already succumbed—it bears mentioning that the regions shared general patterns of social behavior, including notions about male-female roles and relations. Edward Pessen observes that "the antebellum North and South were far more alike than the conventional scholarly wisdom has led us to believe." Even with "all of their distinctiveness," he maintains, "the Old South and North were complementary elements in an American society that was everywhere primarily rural, capitalistic, materialistic, and socially stratified, racially, ethnically, and religiously heterogeneous, and stridently chauvinistic and expansionist." [22] Along similar lines, Michael P. Johnson has argued: "Northern opposition to slavery did not fundamentally challenge patriarchal ideology. In fact, the net result of northern efforts against slavery was to clean up patriarchal ideology and allow it to be exhibited openly in the bourgeois parlor." [23]

Pessen and Johnson write, of course, of a largely masculine-contrived cosmology. In *The Feminization of American Culture*, Ann Douglas, however, identifies and describes a female-inspired sentimentality of the 1800s, which leads her to observe none too charitably that "nineteenth-century American women were oppressed, and damaged; inevitably, the influence they exerted in turn on their society was not altogether beneficial." [24] Carroll Smith-Rosenberg has delved into a private sphere where "women, who had little status or power in the larger world of male concerns, possessed status and power in the lives and worlds of other women." They lived in "a world bounded by home, church, and the institution of visiting—that endless trooping of women to each others' homes for social purposes. It was a world inhabited by children and other women." [25] Barbara Welter, in her carefully drawn study of the "Cult of True Womanhood," has demonstrated

that the "True Woman"—and she writes principally about northern females—was confined to the private sphere, "a hostage in the home."[26]

According to Catherine Clinton, "the same phenomena of restriction
and oppression appeared in both North and South but often took markedly
different forms." The "relative proximity of households" in New England
and the Mid-Atlantic region saved women from the "isolation of their
southern counterparts."[27] Southern women, too, of the colonial era and
later as well adopted visiting as a panacea for their loneliness with the same
enthusiasm as other American women did. "Visiting was the most usual
diversion," writes Julia Cherry Spruill in *Women's Life and Work in the
Southern Colonies.* "Neighbors frequently dined, drank tea, or spent the day
with one another, and those living at greater distances made visits lasting
from a few days to weeks and months." Spruill adds that "young ladies, and
even mistresses of large families, set out on a series of visits, staying at one
house several days or weeks, and moving on to another and then another
until they had made the round of their friends and kindred."[28]

"Traveling alone" represented a gross social impropriety, and accepted
standards dictated the chaperonage of women, ostensibly for their protection. This gave rise to "a system in which women became virtual wards; and
the price for this 'protection' was high, in isolation and limited mobility."[29]
Still, when the opportunity presented itself, well-to-do females amused
themselves with extended visiting (which had the added advantage of ward-
ing off unwanted pregnancies), a diversion less readily available to their
poorer counterparts. Although the common run of women in the South
lived out their days in a style that contrasted starkly with that of their more
fortunate sisters, they shared with them a life often proscribed by rural and
frontier existence and almost always by generally accepted notions, class
not excepted, of male superiority and the realities of male dominance.

Even as the denizens of Dixie closed ranks and the Old South solidified,
the frontier process continued. During the first half of the nineteenth century, westward-moving pioneers strung southern culture from the Tidewater to Texas. With each successive advance along Dixie's ragged frontier,
the South reinvented itself; and the fluidity of the frontier temporarily
ameliorated the relative rigidity in its wake. Pioneers may have cast off all
but the most essential physical possessions for the trek westward, but they
retained much of their cultural baggage. Ultimately the waves of migrants
employed virtually the same images and codes of conduct that they had
known back east to re-create themselves and society; and the women as
well as the men came to bear an amazing similarity to the people they had
left behind. The westward movement in the South resiliently reaffirmed
gender roles and in turn the inferior status of women, notwithstanding
their indomitable pioneering spirit.

"The southern backcountry," writes David Hackett Fischer, "was a vast area roughly the size of western Europe, extending 800 miles south from Pennsylvania to Georgia, and several hundred miles west from the Piedmont plateau to the banks of the Mississippi." Fischer estimates that the English, Irish, and Scottish made up 90 percent of the settlers, most of them from Ulster, northern England, and the Scottish lowlands. They encountered an American landscape "of corrugated ridges and valleys, rising from the coastal plain to the crest of the Appalachians . . . , then falling away to the western rivers." The emerging back-country elite included surnames like Jackson, Polk, Calhoun, Henry, Houston, Graham, and Bankhead.[30]

"That the frontier created a spirit of equality among the sexes could not be farther from the truth," Fischer declares. Men expected women to join them in the most grueling tasks associated with clearing forests, breaking ground, raising crops, and tending livestock; but that was about the extent of sharing and equality. In the back country, "travelers were startled to observe delicate females knock down beef cattle with a felling ax, and then roll down their sleeves, remove their bloody aprons, tidy their hair, and invite their visitors to tea." Still, these relative newcomers "had exceptionally clear-cut ideas of masculinity and femininity in manners, speech, dress, decorum and status."[31]

Exceptions to the feminine fastidiousness that Fischer describes could also be found. A traveler in Arkansas described Rebecca Davis Barkman, the daughter of a hunter, who was known in her youth as "old Davis's 'She Bar.'" George W. Featherstonhaugh declared that he had "never seen anyone, as far as manners and exterior with less pretensions to be classed with the feminine gender." Rebecca "chewed tobacco, she smoked a pipe, she drank whiskey, and cursed and swore as heartily as any backwoodsman, all at the same time." Mrs. Barkman reportedly "had the habit of boxing her husband's ears when he displeased her."[32]

For most frontier women, isolation and loneliness exacerbated an already difficult existence. Following wandering husbands often meant separation from parents, siblings, relatives, and friends. A traveler who had met John Breckinridge and his wife, Mary Hopkins Cabell ("Polly") Breckinridge, on their way to Kentucky from Virginia in 1793 recalled that John had urged him to entertain Mrs. Breckinridge with his "funny stories," adding that "it would keep up her spirits, for she has not even smiled since we set out on our journey."[33] The historian Melinda S. Buza explains that some young women of the Virginia gentry "faced marriage with anxiety and sadness because they feared the impact that relocating and undertaking many taxing new duties would have on their treasured female friendships." Mothers also dreaded having their daughters taken far from them.[34] The historian Joan E. Cashin offers additional insight into the minds of planter

women caught up in but less than enthusiastic about the process of migration: "Only a few, at moments of great unhappiness . . . articulated their
bewilderment, anger, and despair about the dramatic changes in their lives.
They usually confided in other women, however, rather than confronting
the men who wrought these changes." Generally, planter women "did not
assail slavery or the patriarchal family."[35]

Trying as the matrimonial state might have been for both parties,
southern men and women considered it the norm. Indeed, simple existence
almost required a male-female team; prosperity virtually demanded it. The
Olivers of northeast Tennessee provided a classic example. Born in Carter
County in 1793, John Oliver, a collier by trade, had known "grinding poverty [during his] early years" and had "dreamed of owning his own land."
While quite young, Mrs. Oliver, the former Lucretia Frazier, had been orphaned and "bound" out by the court to a local family. John had joined the
militia and fought under the command of General Andrew Jackson at the
Battle of Horseshoe Bend. Lucretia, not wanting to take any chances about
having a husband, entered into engagements with two other men. In later
life she told her grandchildren that she had been determined to marry,
whether John survived his militia experience or not. John and Lucretia did in
fact wed in April 1814 and became the first known white settlers in Cades
Cove.[36]

Married couples of all classes on the southern frontier often spent considerable time apart. Daniel Boone, a quintessential "long hunter," for example, had earned a reputation, perhaps ill founded and incorrect, of not
readily adjusting to family life. One critic complained that the men of the
Yadkin settlements in North Carolina left the work to the women and children and indulged themselves in hunting. In 1762 Rebecca Bryan Boone
seems to have been delivered of an illegitimate child, Jemima, conceived
during one of Daniel's extended absences. Different accounts suggest that
there was not "a whisper to the disadvantage of Mrs. Boone" in regard to
this matter, and Daniel himself seems to have taken it all in stride. In any
event, the most likely candidate for fatherhood in this instance seems to
have been his brother Ned. Whatever the truth of the matter, a special relationship existed between Daniel and this child; and he went to considerable
lengths to rescue her when she was captured by Indians in Kentucky.[37]

Russell Bean, perhaps the first white child born on the northeast-Ten-
nessee frontier, accepted his wife's bastard with less aplomb. Both Russell—
the scion of William Bean, who had claims to being the original permanent
settler in what would become the Volunteer State—and Russell's spouse—
the former Rosamond Robertson, a daughter of the Washington County
sheriff—represented true children of the frontier. Although from prominent
pioneer families and generally respectable, both occasionally ran afoul of the

law. Rosamond, Russell's sister, and another female once managed to elude arrest when an indictment had been returned against them. The warrant went unserved, with this written explanation: "Will not be taken, kept off by force and arms."[38]

A businessman and a noted gunsmith, Russell made extended trading trips, one of which, around 1798, took him to Natchez and thence to New Orleans. According to a biographer, "he spent a number of months enjoying the divertissements of the city, cock-fighting, horse and foot racing, and other sports popular on the frontier, before starting back on the long journey overland." After an absence of several months, Russell returned to find his wife with an infant. Circumstances deemed it unlikely that he had fathered the child. While contemplating the matter, off to town he went and indulged in a rare but "roaring drunk." Then returning home from Jonesborough, "he picked up the child from its cradle, pulled his hunting knife from its sheath and cut off both its ears, saying that he 'had marked it so that it would not get mixed up with his children.'" Russell seems, in this instance, to have appropriated the technique of slitting or cropping ears, which frontiersmen sometimes employed to identify their livestock.[39]

The episode of the crop-eared child apparently contributed to the Beans' divorce, and Rosamond subsequently moved to Knoxville, where her misbegotten offspring died; ironically she and Russell remarried in 1820.[40] The circumstances surrounding Rosamond's bastard represented an exceptional situation, but children expired all too frequently. As a consequence of such circumstances, sadness often trailed women westward, grief hovered over them, and death lay in wait. Calamities and tough choices occurred with regularity. Mary Ingles, for example, was among the first white women in the Kentucky country. The Shawnees had abducted her and her children on 8 July 1755 at Draper's Meadow on the Virginia frontier. When Mary was at Big Bone Lick, where her captors had gone to make salt, this unwilling guest escaped, leaving behind the only child, a baby, who had not been taken from her. Along with an aged Pennsylvania-German woman, she made her way to the relative safety of Virginia after great struggle and hardship.[41]

Most white women probably set foot on the dark and bloody ground of Kentucky and other frontier outposts with some trepidation. Usually subservient to husbands and fathers, they most certainly went under duress; but black women entered the back country as chattels, the slaves of migrating families. In Kentucky, one of the earliest, Molly Logan, the mother of three young sons, had settled on 8 March 1776 at St. Asaph's, near present-day Stanford.[42] Hardship, however, was colorblind. White women with the Donelson party en route to Nashville by flatboat, for example, experienced their share of the vicissitudes visited upon path breakers. On 8 March 1780 the boat of Jonathan Jennings "ran on a large rock" and was attacked by Indians. In the words of Mary Purnell Donelson, "To lighten the boat, Mrs. Jennings & her daughter, Mrs. Peyton [who had just given birth the preceding day], threw some of the articles overboard—& accidentally with the blankets & bedding in the hurry, fear, & confusion, was thrown the young child of Mrs. Peyton, & did not discover the mistake until some time after."[43]

Some women naturally adapted more readily to frontier life than did others. Esther Whitley, of Logan's Fort in Kentucky, enjoyed a reputation as a crack shot. Other women molded bullets, but Esther was valued for her marksmanship, outdoing all of the males in a match staged there in 1777. During a large migration in 1784, Mrs. Jane Trimble, cradling a baby in her left arm while a three-year-old boy held tightly to her, forced her horse across the rain-swollen Clinch River and led a group of women to safety on the other side. Four years earlier a wounded girl with the Donelson party, Nancy Gower, had calmly guided a flatboat through an Indian attack after two young men on board had jumped into the water and fled for their lives. A shot had passed through her thigh in the fracas, but others did not know that she was wounded until her mother saw her blood-soaked clothes.[44]

Imminent death could call forth an admixture of female rage and feminine heroism. At an isolated cabin in Nelson County, Kentucky, in 1787, Indians attacked on a summer night and wounded John Merrill badly. Mrs. Merrill seized an axe, the only weapon at her disposal, and promptly killed or badly injured four of the attackers. When others of their party attempted to come down the chimney, she ripped open the feather bed and dumped the feathers on the coals in the fireplace. Two Indians, overcome by smoke, fell dazed on the hearth and met death from Mrs. Merrill's axe. Into the woods ran the sole survivor, howling from the gash that permanently disfigured his face.[45]

Perhaps the most celebrated example of the heroism of Kentucky women has been drawn from the events at Bryan's (or Bryant's) Station some five years earlier. In August 1782 the halfbreed Simon Girty and the Canadian ranger Captain William Caldwell persuaded a small group of whites and approximately three hundred Wyandot and Lake Indians to turn to the south and attack outposts in Kentucky. For a time this force lurked in the vicinity of Bryan's Station. "Even the women, aided by the slaves, were permitted to milk the cows without being molested. They also went to the spring and carried in as much water as possible, conducting themselves in such manner as to indicate no consciousness of the Indians' being there," according to one historian.[46] Although the attackers seem to have inflicted relatively slight damage at Bryan's Station, they destroyed crops, livestock, and cabins in the surrounding countryside. Furthermore, Bryan's Station signaled the onset of a series of events that produced "the bitterest moment of all for the Kentucky frontiersmen," the Battle of Blue Licks on 19 August 1782.[47]

The women at Bryan's Station had their small triumph, but that same year near Estill's Station, twenty-five Wyandots attacked a mother and her two daughters, raping, tomahawking, and scalping them. History failed to record the names of these unfortunate females. The Widow Scraggs (Shanks according to some sources) of Bourbon County and her family also fared badly a few years later. When the Indians had finished their grisly work, only three or four members of what had been a substantial household survived. Notwithstanding the dangers of daily living, women persevered and subsisted. During the 1770s at Fort Harrod, the much-married and much-widowed Ann Kennedy Wilson Poague Lindsay McGinty reputedly had brought the first spinning wheel into the Kentucky country and, by experiment and happenstance, had begun producing linsey-woolsey. Jane Coomes, another Harrodsburg woman, launched a school in 1776. At Cumberland Gap, Molly Davis owned and operated a tavern during the 1790s.[48]

Prevailing views hold that women exerted a civilizing influence. Even under primitive conditions, a feminine presence at the wilderness outpost of Boonesboro had reportedly occasioned improvements. One authority on Kentucky's past noted that "shaving, hair-cutting, washing, sweeping, knitting, quilting and 'courtin' began—even looking glasses came into use. Times were better at Boonesborough."[49] Still, what passed for late-eighteenth- and early-nineteenth-century Bluegrass society remained "rough and ready." The gauche had not given way to gentility, and some women as well as men often exuded crudeness. One early traveler commented that a woman who made her living as a frontier landlady was "'a Xantippe,' and dirty to boot." Lord Henry Hamilton, a captive at Logan's Station in 1779, reported that Jane Manifee, another Kentucky sharpshooter in skirts, had threatened to kill him. Manifee observed that a tomahawk Hamilton had in his possession had probably been used on women and children and offered to use it on him. About the same time, Colonel William Fleming, a physician, commented on the dirt, filth, and general nastiness at Harrodsburg. Moses Austin later noted that new settlers, families among them, who followed the original pioneers into Kentucky were an unfortunate lot, often barefoot and hardly clothed.[50] His description revealed more about their economic plight than about their character. That some of them managed to sustain themselves and survive seems more revealing.

The historian Elizabeth A. Perkins in a 1991 article concedes that "while some of the hardships of early Kentucky have been exaggerated, severe distance constraints did weaken social and material ties with the East." All the same, "back country women and men were not thrown completely on their own resources. Stores, traders, and consumer goods accompanied the first settlers to Kentucky." Even at Fort Harrod, almost every woman lovingly claimed some bowl or dish that she had carried westward. Tea drinking continued to be a ritual at a fort in Lexington, but when the women took tea together, it was bereft of delicacies—just tea and dried buffalo meat. Frontier women apparently did not forgo that very feminine pastime of shopping. Around 1800, for example, the widow Elizabeth Gillmore "manufactured cloth, the emblem of the self-sufficient household," but "plainly did not intend to dress herself in homespun." On the contrary, "she sold her country produce for goods she wanted more: a hat, two skeins of silk thread, and several yards of imported fabric."[51]

Early Kentuckians obviously succumbed to temporal delights and temptations of the flesh. Laboring in the Lord's vineyard sorely tried the souls of frontier revivalists if their accounts can be believed, and some of the "gentler sex" made their task no easier. Peter Cartwright reported that "upon one occasion a mother sought to remove her daughters from the altar rail by kicking them during prayer." His reaction is reported in his own words: "I took hold of her foot and gave her a strong push backward, and over she tumbled among the benches. Being a large corpulent woman, she had some considerable tussel to right herself again." The passion and religious fervor of camp meetings seemed to give rise to dissolute behavior. The Reverend John Lyle reported in his diary that "Becca Bell,—who often fell, is now big with child to a wicked trifling school master . . . Raglin's daughter seems careless . . . Kitty Cummins got careless . . . Peggy Moffitt was with child to Petty and died miserably in child bed."[52]

Saintly conduct seems to have been equally rare in the Cumberland settlements of Tennessee. Although the local court "attempted to enforce an orthodox, even puritanical, moral code," according to the historian Anita Shafer Goodstein, "adultery, profane swearing, buying and selling or grinding corn on the Sabbath, and bearing or siring bastard children" went on unabated. The prominent no less than the common folk fell to temptation:

Evan Shelby in bed with the tavernkeeper's daughter; Mark Robertson accused of siring a bastard; Elijah Robertson up for assault and battery, and again for swearing in the court's presence, and twice again for drunkenness; Squire Molloy emancipating his slave daughter and making her his heir; Andrew Jackson and Rachel Donelson Robards eloping on the rumor of her divorce—the frontier was not an easy place to maintain standards.[53]

According to Joan E. Cashin, men and women of the landed elite who settled in the Old Southwest between 1810 and 1860 harbored disparate perceptions of migration and resettlement. Some planter-class men of this era relocated west of the Alabama-Georgia line in a determined attempt "to escape the intricate kinship networks of the seaboard," but their women struggled against great odds to preserve family ties. "On the Southwestern frontier, the planter family underwent 'nuclearization,' . . . men, women, and children found themselves alone, far from the many collateral relatives who populated the seaboard." Women, according to Cashin, "experienced all of the isolation of modernity with none of its easy geographic mobility. Freedom of movement was a privilege in the antebellum South, not a right, and most women's kinship networks deteriorated, just as they had feared. The final result of all these changes was that women became even more dependent on men than they had been at home." After resettlement, men "expressed their independence . . . drinking, gambling, and fighting with a new sense of license," which may also have been reflected in relatively uninhibited sexual relations with slave women.[54]

Admirable as certain ideals associated with "southern honor" may have been, one might search the earth for a greater level of hypocrisy than that which coursed through it and still come away empty-handed. Chivalry and chauvinism reposed harmoniously in the minds of most antebellum southern males and still rests comfortably with many of their progeny. The historian Bertram Wyatt-Brown explains:

It might seem paradoxical that men should make demands for sexual restraint on their female relatives, when giving themselves a right to license. But to the traditional mind there was no double standard of morality. The sexes differed. They lived separate lives—one in the world, the other in the home, one in exterior circumstances, the other in the inner sanctuary that required vigilant safeguarding . . . the male identified that inner part of himself with his women. The woman's responsibility was solely to make sacred that internal space.[55]

In a compelling description of "the man at the center" of the southern mind, Wilbur J. Cash pinpoints the masculine "focus": "To stand on his head in a bar, to toss down a pint of raw whisky at a gulp, to fiddle and dance all night, to bite off the nose or gouge out the eyes of a favorite enemy, to fight harder and love harder than the next man, to be known eventually far and wide as a hell of a fellow."[56]

A product of the West Tennessee wilderness, where honor, violence, and alcohol mixed easily, the dashing General Nathan Bedford Forrest of the Confederacy embodied many of the characteristics described by Wyatt-Brown and Cash. When during the 1840s Forrest had asked the Reverend Samuel Montgomery Cowan for his daughter Mary Ann's hand, Cowan had refused: "Why, Bedford, I couldn't consent. You cuss and gamble and Mary Ann is a Christian girl." To which Forrest replied, "I know it, and that's just why I want her." Cowan, all too familiar with the social limitations of frontier life, soon acceded.[57]

Another well-known son of Tennessee and Texas, Sam Houston, ranks as something of a frontier Lothario. "She was cold to me, & I thought did not love me," Houston said of his new wife, Eliza Allen. In 1829, when his marriage quickly went sour, he declared himself "a ruined man," resigned as governor of Tennessee, and headed for Texas. A few years later he managed to obtain a divorce of "dubious legality" at a time when he became interested in another white woman. In the meantime he had married Tiana Rogers, a mixed-breed beauty, in a traditional Cherokee ceremony. They settled down at Wigwam Neosho in Arkansas Territory on the Texas Road. After absenting himself a good deal from Tiana, he made his final farewell, leaving her the wigwam, trading post, two slaves, and all livestock except a broken-down horse. Destiny awaited him in Texas, where he subsequently married Margaret Lea, who, despite his pattern of prolonged and numerous separations, remained committed to him until his death in 1863; she succumbed some four years later.[58]

From the vantage of the late twentieth century, it seems evident that during the antebellum era even the best of southern white men made rigorous and often unreasonable demands on their women; the worst of them misused and abused the females of their own race and exploited African-American and Native-American women. It is impossible to determine the extent of physical violence perpetrated by white men against women on the frontier; that it occurred, however, is evident. A male boarder at the residence of Randolph McAlister in northeast Tennessee, for example, swore that he had been awakened during the night of 31 March 1842 "by a noyse between Said McAlister and his wife and . . . asked McAlister what was the matter[.] He McAlister made no reply but went out of the house and came in directly again and commenced beating her again and beat her three times and swore by his maker that he would kill her and send her to hell."[59]

Although such incidents of physical violence against women may have been exceptional, most men hardly considered their less-than-gentlemanly behavior toward the opposite sex unnatural, instead claiming it as their rightful due. As for the women themselves, they lived in a time and place and under conditions that offered little respite. Around the turn of the century, however, Native-American women had not always yielded to white expectations. Negotiations broke down in 1797, for example, when the Creek Indian agent Benjamin Hawkins outlined his conjugal expectations to his prospective Indian mother-in-law. "The ways of the white people differ much from those of the red people," Hawkins intoned; his wife would bring up their offspring, including hers from a previous union, as he pleased; "the red women should always be proud of their white husbands [and] should always take part with them and obey them, should make the children obey them, and they will be obedient to their parents, and make a happy family." All of this was too much for the old Creek woman, who could not see her way clear to accept his view of marriage and child rearing for her widowed daughter.[60]

Even so, perennial contact with the whites affected the status of Native-American women among their own kind as Indian men appropriated the ways of transplanted Europeans. The advent of the missionaries and the transmission of their "civilizing" influence through the mission schools, accompanied by the usual Christian fixation with clothing the "savages" from head to toe while stripping them of their heritage, gradually had its impact. Theda Perdue has observed that "men of wealth and power among the Creeks, Choctaws, and Chickasaws as well as the Cherokees readily accepted the technical assistance offered through the government's civilization program and gradually adopted the ideology it encompassed." As a consequence, "women began to fade from economic and political life in the early nineteenth century."[61]

"The United States government promised the Cherokees that they could retain their ancestral lands in Georgia if they would adopt the ways of white men and women," writes the historian Joan M. Jensen. "For Cherokee women, this meant withdrawing from field work and confining themselves to traditional white farm women's work: caring for cows and chickens, spinning and weaving cloth, and tending small gardens."[62] The Indian agent Benjamin Hawkins "unlike the missionaries . . . did not try to teach the Indians the mysteries of religion or the intricacies of literature; instead he concentrated on the useful arts of agriculture and manufacture." When his plans met with ridicule from the male chieftains, Hawkins turned to the women. By 1805, apparently as a result of his efforts, Native-American females operated twenty looms in the lower Cherokee towns and ten in the upper ones. Hawkins reportedly advised the women to withhold their sexual favors unless their men cooperated in "the civilizing mission" by taking up farming and raising livestock.[63]

Cherokee willingness to compromise was not strong enough to offset white greed. To assuage the latter, removal emerged as a panacea. In 1818 the Cherokee women had taken a stance against the idea. Meeting in council, their representatives not only opposed the idea of leaving their ancestral lands but also urged resistance, saying:

We well remember that our country was formerly very extensive, but by repeated sales it has become circumscribed to the very narrow limits we have at present. Our Father the President advised us to become farmers—to manufacture our own clothes, and to have our children instructed. To this advice we have attended in every thing as far as we were able. Now the thought of being compelled to remove to the other side of the Mississippi is dreadful to us, because it appears to us that we, by this removal, shall be brought to a savage state again; for we have by the endeavors of our Father the President, become too much enlightened to throw aside, the privileges of a civilized life.

The women likewise mentioned that several of their people had taken up Christianity and been educated at the missionary schools. They reserved their most bitter words for "some white men among us, who have been raised in our country from their youth, are connected with us by marriage and have considerable families, who are very active in encouraging the emigration of our nation." Those who "ought to be our truest friends" have proved to be "our worst enemies."[64]

Not content with "civilizing" the southern tribes, the United States government during the 1830s began one of the sorriest chapters in American history: Indian removal. It would be difficult to exaggerate the hardships that plagued these native people. Inadequately clothed, fed with contaminated rations, and forced on the trail in foul winter weather, "they were crowded together on old, unseaworthy boats . . . and separated from their remaining possessions by emigrating agents, local citizens, and sheriffs prosecuting alleged debt claims," writes the historian Michael Paul Rogin. The elderly, the sick, pregnant women, and the very young received no quarter. "War, disease, accident, starvation, depredations, murder, whiskey, and other causes of death . . . had killed by 1844 one-quarter to one-third of the southern Indians." Among those who died was Quatie, Chief John Ross's wife. When she succumbed to pneumonia, forlorn family members and friends committed her body to a shallow grave and continued their march. Chief Ross had, in principle, opposed removal and, more specifically, the Treaty of New Echota, by which removal was implemented. When all efforts to reverse the federal government's decision had failed, however, he became superintendent of emigration for the move westward.[65]

Indians of Florida fought valiantly during the 1830s in what is known as the Second Seminole War when the federal government had tried to relocate them west of the Mississippi. Hostilities continued for seven years before most of Florida's Native Americans gave up and acceded to white pressure. The government ordered the others to a reservation in the Everglades. During the 1850s, conflict again arose between whites and Indians in Florida; and in 1858 the United States government renewed its efforts to force the remaining Seminoles westward. On 4 March 1858 Chief Billy Bowlegs accepted the government's offer, which included a $5,000 personal cash payment and $2,500 as reimbursement for cattle that he claimed had been taken from him. A warrior received $1,000; each woman and child, $100. Still an estimated two hundred Seminoles remained in the Everglades and only rarely ventured from their isolation to trade with whites. Their numbers had grown to approximately six hundred by the early twentieth century, among them the elderly Annie Tommy and her older brother, Willie Jumper. When Florida's Governor David W. Sholtz and his cabinet visited Collier County in 1936 and asked the Seminoles how the state could assist them during the Great Depression, they responded, "Just leave us alone."[66]

The treatment that was accorded the Indians strongly suggests that greed and racism had superseded the finer aspects of southern chivalry and national honor. The callous disregard for Indian women and children and the indifference to the black family in no way diminished the significance that southern whites attached to their own kinship ties, marriages, and children.[67] Men in the South, shored up by evangelical Protestantism, went about begetting in a manner not unlike that of biblical patriarchs and at least attempted to preside over their wives, offspring, and chattel in much the same manner. In a greatly oversimplified and equally overstated generalization, the historian William R. Taylor likened the plantation to a matriarchy in which "alongside the Southern matriarch, the gentleman planter becomes a shadowy figure, hovering in the background, or . . . he disappears altogether and leaves to woman to preside over the family unobstructed."[68]

"Maternity ward" seems a more apt description than "matriarchy" for the world of southern women of all classes and circumstances. Tiny human graves, so small they hardly indented the landscape, and headstones of young women, dead before they had much more than begun to live, afford ample evidence of the hazards of pregnancy, childbirth, and infancy. Seemingly incessant childbearing marked the lives of most married women. Both men and women remained relatively ignorant of nineteenth-century birth-control techniques, unreliable as they were. Married couples also seemed somewhat reluctant to employ them, as if enjoying marital relations must, of necessity, culminate in pregnancy, at which time men separated themselves as much as possible from the whole messy business.

The historian Carol K. Bleser, in a study about the marriage of Benjamin and Elizabeth Perry of South Carolina, which seems to have been a happy and companionate one, comments on this tendency. She notes that "Perry complained about his wife's fertility as if he had nothing to do with it, but consoled himself with the Victorian cant that 'all women are anxious to have children and none are happy who are married without them.'" According to Bleser, Elizabeth bore four live children, was delivered of two stillborn daughters, and experienced four miscarriages in the first ten years of the marriage. This same remarkable—and resilient—woman took an avid interest in her husband's political career. When Benjamin chose not to seek reelection to the South Carolina House of Representatives, Elizabeth chided him, saying, "the two reasons you give for wishing to leave, namely love of home and finding Legislation hard, I cannot admit of, the first is effeminate, the second selfish."[69]

Women in the Northeast by this time may have begun to assume some control over their own fertility. In a landmark study dealing with motherhood among the so-called privileged classes of the Old South, Sally G. McMillen observes that "if southern women ever tried to control their fertility, their efforts rarely influenced the number of pregnancies." Indeed, "the larger families of the South may signify the husband's retention of power there." McMillen also concludes that "a positive attitude toward having large numbers of children reflected the vigor of the patriarchy, the importance of the southern family, and the prosperity of the region. But women were left to bear and raise the young."[70] Still, self-righteous sages seemed ever ready to offer advice and counsel. Such was the case in the matter of poor relief and maternal obligations in antebellum Charleston. Male commissioners of the Orphan House interfered in the life of the self-supporting chronic-drinking Irishwoman Margaret Boggs by depriving her of her children. Venting her frustrations, she lashed out at them: "My children, Gentlemen, are my own and I am their mother." The pious patriarchs remained unmoved until a "respected man" intervened on her behalf.[71]

Generally, men in the antebellum South seem to have viewed women as inferior beings, some regarded them in the same manner as property, and most believed it best that females fall under men's governance. This pervasive commitment to male autonomy, as well as the sense of license that accompanied it, crossed racial and class lines and intruded into the great majority of feminine lives. In no position to dictate and sometimes unable even to influence masculine conduct, women who personally had no abuse visited upon them might still experience embarrassment and humiliation when male relatives violated standards of conventional behavior.

Bertram Wyatt-Brown and Catherine Clinton alone have dredged up enough evidence of lascivious thoughts, schoolboy boasting, and barnyard language to shock the sensibilities of the stereotypical southern lady. The former explains that "in the American South, as in England and France, sleeping with a woman was an informal rite of virilization. The obvious way was to pursue a black partner. If the initial effort were clumsy or brutal no one would object, in view of the woman's race and status." Writing about the youthful Thomas Jefferson Withers, who later became a justice of the South Carolina Supreme Court, Wyatt-Brown relates how Withers claimed that smells emanating from an outhouse visited by a white female he was admiring "doth make my cock stand as furious as a stud's." When the object of his lust did not return his interest, he sought the attentions of a black girl, but with no more success.[72]

Clinton also recounts instances of youthful fantasy. In 1831 a planter's son admitted to a male counterpart his growing interest in women. A chance encounter with a member of the opposite sex may have further piqued his curiosity: "I met a girl not long since going to plough barefoot riding astraddle barebacked by a crook in the Road. I got up to her before she discovered me. She had a good foot and ankle, a well turned leg up to the knee. She looked to be about 18 years old, had titties as big as your fist, as round as a butter ball and would have weighed a pound." Another young gentleman of similar sensitivities had used the word "meat" when he referred to women. Clinton adds that "licentiousness, when it came to fact rather than fantasy, was costly. The recipe books of southern plantation mistresses are full of concoctions to cure gonorrhea."[73]

Trying to come to grips with the history and historiography of human sexuality and race relations in the antebellum South is always confusing and sometimes bewildering.[74] In this emotionally charged and murky world where miscegenation not only loomed as a possibility but occurred not infrequently, human feelings ran the gamut. Not all white men spent their days despoiling women of their own race or the enslaved blacks. Some gentle patriarchs did exist within this oppressive system. There were saintly white women who tenderly ministered to both races, as well as sadistic ones who vented their frustrations on their husbands' black paramours and the misbegotten offspring of such unions. The vulnerability of black women made them easy prey, but even among those summarily assumed to be victims, seductresses could be found. Professional historians, just as laymen, need to remind themselves from time to time that the great majority of southerners did not own slaves of either sex. It requires nothing less than a vivid imagination to write the antebellum South off as a rollicking harem in which lecherous patriarchs forced their attentions on beautiful dusky handmaidens, while scripture-reading lily-white ladies sat silently on the sidelines.

Still, the South's "peculiar institution," dehumanizing for blacks of both sexes, weighed most heavily on African-American women, who suffered the additional degradation of sexual exploitation. Some scholars are increasingly inclined to criticize white women of the master class for their toleration of slavery. Cruel and abusive mistresses existed, and their behavior should not be rationalized or excused. Nevertheless, most white women were ill equipped to challenge the masculine power structure of the South, which was strongly committed to the continuation of slavery, even had they been so inclined, which most of them probably were not. Any tendency toward a categorical condemnation of southern white women should be tempered by the honest admission that it took four years of bloody warfare and all the powers that could be brought to bear by the United States government to eradicate slavery. The same determined masculine-contrived

system that justified black slavery—advancing many of the same arguments—controlled southern white women.

"God forgive us, but ours is a *monstrous* system & wrong & iniquity,"
diarist Mary Boykin Chesnut wrote. (Quoting her seems almost obliga-
tory.) "Like the patriarchs of old, our men live all in one house with their
wives & their concubines, & the Mulattoes one sees in every family exactly
resemble the white children—& every lady tells you who is the father of all
the mulatto children in every body's household but those in her own."[75]
The English actress Frances (Fanny) Kemble, who was the wife of the
Georgia slaveowner Pierce Butler for several years, had made similar obser-
vations: "Nobody pretends to deny that, throughout the South, a large proportion of the population is the offspring of white men and colored wom-
en."[76] Kemble also commented on the connection between slave women's
fecundity and their own sense of self-worth: "They have all of them a most
distinct and perfect knowledge of their value to their owners as property;
and a woman thinks, and not much amiss, that the more frequently she
adds to the number of her master's livestock by bringing new slaves into the
world, the more claims she will have upon his consideration and good will."
The slaves themselves called out, "Look, missis! little niggers for you and
massa; plenty little niggers for you and little missis!"[77]

Mentioning *Incidents in the Life of a Slave Girl* is about as much a requirement as resurrecting the words of diarists Kemble and Chesnut. In this
text an Edenton, North Carolina, runaway, Harriet Jacobs (under the
pseudonym Linda Brent) recounts alleged episodes from her own life. The
historian Nell Irvin Painter treats the account as an autobiography but acknowledges that the work is controversial; others are less certain of the
genre.[78] "But now I entered on my fifteenth year—a sad epoch in the life of
a slave girl," Jacobs lamented. "My master began to whisper foul words in
my ear. Young as I was, I could not remain ignorant of their import."[79] The
circumstances of slavery ultimately reduced most black women to submission, however repugnant any involvement with white or black men may
have been to them. In the most extreme situations they sometimes retali-
ated. The historian Melton A. McLaurin has provided one such example:
Celia, a slave in Missouri, finally killed her white oppressor and burned his
body in her fireplace; for this, she was hanged.[80]

Rape, forced breeding, casual sex between males of the master class and
slave women, and the dissolution of black families occurred too often to be
exceptional in the antebellum South. In the words of Catherine Clinton,
black women were "caught in the web of the big house." Clinton, who has
demonstrated as much scholarly interest as anyone in how nineteenth-
century sexuality and violence affected women in the South, explains that
"the various strands of intimacies and blood which wove together black

and white in the Old South created a tangle of issues that is enormously difficult to unravel. Even the passage of time does not give us enough distance from these explosive topics."[81]

Slavery, though it was also practiced in southern cities, remains heavily associated with plantations and farms. The relative isolation of rural life may have served to obscure the complexities of slavery and sexuality in the largely Protestant South. In the old French city of New Orleans, however, with its curious blend of Catholicism and cosmopolitanism, the "plaçage" system developed. This contractual concubinage existed in an environment where free women of color outnumbered men of their own kind almost two to one. At "quadroon" or "fancy girl" balls, the *gens de couleur libres* paraded their young women. A well-to-do white man, promising the parents that he would protect their daughter and provide financially for any illegitimate offspring, negotiated for possession of her body and perhaps eventually earned her affection. Octoroon daughters of such a union might be groomed to follow in their mother's footsteps.[82]

Examples of solicitous relationships between white men, slave women, and their offspring can be found elsewhere in the antebellum South. In an account aptly titled *Ambiguous Lives*, set in rural Georgia from 1789 to 1879, Adele Logan Alexander has detailed the lives of the free women of color in her own family.[83] Despite the best intentions of white men to look after their illegitimate families, social conventions and legal restrictions threw up almost overwhelming obstacles. Codification of such arrangements appears to have been unique to New Orleans, even though the trade in light-skinned women occurred in such cities as Richmond, Virginia, Columbia, South Carolina, and Lexington, Kentucky, as well as Charleston and St. Louis.[84]

More interracial sexual unions involved white men and black females than black males and white women, but in *We Were Always Free*, T.O. Madden, Jr., assisted by the historian Ann L. Miller, has provided a narrative with a different twist. His white ancestress, Mary Madden, an indigent Irish immigrant, founded a family of color in America when she bore a mulatto daughter in 1758.[85] Bishop Henry McNeal Turner, a key late-nineteenth-century figure in the African Methodist Episcopal Church and a Georgia legislator during Reconstruction, claimed as his paternal great-grandparents a white woman, Julia Turner of South Carolina, and an unidentified black superintendent on her plantation.[86]

The dialectics of slavery transcended interracial sexual dalliance. Most southern women, both black and white, accommodated themselves to the "peculiar institution"; a few reacted in their own unique ways. Two of Dixie's daughters, Sarah M. and Angelina E. Grimké, formerly of South Carolina, attended the first antislavery convention of American women, held in New York City, 9-12 May 1837. Sarah served as one of the vice-presidents, and Angelina acted as a secretary.[87] Harriet Tubman, known to blacks as Moses, escaped from slavery in her native state of Maryland around 1849, subsequently made at least eighteen trips into the South to "rescue" others of her race, and is credited with helping three hundred or more to escape. "There was two things I had a *right* to," Tubman declared, "liberty or death; if I could not have one, I would have the other; for no man should take me alive; I should fight for my liberty as long as my strength lasted, and when the time came for me to go, the Lord would take me."[88] Neighboring Delaware produced Patty Cannon, a white woman who kidnapped blacks, both slave and free, and sold them to unscrupulous dealers. She was also an accused murderess. Arrested and imprisoned, Cannon reportedly "cheated the hangman by dying in her cell," writes a student of Delaware history, "although an alternative tale says that she escaped, leaving a dead woman in her place." George Alfred Townsend, a Civil War journalist, fictionalized her exploits in *The Entailed Hat*.[89]

The antebellum South gave rise to the stereotypical images of black females as "Jezebels" and "Mammies." American popular culture has sustained them, and they continue to influence contemporary perceptions of African-American women. The historian Deborah Gray White observed in 1985 that it seems that scholars "have come full circle to the conclusions of black sociologist and historian E. Franklin Frazier, who was among the first to point out the central role slave women played in families." At the same time, Frazier had "evoked an image of a domineering woman," which White claims had the effect of maligning black women for holding their families together. She also acknowledges that "for all the differences between bonded women and other American women, the contour, if not the content, of their lives was paradoxically similar." Monotonous and difficult work overwhelmed both black and white women, and neither had much control over their reproductive capacities. Succinctly stated, "white males made the crucial decisions regarding the future of *all* Southern children."[90]

By mid-century, forces that would erode but not eradicate Dixie's patriarchy were gathering momentum on an expanding front. During the decade of the 1850s, as the issue of slavery in the territories destroyed possibilities for political compromise, the United States and the American South moved toward an encounter with destiny. When the cataclysm that convulsed the country had spent itself, military might had eliminated slavery; but the war rendered neither the nation nor the South a utopia. Racism, sexism, and classism remained largely intact. The American South, however, would be different; so, too, would be the prospects for southern women.

FOUR

રીજી

And if a House Be Divided Against Itself

Professional historians have treated the Civil War as a watershed—a great divide—in national and regional history, yet events of that era did not produce a total transformation of either American or southern society. Protracted military action, followed by constitutional changes, eradicated slavery and made legal alterations in the status of blacks in American society. In 1876-77, however, to retain control of the presidency, the Republicans, who had not been particularly concerned about improving the status of free blacks north of the Mason-Dixon line, abandoned their newly liberated southern counterparts. In return for an election victory the party of Lincoln relinquished its efforts to exercise political control in the former Confederate states and acquiesced in the return of native white conservatives to power. The perpetual servitude of African-American women, then, gave way to seemingly indefinite subordination, exacerbated by both race and gender. As for southern white women, gauging the impact of the war and its consequences on their lives, despite the tendency toward expansive estimates, is best done in small incremental measures. For such careful work the skills of historians surpass those of cinematographers and media mythmakers.

Yet much of what contemporary Americans think they know about the Civil War, the American South, and southern women is heavily dependent on Margaret Mitchell's Gone with the Wind and David O. Selznick's interpretation of that great epic for the silver screen.[1] Hollywood history, as well as other fanciful renditions of Dixie's past, has created and fostered the impression that the South was born on the eve of the war, experienced defeat, suffered reconstruction, and thereafter endured essentially intact. As a consequence the Civil War era, in the popular mind, is the region's alpha and omega, its beginning and its end, the South eternal, transfixed in time.

"The conventional image of the American South," write the sociologists Maxine P. Atkinson and Jacqueline Boles, "is one of a rural area dotted with moss covered oaks, fields of cotton, plates of grits, gross bigotry, and beguiling women." The actress Sally Field, who is often associated with the television series "The Flying Nun," won an Academy Award for her role in *Norma Rae*, a film that revolves around the empowerment of a woman in a southern mill town. But when it comes to female images, Americans disdain a "lint head" turned union organizer. "The romantic southern lady descending a curved staircase or sweeping through a crowd of admirers," not a common twentieth-century southern mill girl, continues to capture the public imagination.[2] The "mammies," the long-suffering southern ladies, dashing officers, blockade-runners, dangerous Negroes, loyal old servants, and other stereotypes off the movie sets inspire skepticism in historians, but Mitchell's Scarlett O'Hara deserves some respect. A southern belle who never quite qualifies as a "lady," Scarlett exhibits resilience and strength in crisis; she is a survivor.

In the *Oldest Living Confederate Widow Tells All*, a novel by Allan Gurganus, Lucy Marsden, the ninety-nine-year-old widow of the Civil War's last surviving veteran, spins a tale of two civil wars: the one in which her husband fought as a mere boy and hers as the child bride of a crazed old soldier. According to Lucy's folk wisdom, equal parts of fact and fable constitute southern reality. When a young interviewer comes to the nursing home to record Lucy's story, the old woman launches into a sermonette: "Honey, you don't want the truth. You're just hunting some sharp old gingham gal that'll fit onto a Sunday Supplement Ladies' Page. She'd tell you how to make gentle soap and slow candles. You think the past was just one long class in handicrafts?" Then Lucy confesses that she hated candle making and churning. "All I am is stringy and cross—with a good memory for grudges. . . . I'm too tired to lie, too vain to need to. Staying mad—that's a lot of what's kept me opening these eyes. See, I'm still waiting for a small last way of getting even." Lucy declares, "I ain't a antique, was never such a fine lady. I don't have no blue-book value whatever."[3] It may be difficult to reconcile Margaret Mitchell's Miss Melanie Hamilton (Mrs. Ashley Wilkes) and Allan Gurganus's Lucy Marsden, but they are southern soul sisters all the same.

Almost always subjectively defined, "ladies," like the region that spawned them, have chameleonlike qualities. Drawing on the writings of the German philosopher Johann Gottfried von Herder, the historian Michael O'Brien has observed:

The idea of the South was strengthened, ironically, by the destruction of its political expression, the Confederacy. By a strange quirk, it left the South as the embodiment of Herder's idea of a nation, for Herder had been insistent that a nation was to be sharply differentiated from the formal mechanisms of the state . . . its essence was a free pluralism. Willingly or not, the South no longer had a common political structure. . . . Sentiment was left free to roam, and men could define their South without the awkwardness of an administration in Richmond to check their metaphysical freedom.[4]

Wilbur J. Cash, in *The Mind of the South*, noted that "sentimentality waxed fat on the theme of the Confederate soldier and the cause for which he had fought and died."[5] Southern honor, macabre but alive, masqueraded in Ku Klux Klan robes; and in the words of Bertram Wyatt-Brown, "lynchings were carried out with some attention to liturgy and magical paraphernalia."[6] Cash claims that paternalism was shored up by "the increased centrality of women." Male fears of miscegenation between white females and black males produced "yet more florid notions about Southern womanhood and Southern Virtue" and fostered "yet more precious notions of modesty and decorous behavior for the southern female to live up to."[7]

Atkinson and Boles contend that "the southern lady today is a slightly modernized version of the plantation mistress, without the plantation." At the same time they recognize that finding "women still pursuing the archaic ideals of their grandmothers is initially as incomprehensible as Marabel Morgan's (1975) total woman, but when the role of the southern lady is placed in regional and historical context, its congruency is apparent." When Atkinson and Boles asked contemporary southern women "to identify the characteristics of the ideal southern lady," they found that "with few exceptions, contemporary ladies agreed that the ideal role model has not changed in over a century." Whatever weaknesses may be inherent in this study, not least of which is an exceedingly small sample, it does suggest that the mythical southern lady haunts human memory in Dixie.[8]

Historians who first began to interest themselves in the impact of the Civil War on southern women probably overestimated the changes it wrought. Mary Elizabeth Massey, Bell Irvin Wiley, and Anne Firor Scott all viewed this conflict as the precursor of the expanded opportunities that developed for females below the Mason-Dixon line during the late nineteenth and early twentieth centuries. Massey laid the foundations when she wrote that "the Civil War provided a springboard from which they leaped beyond the circumscribed 'woman's sphere' into that heretofore reserved for men."[9] Wiley claims that "the Southern male, whose dominance both sexes accepted in antebellum times, lost caste by suffering defeat in the war he made and conducted. When he came home from the war, he could not logically regard as inferior the woman who had successfully managed farm or plantation during his absence." Wiley acknowledges, however, that "men were slow to recognize women's changing status."[10] Scott has observed that "the breaking up and remaking of institutions affected the whole society and had profound consequences for the lives of southern women." According to Scott, for all practical purposes, "the patriarchy was dead, though many ideas associated with it lived on for years. Personality styles of southern women were changing to meet the changed time; the new patterns would become increasingly apparent as the century wore on." [11]

More recently some historians have tempered pronouncements like Scott's, among them Catherine Clinton, an early critic of the "New Englandization" of American women's history. (This model seemingly gauges the experience of all females in the United States against that of New England women as recorded and interpreted by feminist historians.) Clinton points out that women "who had shouldered burdens throughout the war felt especially oppressed by postwar hardships. . . . Men filled their heads with talk of the Lost Cause and former glory, but women faced the reality of keeping the household running, the family healthy, and trying to make life more than endurance." [12] George C. Rable, in the most comprehensive study of southern white women and the great conflict to date, essentially supports and expands upon Clinton's synopsis. Rable writes that "by the end of the war, many women wavered in their support for the southern cause, but they seldom questioned the racial, class, and sexual dogmas of their society." Furthermore, they "functioned as members of a supposedly superior race." He also observes that "women's roles and status in Southern society continued to evolve in new directions, creating a crazy-quilt pattern of modest and limited improvements in an atmosphere of ideological reaction." [13] LeeAnn Whites, in somewhat the same vein as Rable but with a bit more cynicism, claims that "the war left white southern men feeling like less than men . . . [and] black men with a manhood that frequently continued to cost them their lives." The South's white females clung "to what was left of white southern men's ability to provide . . . black southern women with no alternative but to work in some white woman's kitchen." Equality and freedom remained elusive. [14]

Drew Gilpin Faust, however, takes a different tack from those of Clinton, Rable, and Whites, although she employs similar data. Faust explains, in exceedingly singular fashion, why "the Confederacy did not endure longer": "I would suggest it was because so many women did not want it to. The way in which their interests in the war were publicly defined—in a very real sense denied—gave women little reason to sustain the commitment modern war required. It may well have been because of its women that the South lost the Civil War." [15] Essentially Faust has coopted and exaggerated the earlier arguments of such historians as Mary Elizabeth Massey and Bell Irvin Wiley. In *Ersatz in the Confederacy*, published in 1952, Massey had

The chronological parameters of southern colonial women's experiences are marked by the arrival of English brides at Jamestown in 1619 (above, Library of Congress) and the contributions of women soldiers of the American Revolution. Below, Molly Pitcher at the Battle of Monmouth (engraving by J.C. Armytage from a painting by Alonzo Chappel).

Unless otherwise noted, all illustrations are from the National Archives and Records Administration, Washington, D.C.

Above left, Martha Jefferson Randolph, daughter of Thomas Jefferson, reflects the Virginia gentry of the late eighteenth and early nineteenth centuries. Abolitionist and rescuer Harriet Tubman (known as Moses, above right, in a painting by Robert S. Pious) represents a challenge to the patriarchal slaveholding society of the antebellum era.

Literate women, North and South, found *Godey's Lady's Book* a pleasant diversion and looked to it for advice on fashion. An 1841 fashion plate is shown (from a copy in the author's possession).

In appearance, Mrs. L.C. White of Abingdon, Virginia (above left), personifies the white "southern lady" of the antebellum and Civil War eras, while Ida Dixon of Richmond, Virginia (above right), provides a less common perspective on her counterpart, the proper black woman of that time.

Mrs. James Longstreet and her husband, Civil War General James Longstreet (right), represent the "Lost Cause." Although Mrs. Longstreet, as late as World War II, exerted considerable effort to promote the general's memory, she was a formidable woman in her own right.

All three photos courtesy of
Tony Marion, Blountville, Tennessee.

"A Daughter of the South" by Charles Dana Gibson, from *Collier's Weekly*, 31 July 1909. This rendering may have been based on Gibson's wife, Irene Langhorne of Virginia. The "Gibson Girl" became an important symbol of the "New American Woman" during the late nineteenth and early twentieth centuries, a time also when southern women entered public employment in increasing numbers.

At right, women workers trim currency in the Government Printing Office in 1907.

Mill work was another common occupation for southern women. The women at left work at spooling tables of the Bibb Manufacturing Company, Macon, Georgia, in 1927.

Right, Mrs. Guilford (Anne Dallas) Dudley, Sr., of Nashville, posed with her children for this propaganda shot to offset insinuations by opponents that women crusaders for the right to vote were "abnormal." Courtesy of the Tennessee State Museum and with the permission of Guilford Dudley, Jr.

Even as some southern women campaigned for the suffrage amendment, a still larger number contributed to the World War I effort in a variety of ways. Below, an American Red Cross parade in Birmingham, Alabama, 21 May 1918.

Access to higher education for southern women eased during the late nineteenth and early twentieth centuries. In addition to the standard academic regimen, women participated in a variety of extracurricular activities, such as this May Day celebration (from the private Josephine Hamilton Collection, in the author's possession) and on athletic teams (Kentucky Library, Western Kentucky University).

All across the South, in war and peace, women have served their families, communities, and country. The twentieth century brought them greater flexibility and expanded opportunities. At left, in 1923 a county agent, home demonstration agent, and rural nurse make home visits in the Booker T. Washington bus from Tuskegee Institute.

Women distribute Food Administration posters in Mobile, Alabama, during World War I.

Packhorse librarians deliver books in Eastern Kentucky, in the mid-1930s (Kentucky Library, Western Kentucky University).

Except for the privileged few, rural women of all races have routinely worked in the fields, a practice that has remained common into the twentieth century. Above, black women pick cotton in Tallulah, Louisiana, ca. 1924-25. Below, the twin daughters of a tenant farmer hoe the family garden plot at Harmony Community, Putnam, Georgia, in 1941.

The depression of the 1930s exacerbated the already hard lot of women across the South. At right, a Cherokee woman does the family washing in Cherokee, North Carolina, 1930s.

At left, Chicano women smock infant dresses as home industry piecework in Texas, 1934.

The plight of the Oakies and Arkies proved especially poignant during the Dust Bowl years. At right, a migrant family from Amarillo, Texas, stand outside their California trailer, which lacks running water and sanitation facilities (1940).

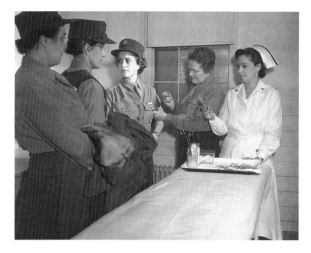

As auxiliary military service units opened to them during World War II, young southern women entered the service of their country and served in every theater available to them. At left, three southern women from the first WAAC unit sent overseas get their shots at Daytona Beach, Florida, in November 1942.

Women from Alabama, Florida, and Texas are among this group of service personnel preparing to return home from Manila, Philippines, in January 1944.

Southerners were well represented among women aviators in World War II (courtesy of the Tennessee State Museum).

As the United States fought a global conflict, women demonstrated their abilities in such traditionally female activities as sewing and running boardinghouses and in such traditionally male occupations as welding. At right, women in a Louisville, Kentucky, garment factory sew army uniforms in January 1942.

Women welders pose at Pascagoula, Mississippi, in 1943.

Mabel Stanley makes miners' lunches at a boarding house in Bishop, Virginia, just after the war, in 1946.

Despite the racist and sexist society in which they lived, many African-American women experienced rich, rewarding, and meaningful lives. Mary McLeod Bethune (above, about 1936, from a painting by Betsy G. Reyneau) was one of the most prominent members of her race, male or female, in the New Deal era. The arts world and the entertainment industry proved alluring for some young black women. World War II evoked the patriotism of African Americans, and they too rallied to meet the needs of the hour.

Young women in a dance class at Atlanta University, 1936-37.

Sgt. Franklin Williams, home on leave, enjoys a soda with his best girl, Ellen Hardin, in Baltimore, May 1942.

Native Americans retained an often overlooked presence in the twentieth-century South. Even those on reservations sometimes embraced the cultural styles and expectations of American society at large. At left, two Cherokee girls are dressed for a prom at Cherokee, North Carolina, ca. 1940s-1950s.

Below, Seminole Jennie Tiger, at seventy, is the oldest learner in an adult class at Brighton Reservation in Florida, ca. 1956.

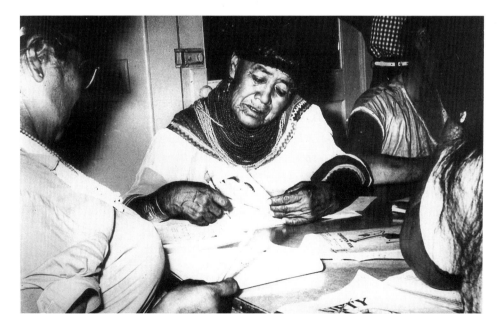

The postwar era brought new opportunities for southern women, along with new challenges. These dramatically different photos of young African-American women reflect the ironies of southern and American life. Above left, Jean Wynona Fleming, a Fisk University student, was jailed after a Nashville lunch counter sit-in in March 1960. Photo by Jimmy Ellis, *Nashville Tennessean* (courtesy of Tennessee State Museum). Above right, Vivian Ellis of New Orleans is shown as a staff nurse at a U.S. hospital in Munich, Germany in January 1964.

Linda King, one of a small number of women to enter underground mining in recent decades, stands outside the Bullitt Mine in Appalachia, Virginia, in 1979.

A few contemporary southern women have made their way into highly visible public positions through election, political appointment, or professional achievement. Above, Dr. Rhea Seddon talks with a fellow astronaut in June 1990 (courtesy of the National Aeronautics and Space Administration).

Right, Janet Reno, photographed in 1993, was the first woman to serve as U.S. Attorney General (photo courtesy of the U.S. Department of Justice). The attainments of both of these women are exceptions to the less glamorous lives of the great majority of women in the South and across the United States.

maintained that "shortages of essential commodities played an important part in bringing about the collapse of the Confederacy." Although "most people at home tried to maintain a spirit of optimism and hope . . . , after 1863 a spirit of war weariness settled over the civilian population."[16] Wiley commented that the "failure of the Confederacy to alleviate the suffering of soldiers' families may have contributed more to Southern defeat than any other single factor."[17] In summary, disenchantment on the southern home front represented but one of multiple factors that produced a Union victory in the War between the States; but before the slaughter had spent itself, men and women on both sides had most assuredly grown weary of it.

The secession crisis of 1860-61 and the fall of Fort Sumter marked the onset of the Civil War, but like a great storm it had been gathering for at least a decade. In the immediate aftermath of the Mexican War—a victory that had been bought and paid for largely with southern blood—politicians, both northern and southern, had tried to avoid the controversy that the acquisition of new land by the Treaty of Guadalupe Hidalgo was sure to bring. Try as they might, however, they could not indefinitely sidestep the issue of slavery in the territories, which ultimately disrupted the nation. When slaveholding Texas had been admitted to the Union in 1845, it carried with it not only the Anglo culture that had been transplanted by Americans but also that of Texas Mexicans, or Tejanos. The Tejanos held expectations for their women that were not unlike those found in other Western cultures; indeed their expectations were compatible with those of the antebellum South. The double standard of morality required that females be virgins at the time of their first marriage and that they be faithful to their husbands, "even if their husbands turned into shameless philanderers." A "paramour statute" existed in nineteenth-century Texas which allowed "a man to kill his wife's lover without fear of legal retribution."[18] The culture of the Southwest had a unique flavor that added to the ethnic diversity of the slaveholding South, but if it had any effect at all on gender roles, it was not to alter but to sustain and reinforce traditional expectations.

The antebellum South had consigned some women of all colors and classes to a gynecological and obstetrical hell. Even "the typical southern woman," Sally G. McMillen writes, "bore and reared several children, suffered poor health, exhaustion, and a variety of physical ailments, grieved over the death of at least one child, and was pregnant or nursing a newborn in every year until her midforties."[19] It is beyond the skills of a historian to give an adequate description of the pain and hardship that women of an earlier era endured as life cycles intersected with biological destiny. One suffering pioneer woman in Kentucky, Jane Todd Crawford, believing that she was carrying twins, rode a horse sixty-four miles from her home south of

Greensburg to Danville to seek medical assistance. On Christmas Day 1809 at his residence, Dr. Ephraim McDowell performed on Mrs. Crawford, without anesthesia, what was reportedly the world's first ovariotomy. She survived and recuperated, and her famous twenty-pound tumor catapulted Dr. McDowell into the medical record books and garnered him one of Kentucky's two places in the National Statuary Collection of the United States Capitol.[20]

In Dixie, assorted fevers in addition to ague, as malaria was known, proved especially virulent, adding to the woes of enceinte females. Both malaria and yellow fever, which routinely visited themselves upon the swampy low-lying areas of the nineteenth-century South, wreaked havoc on the health of pregnant women. In 1853, Zac Robertson, a New Orleans businessman, wrote to a Massachusetts associate about the horrors he had witnessed during the yellow-fever epidemic that had swept the Crescent City that same year: "I saw a woman at the Hospital who suffered from Hemorrhage of the lungs, Hooping Cough, yellow fever and the pains of labor [a miscarriage] all at the same time. Horrible Case!" Although this wretched female experienced the worst combination of circumstances, yellow fever and malaria, so common in the South, severely affected many females of childbearing age.[21]

Struggling with "female troubles" alone during an era when relatively minor problems could create enormous discomfort and when more serious ones might lead to death would have been enough to distract the daughters of Dixie from the lofty details of war, politics, and diplomacy. It may well be, however, that the crisis of the Union, this "American Iliad," was of such momentous proportions that it jolted the private worlds of even those southern females who had been the most comfortable, hastening their entry into public life. In a recent Civil War synthesis, Charles P. Roland observes that "women had never been the fragile and ineffectual creatures they were sometimes pictured as being." The experiences of wartime, which "cast them in roles that were far removed from those usually assigned to them," however, may have "combined with the defeat of southern men on the battlefield . . . to weaken somewhat the region's traditional patriarchal family system and to turn southern women in the direction of public endeavor."[22]

When the slaughter had spent itself, the healing process most assuredly required enormous contributions and compromises by women. The war, leaving in its wake thousands of deaths and debilitating wounds, exacerbated the difficulties already inherent in making a suitable match. Confederates had lost one in four soldiers, and after the war, some young males left the South, hoping to forget the war and start anew elsewhere. Females outnumbered males in the South until the 1880s.[23] Commenting on the importance of matrimony in antebellum America, the historian Robert E. Riegel explains: "No young miss, whether at home with her mother, working in a Lowell mill, or embracing the social whirl, forgot that her main business was the acquisition of a husband. By accepted fiction man was the pursuer, but in fact woman utilized every feminine wile to encourage pursuit and to expedite capture."[24]

Of course, exceptions existed. In the South, reclusive and celibate Catholic nuns, who were scattered about the region, and such utopians as the Shakers shunned matrimony. The Sisters of Loretto, a teaching order, dated its presence in Marion County, Kentucky, from 1812. The Sisters of Charity, who set up operations near Bardstown, Kentucky, that same year, nursed the sick during the cholera epidemic of 1833 and cared for the wounded during the Civil War. In that same state, two Shaker communities—South Union in Logan County and Pleasant Hill in Mercer County—recognized the equality of women.[25] St. Cecilia's Academy in Nashville, established by four Dominican Sisters from St. Mary's Convent at Somerset, Ohio, originated in 1860 and survived the war and Union occupation.[26] For the most part, older females as well as adolescents of the Civil War era tried to live up to traditional social conventions in the South, which included matrimony; but stark realities produced a ghoulish humor. The diarist Mary Boykin Chesnut reported listening to acquaintances discuss the pros and cons of marrying a veteran who had lost a limb; one retorted that it would be her fate to wed a man who had been deprived of his head.[27]

For more southern females than ever before, the war and its aftermath meant "going out to work." Those who labored for the Confederacy found themselves not only in some of the dullest jobs but also the lowest paying ones. Danger hung over those who filled cartridges for the Ordnance Department. Accidents at Brown's Island in the James River of Virginia and at a Jackson, Mississippi, factory, killed and disfigured several young women, many of them just teenagers.[28] Although women had always toiled privately in the South, the idea of having a female sell her time and energy publicly remained anathema to a great many of both sexes in the region. Southern society tolerated the entry into the workplace of some females—widows, spinsters, and those of the lower economic orders whose husbands or fathers could not support them. "During the antebellum decades," according to George C. Rable, "increasing numbers of women worked outside the home, but mostly in traditional female jobs." The Old South, overall, claimed a relatively small number of white female factory workers. Frederick Law Olmsted reported seeing "scantily clad women and children shoveling iron ore and working as hard as any man" in Alabama.[29] Antebellum black women, as slaves, labored in mines, foundries, salt works, and on railroads; they also plowed fields. They reportedly constituted approximately half the laborers on the Santee Canal project in South Carolina.[30] The historian Ira Berlin has also found that "many more free Negro than white women were forced to work. The sexual imbalance of the free Negro caste in the cities placed many black women at the head of their household, and even when a man was present, his income was often insufficient to support the family."[31]

For white women who had occupied the middling and upper social orders before the war, acknowledging their desperate straits proved painful. That venerable old cliche "helpin' out" served as a face-saving device, because it suggested that taking pay for their efforts was only temporary until their husbands or male relatives could retrieve lost fortunes or get on their feet financially. Semantics hardly obscured the dire economic circumstances that forced women to labor in the public arena; "helpin' out" might last a lifetime. Feminists have tended to view "going out to work" as a positive milestone in a female's life because it suggests the possibility of economic autonomy. For more than a few southern women of the Civil War era as well as contemporary times, having to seek employment has not only been frightening but also humiliating and embarrassing. "Many southern women preferred to operate in their own well-defined sphere than to compete with men in public life," George C. Rable explains. "Better to serve as guardians of the home and the humane values that supposedly flourished there than to enter an evil world that showed little respect for female virtue."[32]

As battles raged, circumstances of the moment placed new demands on women; and the exigencies of survival in the aftermath of the war required different approaches to daily life. Still, the antebellum South had harbored uncongealed agents, if not a formal infrastructure, for female involvement in activities that took them beyond the home, farm, and plantation. These agents seemed innocuous at the time because for the most part they posed no challenge to the existing power structure and not infrequently lent support to the status quo. Women could hardly be faulted for religious and benevolent outpourings, which seemed not only appropriate but even becoming to their sex. Circles, clubs, and organizations existed as separate, autonomous, and self-supporting groups during the decades before the Civil War.

The historian Marsha Wedell, in a study of elite women and reformism in Memphis, Tennessee, points out that "these groups kept a low public profile, with their activities confined to aiding their specific church or the poor of their faith, and there does not appear to have been cooperation among them." Yet women interacted with each other within an organizational framework away from their own households. "It was largely these religion-oriented societies that provided Memphis women with an established base from which support activities for the Confederacy would be quickly formed," Wedell adds.[33] Such feminine benevolence was hardly unique to Memphis. Just on the eve of the Civil War, for example, prominent churchwomen in antebellum Mobile, Alabama, led by Mrs. Josiah Nott, a physician's wife, established the Protestant Episcopal Church Employment Society to provide sewing jobs for poor women. The managers solicited orders and assigned work to seamstresses, but the society also maintained a shop on Dauphin Street to sell garments suitable for servants and children. According to the historian Harriet E. Amos, this represented "the only job agency in antebellum Mobile."[34]

Page Putnam Miller, another historian, has documented the presence of antebellum southern women in the vanguard of the Sunday-school movement of the Presbyterian Church. One of them, Margaretta Mason Brown, a native of New York City, had married John Brown of Virginia. Brown had moved to Kentucky in 1783 and, after statehood in 1792, had become one of the Bluegrass State's first two United States senators. The couple's home, Liberty Hall, designed by Thomas Jefferson, became a nucleus of religious, political, and social activity. Margaretta, described as "the most cultured woman of her day in the Capital of her adopted state," initially conducted a Sunday school of sorts at her residence but subsequently established an independent formal one for girls which operated from 1819 to 1826. Apparently her early work met with less opposition than did later efforts after more churches of different denominations had come into existence.[35]

Anne Clay provides another pattern of leadership in religious education. Although she was born in Savannah, Georgia, in 1796, Clay had lived in New England, where her family spent the warmer months; and she had been educated at a girls' school in Medford, Massachusetts. Not only did she establish a school for slave children on her family's plantation and teach in it for sixteen years, but she also quietly advocated Sunday schools for slaves elsewhere in the South. One of her close acquaintances wrote that "she ever regarded the religious instruction of the negroes as the great duty of individual Christians and churches in the southern states." Apparently Clay expressed her opinions unobtrusively to the Episcopal male clergy and laity. Page Putnam Miller maintains that "not only southern women but many women in antebellum America adopted Clay's pattern of leadership." By personal example and through deferential informal meetings with patriarchs, Clay and others like her exerted what may have been significant influence without violating social conventions.[36]

Southern women also expressed themselves at revival meetings and political rallies which generally occurred outdoors. Set against the expansive backdrop of nature, secular outpourings of the latter genre matched the evangelical fervor of the former. Women "engaged in emotional antics evoked by itinerant preachers—falling, jerking, rolling, dancing, running, singing, laughing, and barking—and at political rallies in the emotional responses evoked by orators—singing, waving handkerchiefs, and quivering to the words of the speakers for hours on end."[37] The historian Joe L. Kincheloe, Jr., explains that religious and political meetings gave women "an opportunity to assert themselves in a manner never before allowed in conventional society. The taste of responsibility obtained at these gatherings may have aroused women's appetites for more important and autonomous roles in the society."[38]

Although "evangelical religion encouraged a certain mordant pessimism about human nature, fostered ideals of self-sacrifice, and reinforced notions of female submissiveness, faith seldom remained exclusively private or domestic," George C. Rable observes. On the one hand, evangelical religion tended to preserve male dominance but "implicitly questioned the legitimacy of the premium placed on aggressiveness in secular society"; on the other, it unequivocally sanctioned female church membership and probably "provided wives and mothers with a greater sense of individual worth." Because of the assumption in the antebellum South that women were or ought to be more pious than men, society deemed religious benevolence an appropriate feminine venue. For southern females, then, church membership and the good works appropriate to it provided an access to public life.[39]

Women also attended and actively participated in political rallies during the 1840s. At Clarksville, Tennessee, on 16 October 1844, a "ladies troop" made up of women "all being in uniform and on white horses" surprised onlookers with their snappy appearance. The troop paled by comparison with a reported (but probably exaggerated) turnout of a thousand ladies and gentlemen on horseback from Smyth County, Virginia, who paraded in support of their candidates that same year at Old Kingsport on the Holston River. Southerners, male and female, took pride in their equestrian skills, but southern women also stood on their own two feet and marched in torchlight parades.[40]

Both Henry Clay, the Whig presidential candidate in 1844, and James K. Polk, his Democratic opponent, claimed feminine supporters. Clay had a reputation as a great admirer of the ladies, and apparently some of them returned the favor in political fashion, for Ladies Clay Clubs remained in existence after the election had passed.[41] His wife, the frugal Lucretia Hart Clay, had managed the home front as her high-rolling spouse indulged in games of chance or when he absented himself on governmental business, which was not infrequently. When a New England lady had commented, "Doesn't it distress you to have Mr. Clay gamble?" the levelheaded Lucretia responded, "Oh! dear, no! He most always wins." "Harry of the West" himself credited his wife with saving them from bankruptcy.[42]

When Polk had earlier taken to the stump across Tennessee during the summer of 1839 in a bid for the governorship, his wife, Sarah Childress Polk, assumed the role of unofficial campaign manager. Actually it was she who forwarded relevant political information to him and made sure that local newspapers announced his scheduled visits, which generated large receptive crowds. The techniques that she devised and orchestrated helped to win the governor's seat for her husband.[43] A student of presidential ladies, Betty Boyd Caroli, describes Sarah Childress Polk as "the most outspoken and politically involved wife since Abigail Adams." Mrs. Polk's "excellent health, an inquiring and trained mind, a supportive husband and no children all increased her ability to participate in her husband's career," Caroli explains. Mrs. Polk outlived her husband by forty-two years.[44]

At such public events as political rallies and religious revivals, women may have felt more acutely than men the social and economic distinctions that characterized southern society. During 1914-15, Gus W. Dyer and John Trotwood Moore surveyed approximately sixteen hundred Tennessee veterans of the Civil War. Responses to their questionnaire seemed to suggest that ordinary work experiences as well as shared values and ideas produced male bonding across social and economic lines during the antebellum era. Some veterans observed, in the words of the historian Jennifer K. Boone, that "a stranger could not have distinguished between slaveholders and non-slaveholders grouped together at public gatherings" because of "the generally unremarkable kinds of clothes everyone wore." Despite such shared experiences as limited education, childbearing, and domestic chores, the women who made those clothes "noticed the differences, and the wealthier ones often made enough of them [the differences] that more than one veteran pointed out that women did not mingle together as freely as the men did." Women of the yeomanry had been known to make such comments as "Oh, she is stuck up because she has a Negro." Boone writes that "the ways in which men's lives were intertwined and thereby bound closer together seemed to serve poorly or not at all for women, and divisions that were present for all became more distinct in the eyes of women."[45]

As long as women played supporting roles, southern men of all classes tolerated them. If, however, females dared to challenge the status quo or to contradict the masculine view of appropriate feminine conduct, they could anticipate male disapproval. For lesser offenses, women ran the risk of censure; for greater ones, excoriation. Still, promoting popular causes or taking the moral high ground afforded females limited access to public life. Octavia Le Vert, a gracious lady from Mobile, Alabama, collected a thousand dollars in one day alone to assist in the preservation of George Washington's home as a national shrine. Miss Anne Pamela Cunningham, the founder and first regent of the Mount Vernon Ladies Association of the Union who also was a southern woman, had initiated the campaign in 1853. The organization promoted its work in the pages of the ever-popular *Godey's Lady's Book* as well as in the *Southern Literary Messenger*. Apparently no man came forth to ridicule either Cunningham or Le Vert. Indeed, the governor of Alabama appointed Le Vert as the state's commissioner to the Paris Exposition in 1855. During the antebellum era, Richmond, Virginia, women founded a temperance society; and Caroline Lee Hentz spoke for the "cold water cause" before the Total Temperance Society of Alabama at a Fourth of July celebration in Tuscaloosa. Raising money to build churches and orphanages and for benevolent purposes apparently did not desex women.[46] It behooved the daughters of Dixie, however, to remember their duties and not to speak of their rights or those of the black race.

Antebellum southern women, married or single, could expect little in the way of assistance from a male-dominated, albeit paternalistic, legal system. Describing the situation in Georgia during this era, the historian Eleanor M. Boatwright has observed: "The philosophies, practices and sentiments governing the political and civil rights of white women . . . between the Revolution and the Civil War were confused, fickle, contradictory, and paradoxical."[47] Throughout Dixie as well as the rest of the country, wives searching for a way out of bad marriages found the route to be rough going. Legal separations, though possible, remained exceedingly difficult, and females rarely availed themselves of the option. Divorce, which had once been obtainable only through legislative action, gradually became a judicial matter throughout the region except in South Carolina, where no divorce law existed.[48]

Pierce Butler of Georgia, in a statement prepared for testimony in his divorce suit, attributed the failure of his marriage to actress Fanny Kemble's "peculiar views which . . . held that marriage should be a companionship on equal terms—partnership, in which if both partners agreed all is well—but at no time has one partner a right to control the other." Fanny apparently objected to what in the South was "the customary and pledged acquiescence of a wife to marital control—nothing more." At the same time she seemingly either acknowledged her husband's right to custody of their children or merely found it convenient. Pregnant with a second child when a separation seemed imminent, she informed Butler that if he made arrangements for the child to be brought to him from England, where she expected to be delivered of it, she would comply with his wishes.[49]

A female who sought relief in the courts had to establish her commitment to domesticity, prove her respectability beyond a shadow of a doubt, and demonstrate that she had displayed the submissiveness appropriate to her sex. Even as the judiciary in southern states ever so gradually moved toward the protection of females, the social stigma attached to separation and divorce remained so strong and economic prospects for women remained so grim that very few summoned the courage to exercise these options. Losing control of minor children probably played no small part in the decisions of most women who dared contemplate an escape from matrimonial bonds.

On another front, southern states, along with northern ones, gradually enlarged the property rights of married women. George C. Rable points out that "there was little that was uniquely Southern about this. After all property law was an ancient bulwark of the patriarchal family in the Western World."[50] Some of the impetus for the property legislation affecting married women came from the decline of dower rights. "Most state legislators voted for the Married Women's Property Acts on the basis of conservative economic reasoning designed to protect, not to liberate, women," cautions Joan Hoff. Middle-class women probably benefited most from such legislative changes. "Of the approximately two dozen Married Women's Property Acts passed by states *before* the Civil War," writes Hoff, "none significantly expanded the legal rights of wealthier women from what they had been under equity trusts."[51]

The statute enacted in 1848 by the New York State Assembly came to be regarded as a model for similar measures in other states. Nevertheless, what seems to have been the first Married Women's Property Act in the United States had actually passed the territorial legislature of Arkansas in 1835 just on the eve of statehood. Earlier a Hempstead County, Arkansas, couple had set up its own unique version of separate estates. James Magness and his consort registered a document in the county records that simply stated: "Now it is understood that whatever is his'n is his'n and whatever is her'n is her'n." The number of white females in Arkansas remained exceedingly small during this era, which enhanced their matrimonial prospects, elevated their economic worth, and perhaps influenced the 1835 legislation. Hiram Whittington, a bachelor, for example, had learned upon his arrival in Little Rock and much to his chagrin that only five marriageable females dwelled there. That they were "ugly as sin and mean as the devil" hardly mattered in a town overrun with men. In such a setting, alliances between white European men and Native-American women proliferated.[52]

Interestingly enough, a mixed marriage and tribal law combined to serve as an inspiration of sorts for the Mississippi Married Women's Property Act of 1839. Betsy Love Allen, the daughter of a half-breed Chickasaw chief, inherited substantial amounts of land as well as slaves when her father died, making her a wealthy woman. Tribal customs and laws of the Chickasaw tribe governed her marriage to John Allen, which meant that the property she possessed remained separate from his estate and subject to her control. Subsequently, in 1830, the state of Mississippi claimed jurisdiction over the Indians, at the same time recognizing their customs and usages, which by implication included Chickasaw marital arrangements. When one of John Allen's creditors laid claim to a slave that Betsy had deeded to her daughter Susan, the matter went to the Mississippi State Supreme Court. In January 1837 the court ruled in favor of Betsy Love Allen. The decision, written by Judge William L. Sharkey, recognized her right to retain control of the property that she had inherited. Piety Smith Hadley, a white woman, also figured in the developments that preceded the 1839 legislation. Thomas Hadley, Piety's spouse, who was also a lawmaker, introduced the bill. His interest may have been spurred by his own business setbacks. Piety herself had an opportunity to lobby other legislators on matters of personal interest to her, for she kept a boardinghouse in Jackson where the solons lodged and dined.[53]

Despite milestones like the Arkansas and Mississippi laws, gender-based discriminatory practices abounded. Women who dared to challenge the prevailing order called attention to the hypocrisy that undergirded it; they found little solace in public society. The historian Victoria E. Bynum, for instance, has studied ordinary black and white nonplantation women in central North Carolina who ran afoul of the law or found themselves caught up in legal proceedings both before and during the Civil War. According to Bynum, the desire to maintain the power of the slaveholders and the stability of the slave system permeated the legal systems of Granville, Orange, and Montgomery counties. "Unruly" females proved to be especially troublesome because they "threatened to disrupt the underlying social structure, which depended upon the services and cooperation of all women."[54]

Male legislators drafted the legislation that affected women, and the laws naturally reflected masculine self-interest. Suzanne Lebsock discovered, when she was studying the property rights of southern women during Radical Reconstruction, for example, that female legal rights had little to do with the feelings, thoughts, or opinions of the women themselves. Such matters as homestead exemptions and married women's property laws functioned similarly. They protected families from economic disaster, provided debtor relief, and operated to the advantage of the men who drafted them. Lebsock writes: "The reforms enacted by the radicals . . . continued an established southern tradition of legislation, a tradition of progressive expansion of the property rights of married women for utterly nonfeminist purposes."[55]

From 1848 to 1852, eighteen states had enacted homestead-exemption laws. According to the historian Paul Goodman, "the movement swept out of Texas in 1839 and spread first to the lower South, then across the Midwest and Northeast, and finally into the new territories of the Far West." During the Reconstruction era, several southern states altered the earlier homestead-exemption laws, which had been intended to provide "a measure of security in an increasingly insecure, volatile economy." The "right to waive homestead exemptions" in such states as Georgia "undercut the safety net intent of the laws." Likewise, "even in a state such as Texas with a strong commitment to homestead exemption, powerful mortgage lenders found ways around the law, just as husbands discovered legal means of evading that state's requirement that wives consent to waiver."[56]

Limited education not only contributed to but also exacerbated the sorry circumstances that characterized the lives of southern women. In the Mid-Atlantic region and in the New England states, literacy rates among females exceeded 90 percent. At mid century, those for adult white females in Dixie rose to an estimated high of 86 percent in Mississippi and dropped to a low of 64 percent in North Carolina, which was 4 to 16 points below southern men. "Literacy" is relative, and in all probability, some women who considered themselves "literate" could do little more than sign their names and stumble over words. "Many antebellum South women," according to George C. Rable, "like the wives of twentieth-century sharecroppers, read nothing."[57]

Still, antebellum southerners may not have been as unappreciative of education as they have often been made out to be. "In 1860," according to one source, "the North had a population of 19,000,000 whites, 205 colleges, 1,407 professors, 29,044 students. In the same years, the South had a population of 8,000,000 whites, 262 colleges, 1,488 professors, 37,055 students." In terms of expenditures the North stood at $514,688 and the South at $1,622,419.[58] All the same, during most of the nineteenth century in Dixie, securing an education remained largely a private matter and therefore open to those who could afford it, which basically meant certain middle-class elements and the planter elite. Fathers' attitudes toward learning affected both their male and their female offspring, and some patriarchs chose to educate their sons adequately by the standards of the times but not their daughters. Yet there is a hint of legal acknowledgment that women had a vested interest in public education. Kentucky in 1838 granted "school suffrage" to widows in rural areas who had children of school age. This seems to have been the first such instance in the United States.[59]

Generally speaking, southern parents who privately saw to the intellectual development of their female children did so in an attempt to enhance their matrimonial prospects and to render them better wives and mothers. In this the southern gentry hardly differed from their northern counterparts of this era; but there may have been somewhat more emphasis on manners, social skills, and domestic preparation below the Mason-Dixon line. Pioneers of women's education in the North often trained upper-class women as well, but they focused on those of the middle class, attempting to prepare them for work before they married, to meet the exigencies of widowhood, or to cope with their husbands' declining economic fortunes.[60]

A single-sex approach to education prevailed throughout the country as students advanced beyond the most rudimentary level, and the antebellum South was strewn with female academies and seminaries in which curricula ranged from abysmally inadequate to intellectually challenging. Rare instances of coeducation occurred. Samuel Carrick, for example, admitted women as well as men to Blount College in Knoxville, the forerunner of the University of Tennessee. At least five females had attended during the 1790s, among them Margaret Blount. She claimed William Blount, governor of the Southwest Territory and Tennessee's first United States senator, as her father.[61]

In the most comprehensive study to date of the antebellum education of southern women, *The Education of the Southern Belle: Higher Education and Student Socialization in the Antebellum South*, the historian Christie Anne Farnham details a story that some may find remarkable, one, however, that is not wholly unfamiliar to native-born southerners. A region that seemed to discourage strong-minded women still offered some of them an education comparable to the best available to men. At the same time the educational establishment maintained and nurtured the conventional behavior often associated with the southern "belle." In these antebellum female academies and seminaries, rites of socialization developed around such events as May Day celebrations. Sororities or Greek-letter societies also originated and proliferated on southern soil. According to Farnham, the first sorority in the country took root at Wesleyan (Georgia Female College) in 1851 when Eugenia Tucker, whose father was the second largest landowner in Laurens County, founded the Adelphian Society, later Alpha Delta Pi. Indeed, the establishment of Georgia Female College at Macon in 1839, in and of itself, had represented a landmark event, because it marked "the first self-conscious effort to erect an institution at the collegiate level—whose stated goal was to provide an education for women identical to that available at the highest levels for men and to use the term *college* in doing so."[62]

Northern tutors, teachers, and professors often filled positions in the antebellum South, and many of the better-educated southerners of both sexes owed their intellectual development to transplanted Yankees. Those pedagogues who abhorred slavery usually remained silent or returned to their places of origin. The more action-oriented Delia A. Webster, a native of Vermont who was principal at Lexington Female Academy in Kentucky, however, assisted runaway slaves as a conductor and operator on the Underground Railroad.[63] Almira Lincoln Phelps affords a model of a more acceptable transplant. A New Englander by birth, she took charge of Patapsco Female Institute in Baltimore during the 1840s and presided over it for more than twenty years. Although she was a pillar of society as well as an educator, "in lecture after lecture she held up an ideal of intellectual growth and character development to be achieved by women's own efforts, an achievement which would not only admit them to the company of the greatest minds, but would help them become strong, resilient individuals capable of dealing with any problem."[64]

Northern influence also cropped up in Indian Territory when the Cherokee Female Seminary of the Western Cherokee Nation opened in 1851. Modeled after Mount Holyoke Seminary in South Hadley, Massachusetts, at the behest of Chief John Ross, it steered several generations of young Cherokee women toward "a world and a way of life quite different from that of their tribal past." Relatively few full bloods attended the school; the great majority of students claimed blood that was only half Cherokee or less. Ellen Rebecca Whitmore of Marlborough, Massachusetts, served as the school's first principal, and another Yankee, Sarah Worcester, was her assistant. Worcester dedicated herself to inculcating "social graces and meticulous refinements of good breeding" along with the traditional subjects. When the United States government had forcibly relocated the Cherokees in the northeast corner of what is now Oklahoma, slave owners among the Native Americans took their human property with them. Many of the students who attended the Cherokee Female Seminary came from slaveholding families, and even teachers and ministers who themselves embraced abolitionism remained silent or risked expulsion from the Cherokee Nation.[65]

Ignorance may not necessarily have been bliss, but educating females hardly ensured domestic tranquility. American education in the nineteenth century, for men and women, tended to eschew independent thinking for indoctrination. Indeed, female seminaries and academies usually fostered the established values that kept women subordinate to men. Nevertheless, exposure to ideas, strong role models to be found in some female educators, and pride that educated women occasionally took in their learning sometimes coalesced to produce unexpected results. Better educated than most southern men and women of their day, Mary Todd Lincoln and Varina Howell Davis, the first ladies of the divided nation who were both daughters of the South, demonstrated considerable independence. During the Civil War, Mrs. Lincoln came under suspicion for her southern sympathies; Mrs. Davis, for her northern connections.

In 1805 Mary Menessier Beck, a Frenchwoman by birth, had opened

her academy for young ladies in Lexington, Kentucky, Mary Todd's hometown. Prior to this time the formal education of females in that commonwealth seems to have been confined principally to "sewing, knitting, and
fine accomplishments," according to one source, with music and drawing
teachers providing sporadic instructions. Beck established a six- to seven-
year course of study with subjects meant to challenge the feminine mind,
including rhetoric, astronomy, geometry, belles-lettres, geography, logic,
natural philosophy, composition, mythology, poetry, universal history, and
natural history. She equipped her school with pianos, globes, magazines,
and books. She also believed in the importance of dancing and usually kept
one of the French emigrés on hand to provide instruction. Mrs. Waldemard
Mentelle, who had taught for Beck, opened her own school around 1820 at
Rosehill Road in Lexington. Within five years she counted among her
boarding students the future Mrs. Abraham Lincoln.[66]

Mrs. Lincoln's Confederate counterpart, Varina Howell Davis, sometimes found the ideal of the southern lady overwhelming. The daughter of
William Burr Howell of New Jersey, who had settled in Mississippi after the
War of 1812, she was born on southern soil, his second child and oldest
daughter, 7 May 1826. Joan E. Cashin suggests that Varina Howell may
have "escaped some of [the] strictures, partly because of her family's Northern roots, and partly because she married a man who became a national
figure." Nonetheless, "she too had to struggle all of her life to behave as a
lady, and she was often confronted with her powerlessness in the family."[67]
Varina was educated at an elite girls' academy in Philadelphia and then was
tutored at home by George Winchester of Massachusetts; northern influence permeated Varina's education. The Civil War years and their immediate aftermath proved wretched ones for Mrs. Davis. Her husband took up
residence at Beauvoir, the estate of the widow Sarah Dorsey on the Gulf
coast of Mississippi, and allowed the widow to usurp his wife's role while
Varina herself was being treated for a heart ailment in England. Such circumstances tended to undermine matrimonial bliss.[68]

After Jefferson Davis's death, Varina lived in the North and supported
herself as a writer. She was but one among several recognized southern literary women of the nineteenth century. Pre-Civil War Dixie had produced a
spate of published women authors whose work fell into the general catego-
ries of good, bad, and indifferent. Mary Forrest's *Women of the South: Distinguished in Literature*, which appeared in 1861, included the names of thirty-
six of them.[69] The editor of a subsequent anthology that contained biographical sketches as well as the works of southern female writers complained self-righteously that "dilettanteism . . . has been the bane of Southern literature."[70] Most of the identified women attempted neither to subsist
on their earnings as writers nor to challenge the underpinnings of southern

society in their work. A realistic approach to the world in which they lived left them little recourse except to stifle any heretical thoughts if in fact such thoughts ever crossed their minds.

Some female writers of this place and time may have thought of themselves as "southern women of letters." (New Orleans writer Grace King, in 1932, used the phrase "southern woman of letters" to describe herself.) Anne Goodwyn Jones, an authority on southern women writers, has employed the label "southern literary women." Just using the term "southern literate women," she observes, means excluding "all those women to whom poverty, race, or the law denied access to literacy itself." Most of those who considered themselves "literary" were little more than "chroniclers," who had found "a way to create an identity and to make, rather than simply report, history."[71]

Still, Dixie produced a few of the better-known female literary figures of the nineteenth century. Mary Virginia Terhune, a Virginian born in 1830 who survived into the next century, established herself as one of the era's foremost advisors on domestic matters.[72] Caroline Howard Gilman of Charleston, South Carolina, a native of Boston, Massachusetts, had published the *Rose-Bud*, described as "the pioneer juvenile *newspaper*" in the country. Commencing in 1832, it contained her fiction, poetry, and prose. Mrs. Gilman's daughter, also named Caroline Howard Gilman, operated a successful school in Charleston for fifteen years after the death of her first husband, Wilson Glover. (She married Louis Jervey in 1865.) Her work appeared in various magazines, and the *Southern Literary Messenger* serialized her novel *Vernon Grove: or, Hearts As They Are*; it was subsequently published in book format by Rudd and Carleton of New York in 1858. She copied this novel for her publisher at night after spending her days in the classroom, managing to fulfill "her social duties, visiting, entertaining, and seeming always to be as completely the mistress of her own hours as the idlest fine lady."[73] Caroline Lee Hentz of Alabama attempted to counter *Uncle Tom's Cabin* with *The Planter's Northern Bride*, an apology for slavery; and Louisa Suzanna McCord, a prominent South Carolinian, wrote articles on political economy and social theory, emerging as an outspoken and influential proslavery advocate. The historian Elizabeth Fox-Genovese has observed that elite southern women tended to keep private journals but that most of them seemed disinclined to publish their musings.[74]

Not surprisingly, the private and public writings of mid-nineteenth-century southern women as well as their successors reflected their shared regional heritage. Anne Goodwyn Jones, who has studied seven women authors of the late nineteenth and early twentieth centuries—among them Kate Chopin, Ellen Glasgow, and Margaret Mitchell—describes them as "both romanticists and realists." Although this later generation of pen women tended to either scorn or ignore "traditional images of the beauty of the southern female," they could not escape entirely the "southern lady." "Discarding the fragility of skin like magnolias and eyes like violets," however, they invented "their own definitions of southern womanhood." According to Jones, "the masks they wear as authors, the personae they create, half reveal and half disguise the truth within their fictions. Yet perhaps their ambivalence should be forgiven; it is quite a magician's trick, after all, to make a marble statue live and move, and then to make it speak."[75]

Neither northern nor southern society of the nineteenth century seemed particularly well disposed to receive the avant-garde—and least of all from women. Most females who expected their writings to make it into print, of necessity, pandered to prevailing views. During the troubled decade of the 1850s, however, when Harriet Beecher Stowe—a New Englander by birth who had been living in Cincinnati, Ohio—addressed slavery in fiction, she spoke to the heart of the nation. *Uncle Tom's Cabin* was first serialized in the *National Era*, an antislavery weekly in Washington, D.C., and was subsequently published as a two-volume novel in 1852. President Lincoln remarked facetiously when he met Mrs. Stowe in 1862, "So you're the little woman who wrote the book that made this great war!"[76]

When the battles of that great war had ended and the last smoke from guns, cannons, and burning buildings had cleared, the human and physical devastation forced southern women to take stock of their resources. Access to education and a strong religious commitment may have wrought more significant and lasting consequences for nineteenth-century females below the Mason-Dixon line than the full range of statutes regarding their sex that had been enacted in all-male legislative chambers. What a woman gleaned from formal study and the personal convictions of her faith had the capacity to take interesting turns. Learning may have opened women's eyes to the need for improvements in southern society, and in turn the righteous conviction of evangelical Protestantism may have spurred them into action. When the South lay in ruins after the war, only the most obtuse could ignore the fact that history had happened to them and their region. The defeat of the Old South and the suffering that followed cut across class lines. Women did not necessarily have to be schooled in the classics to recognize that their world lay in shambles and that the course charted by southern men had left their region in ruin; each responded to the crisis of the union and its consequences in her own unique way.

"The mid-nineteenth-century South presents the picture of a society teetering on the edge of a critical racial and gender imbalance, pushed to the brink by changes in the sectional social and economic structure," Lee-Ann Whites observes.[77] Historians and laymen alike recognize the Civil War era as the South's Sturm und Drang. Contemporary experts on racial issues, as well as political activists in the African-American community, point to the overriding importance of slavery in nineteenth-century America, while some overly zealous feminists within and without academia tend to overestimate the importance of the Civil War as a milestone in southern women's lives. Yet most of those who lived through those troubled times focused their attentions on such mundane details of daily existence as birthing babies, doing the laundry, preserving and cooking food, and tending the sick. Ultimately the war that men had made came so close to southern women, literally and figuratively, that they could no longer ignore it. They had to recognize it for the cataclysm that it was when they watched their families being torn asunder, saw their loved ones going off to war, tried to keep farms and plantations operating, buried the dead, and sometimes fled invading armies, becoming refugees in their own land.

"It was from the environs of Washington that the first mass exodus of Southern sympathizers began," according to Mary Elizabeth Massey. In her fifties and suffering from arthritis, Mary Custis Lee, the wife of General Robert E. Lee, counted herself among them. Almost as soon as General Lee assumed command of the Virginia troops, he began urging her to leave Arlington, a home that held memories and heirlooms dating back to her great-grandmother, Martha Washington. Mrs. Lee left Arlington on 14 May 1861 and never lived there again. Refugees, who came from the ranks of the high and the low in the South, numbered tens of thousands of human beings.[78]

As hunger and deprivation stalked them, even those women who had been the most enthusiastic about secession surely questioned quietly the wisdom of the course that the South had charted. In May 1863 a mob made up largely of females vented its fury against speculators as well as German and Jewish merchants when they rioted and looted in Richmond. The personal intervention of President Jefferson Davis and the arrival of Virginia troops ended this civil unrest, but authorities took some forty-four women into custody, twelve of whom were tried and convicted of various offenses. On orders from the Confederacy's War Department, Richmond newspapers suppressed the details.[79]

The great drama that was the Civil War placed men center stage. All the leading roles as generals, politicians, and diplomats went to them, and males constituted the cast of thousands from which both the North and the South forged armies. War only allowed females supporting or lesser parts. LeeAnn Whites notes, however, that "as the fiction of slave servility and childlike dependence upon the patriarchal planter dissolved in the crucible of war, it left only the subordination of southern white women—as the only dependents on whose loyalty the planter could continue to rely . . . Not surprisingly, Confederate men at the time and for years afterward have writ-

ten in self-congratulatory tones of the loyalty that their women demonstrated during the conflict."[80] Some Confederate men have even claimed
that women were the most enthusiastic supporters of the Confederacy and
the Lost Cause, an argument that such historians as Drew Gilpin Faust and
others have essentially neutralized.

As George C. Rable acknowledges, however, "the women of the South
were not simply victims or innocent bystanders to this national tragedy."
He explains:

Female slaveholders had struggled with and profited from a labor system that lay at
the root of the conflict, and most white women had taken pride in the hegemony of
their race. Despite their marginal role in the South's political culture, a few women
had followed public affairs, and the sectional conflict aroused the interest of many
others. They mouthed familiar words: *liberty, honor, Southern rights*; they excoriated the enemies of the white South: black Republicans, abolitionist fanatics,
greedy capitalists; they even implicitly defended and tacitly supported a social system that exalted female subordination.[81]

In Kentucky, which remained in the Union under duress, Mrs. Margaret
Ray of Owensboro supported the Confederacy in direct opposition to her
husband, who served as the Union's provost marshal. When Dr. Samuel S.
Watkins was arrested on Judge George Ray's orders and while he was being
escorted to jail by two Union soldiers, Mrs. Ray called out to the rebel:
"Good morning, Dr. Watkins. You look like Jesus Christ between two
thieves."[82]

Women on rare occasions expressed their frustrations in public remon-
strances. Still, the Confederate States of America was masculine-contrived,
and the Confederate military was a man's world. Very few women actually
took up arms as soldiers in the field, although there are some documented
instances. The miniscule number of them who donned masculine garb and
followed their menfolk into training camps or onto battlefields rarely escaped notice; authorities acted with dispatch to send them home. Bell Irvin
Wiley recounts an item from the Sandusky, Ohio, *Register* of 12 December
1864, which reported: "One day last week one of the rebel officers . . . [im-
prisoned on] Johnson's Island gave birth to a 'bouncing boy.' This is the
first instance of the father giving birth to a child, that we have heard
of . . . it is [also] the first case of a woman in rebel service that we have
heard of, though they are noted for goading their own men in[to] the army,
and for using every artifice . . . to befog and befuddle some of our men."[83]

What Adelicia Hayes Franklin Acklen said or did to Confederate and
Union officers to persuade them to allow her to move 2,800 bales of cotton
from Belmont plantation in Middle Tennessee to New Orleans remains a
mystery. Intelligent and beautiful, Adelicia, a graduate of Nashville Female

Academy with highest honors, first hired a gunboat and gained permission from Union officers to run the blockade. They became suspicious, however, and confiscated her cotton. Later they returned it to her and provided her with wagons and new mule harnesses from Union supplies. She eventually shipped the cotton off to England, with a Confederate soldier standing guard; and it garnered her $960,000 in gold, which made Adelicia, who was hardly a pauper beforehand, one of the richest women in America.[84]

Neither southern nor northern men could be faulted terribly for succumbing to feminine wiles and for paying deference to the ladies. Arms-bearing females clad in gray, however, undermined masculine honor and therefore could not be seriously countenanced. Confederates, after all, found it comforting to imagine themselves fighting for the sanctity of southern womanhood. This provided the rationale for an occasional atrocity. One explanation for the sack of Lawrence, Kansas, on 21 August 1863 by Quantrill's Raiders involved the imprisonment of women who were suspected of having given aid and comfort to the bushwhackers. Among those housed in a dilapidated brick building in that town were relatives of men serving under Quantrill: Mrs. Charity Kerr and Mrs. Nannie McCorkle, John McCorkle's sister and sister-in-law; Susan Vandiver and Armenia Gilvey, Cole Younger's cousins; and Jennie, Mary, and Josephine Anderson, Bill Anderson's sisters. Four of the women died immediately when the structure collapsed on 13 August 1863, one more subsequently succumbed, and a sixth one remained a cripple for the duration of her life. Tragic as this episode was, William Clarke Quantrill's own hatred for Lawrence, the factional bitterness in Missouri, and vengeance for Osceola, Missouri, which the Federals had raided in 1861, were all contributing factors.[85]

The veneer of chivalry, so prevalent in southern culture, yielded up some highly romanticized wartime stories, among them the daring of Miss Emma Sansom. Her mother implored her not to go with General Nathan Bedford Forrest, by saying, "No, Emma, people will talk about you." Emma retorted: "I am not afraid to trust myself with as brave a man as General Forrest; I care not for people's talk." As she led him to a ford across Black Creek near Gadsden, Alabama, several Minié balls passed through her skirts; but brave Emma declared, "They have only wounded my crinoline." After the capture of Streight's Raiders, according to General Forrest, "a Federal officer then stepped up and asked me if it was I who was examining the ford the day before, and if that was a lady I had with me. I replied to both questions that it was, and added, 'and a beautiful young lady at that.' He turned to his men, and said, 'It is no use to fight such people, for we cannot conquer them.'"[86]

Delicate as southern lore would have them be, Dixie's fairer sex came to know all too well the sights, sounds, and smells of war. When the wounded from the fighting in Virginia during May and June 1862 were brought into Richmond, one woman wrote, "We lived in one immense hospital, and breathed the vapors of the charnel house."[87] Early in the war it offended southern sensibilities for white women to nurse the wounded in the "masculine milieu of an army hospital which presented sights that no lady should see." Females "should stay at home and make bandages, knit socks for soldiers, and comfort the menfolk when they returned from the rigors of battle." The escalating numbers of Confederate wounded and sick undermined such notions. Female volunteers came forth as nurses; some women set up small hospitals. President Jefferson Davis himself commissioned Sally Louisa Tompkins a captain so that her hospital, acclaimed as one of the best, could be designated as an army hospital in the capital of the Confederacy. From 1862 to 1865 Mrs. Phoebe Yates Pember served as chief matron of Chimborazo Hospital, also located in Richmond. After the Battle of Shiloh in April 1862, Kate Cummings from Mobile, Alabama, made her way to Corinth, Mississippi, to nurse the wounded among General Beauregard's retreating army. "Nothing that I had ever heard or read had given me the faintest idea of the horrors witnessed here," she recalled. Many of the women who attended the wounded soldiers acted in a purely voluntary capacity, but others, under a September 1862 law passed by the Confederate Congress, subsequently became official army medical service staff. The mostly Protestant rebel soldiers also appreciated the tender ministrations of such Catholic religious orders as the Sisters of Charity and the Sisters of Mercy.[88]

Late in the struggle, Mrs. Eliza Clinedinst Crim witnessed the Battle of New Market on 15 May 1864 from her home. She ran on the field, assisted the wounded and dying, and sheltered others in her home. "I will never forget those brave boy soldiers [from Virginia Military Institute] as they ran down the hill to victory and death," she commented later. In 1904, cadets at Virginia Military Institute presented Mrs. Crim the New Market Cross of Honor bearing the inscription "Mother of the New Market Corps." Union troops subsequently set fire to the military academy in 1864, taking their revenge on the institution whose students had fought at New Market. Lexington during the Civil War years had considered itself a bastion of the Confederacy and continues to be one of its shrines; the remains of two of the Confederacy's greatest generals rest there. When General Thomas J. Jackson died of complications from wounds tragically inflicted by his own men at Chancellorsville, Virginia, his body had been brought back for burial to the little town where he had lived and taught. Jackson's sister-in-law managed to save his sword, when the Federals came to Lexington, by concealing it beneath her long skirts and then, under cover of darkness, hiding it in an outhouse.[89] After the war, General Robert E. Lee took up residence in Lexington when he accepted the presidency of Washington College. When he died and was entombed there, the school memorialized him along with George Washington, General of the Revolutionary Army and first president of the United States, by renaming it Washington and Lee.

Although most southern women probably kept as much as possible to the usual gentle feminine pursuits prescribed for them, the war created a demand for the more exotic, dangerous, and shady feminine wiles. The huge hoop skirts of the times allowed women to carry all manner of goods, including medicines, weapons, food, and clothing, through enemy lines. Female informants and spies assisted Confederate generals. Belle Boyd of Martinsburg, West Virginia, gained the most fame when in defiance of great personal danger she gathered intelligence for the likes of J.E.B. Stuart and the mighty "Stonewall" Jackson in the Shenandoah Valley. The actress Pauline Cushman, a native of New Orleans, spied for northern forces. She toasted Confederates at Wood's Theatre in Louisville and went south in a transsexual disguise as a Federal agent. In 1863 her espionage activities in Tennessee earned her a death sentence. She managed to escape, however, and later enjoyed considerable popularity in the North when she appeared on stage in the role of Union spy.[90]

Rose O'Neal Greenhow of Washington, D.C., became a key figure in a spy ring organized by Colonel Thomas Jordan, a Confederate who had been William T. Sherman's roommate at West Point. The widow Greenhow's great value rested with the fact that she seemed predisposed to use not only her social graces but also her sexual favors to elicit information. The detective Allan Pinkerton discovered a weighty packet of love letters that Henry Wilson, a senator from Massachusetts who was chairman of the Military Affairs Committee, had written to her. Wilson, a future vice-president, apparently was only one of several powerful men in the United States government who considered Mrs. Greenhow an intimate friend. Imprisoned for a time in the Old Capitol, a cold and miserable ancient wooden building, Rose eventually secured a release and made her way through enemy lines to Richmond, where she enjoyed the accolades of the Confederate capital.[91]

Southern men as well as northern ones succumbed often enough to feminine charms. Never let it be said that a pressing military matter prevented a Confederate soldier from noticing the fairer sex. The advent of warfare itself had meant a sizeable number of hastily arranged weddings. Wives and girlfriends visited their men in camps when circumstances permitted; the furloughs of married soldiers, when they could be arranged, usually produced a rash of new pregnancies among their wives. General William Dorsey Pender expressed relief when his wife miscarried but advised her that if she wanted to avoid having children, she should stay away from him. "Hereafter when you come to me," he cautioned her, "I shall know that you want another baby." When she did visit him again, they practiced the "rhythm method" of birth control but to no avail. "I did hope when you left me that you had escaped," the general comforted her, "but we poor mortals know so little of the future. Surely we never need make any calculations again." Before the second child—a son—was born, Pender had been mortally wounded at Gettysburg.[92]

When legitimate feminine companions were not available, camp followers and prostitutes stood ready as substitutes. This represented at least one dimension of the human experience in which military rank mattered little, and women of ill repute serviced the enlisted men and the officers alike. There is no telling how many of those gallant battle-weary soldiers carried home with them the little mementos of carefully executed frontal assaults on whorehouses or how many of their wives and girlfriends quietly nursed "the clap" or other sexually transmitted diseases. Dishonorable as well as honorable fraternization between some native-white southern females and Union troops of occupation likewise occurred, much to the disgust of die-hard Confederates.

The manly attributes of the handsome and dashing General John Hunt Morgan of Kentucky devastated some of the respectable females who had the good fortune to meet him and enjoy his company. Morgan epitomized the southern cavalier, the cult of chivalry, and the southern caste system. At various times in his life he happily indulged himself in wenching until, according to his biographer James A. Ramage, he fell madly in love and married Martha Ready, his second wife, in *the* wedding of the Civil War. The president of the Confederacy and all of the high-ranking generals of the Army of Tennessee attended. One of them, Leonidas Polk, who was also an Episcopal bishop, performed the ceremony. (The first Mrs. Morgan, Rebecca Sanders, had died in 1861, after many years as an invalid.) Indeed, Morgan was so enamored with his "Mattie" that he may have neglected his military duties.[93]

Prior to Morgan's second marriage in 1862, however, he had left his brother-in-law Basil Duke in charge of his troops in Alabama and had gone off to relieve his boredom in Richmond. Absent without leave, he forsook the horseflesh that usually transported him and rode the trains some six hundred miles to the Confederate capital, which Ramage describes as "the most lively center of night life in the upper Confederacy. . . . There beautiful young prostitutes worked in brothels such as Eliza Herbard's on Cary Street, and they plied their trade on the sidewalks and in hacks and carriages on the streets." Along with pleasures of the flesh in Richmond, Morgan could satiate himself with gambling, another of his vices. Although rumors have persisted that Morgan was killed as he was exiting a woman's bedroom in Greeneville, Tennessee, Ramage dismisses that story.[94]

Hardly a wartime phenomenon, prostitution had flourished in southern cities, large and small. The 1860 census, for example, identified "four so-called 'female lodging houses' run by 'mistresses of the house'" in Mobile and similar establishments in Nashville. A busy port city, Mobile attracted a "professional" contingent that hailed from the South, elsewhere in the United States, and even foreign countries. Nashville had counted 207 "professional prostitutes" on the eve of the war, most of them homegrown, in their teens, and of Anglo-Saxon extraction. The brothels of Tennessee's capital ran the gamut from "great affluence" to "abject poverty."[95] Because the flesh trade offended the sensibilities of genteel women, they usually pretended ignorance of its existence in their own communities.

General Benjamin F. Butler, commander of Union troops of occupation in New Orleans, brought whoredom to the immediate attention of the "ladies" there with General Order No. 28, designed to halt their abusive treatment of his troops, which included but was not limited to their spitting on the blue-clad men. Known as the Butler Law, it specified:

As the officers and soldiers of the United States have been subject to repeated insults from the women (calling themselves ladies) of New Orleans in return for the most scrupulous noninterference and courtesy on our part, it is ordered that hereafter when any female shall, by word, gesture, or movement, insult or show contempt for any officer of the United States she shall be regarded and held liable to be treated as a woman of the town plying her avocation.[96]

The walls of houses of prostitution could hardly contain all the illicit sexual dalliances in Dixie. The historians James Lee McDonough and Thomas L. Connelly, in their account of the 1864 Battle of Franklin in Tennessee, comment that "the strange inertia of key Confederate officers remains a puzzle." Referring to what is sometimes called "the Spring Hill affair," they raise again the possibility that a woman may have contributed to the tragedy that befell the South at Franklin. (McDonough and Connelly apparently refer to a minor military action, but the phrase is a double entendre, which, given the circumstances, could mean either a skirmish or sexual dalliance.) At Spring Hill resided Jessie Helen McKissack, the wife of George B. Peters, a physician who had shot and killed General Earl Van Dorn the previous year for having widely rumored trysts with his beautiful wife. Peters had taken refuge in Nashville, but Mrs. Peters remained at home as the Battle of Franklin took shape. She asked Captain H.A. Tyler of Forrest's command to speak with the general. Tyler took Forrest to her and left them talking, and innocence may have prevailed.[97]

Several years later, however, Colonel Henry Stone of the Union army, who had been assistant adjutant general on General George H. Thomas's staff, wrote:

There was music and dancing and feasting, and other gods than Mars were wor-
shipped. During the sacrifices at their shrines, the whole of [General John M.]
Schofield's . . . force moved silently and fearfully by. . . . But in the morning there
was much swearing. . . . Cheatham and Forrest and the others who had given
themselves up to the charms of society the night before were more chagrined at the
disappearance of the enemy than at their own lapse from duty.[98]

Whatever the explanation for the Confederate debacle that led to the Battle of Franklin, McDonough and Connelly call it "the worst five hours in
Civil War history." The South suffered more than six thousand killed and
wounded. Five generals died outright, and another, gravely wounded, died a
few days later; the casualties also included some ninety field officers.

In reality the South seems to have had its fair share of lusty men and
women, but the imagery associated with the "lady" denied or ignored the
sexuality of white females and encouraged the exploitation of black ones.
Sexual harassment, abuse, and violation could hardly be considered novel
to the region, although wartime circumstances placed some southern wom-
en in even greater jeopardy. With most of their men away at war, they felt
especially vulnerable; and some of them fell victims not only to invading
Union soldiers but also to southern riffraff and outlaws. That rapes occurred there is no doubt; how extensively, there is no way to know, for
women understandably hesitated to make rapes public knowledge. The war
brought hope and the promise of freedom to black women, but it did not
spare them from sexual abuse; nor were southern white men their only op-
pressors. Some Union troops harassed and raped black women just as they
did white ones.[99]

When the "glories of war" had spent themselves, the ragtag remnants
of the Confederate armies stumbled home to rest, reflect, and renew
themselves. Their women, for the most part, had eagerly anticipated the
men's return. What warfare did to men physically and psychologically,
however, left many of them ill equipped to live up to feminine expectations. Females found themselves saddled with much of the responsibility
for picking up the pieces of daily life. The Civil War defeated the Old
South, but it did not in one fell swoop destroy all of its underpinnings. "A
peculiarity of civil war is the destruction not only of armies and nations
but of ideologies," wrote novelist Walker Percy. "The words and slogans
may remain the same, but they no longer mean the same thing."[100] The
majority of southern white women still supported the status quo or subscribed to progress as defined by men, but out of the shambles of Confederate defeat, seemingly viable alternatives presented themselves. Previously those who had differed substantially with the prevailing order either
left, submitted to social humiliation, or kept silent. In the post-Civil War
South, female activists, always a numerical minority, set a different agen-

da for themselves as well as for other repressed and oppressed groups of their region. In one of the great ironies of history, it seems that black women, who may have had reason to be the most hopeful during the war and its immediate aftermath, ultimately emerged from those chaotic years with the greatest disappointment.

❧

FIVE

Set Thine House in Order

Those who harbored expectations that a dramatically different South might rise quickly from the ashes of the North's military victory seriously underestimated the tenacity of native-born white southerners. The great majority of the men as well as the women of Dixie clung steadfastly to their traditions. Above all, they continued to share with their northern counterparts a fervent belief in the superiority of the white race.[1] The general acceptance of female subordination also knew no geographical boundaries. Neither northerners nor southerners in the late nineteenth century seemed prepared to come to terms with the radical and fundamental social changes that would have been required to afford the black race and the female gender a fair and equitable status in American society. Yet the years 1865 and 1920 stand as important parameters in both regional and national history. This era, which began with the end of black slavery and ended when woman suffrage began, served up a strange blend of residuals from the past and promises for the future. That transitionary interlude proved to be one of progress and paradox for southern women and their region.

The life of Elizabeth Avery Meriwether of Memphis, Tennessee, which spanned ninety-two tumultuous years, illustrates in part the complexities of southern womanhood in the post-Civil War era. One evening in 1867 Mrs. Meriwether served sandwiches and coffee to some of her husband's friends who gathered at the couple's frame cottage, located on the site of the present-day Peabody Hotel. General Nathan Bedford Forrest, along with Matthew Galloway, editor of the *Memphis Appeal*, and others, discussed how Memphis and the South might be saved from bankruptcy at the hands of "ignorant ex-slaves, elected to City Councils and State Legislatures, and dominated by the carpetbaggers." At a time when former Confederate soldiers remained disfranchised, they reasoned that the Ku Klux Klan, by intimidation and violence, could dissuade Negroes from voting.

This in turn would keep Negroes out of public office and prevent them from running up astronomical sums in bonded indebtedness. Mrs. Meriwether's son reported that Galloway inquired of his hostess, "Well, Betty Meriwether, what do you think of our plan?" To which she responded: "It may work. Negroes are very superstitious. They may become too scared to vote; then when you are allowed to vote you can elect intelligent men to tax you and make the laws that govern you. But when will women have the right to vote?"[2]

Subsequently Mrs. Meriwether became one of the first southern women who publicly endorsed female suffrage. Indeed, she rented a Memphis theater on the evening of 5 May 1876 and informed a large crowd that she intended to support Samuel J. Tilden in his presidential bid. On election day she went to the polls and cast her vote. Local officials who were friends of her husband's allowed her to drop her ballot in the box, though her son assumed that they destroyed it later. Undeterred, Elizabeth Avery Meriwether remarked: "Counting my ballot is not important; what is important is to focus public attention on the monstrous injustice, as well as stupidity, of including educated women with felons and lunatics as persons denied the right of suffrage."[3] Although she did not survive to witness the reality of unrestricted female suffrage, she lived to see both major political parties promise to support the franchise for women. She and other feminine crusaders in Dixie found it possible to rationalize the demand for rights for themselves while denying the same for blacks. Even with their own inherent racism removed from the equation, political realities necessitated this incongruous strategy.

The efforts to forge a new nation below the Mason-Dixon line and to create a separate political identity had met resounding failure, but "the dream of a separate Southern identity" had not been destroyed. Southerners possessed a powerful private determination to elude the consequences of public military defeat. They eventually came to accept the demise of the Confederacy as a political entity, but their "dream of a cohesive Southern people with a separate cultural identity" remained strong. The failed Confederacy, the historian Charles Reagan Wilson maintains, "survived as a sacred presence, a holy ghost haunting the spirits and actions of post-Civil War Southerners."[4] "When the war was over," Daniel Joseph Singal writes, "southerners of all social ranks began searching for a rationale to justify their attempt at secession and to explain their current predicament." They settled on the "preservation of an aristocratic way of life." The advent of such societies as the United Confederate Veterans and the United Daughters of the Confederacy produced "an army of full-time perpetuators willing to suspend all disbelief in their effort to embellish history . . . the only limits placed on the Cavalier's splendor lay in the ample capacities of the southern imagination and in the requirements of the region's wounded pride."[5] "The attachment of white Southerners to their way of life," John Hope Franklin agrees, "was as strong as ever, and they were determined to preserve it." A few may have been "bitter that their lives had been spared in the glorious cause," but he maintains that others "were determined to work and, if necessary, fight to preserve what was left." Indeed, the South would be "regenerated . . . , but only on the basis of *Southern* ideas and *Southern* institutions."[6]

As the nation haphazardly but publicly went about the business of binding up its wounds, private concerns about masculinity and femininity and undertones of gender redefinition prowled the recesses of regional and national consciousness. The myth of the southern lady had sufficiently infiltrated the minds of enough northerners for them to heap considerable blame on southern white women for the crisis that had torn the country asunder. When, for example, Mrs. Meriwether had unsuccessfully petitioned General William Tecumseh Sherman to return rent moneys from property that she (not her husband) owned, she reported that the general had demanded to know why she had allowed her husband to serve in the Confederate army. Not once, but three times, he had posed the question. These rents, which tenants now paid to Sherman's provost marshal, had been used to sustain her and her children, and she explained to him as calmly as she could that "by all the laws you men have made, and by all the religions you men do teach, we women have been brought up to obey our husbands, not to rule them. I had no power to keep my husband out of the army."[7]

During his military career, Sherman had spent time at southern postings; and when the war came, of necessity he vacated his position as superintendent of the Louisiana Seminary of Learning and Military Academy. The nation, he wrote in September 1862, needs to understand that "the entire South, man, woman, and child are against us, armed and determined."[8] Sherman, as few other Union generals, recognized the will of the Confederacy and waged total war against its people. Allowing for the South's propensity to exaggerate its sufferings neither diminishes nor eliminates the pain that Union forces inflicted. In isolated instances during the last horrible days of the war, some Federals perpetrated sexual violence, ravaging white and black women. Nevertheless, just as the defeated South was spared the genocide so often associated with civil wars, so, too, southern women probably suffered comparatively few violations. Susan Brownmiller comments, in her politically important but ahistorical book *Against Our Will: Men, Women and Rape*, that family relations may act as a deterrent to the abuse of women. She suggests that "the American Civil War . . . in some respects, a struggle of brother against brother, is considered a low-rape war by those few historians who have thought about it."[9]

The absence of substantial compilations of evidence hardly negates the likelihood or the reality of such occurrences, because respectable southern white women of that time and place could hardly have been expected to broadcast their humiliation. The testimony that is available tends to focus on the victimization of black females and, in turn, the humiliation of white folks of both sexes who were sometimes forced to watch the invaders abuse their property—that is, their slave women. Supposedly throughout her life, Rebecca Latimer Felton of Georgia, the first female to serve in the United States Senate, reserved a special hatred for northern troops who had sexually assaulted women in the South. (She was a temporary appointee in 1922 with a very brief tenure.)[10]

In Columbia, South Carolina, Sister Baptista Lynch had reason to expect decent treatment from Sherman's army because she was a friend of the general's sister, but his men stole gold altar vessels and set fire to the convent just after the young nuns and schoolgirls had left the building. Three-fourths of the city succumbed to flames that night, and a Union engineer wrote that "the burning houses, lighting up the faces of shrieking women, terrified children, and frantic, roving drunken men, formed a scene which no man of the slightest sensibilities wants to witness a second time." A Columbia newspaper reported that "the steets were full of rubbish, broken furniture, and groups of crouching, despondent, weeping, helpless women and children." Until his death, Sherman denied that he had ordered the burning of Columbia, but in a postwar statement he said, "Though I never ordered it and never wished it, I have never shed any tears over the event."[11]

Although neither Sherman nor his northern contemporaries wasted much sympathy on southern women of either color, they tended to assign blame to the white ones. The historian Nina Silber writes that "postwar observers portrayed southern women as the very foundation of the Confederacy—its main supporters and defenders." A Yankee critic of the time spoke of "bitter, spiteful women whose passionate hearts nursed the Rebellion." Silber observes that "in a society that held women's political participation in contempt, this notion of Southern women's intense commitment to the Confederate cause only underscored the illegitimacy of the government." According to the northern press, southern men had presumably accepted defeat, but the women had wanted "no truce and no peace." Even as northerners castigated southern white women, they attempted to emasculate the same southern white men who had fought so valiantly against the North for four bitter years. With relish, northern journalists embellished tales that Jefferson Davis, the president of the Confederacy, had disguised himself as a woman in an unsuccessful attempt to elude his Federal pursuers. While it seems to have been true that Varina, his wife, threw one of her cloaks or shawls over him at the last minute, Yankee illustrators had a field day employing the imagery of petticoats, hoopskirts, and all manner of feminine apparel.[12]

Before many years had elapsed, however, southerners, in a sense, turned the tables on northerners. "One traditional means the South employed for defining its identity and keeping the image clear was the running critique of Yankee morals it kept going over the years," writes C. Vann Woodward. "The crudities, excesses, and shams of the Gilded Age presented Southern critics and moralists with the broadest target they had ever had above the Potomac."[13] Such prominent Yankee authors as Herman Melville, Henry Adams, and Henry James, with little firsthand knowledge of Dixie or its denizens, still dared to introduce fictional southern characters. In *The Bostonians*, James pits Olive Chancellor, a Back Bay bluestocking, against her cousin many times removed, Basil Ransom, of Mississippi. When Verena Tarrant, who has been somewhat under Olive's tutelage, assertively announces, "Mr. Ransom, I assure you this is an age of conscience," he unleashes a diatribe against "feminization": "The whole generation is womanized; the masculine tone is passing out of the world; it's a feminine, a nervous, hysterical, chattering, canting age, an age of hollow phrases and false delicacy and exaggerated solicitudes and coddled sensibilities, which, if we don't soon look out, will usher in the reign of mediocrity, of the feeblest and flattest and the most pretentious that has ever been."[14]

A belief that bluestocking feminine influence threatened red-blooded American masculinity was hardly confined to fiction. Some contemporary students of nineteenth-century culture have likewise depicted a weak-kneed, uninspired sentimentality associated with females; others have presented a more sympathetic treatment of feminine cultural contributions.[15] Some northern intellectuals of the late nineteenth century, whose reasoning may have been more than a little influenced by male chauvinism, imagined that southern men represented the last bastion of masculinity. Rhetoric emanating from Dixie certainly suggested that southern gentlemen, metaphorically speaking, had developed a relatively successful sexist strategy of lifting females up only to keep them down. On pedestals, on their backs, or under men's heels presumably represented the proper places for members of Dixie's fairer sex. When such writers as Melville, Adams, and James "came to frame their critique of the new order, they turned to the South in search of the values and traditions they had lost," C. Vann Woodward notes. This in turn leads him to speculate that "among the ghosts of the Old Regime that haunted the deep woods across the Potomac there must have been a great deal of wry merriment from time to time over the modern turn of events."[16]

Neither northerners nor southerners held a monopoly on distorted perceptions of their regional counterparts. The former Rebels, who were much given to ancestor worship and preserving the purity of their race, tended to regard Yankees, who were somewhat more ethnically diverse, as mongrels. "In the minds of ministers of the Lost Cause," writes Charles Reagan Wilson, "the Yankee monster symbolized a chaotic, unrestrained Northern society that had threatened the pristine, orderly, godly Southern Civilization." Southerners imagined themselves as "Crusading Christian Confederates" pitted against "marauding Yankees," the products of "an undisciplined, unrestrained liberty." Virtue reposed with the denizens of Dixie, and "the highest symbol of Southern virtue was the Confederate woman." The collective heroic efforts of southern women during the war and their symbolic significance as the guardians of home and family entitled them to the most exalted position in the hierarchy of virtue.[17]

LeeAnn Whites suggests that Confederates "may have gone to war in defense of what they perceived to be their prerogatives as free men and in rejection of the threatened domination of a 'horde of agrarians, abolitionists and free lovers,'" but "the actual demands of fighting the war made them increasingly conscious of their own dependence upon women's love and labor." Confederate men relied on women to continue managing households in their absence, keep farms and plantations in operation, outfit them in the field, and nurse them when they were wounded or ill. "Such men, in fact, became increasingly feminized," according to Whites.[18] Southern males may have become more appreciative of their women. Traditionally they had placed tremendous emphasis on family and religion and the purity of women, but the evidence is hardly convincing that the war led them to forfeit power and authority.

Certainly the rhetoric of the masculine South exalted women. "Central to white Southern culture was the notion that men were more sinful than women," writes the historian Ted Ownby. He notes, however, that "there was a certain highly charged quality about everyday life in the nineteenth-century and early twentieth-century South" that affected both sexes. "The region's saints were more saintly, its sinners more sinful" for "when Southerners sinned, they sinned with a vengeance."[19] Religious services presumably afforded spiritual sustenance. They also provided social outlets for young and old alike, and temptation often lurked nearby. Lusty youths particularly valued churchgoing for the assistance it lent to courting. Evening services had the additional advantage of providing them with cover of darkness as they played the gallants escorting fair members of the opposite sex to the safety of their homes. Most young men who committed their thoughts to writing may have been sufficiently pious (or circumspect) to couch their baser instincts in romantic phrases, but a North Carolinian in 1890 cut right to the chase—that is, if he was truthful in the story he told a friend. "I gave her [his girlfriend of the hour] a little talking Last night as she went on from church. I talked to her about her soul salvation. She said she believed that she had religion. I told her that she did not have no more religion than my 'ass.' I screwed her before she got home." [20]

Northerners and southerners in the wake of the Civil War surely differed on their relative goodness as well as their respective levels of masculinity and femininity and on whether to "rebuild" or "reconstruct" war-ravaged Dixie. Nonetheless, on one issue they found common ground. Northerners and southerners expected the former slaves to work, and they collectively assumed "that black wives and mothers should continue to engage in productive labor outside their homes." [21] John Hope Franklin, the eminent black scholar, observes that "anxious and confused" whites tended to generalize about the labor situation:

If they saw Negroes idling away their time, they were inclined to conclude that Negroes would not work, [but] the plain fact was that some would work and some would not work. Some began immediately to look for jobs. Others delayed this unpleasant search as long as possible. Before the end of the year [1865], it became clear to any who cared to look that in the Negro population the South still had a labor force and, for the most part, the South could employ this force on its own terms. [22]

Farm tenancy and field work awaited rural black women just as it did many of their white counterparts; black women who were already in cities or who gravitated to them in the great dislocation that former slaves experienced usually went into the service of white families. [23]

In 1912 a writer who claimed to be a Negro nurse predicted that "in the distant future, it may be, centuries and centuries hence, a monument of brass or stone will be erected to the Old Black Mammies of the South, but what we need is present help, present sympathy, better wages, better hours, more protection and a chance to breathe for once while alive as free women." [24] The beloved old mammy of the antebellum era in fact became one of the South's icons. "The New South movement frequently used the mythology of the Old South to promote its cause because it helped to present the picture of the South as a utopian community of harmonious relations," the historian Cheryl Thurber explains. From around 1910 to 1923, southerners put forth various schemes to memorialize "mammy." The United Daughters of the Confederacy proposed to honor her with a statue in Washington, D.C., but the United States House of Representatives rejected the idea. Black critics believed, not incorrectly, that the interests of "mammies" and all others of their race might be better served by putting an end to lynching, by improving educational opportunities, by fighting discrimination, by eliminating Jim Crow, and by guaranteeing suffrage. Writing in the Confederate Veteran in 1918, Mrs. W.L. Hammond seemed to agree when she suggested a decent burial for "the old black mammy" so that justice might be done for her (the black mammy's) granddaughters.[25]

Former slave women who wandered the highways and byways searching for family members separated from them or who anticipated an endless "Day of Jubilee" seemed doomed to disappointment. In 1993 actress Halle Berry played the lead role in the television miniseries "Queen," based on Alex Haley's unfinished book about the trials and tribulations of his grandmother in the postwar South. A light-skinned black woman herself, Berry claims to have identified with Queen, "the love child of a white plantation-owner's son and a half-black, half-Cherokee slave."[26] Whatever the historical merits of either Haley's work or the miniseries, Americans increasingly seem to have difficulty in separating fact from fiction and are easily confused by such productions as the Emmy Award-winning CBS-TV special "The Autobiography of Miss Jane Pittman," starring actress Cicely Tyson. Based on a novel by Ernest J. Gaines, it told a make-believe story as if it were the actual memories of a black woman who had endured slavery and had survived to witness the rise of black militancy during the 1960s.[27]

It is relatively certain that during the war itself, "black women's priorities and obligations coalesced into a single purpose," according to the historian Jacqueline Jones, "to escape from the oppression of slavery while keeping their families intact." When Union armies advanced into what had previously been Confederate territory, some blacks essentially declared themselves free and headed for the nearest encampments. One Louisiana mother carried with her a dead child, who had supposedly been killed by the master she was fleeing, "to be buried, as she said, *free*." For the most part, Union military officials offered little aid and comfort, often denouncing these females as vagrants and prostitutes. At Camp Nelson, Kentucky, where a shantytown had been built, soldiers razed it, leaving four hundred women and children without shelter to face bitter weather. Even Freedmen's Bureau wage guidelines discriminated against black women, mandating that they be compensated at a lesser rate than black men. Finally, some black men aggressively asserted themselves as lords and masters in their own households, beating their wives and children and taking up with "outside women."[28]

Just as some southern whites had a tendency to exaggerate and misrepresent their sufferings during the war and its aftermath, so, too, did some blacks who briefly enjoyed the limelight until northern journalists, congressmen, and do-gooders tired of the blacks' trials and tribulations. This statement is in no way intended to dismiss the horrors of slavery or the cruelty and violence inflicted on the black race generally and on women in particular, for they were all too real. Still, some southern blacks prevaricated, and some northern whites proved more than ready to accept outlandish stories. After the Memphis riots of 1866 a congressional committee headed by Elihu Washburn conducted hearings. Mrs. Frances (or Francis) Thompson and her companion, Lucy Smith, a black girl, gave gruesome testimony of their indignities at the hands of seven former Confederate soldiers. Their stories of sexual abuse, horrendous as they were, reportedly moved the politicians to tears. Not long thereafter another black woman filed a complaint against "Mrs. Thompson," who had hired her daughter—ostensibly as a maid—and subsequently had impregnated her. It seems that "Mrs. Thompson" was "a big robust man." Police in Memphis jailed him, and respectable blacks jeered at him from the street.[29]

Most southern whites proved "unwilling to expand their prewar definitions of 'manhood' and 'womanhood' to include formerly enslaved persons," Catherine Clinton declares. "Although the law might dictate an African American woman could now be a person and a wife, and a black man a citizen and voter, Lost Cause ideologues promoted white supremacy with a vengeance both fierce and formidable."[30] As they made the transition from slavery to sharecropping, from forced servitude to segregation, black women "continued to respond to the same human and seasonal rhythms over the generations," structuring their lives around homemaking, child rearing, work outside their households, community self-help organizations, and benevolent societies.[31] During the late 1860s black churchwomen organized groups like the Daughters of Zion, while others joined such fraternal and benefit societies as the Order of the Eastern Star and the Daughters of Calanthe.[32]

Although many whites, in both the North and the South, tended to categorize blacks according to race and race alone, class also striated the African-American community, fragmenting its ranks. Prior to the Civil War, slaveholders had engaged in the "increasingly selective liberation of favored bondsmen." Escaping slavery had become all the more difficult, writes Ira Berlin, and those who were able to purchase their freedom had generally been "more skilled, literate, and well connected with whites than the mass of slaves." Consequently, "even before they were emancipated, most free Negroes had enjoyed a privileged position within the slave hierarchy."[33]

The historian Willard B. Gatewood has found that "in the generation following Reconstruction, blacks engaged in lively and frequent discussions regarding the significance and implications of the evolving social gradations in the black community." The upper class, which is best described as "miniscule," exerted an influence inversely proportional to its size. A small middle class gradually expanded, and the large lower class dwarfed the other two in numbers. The historian Loren Schweninger, in his study of black property owners in the South, identifies a few prosperous women among them. Some possessed such small businesses as laundries, bakeries, grocery stores, and real-estate firms; others inherited property from well-to-do husbands; and Maggie Lena Walker founded St. Luke's Penny Savings Bank in Richmond, Virginia. Gatewood observes that "by the turn of the century, upper-class black women began to express themselves in regard to the double jeopardy that they experienced as a result of being both black and female." Although they assigned most of the blame to whites, they did not excuse black men, who denied them the "chivalry, admiration and even worship" seemingly enjoyed by their white sisters. Some black women also charged that black men, like whites, attached too much significance to the physical appearance of females and too little to their other attributes.[34]

Whatever strife may have punctuated male-female relationships among African-Americans, the black family proved to be a source of strength, and the marital relationship was an important one. Newly freed blacks frequently moved as quickly as possible to legitimize their slave marriages, and others embarked upon new matrimonial ventures with great enthusiasm. The mulatto Bishop Lucius Henry Holsey of Georgia, while himself still a slave, had wed a fifteen-year-old girl formerly owned by Bishop George Foster Pierce of the Methodist Episcopal Church, South. (Pierce had given her to his daughter.) Bishop Pierce performed the ceremony, and, according to Holsey's recollections,

the Bishop's wife and daughters had provided for the occasion a splendid repast of good things to eat. The table, richly spread, with turkey, ham, cake, and many other things, extended nearly the whole length of the spacious dining hall. "The house girls" and "the house boys" and the most prominent persons of color were invited to the wedding of the colored "swells." The ladies composing the Bishop's family, dressed my bride in the gayest and most artistic style, with red flowers and scarlet sashes predominating in the brilliant trail.[35]

Most black unions, however, began with less fanfare and on a much more modest scale.

The threat of violence, particularly against black males, loomed over African-American families in the post-Civil War South. In the aftermath of defeat, the desire to keep the South a white man's country contributed to remarkably incongruous stereotypes of the black male as the incompetent "Sambo," on the one hand, and the virile, aggressive "black rapist," on the other. Black women, by general consensus among the dominant race, remained morally bankrupt. Otherwise the mulatto presence "might not be a result of slave women's promiscuity, but rather of white sexual coercion."[36]

Nothing stirred the anger of southern whites quite so quickly or to such feverish proportions as allegations that their women might willingly enter into liaisons with black men. Such relationships, although infrequent, did occur. Indeed, some relatively sketchy evidence suggests that a few women of the slaveholding class had either coerced black males into having sexual intercourse with them or persuaded them into mutually agreeable coupling. According to the historian Martha Hodes, "white ideology about the hypersexuality of all black men developed swiftly from emancipation forward, [but] the twin ideology about the purity of all white women never took on the same ironclad quality. Rather, class distinctions in white ideology about white female sexuality remained." Hodes observes that "ultimately, it was the conflation of politics and sex in the minds of white southerners that would generate so much of the Reconstruction-era violence in the South." After all, former black male slaves had gained political recognition. Hollow as that newfound status proved to be, it seemed to cause southern whites to focus "on the taboo of sex between white women and black men with a new urgency." Such liaisons, which formerly had "been the province of local communities and courts . . . took on national political dimensions after the war." [37]

White supremacists regarded any reference to black females as "ladies" to be insulting to all white women. The supremacists' exaltation of the fairer sex, however, hardly extended to the wives of Union officers or to southern white women whom they considered to be in league with the "enemy." Even Mrs. Louise de Mortie, a native of South Carolina who operated the Orphan Asylum in New Orleans, found it necessary to appeal to Freedmen Bureau officials in Louisiana for protection. Although Mrs. Mortie kept her facility—which was located in the confiscated home of Pierre Soule, a former United States senator—essentially independent of the federal agency, she relied on the agency for some assistance; and when the Soule home reverted to its owners, Mrs. Mortie moved the orphanage to a wing of the Marine Hospital, which was partially occupied by the Freedmen's Hospital.[38] After the Memphis riots, a Union officer testified before a congressional committee: "Neither I nor any other Union Officer occupy any social position in Memphis; the whites, being all rebels, keep to themselves. They have nothing to do with us socially." According to Elizabeth Avery Meriwether, "this was true; when we saw a Union officer or a Union officer's wife or sister we simply didn't see them—we just looked straight through them, as if they didn't exist." [39]

Even something as relatively innocuous as fashion entered racial discourse. When young black women took to wearing veils, thereby appropriating the styles that southern belles had adopted to mourn the Confederate dead as well as to deny Union soldiers the privilege of seeing their faces, white females quickly forsook this affectation.[40] Black females, however, gradually emerged from political dormancy in a more meaningful manner than dress. On 4 May 1884, twenty-two-year-old Ida Bell Wells, a native of Holly Springs, Mississippi, climbed aboard a Chesapeake and Ohio Railway train for the short ride between Woodstock, Tennessee, where she taught, and Memphis, where she lived. She took a seat in the first-class "ladies car," but a conductor ordered her to the second-class smokers' section. She refused to go, braced herself against the seat in front of her, and bit the conductor when he reached for her. In the ensuing melee, three railroad employees managed to push her off the train, tearing her dress in the process. She sued the railroad (which tried to bribe her to abandon the case) and won $500 in damages. The Tennessee State Supreme Court, however, reversed the decision in April 1887.[41]

A few years later on 21 May 1892, this same black female activist, then a journalist for the weekly *Free Speech and Headlight*—at considerable risk to her own life—wrote an editorial in which she denounced lynching. She was reacting to mob violence that had just taken the lives of several black men in Memphis. The first episode had resulted in the deaths of three, one a close personal friend of Wells. The lynching of another eight soon followed. Wells declared: "Nobody in this section of the country believed the threadbare lie that Negro men rape white women . . . if southern white men are not careful . . . a conclusion will be reached which will be very damaging to the moral reputation of their women." The suggestion that white women might enjoy the attentions of black men incensed the local citizenry; it led to Wells's timely self-imposed exile from the South. Some whites not only destroyed the newspaper office but talked openly of lynching her. They apparently sent word to Wells, who was out of town, that "she would be hanged from a lamppost if she were to return to Memphis."[42]

Virulent as the racism of this era was, all blacks and whites in the South did not hate each other; toleration, if not outright affection, often existed. Black women and white women in the postwar South sometimes maintained close relationships, not just those foisted upon them in their roles as employees and employers; in some instances they were great friends. A South Carolina man, Woodrow W. Long, recalled that as late as World War I a former slave girl, by then an elderly woman, visited his grandmother about once a week even though they lived several miles apart. According to Long, "this ex-slave [I should just call her my grandmother's friend, I guess, close friend; and leave the slave part out.] would walk to my grandmother's and they would sit and talk, and they would walk around and talk, and they would work some and talk, and they would eat some and talk." He explained how these were "happy days and precious days to them. . . . I guess that they shared hardships together and shared good times together. And in their old age, they shared with each other."[43]

Such harmonious relationships occasionally existed among some whites and blacks in Dixie. Still, whatever mitigating private influences may have been at work, the late-nineteenth- and early-twentieth-century South had its share of human misery, gross inequities, indifference, and callousness. Gone were the armies of occupation and the influence of unscrupulous carpetbaggers, the hated scalawags, and the taunting Negroes; the Democratic party prevailed. Homegrown mistreatment and intolerance crossed the color line. Grandfather clauses and lynchings kept blacks at bay, and mill owners joined ranks with planters to control poor whites. Southern honor oftentimes neglected blacks and whites of the lower socioeconomic orders, and the much-vaunted chivalry reserved for middle- and upper-class white women hardly extended to such less-fortunate members of society as female prisoners and prostitutes. According to C. Vann Woodward, "the South remained basically pessimistic in its social outlook and its moral philosophy." He explains that "an age-long experience with human bondage and its evils and later with emancipation and its shortcomings" had not prepared southerners to look with favor on "such popular American ideas as the doctrine of human perfectibility, the belief that every evil has a cure, and the notion that every human problem has a solution." Neither "utopian schemes" nor the "gospel of progress" flourished or found acceptance below the Mason-Dixon line during the nineteenth century.[44]

This may at least partially explain why prison reform came slowly to the late-nineteenth- and early-twentieth-century South. When Tennessee had opened its penal institution in Nashville in 1831, prisoners, both men and women, labored together silently during the day, the females mostly engaged in sewing. Probably no more than thirty-five women inmates entered the gates of the prison in the prewar period, although some twenty-five hundred men at one time or another called it home. Females occupied cells adjoining those of males. In 1843 the prison received "Pricilla [Priscilla] Childress, a convict from the county of Giles, [and] her infant child." Bridget Tienoay, who was found guilty of larceny in 1861, received an early release because she was pregnant. Whether she was with child when she entered the penitentiary is not clear, but the potential for sexual fraternization between prisoners existed, as well as the victimization of the female inmates by the all-male prison staff.[45]

During the 1870s the state leased out female as well as male prisoners. The names of women appeared on the lists of those who worked at the Sewanee, Vulcan, and Battle Creek coal mines and on the Cumberland and Ohio and the Paducah railroads. A legislative report described such privately operated branch prisons as "hell holes of rage, cruelty, despair, and vice." Not until 1892 did the lawmakers provide for a separate wing for female prisoners. The construction took several years, and the new prison, with special accommodations for women, did not open until 1898. As late as 1894, forty-five women had occupied sixteen cells; at the same time they had no employment or program, not even a place to exercise. Officials allowed some to go "outside the wall" to work, but the General Assembly made such practices a misdemeanor in 1897. Although state lawmakers had established the position of matron to supervise female prisoners during the 1890s, it went unfilled because they failed to appropriate funds to hire any-one, a not-uncommon practice in Tennessee as well as in other financially strapped southern states.[46]

Female prisoners in neighboring Kentucky fared no better. Not until 1872 did the commonwealth provide them with separate quarters; previ-ously they had slept in a large room over the penitentiary hospital. Male staff supervised women inmates as late as 1917, which gave rise to "re-peated charges of illicit sexual relations." During a legislative investigation in 1897, an inmate, Ruth Martin, had testified "that the guards were 'all gentlemen' except for [one], with whom she had intercourse three times on the top walk." When asked if she had been forced, she replied, "No Sir." "What did he do?" demanded her questioner. Pressed for additional details, she stated simply, "Just set the block to me." Also during the 1920s, accord-ing to one account, "it was a common occurrence for the men and women to loosen the boards in the fence that separated them so that the women might slip into the men's prison. Although iron bars remained between the men and the women, they succeeded in having sexual intercourse." Fre-quent fights arose among the women "engendered by the never-ending flir-tations with male prisoners."[47]

A state prison employee, whose first job, in 1931, had been that of a guard, later claimed that the lash was still being used on both male and female prisoners after this punishment had supposedly been discontinued. Robert Gunn Crawford, a student of the Kentucky penal system who con-ducted the interview, reported that his subject "recounted with gusto the experience of a 'high society' lady who was in prison for murdering her hus-band." According to the guard,

she would not perform any of the tasks assigned her, such as laundry or cleaning; nor would she wear the standard prison dress. She defied the matron and the super-intendent to force her, on the threat of using political influence to cost them their jobs. At long last . . . the superintendent ordered her taken to the "bull." [The guard] interspersed his remarks with loud guffaws when he described how she was placed on the "bull," with her hands tied to her ankles. A guard then jerked her dress up and her "drawers" down to expose her "white ass." When the guard picked up the wet and sandy leather strap and hit her full on the buttocks, she screamed and . . . "pissed a bucketful."[48]

The economic problems that plagued the region during this era account for some of what at first glance seems to have been monstrous indifference to social challenges. Still, deviant behavior exacted all too little sympathy in the masculine-dominated South. Public officials wasted little pity on the mentally disturbed or on those they assumed to be so, as the case of Andrew Moore Sheffield of Guntersville, Alabama, demonstrates. Sheffield, a woman with a man's name, "never married, never managed to conform to standards of ladylike behavior, and never succeeded in pleasing the men of her prominent family." She had become addicted to chloral hydrate, commonly used to induce sleep, which was being supplied her by an abusive doctor with whom she probably had a sexual relationship. She had tried to torch a house whose owner was at odds with her physician, supposedly at the latter's behest. This incident immediately preceded the decision of her half brother and father to commit her to Bryce Hospital, the state mental institution in Tuscaloosa. Although she was indeed an addict and a criminal, her assertiveness and her adeptness in articulating her views led doctors to diagnose her as "morally insane." This was a "highly charged and controversial" diagnosis during the late nineteenth century, according to the historian John S. Hughes. "Morally deranged persons showed no delusions and no impairment of reasoning. Only their moral sense or, more correctly, their ability (or desire) to live in accordance with accepted morality seemed insane." Throughout her incarceration, Sheffield asked to be tried and imprisoned as a sane person. Instead she remained at Bryce Hospital from 1890 until her death in 1920, when she was buried on the grounds of the asylum at her request.[49]

The situation of at least one other patient, Ruth Smalley, resembled that of Sheffield. Smalley entered the facility in 1890, the same year as Andrew Sheffield, and remained there until her death in 1918. She "too was well educated (a music teacher), articulate, and by all accounts extremely difficult to live with. Married twice, she was deserted by both of her husbands. Members of her family also could tolerate her only for short periods." Sometimes, not surprisingly, Smalley threatened suicide, which Sheffield apparently never did. Andrew Sheffield herself "advanced the theory that her half-brother arranged her commitment to the Hospital specifically to keep her away from her father's trial [he had shot and killed the disreputable physician with whom his daughter had been involved in Guntersville] and generally to help salvage the family's wounded reputation." Her assessment may have been on the mark, for she had hardly been the "typical woman of her age in the deep South."[50]

Southern women who became prostitutes likewise deviated from societal norms and expectations, but the masculine guardians of the community proved to be conspicuously inattentive to circumstances that promoted such vices. In Lexington, Kentucky, Belle Brezing, born in 1860 the illegitimate child of a prostitute, seemed almost doomed to follow her mother's calling. Bearing the onus of her family's unsavory reputation, she had become sexually involved with a man several years her senior by the time she was twelve. (In another era this would be considered statutory rape if anyone cared enough to report it; but apparently at that time in Kentucky, twelve was the age of consent—that is, the age at which a female could legally marry and, by inference, be mature enough to engage in sexual relations.) At fourteen, Belle became pregnant and entered into a brief marriage. Left to fend for herself, she turned to prostitution to support her child, rising to a stellar position in her "profession." Brezing presided as the madam of what was reputedly one of the finest "houses" in the South and may have been the prototype for Belle Watling, Rhett Butler's disreputable female friend in *Gone with the Wind*. During her last years, Brezing found herself in a losing battle with poverty; but when she died in 1940, *Time* magazine noted her passing.[51]

On the eve of the First World War a survey of urban America found prostitution well entrenched in several southern cities, among them Atlanta and Savannah, Georgia; Baltimore, Maryland; Dallas, El Paso, Fort Worth, and San Antonio, Texas; Louisville, Kentucky; Memphis, Tennessee; New Orleans, Louisiana; Norfolk, Virginia; St. Louis, Missouri; and Washington, D.C.[52] During the late nineteenth century, New Orleans had adopted an approach not wholly unknown in other municipalities during that era. The administration of Mayor Walter C. Flower attempted to confine prostitution to a particular section of the Crescent City. Storyville, as the red-light district of New Orleans was known, enjoyed a thriving business, which the nation's call to arms in 1917 would almost certainly have aided and abetted if circumstances had been allowed to run their natural course. Instead, "The Great War" proved to be the undoing of this particular vice district, for Secretary of the Navy Josephus Daniels ordered that it be closed.[53]

The red-light district in New Orleans may have been one of the most notorious vice dens in the South, but it was hardly unique. El Paso, Texas, for example, published rules for its "reservation." Municipal regulations confined the women to their "cribs" until after twelve o'clock (presumably midnight) and required them to perform their assigned tasks in an illuminated room. The Monte Carlo in San Antonio attracted a somewhat more prosperous clientele than the down-at-the-heels but no-less-eager assortment of men who frequented the cheap whores of the border towns. The Monte Carlo's published prices ranged from three to twenty dollars, depending on the time the customer required. Although the "girls" at this particular house enjoyed the luxury of a night off every week, the management discouraged them from lolling about the live-long day. Only if business had been especially brisk the previous evening could these "soiled doves" expect the privilege of having breakfast served after one o'clock (presumably 1:00 P.M.). The fallen women of Hell's Half Acre in Fort

Worth fared no better. "On any given day," the historian Richard Selcer explains, "a prostitute might be beaten up—or worse—by one of her competitors, 'stiffed' by a cheap customer or thrown out of her living quarters by her madam or landlord." Fear and violence remained her most faithful companions and served as constant reminders of the dangers that lurked in the vice districts of American cities.[54]

When the National Guard had been mobilized and dispatched to the Mexican border during 1916-17, prostitution flourished. In an urban area that an investigator identified as Community D, both the segregated vice district and "cribs" experienced a boom. "From noon until early morning soldiers in great numbers were found in these districts," according to M.J. Exner, M.D. "In the evening they were thronged, and before many of the 'cribs' doors soldiers stood in line." A woman, whom Exner considered not very attractive, reported "that on a good night she served about 50 men, and that on the previous Saturday she had served 60, and on Sunday 40." The doctor claimed that "reliable sources" suggested that other prostitutes "served a much larger number."[55] The National Board of the Young Women's Christian Association attempted to counter the appeal of the vice dens by offering wholesome entertainment. This organization also hoped to prevent young women in marginal economic circumstances from falling into a disreputable life. It is doubtful, however, that its three centers—in the Texas cities of San Antonio and El Paso and in Douglas, Arizona—offset either the lure of easy money or the compelling drive of base instincts.[56]

Despite the human degradation to be found in Dixie during the late nineteenth and early twentieth centuries, the South retained much of its rural heritage even as it urbanized, and it was not devoid of pleasantries. Still, as the historian William A. Link has observed, southern traditionalists thought of "community" in local terms and took a passive and indifferent approach to social problems. They valued parochial control and personal liberty, and they resented outsiders who attempted to change them or their opinions.[57] The nation, which had conducted a historic love affair with arcadia, often waxed nostalgic about the pastoral life. Agrarian existence, however, placed harsh demands on the southern region's inhabitants, especially its women. Their male counterparts may have marked the milestones of their lives with such public events as elections and wars or the private thrills of hunting small game, listening to their dogs chase foxes, womanizing, or tending their stills. Females most often measured theirs in such private aspects of the human continuum as courtships and marriages, the births of children, and the deaths of loved ones. Some women probably found beauty and goodness in nature and possessed a strong attachment to place and a deep affinity for the land. Others attempted to improve the appearance of drafty cabins and ramshackle old farmhouses with plantings of violets, daffodils, and roses; almost all of them employed their skills with needles, looms, and sewing machines to make necessary items, while a smaller number created artifacts of great and lasting beauty.[58]

The Farmers' Alliance of the late nineteenth century proved receptive to women members; females constituted a fourth of its total membership and made up half of some local organizations. Female participation ran the gamut from voting on prospective members and participating in all business to sharing the passwords and signals, holding local offices, delivering addresses, and writing for the Alliance's publications. Nonetheless, some male members resented the outspokenness of the opposite sex, and more than a few of them valued the females mostly for their culinary skills. Women always had the dubious honor of preparing food and serving the men.[59]

Despite the fledgling camaraderie among both sexes to be found in the agrarian organizations and the community of interests that transcended gender, the great majority of southern farm women of this era were dogged by isolation, loneliness, and drudgery. Few ever traveled more than a few miles from home, and the men were far more likely than the women to go into nearby towns and villages to trade, sit in on trials, and gossip. Rare was the female who escaped caring for animals or laboring in the fields. While the women stopped to prepare noontime meals or late suppers, the men took their ease under a shade tree or on the porch. Women served husbands, sons, male relatives, and occasional hired help first, then made do with the leftovers for themselves. Rebecca Latimer Felton, who was a power in farmers' politics in Georgia and a crusader for women's rights, reserved her special ire for "men who went to town on Saturdays to hold forth about the state of 'my crop,' 'my house,' and 'my farm,' with their fellow farmers." If it were not for the subordination of his wife and daughters, Felton railed, a man could not "spread himself like a green bay tree, and bray like a son of thunder." She proclaimed herself unable to determine whether she should feel the greater disgust for the "masculine tyrants" or "the slave-women who accept the yoke without a protest."[60]

It can be safely assumed that most women in the rural South never had much cash at their disposal, because well into the twentieth century, farm income fell in the range of a very few hundred dollars or less per year, which guaranteed a lifestyle of minimal subsistence. Nonetheless, women pored over the pages of mail-order catalogs and carefully considered the wares from a traveling-salesman's case, cherished a bit of lace or a nice piece of jewelry, and found pleasure in a particularly lovely flower or a carefully concocted culinary delight. Theirs was a world of chickens, washtubs, wood stoves, hungry men, and demanding infants and small children. Women took comfort in religion, enjoyed occasional visitors, and sustained themselves with webs of kinship. They often measured their accomplishments by the height of the meringue on their pies or the accolades heaped on their biscuits and fried chicken at "dinners on the ground" or at church socials.

The diaries of Magnolia Wynn Le Guin afford a rare insight into the life of a rather ordinary Middle Georgia farm woman of the early twentieth century. Her life—particularly the drudgery, monotony, and confinement to "'small" places—resembled that of the fictional Ellen Chesser, developed by the Kentucky novelist Elizabeth Madox Roberts in *The Time of Man*, published in 1926.[61] Still, Ellen hailed from the tenant-farmer class, while Magnolia came from the yeomanry. Written during years that undoubtedly represented some of the worst of Le Guin's life but a time of fascinating politics and domestic reform on the national and regional fronts, her diaries revealed nothing about the world beyond Wynn's Mill on the banks of Tussahaw Creek in Henry County. By her own description she was "a home-concealed woman," who during her entire life never traveled more than thirty miles from her birthplace. What set her apart from thousands of other rural women who were constrained by their prescribed roles as daughters, wives, and mothers was not only her self-confessed love of writing but also the fact that her ruminations eventually made their way into print. Magnolia seemed compelled to commit her thoughts to paper as she struggled to be a dutiful wife, concerned mother, and loving daughter. Indeed, venting her frustrations in this manner shielded her from ridicule and may have saved her sanity. All the same the diaries gave voice to a life of seemingly incessant childbearing, caretaking, and deprivation.[62]

During 1892, 1899, and 1900, Magnolia Wynn Le Guin made sporadic entries, but her diaries began in earnest on 18 February 1901. At that time she was thirty-two years old, the wife of a cotton farmer, the mother of three boys under five and a daughter who had died at birth, and caretaker to two elderly and ailing parents in whose home they all lived. The entries concluded on 11 September 1913. During those twelve years, Le Guin gave birth to five more children and buried her father and mother. Along the way she wrestled with ill health and poor medical services, what seemed to be an endless stream of overnight and extended visitors and boarders, and the burden of trying to maintain a household with little help and no electricity. Occasionally she enjoyed a telephone in her house, but a shortage of cash kept it from being a permanent fixture. Ironically, Magnolia's own father, a physician, had been graduated from the Medical College of Georgia, and it might have been expected that his daughter would have had a better quality of life than she did. The doctor had sired at least eleven children, which may or may not have taxed his physical stamina but almost certainly affected his financial resources. Magnolia's life had the makings of an awful southern melodrama, for she was married to a man named Ghu, whom she outweighed, by her own admission, by at least thirty pounds. According to her accounts he cut trees, picked cotton, and occasionally frequented a local establishment where he drank beer and ate pickles and crackers, which met with her disapproval.[63]

At late as 1880 "the southern landscape" had borne "the signs of the preceding twenty years," writes the historian Edward L. Ayers. "A jumble of tenant shacks" had replaced "symmetrical rows of slave cabins," but abandoned lands lay fallow, and the wartime rubbish of weapons and bones had not been completely cleared. "Confederate veterans at the court house or the general store bore empty sleeves and blank stares. Black people bitterly recalled the broken promises of land from the Yankees and broken promises of help from their former masters and mistresses." The depression of the 1870s had affected almost everyone.[64]

In the late nineteenth century, however, new sights, sounds, and smells were emanating from the monotony and poverty that characterized much of the rural South. In the words of Colonel A.S. Colyar, a strong proponent of the "New South," "blast furnaces are lighting up the darkness of a dead past, and smokestacks are burning incense to the brighter skies of a more hopeful future."[65] "Textile mills built the New South," write the historians Jacquelyn Dowd Hall, Robert Korstad, and James Leloudis. "Beginning in the 1880s, business and professional men tied their hopes for prosperity to the whirring of spindles and the beating of looms. Small-town boosterism supplied the rhetoric of the mill-building campaign, but the impoverishment of farmers was industrialization's driving force."[66] Edward L. Ayers agrees that "the pervasive decline of Southern rural life created a sense of dissatisfaction and desperation among white farming families that made it easier for mill operators to find a work force."[67] In J. Wayne Flynt's opinion, poor southern whites made the sad discovery "that industry was a Frankenstein, beckoning them from a hard, monotonous life on the land with beguiling promises, then providing only more poverty amidst the choking lint of the textile mills or the unrelenting gloom of the coal mine."[68] Although the mill villages and the coal camps may not have been quite the hellholes that some students of southern labor have made them out to be and although they did indeed present alternatives to rural poverty, they were hardly utopias. Ayers writes philosophically of mill towns: "These villages exhibited a broad range of conditions and elicited a broad range of reactions."[69]

In this nether world that straddled rural and urban life, the tempo of labor and the rhythm of women's lives as well as those of their families experienced a not-insignificant transformation; work in the mills was not altogether negative and was at least a cut above tenant farming. Widows and other female heads of households sometimes found solace as well as employment in the mill villages. They "could keep their families together and live without dependence on others," Edward Ayers explains.[70] Gangster moll Virginia Hill, a close personal friend of Bugsy Siegel and other mobsters, sprang from such circumstances. Born in Lipscomb, Alabama, in 1916, the seventh of ten children, Virginia grew up in a household tyrannized by her drunken, abusive father. Margaret, the mother, took whatever odd jobs she could find, including factory employment, to sustain the family. By the mid 1920s, she had suffered enough, so she and the children walked out. The family settled in Margaret's hometown of Marietta, Georgia, where she worked at the local hosiery mill.[71]

Some female factory workers took pride in their work, while others, only out of desperation, conformed to the relentless rhythms of the machines. Alice Caudle boasted that only women performed the work of the spinning room at Cannon Mills in North Carolina. She had received a thirty-year service pin from the owner, Charles Cannon himself, and she recollected in 1938 that she had entered the mills when she was ten years old. "Law, I reckon I was born to work in a mill. . . . When I started down here in plant Number One, I was so little I had to stand on a box to reach my work."[72] In 1935 Mabel Lee Poindexter recalled her first experience with mill work somewhat less enthusiastically. Born in Forsyth County, North Carolina, in 1903 and orphaned at fifteen, she had been left with little alternative but to seek paid employment. Mabel's father, a prosperous farmer, had committed suicide when she was six; the mother had subsequently married a hardworking and hard-drinking man; but broken in health, she, too, had expired a few years later. "My uncle helped me to get a job in the silk mill," Mabel recollected. "I wound silk from the skein onto a bobbin. It was hard and very tedious. I had been used to hard work on the farm but the work in the mill was more tiresome."[73]

Another woman, Bessie Harris, described her introduction to the southern factory system. Harris grew up about sixty-five miles from Atlanta "in a backwoods section of the country." "I was a great big girl," she wrote, "before I knew that there was anything which could be bought to eat except sugar and coffee and sometimes we could get some rice." Her father had once taken her sightseeing in Atlanta. After his death, all that the family had left was "the little rough farm, a mule, a milk cow, and some chickens." Bessie headed for the city. "The first morning after I got there I went to hunt a job," she reported. The next day she was at work in Carhartt's Overall Factory. "I found the work quite different to what I had been doing in the field. The machinery was making so much noise I could not hear anything so I thought because I could not hear the others that they could not hear either, so I talked at the top of my voice. Everybody laughed."[74]

Obviously some white females found the farm-to-factory transition less difficult than others. The historian Dolores Janiewski also offers reminders of the racial dynamics that affected this transformation. Both black and white females knew sexual subordination, but "racial domination gave white men greater power and white women greater privilege." Although both races may have been economically servile to the same master, "white women still enjoyed greater freedom from drudgery at all but the most depressed levels of white society." The existing "system of racial domination" often made black women and white women "antagonists" instead of "sisters or allies."[75] Sharon Harley, an authority in African-American studies, has found that the federal government demonstrated a "clear preference for white women to fill clerical positions" and that "more black men than black women" gained access to such jobs in Washington, D.C. In the urban South, however, including the nation's capital, during this era, adult black females outnumbered black males. As late as 1920 the ratio was 1.000 to 0.822 in the nation's capital; on average, 1.000 to 0.962 in northern areas. Sexual and racial discrimination, as well as the inability of many black women to pass the civil-service examinations, kept them out of most higher-paying positions; a few could be found doing work classified as semi-skilled and skilled at the postal and printing offices. Black women, however, claimed a virtual monopoly on federal char work.[76]

Clearly the *fin de siècle* South trailed the trappings of the old and reached out for the new. As native-born whites and blacks abandoned the rural South for mill villages and coal camps or the cities, recently arrived immigrants from southern and eastern Europe likewise made their appearance in the core areas of the urban South. Railroad construction camps and smoky coal and iron enclaves of the Appalachian region attracted the immigrants like magnets. They came to Dixie in relatively small numbers, sometimes with wives and children in tow; a few intermarried with local women.[77] During this same era Mary Noailles Murfree, a Tennessee novelist and local colorist, writing under the pen name Charles Egbert Craddock, romanticized and stereotyped the lives of native-born white mountain people.[78]

On another front the *ancien régime* went about decorating the graves of Confederate soldiers, erecting memorials to fallen heroes on courthouse lawns, staging balls and cotillions, and conducting ring-and-lance tournaments—"the most colorful of elite recreations" and "the closest Southerners ever came to the days of Sir Walter Scott."[79] A year after the Civil War ended, 26 April became Confederate Memorial Day; it marked the day on which the last major southern army had surrendered. Ladies' Memorial Associations sprang up across the South. The first probably appeared in Columbus, Georgia, but others also claimed that distinction. In Nashville,

Tennessee, Mrs. Caroline Meriwether Goodlett, president of the local Ladies Auxiliary to the Confederate Soldiers Home, founded the United Daughters of the Confederacy (UDC), which was chartered on 10 September 1894. Serving as a unifying force, the UDC soon superseded all other female patriotic societies devoted to the Lost Cause.[80]

As late as 1941, Helen Dortch Longstreet, General James Longstreet's widow, wrote from Washington, D.C., that she was "in the east now to try to arrange for a national broadcast of the dedication of the site for the Longstreet monument on the Gettysburg field the coming 2nd of July."[81] The next year she complained: "The U.D.C. Conventions have degenerated into frolics and publicizing events for the officials. We once had great Southern women to lead the U.D.C., but they have died, and the control has passed into the hands of a group that seem to care no more about the few Confederate veterans who are still with us, than about the dirt under their feet."[82]

The second Mrs. Longstreet, a native of Georgia, had married the general on 8 September 1897, when he was about seventy-six years old and she was still a sweet young thing. Although she had a career as a journalist and as a librarian, she dedicated considerable energy to memorializing the general after his death in 1904. "General Longstreet would have lived longer," she claimed, "if I could have prevailed on him to take proper care of himself." She recalled that "the morning he walked out into the sleet [on the way to the barbershop], which gave him pneumonia, from which he died two days later, I implored him not to go." "Precious," he reminded her, "I was sleeping on the wet ground before you were born." Blessed with "a powerful constitution, [he] could never be convinced of the necessity for taking care of himself."[83]

In November 1943, from Fair Oak Trailer Park in Marietta, Georgia, Mrs. Longstreet advised Mrs. J.F. Howell that she had entered a vocational school for aircraft training and had "scarcely had time to bat [her] eyes," working "at the school 'til nearly midnight and half the day to finish sooner" and getting in bed "between one or two o'clock in the morning. I shall aid in building flying fortresses. The Manufacturers name them by numbers, such as A29; A30, etc. etc. But the pilots are permitted to give any pet name they wish. I am going to ask the pilots to name one fortress for General Longstreet and one for General [Julius Franklin] Howell."[84]

Many able, intelligent, and educated southern women of the late nineteenth and early twentieth centuries, like Helen Dortch Longstreet, still reveled in the past, and, more accurately, some even wallowed in the Lost Cause. Others, equally proud of their heritage, looked to the future. Only the frivolous few devoted themselves entirely to high society and haute couture. In this era the illustrator Charles Dana Gibson, a talented artist, created the "Gibson girl" and the "Gibson man." Young women of the period "tried to model their clothes, their gestures, their hair and features on the Gibson specifications," which suggested "a message of hope, a tantalizing reach for a superior life." The Gibson girl not only looked healthy and athletic but she also contradicted certain popular notions of the nineteenth century that assigned beauty to frail, tubercular-looking creatures.[85]

The Gibson girl became the artist's "crowning success and, for the public, an ideal." "Hauntingly mysterious and yet very solid and real . . . , she was the heroine of many plays, appeared on an untold number of products and in many ads, and most fanciful of all, became a design for wallpaper meant to adorn the walls of the most discriminating bachelors." Although he had several different models, Gibson "met—and—married—his very own Gibson girl. She was the gorgeous and spirited Irene Langhorne, daughter of a very wealthy social family" from Virginia. Recognized nationally for her beauty and acclaimed as one of the "Four Southern Graces," Irene had captured the limelight in 1893 at the Patriarch's Ball as the social butterfly who led the grand march.[86]

Irene Langhorne Gibson's sister Nancy became Lady Astor, the first woman to sit in the British House of Commons.[87] Ralph G. Martin, biographer of both Jennie Jerome Churchill and Wallis Warfield Simpson, describes Lady Astor as "an American from Virginia who had become more British than the British." She hardly sympathized with another southern woman, Wallis Warfield Simpson, a native of Baltimore, Maryland, during the abdication crisis of the 1930s. Lady Astor admitted that she had begged Edward VIII "not to do as he was doing" and that she had spoken "hotly and loudly" when he proved unamenable to her point of view.[88]

In *Homeland*, the novelist John Jakes introduces the character of Willis Fishburne, who amply qualifies for the role of "new American woman" of the late nineteenth century. Thrice married and more often loved, she sometimes counsels her niece Julie, a denizen of Chicago. Aunt Willis, when still the fifteen-year-old daughter from a "secesh" family in the Bluegrass State, ran off with Billy Boynton, her first lover. He was a loyalist who donned Union blue and died at Chickamauga, but Willis never has any regrets and remembers her six days and nights with Billy Boynton as "among the happiest" she has ever known. "I wouldn't trade them if they offered to make me Empress of China," she declares. Willis speaks of Henrik Ibsen's plays, but Julie has only heard of Ibsen and knows that "people say he writes dirty plays." Aunt Willis counters: "For a man, he knows an astonishing amount about our sex. A woman needs a purpose, Julie. A mission she believes is important. That and a glass of fine Kentucky bourbon, a bracing swim, or a vigorous lover will cure almost anything that ails you."[89]

Helpful as a stiff drink, physical exercise, and good sex might be, the plight of Kentucky women and their southern sisters during the late nineteenth century required more stringent measures. In 1890 Josephine K. Henry, a crusader for women's rights from Versailles, Kentucky, offered the following assessment of married women's legal status in her state:

A woman worth one hundred thousand dollars, that has not been settled upon her as her separate estate, marries a man not worth a penny, and it all becomes his in the instant he promises "With all my worldly goods, I thee endow." The woman comes from the marriage altar not even the legal possessor of the clothes she has on her back. She cannot make a will, and, if the husband died one week after the marriage, fifty thousand dollars of the wife's money goes to his nearest male relative, unless he generously wills the defenseless wife her own estate.[90]

Similar circumstances existed throughout the region.

Southern women, like their American sisters elsewhere in the country, had been socially conditioned to speak not of their *rights* but of their *responsibilities*. "During the Nineteenth Century," according to the historian Paula Baker, "women expanded their ascribed sphere into community service and care of dependents, areas not fully within men's or women's politics," an approach she labels "domestic politics."[91] With all the callousness and indifference to be found below the Mason-Dixon line, the relatively simple but terribly important concept of respect for human dignity remained omnipresent in the lives of some southerners of both sexes. In part, it influenced a small cadre of activist southern women, black and white, to move into the public arena in a more aggressive manner. Within the conundrum of reform and reaction, progressive philosophy and "New South" propaganda, religiosity and racism, and ambition and altruism, "domestic politics" arrived in Dixie. As this generation of activist southern women assumed their *duties*, they likewise expanded their own *opportunities*.

Race and class differences have affected the women's movement throughout the United States as well as on the international front; the same has been true of the South. Rebecca Latimer Felton, for example, was one of Georgia's "most prominent advocates of the vote for white women" and, at the same time, "one of the state's most outspoken racists."[92] To a degree unrivaled anywhere else in the United States during similar time frames, "femininity" and "feminism" have been at odds in the American South.[93] Throughout the centuries, females below the Mason-Dixon line have been haunted by the specter of "the southern lady." Regional feminists have experienced firsthand the burden of southern history, their difficulties compounded by this female nemesis. In a turn of events riddled with irony, being ladies proved to be a blessing rather than a bane for the first generation of southern female activists. "Southern lady," with all that it implied, was an entree to public participation, helping bridge the gap between the private and the public sphere.

Churches afforded the first significant opportunities. According to Anne Firor Scott, "religion continued to be a central aspect" in the lives of many southern women as the twentieth century dawned, but it was transformed from "intense personal piety to a concern for the salvation of the heathen and for social problems."[94] Church work brought ladies into contact with the plight of the less fortunate and in turn raised questions about the prevailing order. Clothed in Christianity and bedecked in hats, gloves, and seemly garments, this cadre seemed innocuous enough even as its members challenged the public bastions of male dominance. Although the "poor dears" might be misguided, it was not chivalrous to fault them. Their initial efforts hardly commenced in calculated fashion, but most assuredly the course that they charted led them into somewhat unfamiliar terrain beyond the boundaries of the religious establishment.

Once feminine religiosity had shifted from personal piety to public concern, southern women partially bridged the chasm between the sectarian and the secular. The range of interests expanded to include important socioeconomic and political issues, among them race relations, labor conditions, the origins of poverty, and finally the status of women. Like females elsewhere during this era, southern women enthusiastically embraced the club movement, which allowed them to dabble in respectable reform. Belle Kearney, a Mississippi temperance leader, for example, referred to the Women's Christian Temperance Union as "the generous liberator, the joyous iconoclast, the discoverer, the developer of Southern women." Some North Carolina women, as well as their southern sisters in other states, chose to regard their public activities as feminine "duties," not yet daring to speak of feminine "rights."[95]

The mere recognition that problems existed and cried out for public attention indicated a fissure in the southern ideology. In effect the women activists and whatever male allies they could muster found fault with the masculine-determined world. LeeAnn Whites hit upon at least a partial explanation for the peculiar degree of tolerance that some of the female dogooders of this era enjoyed. She argues that "domestic politics was permitted and even encouraged to develop because at different times and in different ways it met the needs of both organized labor and the capitalist elite in mitigating the crises and contradictions of early industrial capitalism." Elite women "taught schools, Sunday schools, and generally inculcated bourgeois values into the working class."[96]

Whites's study centers on Augusta, Georgia, from 1870 to 1890, but the bourgeois culture that she describes was just as common to many other national and regional urban settings. Girl Scouts of America, a model main-

stream middle-class organization par excellence, originated in another
Georgia city. Juliette Gordon Low, a talented sculptress who was married to
a wealthy Englishman, established Girl Guiding in the United States. She
soon changed the name to Girl Scouting. Although deaf and in poor health,
she conducted the first troop meeting in her Savannah home on 12 March
1912. In the next year the national headquarters opened in Washington,
D.C., but later moved to New York City.[97]

While some women activists of this generation moved into the public
arena out of Christian commitment, others—especially those who had
gained access to higher education—discerned the personal possibilities that
reform held: to influence the world in which they lived, to carve out a
public role, to find legitimate careers for themselves. "Reflecting their natural gregariousness and their quest for the 'bonds of sisterhood,'" writes the
historian Martha H. Swain, "southern college women founded in the post-
Civil War years a number of Greek-letter societies. Such collegiate groups
and related literary societies have remained popular in southern universities." Swain explains that "many women have 'graduated' to high-society
organizations that flourish in southern towns and cities, best represented by
the Junior League and other benefit groups, whose principal functions are
to raise funds for community arts and social services." "Society" also sometimes meant membership in the Order of the Eastern Star and similar fraternal auxiliaries.[98]

Still other women turned to organizations that were not only service-
oriented but also somewhat less provincial and more professionally inclined.
The Southern Association of College Women (SACW), for example, originated in Knoxville, Tennessee, on the University of Tennessee campus in
1903. Under the leadership of Elizabeth Avery Colton the SACW demonstrated a powerful commitment to improving academic standards at female
colleges in the region; it merged with the American Association of University Women in 1921. In 1919 Annie Webb Blanton and a group of Texas
teachers established Delta Kappa Gamma, which became an international
society for female educators. Altrusa International originated in Nashville
in 1917, and Lena Madesin Phillips, a Kentuckian, founded Pilot International.[99]

When associative women from across the United States gathered in
New York's Madison Square Garden in March 1889, Tennessee and Louisiana were represented. Responding to the invitation issued by the Sorosis
Club of that city, the southern delegates shared the company of almost one
hundred women from nineteen states. They had convened to form a national federation of clubs whose interests spanned the full range of social
and civic issues of the times. Katherine Nobles of New Orleans, Louisiana,
explained that "associative bodies of women exist in nearly all our southern

cities and towns, but they are not known as clubs; some philanthropic or benevolent purpose or name hides the desire for associative life." Southern women communed under such rubrics as the Fortnightly in Meridian, Mississippi, the Covington Woman's Club in Kentucky, and the Village Improvement Association of Green Cove Springs, Florida.

In 1890, representatives from women's clubs across the country again converged on New York City to put their final stamp of approval on the national federation. Sixty-three delegates from seventeen states attended. Delaware, Louisiana, Missouri, and Tennessee each had one club represented. Four years later, in July 1894, the national organization met in Louisville, Kentucky, and heard Patty B. Semble of that city assure the delegates that the South was "united . . . in a desire to take its place in the march of progress." A southerner, Rebecca Douglas Lowe of Atlanta, Georgia, assumed the presidency of the General Federation of Women's Clubs in 1898.[100]

"You can't appreciate home till you've left it, money till it's spent, your wife till she's joined a woman's club, nor Old Glory till you see it hanging on a broomstick on the shanty of a consul of a foreign town," opined O. Henry (William Sydney Porter) in *Roads of Destiny: The Fourth in Salvador*. More than one man of the late nineteenth century surely agreed with that author, for middle- and upper-class women became increasingly peripatetic during the late nineteenth and early twentieth centuries. Such women, according to the historian Allen F. Davis, embraced the social settlements and other progressive reforms because they felt a "sense of uselessness" which "rested most heavily upon the growing number of college women—who felt they had to prove their right to a higher education by doing something important."[101]

Davis concerns himself mostly with the motivations of northern women, but educated southern women also shared some of the same urgency. Whether private or public, segregation by sex remained the norm in southern institutions of higher learning. Around 1900, 66 percent of the nation's female colleges could be found in the South. Lawmakers and educators there exhibited some preference for the establishment of new colleges for females. The alternative meant denying them access to higher education or admitting them to the already-existing schools for males. Mississippi took the lead in establishing the first public college for women. Within twenty years, Alabama, Florida, Georgia, North Carolina, Oklahoma, South Carolina, and Texas had followed suit.[102]

Indeed, the establishment of the Mississippi Industrial Institute and College (also known as the Collegiate Institute and still later as Mississippi State College for Women) in 1884 marked the beginning of state-supported colleges specifically for females in the United States. Sallie Eola Reneau, an

1854 graduate of Holly Springs Female Institute who was a resident of Grenada, Mississippi, had initiated a campaign to establish such an institution during the 1850s. She succumbed to yellow fever in 1878, but Annie Coleman Peyton of Madison and Copiah counties and Olivia Valentine Hastings of Claiborne County continued the crusade after Reneau's death.[103] During the 1890s, Georgians expressed interest in "a first-class college for the education of white girls," which led to the establishment of Georgia College at Milledgeville. About the same time, however, the state normal school in Athens, previously all male, opened its doors to females. It evolved into the University of Georgia's Department of Education, and the 1893 legislation that granted women entry marked the first time that any unit of that institution had been opened to them. By 1912, seven southern universities, heretofore existing only to educate the masculine sex, also admitted females.[104]

Naturally enough, educated, socially conscious women looked for opportunities to put their knowledge to work. During the late nineteenth and early twentieth centuries, Appalachia, the reigning fantasyland in the American consciousness, experienced one of its several "rediscoveries" and loomed as a legitimate missionary field and outlet for their energies. Many answered the call, giving rise to that quaint phrase "fotched-on women"— that is, females who ventured into the mountains to assist the downtrodden mountaineers, among them Katherine Pettit, May Stone, Mary Breckinridge, and Marguerite Butler.[105] One of the founders of the Pine Mountain Settlement School in Kentucky, Ethel de Long Zande, a 1901 graduate of Smith College who had spent most of her youth in Montclair, New Jersey, "went out into the world carrying with her a keen sense of loyalty to her alma mater." She also possessed an "equally keen awareness of the responsibility that she had to be true to the ideals she had absorbed there and to make her education count for something."[106]

Ironically, as a study of Vassar College's early years reveals, women "given a men's education . . . were not to seek a man's career." Debra Herman noted that "to educate women in the same manner as college men was to prepare them for possibilities the college itself believed to be outside of women's province."[107] All the same, the subsequent activities of Vassar graduates, as well as those from other women's colleges, North and South, suggest that imaginations had been fired. Louise Leonard, a 1907 Vassar graduate who was one of the founders of the Southern Summer School (SSS) for Women Workers, left her native Pennsylvania to come south in 1920 as industrial secretary for the National Board of the YWCA in the southern region. Born in 1897, Lois MacDonald, a native of Winnsboro, South Carolina, who was the cofounder of the SSS, initially enrolled at the South Carolina College for Women but later transferred to Erskine; she first became involved with the YWCA in New York. Zilla Hawes, who worked with the Highlander Folk School of Tennessee during the 1930s, had graduated from Vassar; she was also an organizer for the Amalgamated Clothing Workers Union.[108]

Georgia O'Keeffe was another southern transplant during this era; her family had moved from her native Wisconsin to Williamsburg, Virginia, in pursuit of a more agreeable climate. Because Georgia's mother was suffering from tuberculosis, they abandoned Williamsburg for Charlottesville.[109] Georgia, who held temporary positions as an instructor in summer art classes at the University of Virginia, accepted teaching positions in South Carolina and Texas to support herself. In 1914, the year before O'Keeffe arrived at Columbia College in South Carolina, some of the students had skipped classes to attend a suffragist rally in town. Such youthful idealism fell like the proverbial pearls before swine; college authorities remained unmoved. For their troubles the errant students cleared rocks and bricks from the campus for the remainder of the semester. In 1916 destiny awaited the fledgling artist in Canyon, Texas, where she accepted a position at West Texas State Normal College. The academic administration in Columbia hardly appreciated her hasty departure, which left the Art Department shy a teacher for the remainder of the academic year; and an ugly exchange occurred. The lure of the Southwest was just too strong. Earlier, in 1912, O'Keeffe had gotten her first taste of that section of the country in Amarillo, Texas, where she had served as supervisor of drawing for the public-school system. Painting, not teaching, consumed her. She taught only to sustain herself, abandoning such stopgap employment to pursue her real passion as quickly as circumstances would allow.[110]

A few native-born southern women of this era also dared to pursue their individual artistic impulses, among them the novelist Kate Chopin, a native of St. Louis who spent several years of her life in and around New Orleans. Her novel *The Awakening*, which involves a woman's gradual self-discovery and ultimate suicide, proved shocking when it was published in 1899. In 1913, Ellen Glasgow of the Old Dominion published *Virginia*, a fictional study of the southern lady, which relied on the morals and manners of the past. Appearing in print that same year, *Hagar*, a novel by another Virginian, the writer and suffragist Mary Johnston, featured a new, independent woman poised for the future.[111]

More of the region's females seemed inclined to express themselves via a group that was collectively engaged in social uplift, but embracing reform did not necessarily cloak them in righteousness. Not surprisingly the first generation of southern female activists reflected their times, places, and personal values. Class and race served as omnipresent reminders of the distinctions between the reformers and those whose lives they were attempting to change. This generation was not able to eradicate the mutual suspicion be-

tween blacks and whites, or even between churchwomen, clubwomen, and
female activists. Females of both races first gingerly felt their way toward
cooperation in temperance societies, according to Gerda Lerner. "Timid
contact" at first between leaders of segregated locals helped somewhat to
dissolve the myth of black female depravity. As white women were able "to
see a connection between the protection of their own homes and the protection of the honor and rights of black women," a climate developed for an
assault on the practice of lynching. Because of the bloody race riots of the
World War I era, "women of both races felt impelled to make stronger efforts than ever before to bridge the gap between the races."[112] Jacquelyn
Dowd Hall claims that evangelical religion provided the basis for single-
gender biracial alliances. Tension nonetheless persisted among black and
white women, even those associated with the Commission on Interracial
Cooperation. Residual racist stereotypes stung black women—comparing
exemplary black females to Negro mammies, not according them the title of
Mrs., asking a speaker who had come to talk "about the work of the niggers"
to enter by the back door.[113]

Especially troublesome is the approach that was taken by some of the
prominent southern suffragists. It seems more than a little hypocritical to
attempt to establish one's rights by denying or threatening those of others.
Southern women activists frequently argued that granting themselves the
right to vote would guarantee white supremacy; they offered statistical
tabulations to prove their contentions.[114] The historian Marjorie Spruill
Wheeler points out, however, that this line of thought was not peculiar to
Dixie. "Carrie Chapman Catt and women who took over the leadership of
the woman suffrage movement [at the national level] in the late nineteenth century shared many of [the] attitudes" of most Southern Democrats. From the 1890s to 1910 the "Southern woman suffrage movement,
with the full support of the National American Woman Suffrage Association [NAWSA]," followed an essentially racist strategy. "Suffragists from
both South and North believed the South's 'negro problem' could be the
key to victory for their cause." They argued that "the enfranchisement of
women (with qualifications that would in effect restrict the suffrage to
white women) would restore white supremacy without the risks involved in
disfranchising blacks."[115] After 1910 the National American Woman's Suffrage Association and the Congressional Union supported a federal constitutional amendment to effect women's suffrage, while southern advocates of
female political participation concentrated on state suffrage amendments.
Kate Gordon of Louisiana and others organized the Southern States Woman
Suffrage Conference, which pledged itself "to support 'states rights' and to
campaign for woman suffrage through state action."[116]

Laura Clay of Kentucky, for example, kept a cautious eye on suffrage measures that would either expand the powers of the federal government at the expense of the states or permit the federal supervision of state elections. On 16 February 1919 she sent a letter to Desha Breckinridge (the husband of Madeline McDowell Breckinridge) of the *Lexington Herald* in which Clay argued that "the chief effect of the [Susan B.] Anthony amendment in conjunction with the Fifteenth Amendment would be to add another to the enumerated powers of the Federal Government, and that without any Constitutional check. All that woman suffrage requires for success is for the Republican and Democratic parties to fulfill their pledge given to the people in 1916 and faithfully to submit and sustain at the polls state suffrage amendments."[117] In spite of the states'-rights position of many southern suffragists, including Kate Gordon of Louisiana, Alice Paul's more strident Congressional Union—later the National Woman's party—had southern partisans, even in South Carolina; and NAWSA garnered considerable support from such prominent southerners as Madeline McDowell Breckinridge.[118]

Such Bluegrass blue bloods as Clay and Breckinridge used the trappings of class, chivalry, and kinship networks to effect their objectives; they needed little or no prodding from outside the region. The national leadership of the suffrage movement, however, had "deliberately recruited Southern suffrage leaders from prominent families" because they "could demand and receive a respectful hearing." They also had the advantages of education, economic means, and leisure. Some even had sufficient wealth to underwrite the crusade for the vote in Dixie. Nellie Nugent Somerville and Belle Kearney of Mississippi, Kate and Jean Gordon of Louisiana, Rebecca Latimer Felton of Georgia, Mary Johnston and Lila Mead Valentine of Virginia, and Pattie Ruffner Jacobs of Alabama—all had distinguished family connections that crossed state lines in Dixie; they also enjoyed relatively comfortable circumstances. Sue Shelton White of Tennessee lacked the wealth and social standing of some of the others, but she claimed the Jeffersons and Marshalls of Virginia as ancestors.[119]

Along with the accoutrements of distinguished family names and sufficient capital, a good wit and a healthy sense of humor stood southern suffragists in good stead. Mrs. Guilford (Anne Dallas) Dudley of Nashville, who was often described as an attractive matron but a suffragist all the same, disarmed her opponents by pointing out that "the cradle will still be rocked, the dishes washed, and still by feminine hands, even if women should take thirty minutes of their time a year for casting a vote." A descendant of Confederate and national leaders, one of the principal organizers of the Nashville Equal Suffrage League as well as its first president, Dudley had the pedigree and manners of a true southern lady by any standard. Guilford Dudley, Jr., recalled that his earliest memories of his mother were of walking in parades with her and his sister. As a boy he also attended the 1924 National Democratic Convention and heard her second the nomination of John W. Davis. "My mother's life has always been my greatest inspiration," he said of her in eulogy, "and she will live on in my heart forever. Her innate beauty and charm were legend. She was a great lady, the loveliest and the best, and I was awfully proud of her." In conclusion, he added that "nothing that I have ever done in this life has made me as proud or made me feel so blessed as being my mother's son."[120]

According to Sophonisba Breckinridge, her sister-in-law Madeline McDowell Breckinridge—Laura Clay's successor as president of the Kentucky Equal Rights Association—would have resorted to militant tactics if they had been practical. As a great-granddaughter of the Henry Clays, a descendant of the famous Dr. McDowell, and the wife of the editor Desha Breckinridge, her social status was "unassailable." She possessed "an aristocrat's indifference to conformity and . . . the charm and intelligence to elicit support for her undertakings." She could be moved occasionally by a sense of righteousness to deliver words in stilettolike fashion. In a letter to the governor in 1915 she wrote, "Kentucky women are not idiots—even though they are closely related to Kentucky men." While crusading in North Carolina, she was the butt of an April Fools Day joke delivered by a Raleigh newspaper, which reported that she would be met at the train by a brass band. She retorted that it was enough to "make the suffragists tear their hair," because they had been "trying to get suffrage there in the most lady-like manner, without having anybody find out they want it."[121]

Pervasive racism across gender lines, the attendant states'-rights philosophy, the overriding influence of male chauvinism, and division within the ranks of women's rights activists themselves diminished possibilities for the national suffrage amendment in Dixie. Despite the best efforts of proponents of the Anthony amendment in the South, only Texas, Tennessee, Kentucky, and Arkansas ratified it, with Tennessee being the thirty-sixth and pivotal state. Under pressure from suffrage forces in the Volunteer State and from national Democratic leadership including President Woodrow Wilson, Governor A.H. Roberts, a less-than-enthusiastic supporter of woman suffrage, called the legislature into special session. The senate approved the measure 25 to 4, but it squeaked by in the house, 49 to 47; then the Speaker, Seth Walker, hastily changed his vote, making the count 50 to 46. This represented a parliamentary maneuver designed to allow him to move for reconsideration if he could muster enough votes to hand the suffragists a defeat; only a representative from the majority position could so move. This ploy was not used, and other maneuvering came to naught. The high drama in the legislative battle had occurred when Harry T. Burn of McMinn County had changed his position. Earlier he had been among those who had voted to table and kill the amendment. (The count had been tied at 48 to 48.) Burn had then reportedly succumbed to his mother's urgings in support of female suffrage and had changed his vote.[122]

Texas had been the first of the former Confederate states to ratify. The historian Elizabeth Hayes Turner, who has studied the local dynamics of the suffrage campaign in Galveston, calls the crusade for the vote in the South "an urbanized phenomenon." Although females in the region "may have been slow to respond to the national suffrage campaign," Turner concludes that they could be "stirred to action on behalf of their own communities and their equal political and economic involvement in them."[123] A. Elizabeth Taylor's earlier study of the suffrage effort in Arkansas, centered in Little Rock, tends to support Turner's findings.[124] Although able to win over only four southern states for the Anthony amendment, the activists of the suffrage generation possessed a better understanding of the importance of grass-roots organizing than did the later strategists for the Equal Rights Amendment (ERA). Failure to build a strong base of local community support doomed the ERA in Dixie and in turn undermined its strong support nationally.

The suffrage fight specifically indicates the weaknesses of feminism in the South, but it also suggests more generally the tremendous barriers to public life that women had to overcome. According to the historian Nancy F. Cott, "feminism" means a belief in sex equality, the presumption that women's condition is socially constructed, and the supposition that women represent not only a biological but also a social grouping. Cott maintains that "feminism" as a word and as a movement made its appearance in the United States between 1910 and 1920.[125] Some historians of southern women believe that the suffrage movement in the South actually represented what Marjorie Spruill Wheeler as early as 1984 called "full-blown feminism." As Wheeler subsequently explained in her book dealing with southern leaders of the suffrage movement, "Throughout its thirty-year history, the suffrage movement in the South was a full-fledged women's rights movement, seeking an expanded and more equitable role for women within Southern society."[126]

Semantics aside, the first generation of women in public life, whether "activists" or "feminists," by 1920 had partially bridged the gap between private and public spheres by challenging the ragged edges of the New South and the residual callousness of the Old South. Whatever their limitations, and they were many, they had recognized in outline, if not always in substance, most of the problems that attracted the attention of subsequent generations of southern feminists. Southern women, like their American counterparts, had crossed into a new century and along the way had gained access to the polls. They had received limited assistance from southern pol-

iticians but little sympathy and even less support from some of their southern sisters.

Explaining the divisions between women in conventional masculine
folk wisdom, that great sage of southern literature William Faulkner, in
Light in August, speaks through his character Armstid, who says of the pregnant, unmarried Lena:

But that's the woman of it. Her own self one of the first ones to cut the ground from
under a sister woman, she'll walk the public country herself without shame because
she knows that folks, menfolks, will take care of her. She don't care nothing about
womenfolks. It wasn't any woman that got her into what she don't even call trouble. Yes, sir. You just let one of them get married or get into trouble without being
married, and right then and there is where she secedes from the woman race and
species and spends the balance of her life trying to get joined up with the man race.
That's why they dip snuff and smoke and want to vote.[127]

Although much touted, suffrage represented a relatively minor piece of a
confusing, complex, and contradictory puzzle. The ballot in and of itself
provided neither a panacea for gender inequality nor a quick solution to the
myriad problems that plagued the lives of southern women. Suffrage was,
however, a monumental landmark for American women and a touchstone
from which the particular needs of southern women could be addressed and
from which subsequent feminist campaigns of the twentieth century could
be launched.

❧

SIX

Looking for New Heavens
and a New Earth

I n America and in the South the right to vote marked an important
watershed in the crusade for women's rights. In some respects, however,
suffrage may have been little more than a façade, a pretty face that served
as a distraction from the continuing sexual discrimination, injustice, ineq-
uity, and outright degradation. More than a few southern females of the
interwar period possessed an intimate acquaintance with hardship, and
their lives often bore the stamp of a persistent, demanding, and sometimes
cruel rural tradition. Others traded hardscrabble farming for a harsh, monotonous existence as mill hands. All told, they belonged to a generation
of Americans who, as they rode out the decade of the 1930s, found themselves impaled on the horns of a great dilemma—a despair occasioned by
the worst economic depression in the nation's history and a world scene
growing increasingly ominous with each passing day. The youth who grew
to maturity during that era were often ill housed, ill fed, and ill clothed.
Yet they survived the Great Depression and rallied to fight an awesome
global war. This may have been the most extraordinary run of common
people that the United States ever produced. Some of them were southerners, and about half of those were female.

In 1938 the National Emergency Council (NEC) presented its findings
to President Franklin Delano Roosevelt in a document entitled *Report on
Economic Conditions of the South*. Earlier, in a letter addressed to the conference on the same subject, Roosevelt had declared: "It is my conviction
that the South represents right now the Nation's No. 1 economic problem—the Nation's problem, not merely the South's."[1] The NEC confirmed
the president's view. Written in the sterile language of bureaucratese, the
official report still painted a vivid-enough picture of life in the South,
where already-grim conditions had been exacerbated by the most severe
depression in the nation's history. Only four of the sixty-four pages dealt

specifically with the topic of women and children, and those focused on employment and wages.[2] Nonetheless, other passages revealed dismal circumstances that affected female lives.

The South possessed an abundance of natural resources, but the region's people remained "as a whole . . . the poorest in the country." In 1929, prior to the stock-market crash, farmers below the Mason-Dixon line had earned only about $186 per year, whereas elsewhere in the country their counterparts took in $528. A majority of southern farm families toiled as landless tenants. Only 5.7 percent of the three million rural houses in fourteen southern states, West Virginia among them, had water piped into them for any purpose; 3.4 percent, for bathrooms. Over half of the dwellings remained unpainted, and more than one-third possessed no screens to ward off mosquitos and flies. According to the 1938 report, "the low-income belt of the South is a belt of sickness, misery, and unnecessary death." Common diseases included syphilis, malaria, pneumonia, and tuberculosis, as well as pellagra, which was caused by nutritional deficiencies. Standing at 8.8 percent, illiteracy in Dixie exceeded that of any other section of the country. The document stated categorically that southerners needed clothing and estimated that farm families in Mississippi and Georgia spent $15 annually to outfit the husband and $12 for his spouse.[3]

In this financially strapped region the birthrate also surpassed that in other parts of the United States.[4] "An easy acceptance of sexuality" prevailed among whites as well as blacks, according to the historian Rosalind Rosenberg, who writes: "In the Ozarks, couples regularly copulated amid their newly planted fields, a practice meant to ensure a good crop. This bawdy approach to life carried over into local square dances, where fiddlers sawed out such tunes as 'Grease My Pecker, Sally Ann' and 'Fucking in the Goober Patch.'" A Missouri fiddler explained that "these dances remained popular until 'the folks that knowed 'em . . . got religion.'"[5]

"Next to China's, the American population growth rate in the nineteenth and early twentieth centuries ranks as a major phenomenon of modern history." Southerners "gave birth most often," according to the historian Jack Temple Kirby, with whites of the Appalachian highlands and blacks throughout Dixie in the lead. The forty-nine-year-old wife of a Florida squatter, the mother of fourteen children, declared, "I never thought of trying to limit my family. . . . What could I have done about it? It's not nature to say if you will have children or not." Yet another downtrodden female lamented that it "seems like all pore folk has is younguns." So great was her suffering after the birth of her last child that she banished her husband from the marital bed. "I tole Sam when 'twas over, he could sleep in one bed and I'd sleep in the other . . . nothing's happened yet. I ain't goin' to say it won't though." A black Alabama farmer, the father of eight children, reported that he and his wife "ain' never interfered with nature a-tall." A man from Harlan County, Kentucky—a father many times over—had no fundamental objection to limiting the size of his family if he or his wife only knew what to do. All the same, he reportedly offered the uncorroborated observation that there was "more fucking going on in Harlan County than any place in the world its size, no wonder there is a lot of kids . . . a big family just creeps up on [you] like, and before you know it you have a whole bunch of kids."[6] Although some couples, faced with the dire economic straits of the 1930s, attempted to limit the size of their family, others most assuredly did not. From all of this the inference can readily be drawn that a fair number of southern females fell into the proverbial category of being *pregnant* and *barefoot.*

These were the hard, cold realities of the lives of many southern women during the 1930s as Americans of both sexes found themselves ensnared by the gripping economic problems of the decade, with international turmoil bearing down upon them.[7] Uncomfortable with the present, the more prescient also feared the future; even the less perceptive among them may have experienced some measure of anxiety. As sexually active as married couples and freelancing singles seem to have been in the southern states (that is, if fecundity serves as any measure), prostitution still had a loyal following. In Bowling Green, Kentucky, for example, Pauline Tabor's famous house on Clay Street flourished during hard times. Indeed, on Armistice Day 1933 she had officially launched her new business on Smallhouse Road in a dwelling "rented from an unsuspecting preacher who had been called to tend a new flock in another town." Pauline's friends, both male and female, "had come calling with soda pop, liquor, beer, sandwiches, and all the other ingredients for a 'bon voyage' party for one of the good girls of Bowling Green who was embarking on a life of sin." Prior to establishing her own business, Pauline had studied the finer points of management at the knee of another well-known madam, Miss May of Clarksville, Tennessee.[8]

As some men found their diversions in the vice districts during this troubled decade, moviegoing provided a more wholesome escape for greater numbers of the depression-ridden populace. In 1936 Margaret Mitchell published *Gone with the Wind*, the great epic of the South during the Civil War and Reconstruction. In due time, Hollywood had its way with this panoramic novel of the Southland. In 1939 the motion picture received the Academy Awards for best picture, best director, best actress, and best supporting actress. This film, in the words of one authority, perpetuated "a legend [of] an opulent South . . . at the expense of progress . . . in race relations [or] a more accurate perception of the South's past and present problems."[9]

Alluring as the fantasy of a mint-juleped South may have been for a depression-weary population, most southerners of the interwar years rooted themselves in terra firma and stoically confronted life's vicissitudes. Nonetheless, even as the twentieth century presented new challenges, old myths still gripped certain elements in Dixie. With lights dimmed in the ballroom, the Key-Ice Club at the University of Alabama performed an extraordinary ritual during intermissions at dances. As flaming torches, borne by some of the members, illuminated the darkness, other men escorted an ice-laden cart about the floor. One of their number customarily toasted southern womanhood thus: "To woman, lovely woman of the Southland, as pure and chaste as this sparkling water, as cold as this gleaming ice, we lift this cup, and we pledge our hearts and our lives to the protection of her virtue and chastity."[10]

It would be overly dramatic to associate schoolboy antics with deep-seated male psychoses in Dixie, but in all seriousness, the portrayal of females as ice goddesses may reveal as much or more about the men as about the women. Lifted from their rightful context, the lines "And fire and ice within me fight/Beneath the suffocating night," penned by the poet A.E. Housman, seem to apply to the contradictory world of the "southern belle" or "lady." Even among the crème de la crème, overt and fiery feminine sensuality, though somewhat exceptional, was hardly unknown in Dixie. During the summer of 1918 a midwesterner stationed at Camp Sheridan, First Lieutenant F. Scott Fitzgerald, encountered a restless southern belle, Zelda Sayre, at the country club in Montgomery, Alabama. She was fresh out of high school, and according to Zelda's biographer, Nancy Milford, "If there was a Confederate Establishment in the Deep South, Zelda Sayre came from the heart of it." Still, Zelda had "chafed against the emotional restraint of her family, and she felt herself being suffocated in the small arena that both her family and Montgomery offered her." World War I released her as "thousands of soldiers and aviators poured into the city to train at Camps Sheridan and Taylor," and "the country club became almost an auxiliary officers' club." Some old Confederates had well-placed doubts about quartering Yankees on the outskirts of their fair city, but such cautionary opinions fell on the deaf ears of the young. Furthermore, one female remembered, "the Yankees were such good dancers."[11]

Smitten with each other, F. Scott Fitzgerald and Zelda Sayre became husband and wife, and "together they personified the immense lure of the East, of young fame, of dissolution and early death." "It was not her beauty that was arresting," Milford observes. "It was her style, a sort of insolence toward life, her total lack of caution, her fearless and abundant pride."[12] To paraphrase Edna St. Vincent Millay's "A Few Figs from Thistles," written in 1920, their candles burned at both ends. Scott drank himself into oblivion, and Zelda suffered a mental breakdown. In her heyday she represented the very embodiment of the flapper, a female persona far removed from the mythical feminine figures of the Old South and equally alienated from most of her contemporaries in Montgomery.

Over in Georgia, the neighboring state of Zelda's native Alabama, lived the debutante Margaret ("Peggy") Mitchell. In 1922 a gossip columnist in Atlanta with the nom de plume Polly Peachtree wrote of the future novelist that "she has in her brief life, perhaps, had more men really, truly 'dead in love' with her, more honest-to-goodness suitors than almost any other girl in Atlanta."[13] Mitchell's biographer, Darden Asbury Pyron, labeled her "the baby-faced vamp" during this interlude in her life. Only four feet eleven inches tall, Peggy struggled to keep her weight above one hundred pounds. Pyron wrote that "she was well-proportioned . . . , prided herself on her good figure . . . [and] dressed like a high-style if miniature mannequin." Furthermore, "she could dance all evening, yet arise the next day early to swim, to camp, and to hunt possum that night. Yet even her physical grace and energy paled beside her social charm."[14]

The biographer added that "men adored [Peggy], and she, in turn, needed men. Males, however, exerted the most ambivalent attraction for her. While she relished male company and flaunted her collection of suitors, marriage failed to interest her. Sex repulsed her." All the same she had written to an acquaintance that she believed "a man who makes improper proposals is a positive necessity in a girl's life—just as much of a necessity as a man whose intentions are honorable and who believes you the personification of all ignorance and innocence."[15] When Margaret Mitchell decided to take up journalism, she received virtually no encouragement from her family or from Atlanta "society." In fact, "society sharply circumscribed legitimate employment for women." Medora Field Perkerson, who hired Mitchell, claimed that "there had been some skepticism on the Atlanta Journal Magazine staff when Peggy came to work as a reporter. Debutantes slept late in those days and didn't go in for jobs."[16]

Another southern belle out of this era made a name for herself in English and American theater. Born 31 January 1903 in Huntsville, Alabama, Tallulah Bankhead claimed distinguished parentage. Her father, William Brockman Bankhead, served as Speaker of the United States House of Representatives; her mother, Adalaide Eugenia Sledge Bankhead, who died shortly after Tallulah's birth, has been described as "one of Virginia's most beautiful women." The actress's unusual name came from her maternal grandmother, another of Dixie's lovelies. In 1937 Tallulah married the actor John Emery. She had met him in Jasper, Alabama, her childhood stomping grounds. Referring to John, Tallulah proclaimed, "He is crazy as a hatter, but then so am I." When she later divorced him in June 1941, she gave the reason as "that old debbil career." Although Bankhead was an avid baseball fan, she declared, "I just couldn't root for a team named Yankees." Despite her southern connections and despite being considered a front-runner to play Scarlett in the movie version of *Gone with the Wind*, Bankhead lost the role to Vivien Leigh. Stronger on the stage than on the screen, Bankhead shone as the character Regina Giddens, a predatory southern female in Lillian Hellman's play *The Little Foxes*, which opened at the National Theater on Broadway in 1939.[17] That playwright also hailed from the Deep South; born in New Orleans, Louisiana, in 1905, she bore the imprint of her youthful beginnings in that colorful city.[18]

Zelda Sayre Fitzgerald, Margaret Mitchell, Tallulah Bankhead, and Lillian Hellman had done their "flapping" during the 1920s. The gin-and-jazz style, however, despite its enduring presence in the nation's memory, pervaded neither the culture nor the times that gave rise to it. Few Americans—southern, northern, eastern, or western—permitted themselves to be so self-indulgent. The lifestyle of the flapper bore little resemblance to the daily existence of an ordinary southern woman and held little attraction for the exceptional one who might have been either able to afford it or sophisticated enough to embrace it and withstand the repercussions. As battery-powered radios made their appearance and became increasingly common in rural dwellings, the "lady of the house" may have been as likely to tune to the "Grand Ole Opry," with its hillbilly music and western swing, as she was to scan the static-ridden airways for the sultry strains of jazz. Many of Dixie's daughters had more in common with Maybelle Carter, a rising star of the country-music set, than they did with Clara Bow, Hollywood's "It Girl," or other symbols of the reckless decade of the twenties.

Mother Maybelle Carter and her daughters joined the Grand Ole Opry in 1950. (One of them, June, eventually became Mrs. Johnny Cash. The alliance of a "hillbilly princess" and a hulking southern male who exuded raw virile talent gave rise to the House of Cash.) Maybelle, a native of the Southern Appalachians out of Maces Spring, Virginia, had been one of the three members of the original Carter Family. Her pursuit of a musical career led her not only to venture far from the insular existence of her hollow but also to abandon the traditional role of mountain women. Maybelle, her brother-in-law A.P. ("Doc") Carter, and her sister-in-law Sara Carter Bayes held their first recording session in Bristol, Tennessee, during early August 1927. They traveled and performed together until the act broke up in 1942. June Carter Cash later wrote: "There was never any talk about whether or not I'd be part of the Carter Family. I was part of the Carter Family, but to join the singing and strumming Carters I had to learn to do something people thought was worth coming to town for."[19] According to Bill C. Malone, an authority on southern music, "no group better embodied the mood and style of the family parlor and country church than the Carters; their three-part harmony, Maybelle's unique guitar style, and their large collection of vintage songs (such as 'Wildwood Flower' and 'Will the Circle Be Unbroken') still influence country singers today."[20]

In an era of primitive recording technology, the original Carter Family managed to develop a personal following. "Back about 1930," James Marion Ripley, a resident of northeast Tennessee, recalled more than half a century later, "Dad bought a second-hand Victrola. . . . At that time, the Carter Family was extremely famous in this part of the country here. Times were hard and Mother loved this good country singing like the Carters put out. . . . Dad would buy a 75-cent record and bring it home. . . . And they enjoyed that so much, and Mother especially." Ripley explained that his mother showed "more emotion when they would sing those good old songs than she would generally about things like that. . . . Back there in the thirties . . . there at home when things were scarce . . . we lived on love and Carter Family records."[21]

This lone survivor of a four-member nuclear family conjured up an image of a kinship unit that was braced by its love and steeled by the spiritual fortitude of a woman whose physical health was declining rapidly as he recounted one of his most precious memories of her:

We didn't know whether she'd ever be able to manage to make it up on top of the hill or not where we wanted to go to have our picnic. But she wanted to go, and she said she was going to try . . . so we eased up a hill, and we went completely upon the highest hill we could find. We placed our lunch there, put some cloths down on the ground, fixed our lunch. We'd put our dopes [soft drinks] in the springhouse the day before and we had them good and cold. . . . We had an awfully good time. We were so close; we were so close in spirit, in person and spirit, too.[22]

Eva Parker Ripley, the woman just described, inspired such love and devotion in both of her sons that her younger one, though ill and weak some two months before his death at the age of sixty-seven, still managed to pluck a pink rose and carry it to his mother's grave on the anniversary of her birth.[23]

If the family has been "the centripetal force in southern culture," as the historian Carol Ruth Berkin has written, then the wife and mother surely represented the center to which the force was drawn.[24] In countless ways throughout the centuries all across the South, such beloved women as the one described above have exerted positive private influences on their families and friends. Indeed, many of them may have been perfectly content to confine their contributions to the domestic front. By the late nineteenth and early twentieth centuries, however, they counted among themselves females who were impelled to move into the larger realm of public life. For the latter, altruism and ambition coalesced and proved to be not necessarily incongruous.

Although the female suffrage amendment had been ratified in 1920, veteran crusaders as well as other well-informed individuals in Dixie readily understood that securing the right to vote hardly represented a miracle cure for all that ailed southern womanhood. The historian Eleanor Flexner has written that even at the national level "the suffragists in 1920 were not only . . . weary of campaigning; they were confused." The League of Women Voters, into which Mrs. Carrie Chapman Catt, who had been at the helm of the National American Woman Suffrage Association, steered the suffragists, may have "short-circuited the political strength of the most gifted suffragist women [instead planting] firmly in the minds of a goodly number of politicians the idea that 'the ladies' were not really interested in politics—as politicians understood the term—but rather in 'reform,' which was quite another matter."[25]

Strange as it may seem, Belle Kearney and Nellie Nugent Somerville managed to win their 1923 bids for seats in the legislature of Mississippi, a state that had staunchly resisted their best efforts to secure the ratification of the Anthony amendment. Of the most prominent southern suffragists, they alone moved into elected public offices. Kearney became the first southern woman to serve in a state senate, and Somerville took her seat in the Mississippi House of Representatives, where she was followed by Ellen Sullivan Woodward two years later. In 1931, when Somerville's daughter Lucy Howorth, an attorney, campaigned successfully for election to the lower chamber of the state assembly, she identified herself as the granddaughter of a Confederate officer. Earlier, as the flamboyant Kearney, clad in a black crepe dress, took her seat in the Senate, male lawmakers rose to their feet, and the hall resounded with their applause. Somerville, sporting a hat on her first day as a solon, thereby violated House Rule No. 10, which prohibited headgear in the legislative chamber. Elsewhere in the South, "Miriam A. ['Ma'] Ferguson's election as governor of Texas in 1924 as a stand-in for her discredited husband was not applauded as a victory for women then," Martha H. Swain reports, "and she has won no apologists since." Likewise, "Rebecca Latimer Felton's half day as a Georgia [United States] senator in 1922" amounted to little.[26]

All told, thirty-two women served as lawmakers in ten southern states (all but Louisiana) during the decade that followed the ratification of the National Woman Suffrage Amendment. The nomination of the South's first female legislator, Lillian Exum Clement of North Carolina, an attorney, actually antedated ratification; she took her seat in 1920. The next year in Tennessee, Ann Lee Worley filled the position left vacant when her husband, J. Parks Worley, died in office. He had been an opponent of woman suffrage, claiming that it violated "both moral and spiritual law." When J. Parks had opposed both a presidential and a municipal woman-suffrage bill in 1919, he purported to represent the "women of Tennessee who were not present, but who were at home tending to their home duties." According to him, "90% of Tennessee's women opposed woman suffrage." As for the remainder, they "were deluded." His widow, Ann Lee, however, sponsored a bill to open all public positions in Tennessee to female office seekers.[27]

Forty-seven-year-old Hattie Hooker from Selma, Alabama, won election to the state legislature in 1922; along with teaching experience to her credit, she had also crusaded for woman suffrage and other civic objectives. The *Montgomery Advertiser*, however, considered her greatest accomplishment to be that she maintained a "beautiful home that [was] a center of refinement, and those lovely characteristics that go to make the perfect home life."[28] Not until 1928 did the first women lawmakers arrive in Columbia, South Carolina, and Tallahassee, Florida. Mary Gordon Ellis of Jasper County served in the South Carolina Senate, and Edna Giles Fuller, a widow from Orlando, sat one term in the Florida legislature, won reelection in 1930, but went down to defeat in 1932, along with several other incumbents.[29]

The first female legislators in the South did brief stints in government, the pattern being single terms. A tenure of more than four years proved rare. The historians Joanne V. Hawks and Mary Carolyn Ellis found that when the first decade of southern feminine participation in the legislative process had passed, Dixie's statehouses remained intact: "Neither Armageddon nor the millennium had occurred. Legislative chambers still stood, and proceedings droned on much as they always had." "Although many of their male colleagues praised the women publicly," Hawks and Ellis refuse to attach much importance to ceremonial trappings. "Many of the flowery statements may have been motivated more by Southern chivalry than by the legislators' true feelings," they caution. "Supporters and critics . . . continued to hold their conflicting opinions, although critics were probably a little relieved and supporters somewhat disappointed with what the pioneers had accomplished."[30]

At the national level, Eleanor Roosevelt Roosevelt attempted to work within the party structure, but she soon came to the troubling realization that style sometimes took precedence over substance in American politics. During the postsuffrage decade, Eleanor, an accomplished woman in her own right, enjoyed a prominent if perfunctory status in Democratic ranks. Her husband, the future president Franklin Delano Roosevelt, had served as assistant secretary of the navy in the Wilson administration and had run on the Democratic ticket for vice-president in 1920. Though Eleanor was identified with the northern-based Roosevelts of Sagamore Hill-Oyster Bay and then by marriage with those of Hyde Park, she claimed southern ancestry.

Eleanor was the granddaughter of a Georgia woman, Martha ("Mittie") Bulloch. Financing Mittie's wedding to Theodore Roosevelt Sr. had required the sale of four slaves. Because of declining fortunes, Mittie's mother and sister left Georgia to live with her in New York City. The old lady (Mittie's mother) reportedly "cried for three days when Port Royal fell in November 1861 [and] announced that she would rather die than live under a triumphant Yankee government." She expired after learning that two of her sons had fallen just before Richmond capitulated. According to Blanche Wiesen Cook, Eleanor's biographer, "it was rumored that Mittie hung a Confederate flag out the window every time the South won a victory, and everybody knew that she and her family sent packages of contraband supplies (woolens, cosmetics, food) through the Yankee blockade via the Bahamas to relatives and friends in Georgia." The heroes of the family, James and Irvine Bulloch, Mittie's brothers, served the Confederacy with distinction. Captain James Bulloch designed and helped build the *Alabama*, a raider that took its toll on Union shipping, and Irvine served aboard the vessel until it was sunk.[31]

With considerable hoopla in March 1924 the male-dominated Democratic establishment proclaimed itself to be "the first political group to seek women's views on important questions of peculiar interest to them so that these social legislation planks as incorporated in the national Democratic platform may represent their ideas." Eleanor Roosevelt headed the women's platform committee for the Democratic National Committee. She surrounded herself with able females, among them Pattie Ruffner Jacobs of Alabama and Charl Williams from Tennessee, the latter being "credited with lobbying the final vote needed for ratification of the suffrage amendment." Eleanor's committee worked diligently and set forth a progressive liberal agenda. The women supported the League of Nations, called for a department of education at the federal level, committed themselves to equal pay for women and restrictions on child labor, endorsed a forty-eight-hour workweek, and suggested establishing employment bureaus and making efforts to guarantee safe environments for American laborers. Not admitted to the proceedings of the all-male Resolutions Committee, which met behind locked doors, Eleanor and her cohorts sat just outside; the future first lady passed the time knitting. In the end the Resolutions Committee decided not to hear the women's proposals.[32]

The fact that male chauvinism still pervaded American society could hardly be considered surprising, but the ambivalence that characterized the approach of activist women weakened their strategy. "Progressive women's ideology and goals are . . . difficult to appreciate today because they seem contradictory and ambiguous," acknowledges Joan Hoff, a constitutional historian and legal scholar. "On the one hand [they] explicitly committed themselves to women's rights—the right to equal political participation and to the opportunity for meaningful, productive, and well-paid work. On the other hand, the very same women successfully set in motion legal constraints on women's rights in the workplace." Obviously, "they did not practice what they preached *for themselves*; instead, they promoted what seems today an idealized and dangerously romantic vision of maternity, home, and family *for other women* (not unlike Phyllis Schlafly several generations later)." While "these Progressive female reformers" claimed autonomy for themselves, they maintained that "others had to be protected because they could not take care of themselves."[33]

More radical than most of their politically inclined contemporaries, members of the National Woman's Party (NWP, originally the Congressional Union), in convention during February 1921, had quickly reorganized. The membership had committed itself to an activist agenda that was directed toward removing the remaining legal disabilities that affected adult females in America. Before 1920 had ended, one of the NWP's younger members, Sue Shelton White, a suffragist from Tennessee, was already doing spade work for a "blanket bill . . . to sweep away these discriminations." At the national level the NWP staked its case on constitutional revision. The Equal Rights Amendment, also known as the Lucretia Mott Amendment, made its appearance in the United States Congress during 1923.[34]

Prior to the introduction of the ERA in Congress, the NWP, which claimed Alice Paul as its founder, pursued a state-by-state strategy. The NWP aimed at securing wide-ranging rights for women, among them "suffrage, office holding, jury service, choice of domicile and name, property rights, ownership and control of labor and services, freedom of contract, custody and control of children equal to that of the father, equal grounds for divorce, and equal immunities or penalties for sex offenses." The League of Women Voters (LWV, formerly the National American Woman Suffrage Association) joined the NWP to win passage of such a measure in Wisconsin in July 1921. The coalition split, however, when the NWP turned away from protective legislation for women in industry, which was a cardinal issue for the LWV. The LWV refused to endorse and support any "blanket bill" that excluded this concept.[35] In the same vein, Mary Anderson, the director of the Women's Bureau of the United States Department of Labor, predicted that the passage of the Equal Rights Amendment would have an adverse effect on women's working conditions. The Women's Bureau conducted surveys and drafted reports during the interwar period, turning up a wealth of information and cranking out reams of documents. For all of its efforts, its long-term impact on the lives of women employed in American industries may have been less significant than individuals like Anderson imagined.[36]

The NWP's strategy had little impact on the national front, much less in the South. Focusing on the Magnolia State, Martha H. Swain observes that "the Woman's Party was too doctrinaire for Mississippi and it suffered the stigma that outsiders have traditionally faced in the state." She explains that the "few emerging career and professional women . . . were too concerned about establishing themselves among their clients to become involved with an organization whose notions about full equality would jeopardize advancement in their own professions." Furthermore, "a vast majority of Mississippi women were homemakers who were not alienated by the league and the federated clubs whose emphases upon protection for mothers, children, and working women seemed far more appropriate for them than the NWP's militant careerism and total equality." Indeed, Mississippi shied away from ratification of the Nineteenth Amendment until March 1984, when both the House and the Senate gave it unanimous approval. Lawmakers in the Magnolia State finally had opened jury duty to women in 1968.[37] Although omnibus bills for women's rights met with little enthusiasm, southern lawmakers occasionally approved changes in the legal status of females. In keeping with national trends, Tennessee, for instance, had passed the Married Women's Emancipation Act in 1919, granting married women the same authority to manage their property that a single woman possessed and recognizing their rather dubious right to sue and be sued.[38]

The legal termination of matrimony likewise became a somewhat more viable possibility during the early twentieth century than it had been previously. The nation's divorce rate represented one of the many social statistics with which the United States Bureau of the Census concerned itself. Findings for the period 1887-1906 indicated that terminations of marriage were on the rise throughout the country, with the western states and territories experiencing the highest incidence and the South having the lowest. Although restrictions governing divorce gradually eased in the southern states during the twentieth century, they remained well entrenched at the turn of the century. Louisiana, for example, forbade remarriage by an adulterer or an adulteress (the guilty party in a divorce suit) or his or her "accomplice." That state also prohibited a female from remarrying for ten months, presumably to allow time for a pregnancy to run its natural course, should one have been under way when the marriage dissolved. By the 1980s the West still claimed the highest divorce rate, but the South had moved into second place.[39]

Some married couples have always dispensed with formal proceedings, exercised their God-given right to independence, and arrived at their own remedies. After having been married just over a decade, Mary McLeod Bethune of South Carolina, a black woman who rose to prominence in public life during the New Deal era, left her spouse but never divorced him.[40] "Divorce in the formal, legal sense was a luxury few poor people could afford, and in any case, they shared the belief of the middle and upper classes everywhere that marriage was sacred," Jack Temple Kirby explains; "traditional morality thus conspired with poverty to bind marriage partners, whatever the quotient of unhappiness. Nonetheless folks split, usually without the assistance of the legal profession and the courts."[41]

Male-controlled southern legislatures carefully scrutinized measures having to do with the "sanctity" of marriage as well as a plethora of other "sacraments" that affected women's lives. The strategy employed by the NWP—that is, the "blanket bill"—made no serious inroads on southern legislative halls after the addition of the Nineteenth Amendment to the United States Constitution. According to Martha H. Swain, however, "the National Woman's Party (NWP) headquarters became a mecca for energetic young southerners who believed in full equal rights for their sex"; among them were a feminist attorney from Mississippi, Burnita Shelton Matthews, and a Tennessee lawyer and women's-rights advocate, Sue Shelton White. White subsequently left the NWP to head the Women's Division of the Democratic party.[42]

Later, in the New Deal era, Ellen Sullivan Woodward of Mississippi garnered the "biggest non-Cabinet job" of any southern female appointee. She directed women's relief programs under the auspices of the Federal Emergency Relief Administration and its successor, the Works Progress Administration. Of black women, only the southern educator Mary McLeod Bethune, a powerhouse in the National Council of Negro Women, landed a high-level position in Washington, D.C. Originally an advisor to the National Youth Administration (NYA), she moved in 1936 to the helm of its Office of Minority Affairs. In that year she also organized what was then commonly called the "black cabinet"—that is, the Federal Council on Negro Affairs.[43]

Although a few southern female activists clearly viewed suffrage as a springboard into public life, the frustrations of politics caused others to turn instead to favorite reform efforts. From the 1920s to the 1950s many of the second generation of southern female activists concentrated on anti-lynching efforts, labor education and organizing, and limited racial integration. Some earlier crusaders who were identified with the first generation of southern female activists had adopted an approach to public life somewhat in keeping with what Paula Baker has termed "domestic politics." The South's second generation, however, not only moved beyond "domestic

politics" but also shied away from "adopting formerly male values and behavior," an approach that Baker claims was taken by the "new [American]
woman" of the 1920s.[44]

Second-generation southern feminists who were predisposed toward
social and economic reform developed a somewhat more sophisticated approach than had their predecessors, which is not to suggest that all aspects
of "domestic politics" had vanished but that this style did not dominate the
emerging feminist strategy in the South during the twenties and thirties. By
the same token those women activists neither enthusiastically embraced
nor successfully practiced mainstream male politics. Although disdaining
traditional politics—problematic in and of itself—in favor of grass-roots
organizing, this phase of southern feminism was probably the most successful in recognizing and responding to the *particular needs* of *southern women*.
In both substance and organization, this may have been southern feminism
at its best.

Even as the suffrage crusade attracted public attention, a cadre of educated, socially conscious southern women, unobtrusively but in their private and usual matter-of-fact way, had been developing an infrastructure
for regional change. Small female colleges throughout Dixie transformed
young women's lives, among them such schools as Marion Female College,
established in Virginia in 1873, and Greenville Female College in South
Carolina, which opened its doors in 1855, thus antedating the Civil War.
Spelman in Atlanta, the nation's first college for black women, traced its
origins to 1881. A sprinkling of southerners likewise matriculated in the
North's "seven sisters." The pride, self-confidence, and commitment that
access to higher education instilled in these young women remained with
them throughout their lives and still shone through in their later years
when they recounted the precious unblurred memories of their youth. Although many of these females took up gainful employment at least for brief
interludes, most of them along the way became wives and mothers.[45]

Southerners, both men and women, still considered matrimony natural
and spinsterhood unnatural. Nonetheless, a few women enjoyed alternate
arrangements. A former southern belle recalled the position of her Cousin
Effie, whose marriage had lasted only three days but whose repudiation of
her new husband as a "brute" and her return to her parents' home had
"gained some kind of honor for her . . . which was widespread." When as a
child the future belle had inquired of her older relative why she had not
liked being married, Effie reportedly had replied: "Well, darling, marriage is
all right for those who like it. I would never dream of criticizing anyone for
getting married. After all my dear Father and Mother were married and I
had the highest respect and devotion for them. But personally, darling, I
have never seen how a LADY could do it."[46]

Presumably, females who married surrendered their virginity, but that hardly meant that they likewise forfeited their minds. Some of them maintained their contacts with their female contemporaries, nationally and regionally, through such agencies as alumnae associations, local chapters of the Young Women's Christian Association, the federated women's clubs, the American Association of University Women, and similar civic enterprises. With access to their husband's earnings and wealth as well as their own resources, some of these middle- and upper-class women found it not only agreeable but also possible to underwrite liberal or even radical causes in Dixie.[47]

Although activists tended to be centered in urban areas, the Smith-Lever Act, passed by Congress in 1914, contributed to alliances of like-minded rural women. This legislation provided for the establishment of the Cooperative Extension Service, thus paving the way for extension home-economics programs, home-demonstration clubs, and the extension home-makers groups across the country. Such organizations, which sometimes grafted themselves onto preexisting school, church, and community networks among rural females, provided opportunities for fellowship and socializing, creative crafts and cooking projects, and the systematic study of issues relevant to women's lives. Organized rural women addressed many of the same topics as their urban counterparts, among them prenatal care and childrearing, nutrition, and health and hygiene (often a euphemism for birth control). Likewise, they were hardly indifferent to current events involving politics, economics, and diplomacy. Some local groups also experimented with interracial cooperation in their collective projects; in Tennessee, for example, black and white women worked together during the interwar period, making mattresses from surplus cotton.[48]

Female activists of this era were neither obsessed with gender-determined issues nor blind to other dimensions of social reform. In the South as elsewhere, however, divisions sometimes occurred along race and class lines, which always presented challenges if not outright obstacles to grassroots organizing. The conservative establishment often accused southern liberals and radicals of being Communists or Communist sympathizers, which in some instances they were. Most more aptly qualified as liberal Democrats or Socialists. Similarly, the femininity and sexuality of those who challenged the status quo came under attack, particularly in a region plagued with the notion that free-thinking well-informed women ran the risk of "desexing" or "unsexing" themselves.

Occasionally, maybe even more often than not, the "sisterhood" marched to a different drummer than did the "sisters." Ironically, women activists of white middle- and upper-class origins, lacking firsthand personal experience with many of the conditions that they have attempted to remedy, have always directed a considerable amount of their energies toward ameliorating the plight of downtrodden whites and blacks. Given the value system that these activists have brought to their work, which, in turn, has influenced their judgments, it is not surprising that they sometimes failed to appreciate fully the positions of those whom they expected to uplift. The extraordinarily talented and self-effacing Eleanor Copenhaver Anderson, a national staffer and southern industrial secretary for the National Board of the Young Women's Christian Association (YWCA), once remarked of her own family, "We were so poor, but we always had servants" (in the southern highlands, "servants" usually meant blacks; "help" meant whites).[49]

Another YWCA staffer out of the Industrial Department found herself traveling with a black female organizer when they came to one of the smaller towns. In spite of the segregation laws, they shared a room. According to an individual who had been told about the experience, "There was only one double bed and one twin bed in the room. The black lady who was also no featherweight insisted that she and Elsie Harper both had to sleep in the same bed, to prove that Elsie had no residue of prejudice." Although Elsie had proved herself on this issue many times before, she was being put to the ultimate test. "They both had to spend a cramped and uncomfortable night in that one not-so-wide bed."[50]

Such discomfort represented a minor passing inconvenience, but during this same era, little black children all over the South, like Fannie Lou Hamer (née Townsend), grew up "poor and unlettered." Fannie was the youngest of Jim and Ella Townsend's brood of twenty—fourteen males and six females. Her arrival garnered her family $50, which sustained them through one more hard winter. This was a time when plantation owners in Mississippi paid a bonus to a tenant woman who produced another field hand. Anticipating no fundamental change in the racial and economic climate, planters could afford to be patient. There seemed to be time enough and worlds enough to realize the newborn's potential. So great was man's inhumanity to man in the Deep South that someone who was known to the Townsend family poisoned "three precious mules" that Fannie's father had struggled to acquire. "That white man did it just because we were getting somewhere," she recalled. "White people never like to see Negroes get a little success."[51]

Virginia Foster Durr of Alabama, a noted southern liberal of the interwar period who was a sister-in-law of the United States Supreme Court Justice Hugo Black, recalled that as a student at Wellesley College during the Jazz Age, she had been distressed about eating with a Negro girl because her "father would have a fit if he knew." The woman in charge of the particular college residence, to whom Durr complained, responded: "Well, dear, your father is your problem, not ours. Our problem is to see that you obey the rules of Wellesley College and if you do not choose to do so, then you will or you can withdraw. It will be your choice not ours. Now go and think about it overnight and let me know in the morning." According to Durr, "That was that," and she stayed.[52]

In the larger scheme of things the unwillingness of the great majority of whites to share a meal with blacks seems relatively benign though admittedly insidious. Far more serious was the systematic violence and bigotry whipped up by such organizations as the Ku Klux Klan (KKK). Such scholars as Nancy MacLean and Kathleen M. Blee have demonstrated that the KKK of the 1920s was hardly an all-male phenomenon. "Not only were women a significant portion of the Klan's membership," Blee asserts, "but their activities and ideologies differed sufficiently from those of Klansmen that an examination of the women's Klan changes our interpretation of the Klan as a whole." Furthermore, not only in the South but elsewhere in the country, right-wing extremist women's groups had not only antedated but also coexisted with the second Klan. One of the better known of such organizations of this era, the Grand League of Protestant Women, originated in Houston, Texas, in 1922. Calling for "'white supremacy, protection of womanhood, defense of the flag' and with its social work," it garnered members in the South and the West. As MacLean has found in her study of local Klan activities around Athens, Georgia, some females looked to the Klan to deal with abusive or errant husbands when no other remedy seemed available to them. The KKK's "moral clean-ups," just as its bigotry— neither of which were gender specific—appealed to a certain element of women.[53]

Although some white females appreciated the Klan for its chauvinistic commitment to "southern womanhood," many others, who were not identified with right-wing organizations, simply found contentment with their own individual bigotry. Nevertheless, the concerns that a relatively miniscule number of white women had about racial injustice took such disparate expressions as Jessie Daniel Ames's establishment of the Association of Southern Women for the Prevention of Lynching in 1930 and Lillian E. Smith's literary approach in *Strange Fruit*, completed in 1941. Ames hailed from Texas while Smith, though born in Florida, spent most of her life in Georgia. Ames's organization of southern white women challenged the assumption that they needed lynching to protect their honor and pitted them—urban and middle class at least in leadership—against the demagogues who dominated southern politics and fanned racial hatred. They employed moral suasion to pressure elected officials, and they made direct contact with local law-enforcement officials when their prisoners' lives seemed to be in jeopardy. Such tactics may have saved some incarcerated individuals from untimely deaths.[54]

Mob violence in Dixie manifested itself most egregiously in the lynching of blacks, but it also occasionally targeted indigenous whites. Non-southerners—indeed anyone who seemed somewhat alien to local culture—ran something of a risk. After the conviction of a factory supervisor, Leo Frank, for the murder of Mary Phagan, a thirteen-year-old worker in Atlanta, the northern-bred Jew found himself in the company of men who had taken the law into their own hands. Frank had just had his death sentence commuted after an unsuccessful appeal to the United States Supreme Court when his abductors transported him to the county of Phagan's birth and summarily lynched him.[55]

The psychology of racism and violence in the twentieth-century South fascinated Lillian Smith, who has been described as "the quintessential atomistic individual." According to the historian Randall Patton, she "was a perceptive critic of her region and her fellow liberals. She knew everyone, and at some time she disagreed with virtually every liberal organization" in the region. Such independence proved expensive, costing her many personal and professional disappointments.[56] Smith's interests and writings, which have been described as avant-garde, differed rather dramatically from those of her contemporary Caroline Gordon, another daughter of the South. Gordon—a native of Kentucky, a product of the southern literary renaissance, and the wife of the writer Allen Tate—showed herself to be something of a traditionalist. Her identification with the region's history is particularly vivid in her Civil War novel *None Shall Look Back*, published in 1937.[57]

For all of their concern for the masses, some of the native liberals and radicals of the interwar period had little in common with the region's people. Nowhere in the South is the chasm between the "people" and their "saviors" more apparent than in the labor movement in which the second generation of southern activists heavily immersed themselves; at no time is it more poignantly addressed than in a 1929 letter written by Minnie Fisher of East Marion, North Carolina, to Louise Leonard, director of the Southern Summer School for Women Workers. On 16 October, Leonard wrote to Fisher that she had been "horrified to hear of the massacre of workers at Marion" and had "been thinking a great deal about all of [her] friends there" and had "wished that [she] might do something to get justice for those accused of the murders since that may help prevent such outrageous things in the future." From the safety of her vantage point away from Marion, Leonard exhibited the not-unusual hypocrisy of passing judgment on those at the scene of labor violence. After expressing her "horror," she chided Fisher for rumors that she had "been scabbing in the mill ever since the murders." "You will remember what you wrote in your last letter about mountain people convinced they are right, sticking together, and I thought you would be the last one to desert the others when it is so important to stick together."[58]

Fisher replied a few days later:

Louise I am sorry you heard that I was scabbing. I will tell you how it was and you can be the judge. I haven't worked but 2 days and they asked me not to go back and now I am back at home and all the mill filled up and I have got no job no money nor anything and my man is gone and I can't find out where he is whether dead or alive and I am [so] in debt that it looks like I am going to have to do some scabbing so you can imagine what kind of shape I am in and I have got a little girl that has to be clothed and fed. . . . What would you do if you was in my place?[59]

Exchanges like this tend to support the writer Sherwood Anderson's claim that the people in the mill villages were "as separate from the people of the town as though they lived on another planet."[60]

The thrust that gave this generation of female activists its identity was directed toward building a sisterhood that would transcend class and to a lesser extent even race to improve the quality of life of women workers and their families. Such impetus and direction clearly placed women activists on the cutting edge of southern liberalism and radicalism during the interwar period.[61] Eleanor Copenhaver (who subsequently married Sherwood Anderson in 1933) operated in this largely indigenous organizational web during the 1920s and 1930s. She formed contacts and friendships with like-minded contemporaries, among them Tom Tippett, a labor organizer; Myles Horton, a cofounder of the Highlander Folk School; Howard Kester, secretary for the Fellowship of Reconciliation; and Louise Leonard, who subsequently wed and used her married name, McLaren. Leonard had been a YWCA industrial secretary who, along with the labor economist Lois Mac-Donald, founded the Southern Summer School for Women Workers in 1927. Copenhaver found herself in the thick of the strikes and labor disturbances that swept the textile industry of the Upper South in 1929 and the following years. This milieu placed activists' lives, not just their sacred honor, in jeopardy.[62] On 14 September 1929 near Gastonia, North Carolina, for example, armed men forced off the road a truck carrying union members and fired on them when they abandoned the vehicle. Ella May Wiggins, a balladeer who conveyed her message through music and was considered "the union's most effective local organizer," died at the scene from a gunshot wound. Her assailants, who were tried only after the governor intervened, went free.[63]

Southern ancestry and social status obviously worked to the advantage of such individuals as Eleanor Copenhaver Anderson and Lucy Randolph Mason, an organizer for the CIO (Congress of Industrial Organizations, which later merged with the AFL, American Federation of Labor). Mason, a Virginia patrician, ventured into mill towns of the South to proselytize for labor organization in much the same manner as YWCA industrial secretaries did.[64] Although Anderson reportedly had brushes with the Ku Klux Klan, she and others of similar persuasion benefited from the omnipresence of the "southern lady," even as they mocked the image. The "lady," however, could hardly be expected to approve of labor agitation. In 1935 at Daisy, Tennessee, gun thugs fired on pickets, wounding Hilda Hulbert, the librarian at Highlander Folk School. Reporting that nurses who treated her at the hospital "were disdainful," Hulbert observed: "It suddenly occurred to me that it wasn't exactly considered ladylike to get shot."[65] The "lady" hovered close by in 1946 as Brooks S. Creedy, a southern-born official of the YWCA, negotiated with community leaders at Hendersonville, North Carolina. Distressed by racially and sexually integrated conferences at Camp Highland Lake, local people made threats and gossiped about impending Klan intervention. When Creedy met with the newspaper editor, he refused to discuss some of the conduct that had allegedly occurred at the camp in the past because she "was a lady." Explaining that her "conference was all women," she "was fairly sure that in his mind the idea of molesting a women's conference was different."[66]

Southern feminism of this era hardly confined its influence to all-female activities, yet some of the most fascinating experiments involved single-sex approaches. The YWCA conferences for female industrial workers and business and professional women, as well as the Southern Summer School camps, focused on the peculiar problems of southern society and the particular needs of southern women.[67] These programs—organized, attended, taught, and financed mostly by women, lasting a few days, as the YWCA conferences did, or a few weeks in the case of the SSS camps—touched the lives of hundreds directly and thousands indirectly. Not content with short-term summer activities, such organizers as Louise Leonard McLaren and Eleanor Copenhaver Anderson forged a network of socially conscious women through a steady correspondence with local chapters of the YWCA and with alumnae of the camps and conferences.

The staff of the National Board of the YWCA and the SSS enthusiastically observed that indigenous southerners came to the forefront of the labor movement. Copenhaver, herself a southerner from Virginia, wrote in her biennial report for 1928-29: "Except at Gastonia it is clear that the idea of getting together and protesting came to workers without outside agitation; in Gastonia even if the first impulse was from the outside, the leadership was largely native." Referring to the rash of strikes, she commented: "Students [at YWCA conferences] in the South see in the upheavals of 1929 a mass movement touching many kinds of people, which they liken in its potentialities to the Reformation or the Renaissance. It is hard to convey to the outsider the magnitude and subtlety of this revolution."[68] For Leonard of the SSS, the most significant aspect of the Elizabethton strike was that southern women had led the walkout. For several years afterward, the SSS arranged for one of them, Bessie Edens, to attend the annual camps. When she was not identified as a student, they hired her to cook; but they clearly valued her more as a source of inspiration for others than for her culinary skills.[69]

Although class differences existed between the ranking officials of these organizations and the alumnae, noticeable bonding occurred.[70] The settings and the shared experiences created an almost mystical female-centered environment. Natural beauty surrounded the church retreats and small college campuses (primarily in North Carolina but sometimes in Virginia, Tennessee, and other states as well) that were used for the camps and conferences. The retreat to nature, as a respite from noisy mills and the daily monotony and strain of human existence, played a role in the ritualistic tactics of grass-roots organizing. Training sessions took on the aura of monasticism in these remote enclaves, which had the added advantage of exciting little outside interference. Indigenous activists also understood fully the power of religion in southern society, so they employed religious analogies and familiar hymns whenever these might produce the desired results.

Course outlines and lists of speakers clearly suggested a philosophical challenge to southern conservatism. Labor history, public speaking, and the preparation of pamphlets, flyers, and yearbooks inspired serious reflection and provided practical lessons in organizing techniques. Discussions of black literature and history and the presence of prominent black visitors tended to undermine rationalizations for segregation. Howard Kester, Myles Horton, and other southern radicals spoke about "a new social order." Although the program in and of itself was substantive, ceremonial trappings also played an important role. Candlelight services, the recitation of litanies written by campers, talk of carrying away symbols of the conferences as lasting reminders, common meals, songfests, and recreation took on the function of ritual.

At a 1934 YWCA business women's conference, the campers recited what was termed a litany written by one of the conferees, which included the following: "I believe in my oneness with the workers of the world" and "I believe in the interdependence of nations and races." Afterwards the conferees "sang the Negro national anthem and went down to the water to sing taps." They returned to the buildings to find that "the entire Negro staff had come out and were singing 'God be with you till we meet again,' 'Lord, I want to be like Jesus,' and 'Ain't going to study war no more.'" In the wake of this obviously moving experience, those in attendance voted to ask representatives of other races and nationalities to be resources in the following year.[71]

Organizers also arranged physical examinations and medical treatments for the women in attendance. Nutritional deficiencies received attention—at least while the camps and conferences remained in session. Scheduled discussion centered on personal problems involving female-male relationships that might have shattered the sensibilities of the mythical "southern lady." Courses in personal hygiene afforded instruction in feminine health-care and access to birth-control information at a time when the dissemination of such material ran counter to existing state and federal statutes which had been inspired by the likes of Anthony Comstock. YWCA and SSS leadership understood full well that females who had no control over their own bodies (that is, their reproductive capacities) likewise had no control over their own lives and in turn were in no position to effect changes in their native region.

Brownie Lee Jones—a director of the SSS during the 1940s who had earlier been a local YWCA industrial secretary in Richmond, Virginia—recalled that she had kept condoms at her desk in the state capital. Jones explained that the local Y provided contraceptives after "one girl who had an abortion . . . almost died . . . and we decided it was time to do something about it. A lot of these girls were married but they had to go on working and they couldn't stop and have children."[72] A native of Alabama reported having been told by his mother that when his parents had lived in Baltimore during the 1920s, his father had forced her to see an abortionist, who made a failed attempt to end one of her pregnancies. Instead the fetus went full term. The child, a boy, survived but had severe birth defects (mostly facial) for which he had to be hospitalized and treated at Johns Hopkins for three years. Ultimately he managed to live a reasonably normal life. The father later deserted his wife and his three sons.[73] It was common knowledge among the folk that granny women and midwives in rural areas throughout the South sometimes functioned as abortionists. Their margin of error, however, or what mutilations their ministrations may have occasioned remain undocumented and unknown.[74]

As the interest in birth control demonstrates, the experiments of the YWCA and the SSS not only reached into the public lives but also into the private intimate existences of female laborers with whom these organizations established contact. Although they sustained themselves throughout the depression years, these programs in worker education declined with the onset of World War II. YWCA conferences waned during the 1940s, and the upper echelon of the Y's leadership, discomforted by redbaiting, fazed out its Industrial Department; by the 1950s the SSS had halted operations. The latter had become coeducational along the way and had abandoned summer camps in favor of weekend training sessions. In the words of the historian Mary Evans Frederickson, The "chief and lasting influence [of the SSS] was transmitted through the lives of its students who came to believe in the possibility of fundamental social change and who pursued the goal of creating a humane industrial society in the South."[75]

Throughout Dixie, however, "factory girls," as they were often called by middle- and upper-class reformers, proved more strident than most of the YWCA members and some of its leaders. The industrial members of the Y had first gained the right to full participation at annual conventions during 1922. That very year, this new element of the organization recommended a study of industrial employment and presented Florence Simms, the YWCA national industrial secretary, with a golden opportunity to educate the entire membership to the special problems of females in industry. At the National Board's headquarters, legends persist about women in its upper echelon (usually officers, not staffers) who had moved or been maneuvered into positions that were philosophically, politically, and economically at variance with those of their own husbands. The rift between members who just wanted to believe in Jesus Christ and those who actually practiced his teachings as social activists left scars, and official records of the organization suggest that these differences remained unresolved for the duration of the Industrial Department's existence. That "factory girls" continued to be catalysts for social change seems evident. In a 1936 diary entry, Eleanor Copenhaver Anderson mentioned a High Point, North Carolina, council meeting at which the "industrial girls" had seemed "bent on [having a] Negro girl as well as [a Negro] leader at [their] conference." Apparently the same was true of the Charlotte council. "It will be hell to pay in New York," Eleanor wrote, "but a real sophisticated decision."[76]

Southern female activism during the interwar period was not confined to the relative moderation of upper- and middle-class organizational structure and the somewhat less combative philosophy of the YWCA and the SSS. In stark contrast stand such women as Katie Richards O'Hare, a moving force and financier in the establishment of Commonwealth College at Mena, Arkansas, during the 1920s. Commonwealth took top billing as one of the most radical experiments in labor education in the twentieth-century South. One writer described O'Hare as "a feminine dynamo" and "a fiery reformer who led the fight in the 1920s to stop prison garment shops from competing with free-enterprise clothing manufacturers." She enjoyed the distinction of having been "the first woman member of the International Association of Machinists"; she had also done time in the Missouri State Penitentiary for violation of the wartime Espionage Act. Convicted in 1918 for delivering a speech against conscription, she was pardoned by President Woodrow Wilson after she had served fourteen months.[77] Another radical female, red-haired nineteen-year-old Charlotte Moskowitz of Syracuse, New York, arrived at Commonwealth in 1927, at which time she was "about the only outspoken voice for the Communist cause" at the school.[78]

During the depression decade, Ida Mae Sledge, a Wellesley College graduate from Memphis, Tennessee, was an organizer for the International Ladies Garment Workers. In 1937 she targeted Tupelo, Mississippi; her objective was to unionize the thousand or so workers, mostly women, in the four garment mills. On two occasions, locals escorted her to the city limits and warned her that "blood would flow unless she quit coming back"; but she persevered. The National Labor Relations Board (NLRB) filed charges, which led Congressman John E. Rankin to complain that "the board was persecuting his town." Meanwhile the Tupelo Chamber of Commerce secured a charter from the state of Mississippi for a local union that soon claimed to represent 90 percent of the labor force. With NLRB action pending, Sledge left the battered remains of her local union in the hands of Sarah Hunt Potter, a hometown girl, and moved on to Baltimore to organize another drive.[79]

Although divisions occurred, occasionally along class lines and even in reformist organizations, they seemed almost insignificant when compared to the distance that separated activists of all classes from many other southern women of the era. Private battles and just plain drudgery, not public crusades, often sapped their vitality. The National Emergency Council reported in 1938, for example, that tenancy prevailed among 53 percent of the South's farm families. Income per person among the average tenant family stood at $73 per annum, whereas among sharecroppers it ranged from $38 to $87.[80] Women of the tenant class, black and white, occupied the lowest economic rung in the South. As a group they confronted the most difficult circumstances to be found among agrarian women.

In 1939 a North Carolina farm tenant, Mary Green, who described herself as "tired, wore out, and ready for the joys of heaven," detailed the cruelty of her husband and the loutishness of her stepsons. The principal rebellious act of her long-suffering life seems to have occurred when her spouse sold her pet calf without consulting her and denied her the proceeds: "When he santered 'round the house with no more to say, I just flew mad all over. I run in the house and grabbed a gallon jar. I put it in a tow sack right quick and ran through the house to the kitchen door. Right thar I met Pap fair, and I just up and bashed him good over the head with that jar. When he dropped [not dead] I got my dollar and went on to the fields to my hoein'."[81] Usually the situation was reversed, as wife beating was much more common than physical attacks by females on their male counterparts. Few southern "gentlemen," however, spoke as freely as a white logger out of

Alabama: "A woman's like a dumb animal—like a cow or a bitch dog. You got to frail 'em with a stick now an' then to make 'em look up to you."[82]

Oppressed southern women often demonstrated a fierce allegiance to their southern heritage. The writer Sherwood Anderson described a South Carolina woman, a weaver for thirty years, who had entered the mills as a twelve year old. She attended a class to learn to read and write after she had put in a ten-hour workday. "I had asked her . . . a logical question I thought . . . why she should bother," Anderson recounted. "She said that she had been told that to have many illiterates in the state would be a disgrace to the state. 'I didn't want to do anything to disgrace my state,' she said proudly."[83]

Meanwhile, southern middle- and upper-class female activists and reformers, most of them town and city dwellers, traveled at will, sometimes drove their own automobiles, enjoyed modest expense accounts, presumably earned and controlled their own income, and spent little time with domestic chores. Before rural electrification their less fortunate sisters carried water, chopped wood, cooked, canned, did the washing with a tub and a board, and ironed (with real "irons" that had to be heated on wood stoves). "Yes, we had running water," a woman from Blanco, Texas, reported; "I always said we had running water because I grabbed those two buckets up and ran the two hundred yards to the house with them."[84]

"They wear these farm women out pretty fast," a denizen of the Hill Country of Texas observed. Along with their arduous household chores, they not infrequently suffered chronic health problems, some occasioned by pregnancy and childbirth. Deprived of adequate medical care, they often experienced perineal tears. During the 1930s, when the federal government dispatched physicians to this section to conduct a survey, they discovered that 158 of the 275 females they examined had "tears so bad that it is difficult to see how they stand on their feet." "But," Robert A. Caro, President Lyndon B. Johnson's biographer, wrote, "they *were* standing on their feet, and doing all the chores that Hill Country wives had always done—hauling the water, hauling the wood, canning, washing, ironing, helping with the shearing, the plowing and the picking."[85]

A woman who had grown up in South Carolina during this era recalled her mother's strength. The family's husband and father worked for a railroad, which required him to leave on Sundays and return on Saturdays. Alone and without help, his wife, who weighed about a hundred pounds, worked the land. "Lockie Ann rose at dawn, milked two cows, fed two horses, three to four pigs, and a yard full of chickens," her daughter wrote, "and returned to fix the morning breakfast before the dew had dried on the grass." She took with her the children who were too little "to help in the fields," and they played on a quilt as she tended "a big garden, a tobacco patch, or fields of green beans." When her daughters became teenagers, "little extras for them [like having their hair done at beauty shops in town] came from egg money or milk she sold to the milk truck and from the weekly house cleaning for the local high school principal." Lockie Ann "never visited a doctor, never complained, never gossiped, and would never make a debt." She believed in God but had no time for Bible reading. When her neighbors came to visit, she offered them "popcorn, baked apples, chestnuts, and *moonshine*." During the winter months she pieced quilts. For entertainment she might "dance to the fiddles at a Saturday night 'get together.'" While others looked askance, "she allowed her daughters to wear shorts to the grocery store and sun-back dresses to church." When her "man" left on Sunday, she "told him she loved him but she called him [an] S.O.B. when he offended her."[86]

Factory women of this era, as well as farm wives, knew hardship; they also experienced discrimination because of their gender and their class. Discontent over long hours and work discipline had produced several walkouts at the J.P. Bemberg Corporation, a German-owned rayon plant at Elizabethton, Tennessee, during the 1920s. On 12 March 1929, however, Margaret Bowen had led a walkout at the sister plant, Glanzstoff, which set off a general strike. No union existed when the standoff began. Described as a girl with black hair and high cheekbones, suggesting Indian heritage, Bowen had previously been employed at a silk mill in Old Hickory, Tennessee; but company representatives had lured her to Elizabethton with the promise of high wages. On the day of the walkout the superintendent had attempted to separate her from the women whose grievances she had voiced. At noon on that same day she led approximately 340 women out of the factory; other workers, both male and female, soon joined them. Eventually about 3,000 struck the plants, but they faced almost insuperable odds. Arrayed against them, as was to be expected, was the company's officialdom. Local entrepreneurs and the political establishment at the county, city, and state levels allied with the owners and managers. The former groups turned on their own kind—that is, the native-born white workers— and supported the German owners. Outside union representatives served the mountain people poorly, and Anna Weinstock, the first female federal negotiator, sold them out. Work resumed on the company's terms.[87]

Females constituted approximately 40 percent of the workers in the rayon plants at Elizabethton, where they toiled 56 hours per week at pay scales in the range of $8.64 to $10.08 (with the average about $8.96), which was roughly 16 to 18 cents per hour. The best wages topped out between 25 and 30 cents. Not only were women paid less than the men (approximately 65 percent of what men could expect), but they also faced rules that discriminated against them on the basis of sex. One of the so-called hard rules specified that females should only be allowed ten minutes in the washroom during the morning, with another ten in the afternoon. The women workers also had to secure a pass from their forelady before they could use the facilities. If a supervisor determined that they spent too much time on such breaks, they lost pay; they might also be dismissed. No such regulations applied to the male workers. Menstruating women, especially, found such regulations unnecessarily onerous.[88]

Elsewhere in the Southern Appalachians, nonfactory women likewise suffered during the depression years. Although it was extremely uncommon, an occasional female worked as a coke drawer or a miner during the interwar period. In the best of times, mining families lived from hand to mouth; their circumstances, bad enough in prosperous times, grew worse during the nation's economic catastrophe of the 1930s. A Toms Creek, Virginia, miner recalled that during the especially difficult month of July 1932 he had worked only one day a week, which netted him $1.96. During most months he earned approximately $12.00. Out of that, $8.00 went to pay the rent on company housing, plus another dollar for electricity; his family sustained itself by gardening. The deprivations of children strained everyone's emotions. After watching five die from dysentery in a twenty-four-hour period, one company doctor cried and said that what they needed was food.[89]

The Reverend Clarence Meyer, a Benedictine priest from St. Bernard's Abbey at Cullman, Alabama, conducted a ministry in the mining camps of southwest Virginia, northeast Tennessee, and southeast Kentucky during the late 1920s and early 1930s. He remembered seeing miners and their families "living in burlap tents on the top of a mountain in the dead of winter rooting in the wilds for something to eat."[90] The journalist Lorena Hickok, working under New Deal auspices, reported from Clay County, Kentucky, that when men and boys passed one cabin, they "pulled their caps down over their eyes." They explained the reason thus: "Well, you see the women folks in that thar place hain't got no clothes at all. Even their rags is clean wore out and gone!"[91] James Still's *River of Earth*, set in the mining camps of Appalachia during the Great Depression, tells the story of a family confronting starvation that rivals John Steinbeck's *The Grapes of Wrath*. Steinbeck based his novel on the experience of thousands of Arkies and Okies who forsook the Dust Bowl and made the often futile trek to California.[92] The hopelessness that wives and mothers must have felt in such predicaments defies description.

During the Great Depression, poverty granted no immunity to women and their families in southern towns and cities, any more than it did to those in rural areas and remote mining enclaves. The historian Julia Kirk Blackwelder's comparative case study of San Antonio's Anglo, black, and

Mexican women during the 1930s in an urban area that she describes as "one of America's poorest" is uniquely insightful. "The caste system based on race, color, or ethnicity was a dominant force shaping women's lives," Blackwelder observes. "Both employers and relief agencies discriminated among women on the basis of caste, and the kind and the degree of discrimination deeply affected women's abilities to cope." Anglo women fared best, according to Blackwelder, and blacks, accustomed to being poor, cooperated to survive circumstances that were all too familiar. Mexican-American females, however, not only dealt with grinding deprivation but also feared deportation, which kept many of them from seeking relief from governmental agencies. They likewise found that their old standby—employment as migrant agricultural workers—declined as the economy bottomed out and responded ever so slowly to recovery efforts. Because they had no solid employment history in an urban environment, their feeble attempts to ride out hard times in San Antonio proved not merely difficult but truly pitiful. Unlike urban blacks, who had some foundation of sharing and support on which to draw, the Hispanics could not count on benevolence from their own ethnic community.[93]

Meanwhile in towns and cities across the South a contingent of black and white women, even in the face of the national economic catastrophe, maintained the give-and-take cadence of their customary relationship—that is, black as domestic and white as employer.[94] Economic conditions of the 1930s exacerbated the double hit that black females had routinely taken because of race and gender. All the same the young among them still looked to a brighter future and cherished dreams; a talented few enjoyed successes. For example, the performer and writer Maya Angelou, born Marguerite Johnson on 4 April 1929 in St. Louis, Missouri, lived briefly with her parents on the West Coast; but the future author of the poignant autobiography *I Know Why the Caged Bird Sings* spent much of her childhood in Stamps, Arkansas, with her paternal grandmother. "One would say of my life—born loser—had to be: from a broken family, raped at eight, unwed mother at sixteen. . . . It's a fact but it's not the truth. In the black community, however bad it looks, there's a lot of love and so much humor," Angelou observed during an interview that followed the publication of that book.[95]

With its promises of fame and fortune, the entertainment world beckoned to the younger generation. An authority on blues-singing women, Ruth A. Banes, writes that "the most successful classic blues singers were southern black women, and their themes are written predominantly from a woman's point of view." Most of them "died poor and unrecognized." Bessie Smith, from Chattanooga, Tennessee, enjoyed some popularity in the North, but her true fans, black and white, came from the South. Her career declined during the Depression years, and she died in an automobile accident in 1937.[96] Billie Holiday, a native of Baltimore, also achieved recognition. She even recorded with Benny Goodman in 1933, had a major film role in *New Orleans* (1947), and along the way dared to sing a protest song, "Strange Fruit," about lynching. A beautiful woman who usually wore a gardenia in her hair, she succumbed to the drug addiction that affected both her health and her career.[97]

Josephine Baker, who hailed from St. Louis, Missouri, debuted during the 1920s as a chorus dancer in the black night clubs of New York City. Around the middle of the decade she moved to France, where she was featured in revues at the Folies Bergère and other Parisian establishments. After garnering international recognition she returned to the United States in 1936 to perform in the "Ziegfeld Follies." Critical of her native country's treatment of blacks during the 1950s, she discovered a somewhat different social climate in the United States a decade later; she, too, had mellowed along the way. Baker participated in the march on Washington, D. C., in August 1963, and she played Carnegie Hall to raise funds for the civil rights movement. She lived until 1975 after having spent much of her adult life in France.[98]

The South also produced what the jazz historian Rosetta Reitz calls "the hottest all-women's jazz band of the 1940s." The International Sweethearts of Rhythm, whose origins were in the Piney Woods Country Life School located in the Mississippi Delta, was "the first racially integrated women's band, and it lasted for over a decade." The band played Harlem's Apollo Theater in September 1941, as well as many times thereafter, and enjoyed the support of such greats as Louis Armstrong and Count Basie. Laurence Flifton Jones, the founder of the Piney Woods School, organized the group from among his charges in 1937 and sent them off to earn money for the institution in much the same manner as the famous Fisk Jubilee Singers from Nashville, Tennessee. Although Piney Woods was a foster home and the only place that the racially and ethnically mixed girls in the band could really call home, they rebelled against Jones in 1941. This development was hardly surprising, because touring deprived them of educational opportunities, which they resented, and Jones was miserly with the money they earned. When the seventeen original members cut their ties with Piney Woods, the band seemingly flourished. Its makeup changed over the next decade as some members dropped out and replacements moved in to fill their slots. During World War II the band joined forces with the USO to entertain—mostly white troops—in Europe. By the 1950s, women musicians like the Sweethearts had lost whatever favor they had enjoyed with American audiences for a relatively brief interlude, so their engagements dwindled.[99]

Well before Congress had formally declared war, the United States, with a realistic president at the helm who understood the dangers that lay before him and his country, had been preparing for hostilities. At the same time, unrealistic voices cried out for peace at any price and excoriated Franklin Delano Roosevelt for his leadership. When the news of Pearl Harbor came across the airways on that fateful Sunday of 7 December 1941, southern women, like those elsewhere across the nation and the planet, braced themselves for what lay ahead. This was hardly the first time, nor would it be the last, when mothers, wives, sisters, and friends all over Dixie watched their men prepare to do battle. War was hell on the home front, too; it tried the souls of females in myriad ways. All the same, most women drew on the same natural residual strength that steeled them in their everyday lives as they prepared to deal with what the evolving international circumstances had thrust upon them.

"I was listening to the radio," recalled Tennessean Grace Paysinger Roland, "when all of a sudden the news of Pearl Harbor came loud and clear. . . . I have never been more depressed. I knew just about what that meant for our family of boys." A few weeks later, one of them, Charles, came home from Washington, D.C., where he had been working. "I shall never forget the day C.P. [Grace's husband, Charles's father] took him to Alamo [a small Tennessee town where he was registered] to report and he was made officer in charge of all the Crockett County boys who were leaving that day." The cold temperature and "snow on the ground" only "added to the dreariness and depression. I hardly knew where I was and what I was doing except that I cried and prayed all day."[100]

Shortly after the United States declared war on Japan as well as the other Axis powers, General Julius Franklin Howell of Bristol, Tennessee, representing the surviving band of United Confederate Veterans whom he commanded, assured President Roosevelt of their support: "In behalf of the small remnant of the six hundred thousand soldiers who served under General Robert E. Lee and his Lieutenants, during the War between the States in 1861-5, . . . [I] express our unbounded confidence in you as our Chief Magistrate and . . . assure you of our complete loyalty in this crisis of our Nation." The old soldier's letter reportedly moved the president deeply.[101]

Howell and his comrades may have changed their mind about the Union, but he had not altered his opinion on the proper venue for women. In October 1940 a very excited Howell had adjourned the Fiftieth Annual Reunion because General R.P. Scott, who was in the chair at the time, "allowed a woman to speak for a veteran whose voice could not be heard." Howell was also irritated that one of his predecessors had conferred a general's commission on a female. Although Howell praised the work of the United Daughters of the Confederacy, he still maintained that "it was never intended by our earlier comrades that women should be granted military authority over us old boys of the war." He also declared that "it has always been repugnant to me to confer on any of our fine southern women a military title. To me it is lowering of refined womanhood."[102]

General Howell, whose chief enemy was old age, survived World War II. In 1948 he celebrated his 102d birthday at a gala attended by his friend the actress Mary Pickford, and he felt feisty enough to dance the Virginia reel with pretty Jean McIntyre, a seventeen-year-old student at Virginia Intermont College.[103] His innermost thoughts about the contributions that southern women made to the war effort seem to have gone unrecorded. Although the passage of the better part of a century had changed the circumstances of armed conflict, females of this generation met the challenges of their time and place with no less determination than had those who had gone before them.[104]

Southern women had always made substantial contributions to war efforts, including those of 1861-65, 1898, and 1917-18; they expanded the level and range of feminine activities as war ravaged the planet. The intensification of courtships and the usual rash of hastily arranged weddings and abbreviated honeymoons and the proliferation of births accompanied the country's formal entry into World War II. Females did their volunteer time with the Red Cross, the United Service Organizations, and similar associations. They likewise mailed morale-boosting letters and care packages. Sometimes, though, having found comfort in the arms of others, they fired off Dear John letters.[105]

Very few women came through the war unaffected, not even those in relatively remote rural areas of the heartland. Much-feared telegrams from Washington, reporting that loved ones had been killed or wounded or were otherwise missing in action, made their way into hollows and bayous with the same relative ease that they traveled down treelined village streets and broad city avenues. Sometimes families knew only enough to be terrified. Remembering the horrible days of December 1944, Grace Paysinger Roland wrote that "Christmas of that dreadful year came and all the other children were home for the occasion [except Charles] and I had planned a big feast, a turkey we had raised and all the trimmings." Circumstances, however, cast a pallor over the festivities, for "just two days before we learned that the 99th division had been surrounded in the Battle of the Bulge and that the snow was from a foot to four feet deep from drifting in that section of Belgium." Of their son and brother they "only knew that he was a captain in the 99th division. . . . The radio was bringing news of this terrible fight and telling that only a few of this division were able to retreat back to Elsenborn." Not until February 1945, when a card arrived saying that he was safe but little else because of censorship, did the family know for sure that he had survived.[106]

This story had a happy ending; others did not. A native of southwest

Virginia has often recalled the grief that struck her family when a troopship went down and her eighteen-year-old cousin was lost forever. There was no body, which only added to the tragedy; relatives could not even give him a decent burial.[107] In her last days, Eva Parker Ripley reportedly stood weeping on the porch of her country home in northeast Tennessee, saying that she wished she "could see her baby" one more time. She died before her younger son, who had received a battlefield commission with the Fifth Army in Italy, returned to East Tennessee several months later.[108]

Though insignificant by comparison with lives lost or jeopardized, shortages of every imaginable consumer item made daily existence difficult; and the rationing system reached into the female psyche. With her husband off to war, a Middle Tennessee farm woman, aged twenty-four and with a child of her own, remembered that she had become "Big Mama" when a sister and sister-in-law, both pregnant and both the recent brides of soldiers, joined her household. To supplement their diets and to have a little variety, she kept chickens. She also had an old automobile. When enough gas could be hoarded, the women and children enjoyed the luxury of overnight trips away from the farm. When such rare outings occurred, Big Mama caught the chickens, put them in a coop, and strapped them on the back of the car. Of such importance was the well-being of the feathery fowls that they went wherever the humans went.[109]

Southern women kept the home fires burning in traditional fashion, but they also ventured into somewhat more unconventional areas during the war years. They constituted approximately 40 percent of the on-line force at Holston Ordnance Works (HOW) in Kingsport, Tennessee, which manufactured RDX and Composition B. At the end of hostilities, HOW was the world's largest manufacturer of explosives. Many of the employees had not previously been exposed to so much as a high-school chemistry class, but for the duration of the war, not one single death occurred at the plant as the result of an explosion, and only three for any other reason. Women also helped to fill the ranks of labor at Oak Ridge, Tennessee, where the Y-12 plant produced the U-235 that went into the atomic bomb dropped on Hiroshima.[110] They could also be found brandishing welding equipment in heavy industries like shipbuilding at Pascagoula, Mississippi, and Mobile, Alabama; riveting tail sections of military aircraft at the Glenn L. Martin Company in Baltimore, Maryland; and manufacturing all manner of war materiel at numerous locations below the Mason-Dixon line.[111]

Dixie's daughters also joined the armed forces and auxiliary units and received assignments as noncombatants, but where Mars presided, those of either gender could be caught in harm's way. The same sense of patriotism that was found in young men also manifested itself in their female counterparts, and there was no dearth of adventuresome spirits in either sex. The first Women's Army Auxiliary Corps (WAAC) unit to be readied for overseas service contained southern women. WAACs, southerners among them, also served in the Philippine Islands and, in some capacity or other, almost everywhere else that the United States dispatched troops.[112] The sister of United States Attorney General Janet Reno, speaking about the Wood sisters, said, "None of the women in the family [out of Florida] ever did what women were supposed to do." Her Aunt Daisy was a World War II army nurse who landed in North Africa and followed General George Patton's army through Sicily, and her Aunt Winifred took to the air with the Women's Airforce Service Pilots (WASP).[113]

The idea for the WASPs originated with Jacqueline Cochran, a pilot who had won the Bendix transcontinental air race in 1938, outdistancing the nine other pilots, all of whom were men. In March 1939 she received her second Harmon Trophy, which at that time represented the stellar award for American aviators. To say that she had risen from humble circumstances is a gross understatement. Abandoned as an infant, she had been taken in by itinerants who barely scraped together an existence working sawmill jobs along the Florida-Georgia line. Jackie created her own identity, even selecting her birthday, 11 May, and adjusting the year from 1906 to 1910 at will. According to one account, "Jackie got a kick out of telling about going to work in the mills at age eight for six cents an hour on a twelve-hour shift, and about the good Catholic priest who saw such promise in a skinny, little blonde girl." She considered the Catholic Church a "good-luck talisman" for the remainder of her life.[114]

Cochran tried nursing for a while, but "one night after the long and bloody ordeal of delivering a malnourished mother of a sick, scrawny baby," she decided to try her luck in the beauty business. While she was working at a shop in Pensacola, she met fliers from the Naval Aviation Station. The planes, as well as the young men, excited her. By 1932 she had made her way to Miami Beach, where she became acquainted with Floyd Bostwick Odlum, who was approximately fourteen years her senior. He was wealthy, and he was married. Odlum bet her the price of the lessons that she could not earn her private pilot's license in six weeks; she did it in three. On her birthday in 1936 they were united in holy matrimony.[115]

Life magazine reported on 19 July 1943: "The time-honored belief that Army flying is for men only has gone into the ash can. At Avenger Field, near Sweetwater, Texas, girls are flying military planes in a way that Army officers a year or so ago would never have thought possible." Jacqueline Cochran had persuaded General Henry H. ("Hap") Arnold of the practicality of training female pilots. Nancy Love and other women aviators had already formed the Women's Auxiliary Ferrying Squadron (WAFS), which flourished under the command of Major General Barton K. Yount. The difference between the WAFSs and the WASPs was that the military trained the latter. To qualify for the program a woman had to be a pilot between the ages of twenty-one and thirty-four with at least thirty-five hours of flying time in light planes.[116] In June 1944 General Arnold terminated all recruiting efforts as well as the training program at Avenger Field; those already in flight school were allowed to finish. By the end of 1944, after an ongoing debate and a raging controversy over the proper role for women, the WASPs were being phased out. Women aviators would not become part of the armed services, they would have no benefits as veterans (a wrong that was finally righted in November 1977), and they were being grounded.[117]

Between the two groups, the WASPs and the WAFSs, female pilots had flown virtually everything in the U.S. arsenal. Of the southern women fliers—and southern women were well represented—Cornelia Fort of Nashville, Tennessee, became one of the more famous by virtue of her untimely death in a crash.[118] When they lost their lives in the service of their country—in the line of duty—the federal government provided no burial insurance and made no arrangements. A former WASP recalled that in at least one instance the women themselves took up a collection to send a girl's remains home for interment.[119] Indeed, during these years, American society sent and women in turn received what Elizabeth Fox-Genovese refers to as "mixed messages."[120] An understated phrase, its two words, though brief, represent a fitting commentary on the passage of southern women through the troubled decades of the thirties and forties. The short-lived but relative calm and the considerable prosperity of the postwar era hardly erased the ambivalence.

President Franklin Delano Roosevelt declared 7 December 1941 "a date which will live in infamy," and in one way or another, it punctuated the personal histories of virtually all Americans, male and female, who lived through it. Before America formally entered World War II, the nation's economy had shown infrequent but faint blushes of prosperity, and southerners no less than other Americans had felt the ameliorating influences of the New Deal's various alphabetical programs. Still, the Great Depression had already placed its irrevocable stamp on the rising generation of young adults before the challenges of what was to be a monstrous global war made its indelible mark. When the furies of bellicosity had spent themselves, not just the individuals who had made the crossing from peace to war and back to peace again, but indeed the world itself would never be quite the same.

❧

SEVEN

A Time to Get,
and a Time to Lose

I n August 1945 the horrors of the global war, after grinding on for half a decade in seemingly endless fashion, came to an abrupt halt, punctuated by the detonation in quick succession of two atomic weapons. Americans breathed an almost audible sigh of relief, and postwar readjustment began. For the American South the next five decades brought what one eminent scholar has termed the Improbable Era and another has labeled the Promised Land.[1] As the crucible for the civil rights movement of the 1950s and 1960s, the region experienced its "Second Reconstruction." Political realignments also gave rise to a relatively viable two-party system. Furthermore, economic changes, wrought by the forces of modernization, visibly transformed the South. Few would deny that the region and its people have been affected by the winds of change that have swept over it. Southerners, however, have performed the masterful feat of publicly accepting integration, sometimes voting Republican, and embracing "progress," but they have done so without privately renouncing "tradition."[2] Even as the region and its people, during the post-World War II era, have moved ever closer to the American mainstream, the coexistence of progress and tradition, along with the paradox of change and continuity, has figured prominently in the lives of southern women.

As fighting men returned to farms, villages, towns, and cities all across the nation and as some families arranged to have the remains of soldiers who had died overseas retrieved from foreign burial grounds and reinterred in native soil, personal readjustments proved necessary. Women who in wartime had risen to all manner of personal and public challenges often reverted, by choice or because of circumstance, to the customary roles. The advent of peace, however much most people of both sexes had desired it, meant fewer jobs for females as well as less challenging and lower-paying employment possibilities. World War II itself had imposed severe restraints

on the home front, and most women had found even the possibility of travel severely proscribed because of the priority that the military and defense
industries had on transportation systems. The rationing of gasoline, tires,
and spare parts limited the movement of those who were fortunate enough
to have an automobile at their disposal, and public accommodations were
jammed to capacity.

Kitty Wells, born Muriel Ellen Deason, who became the first female
superstar in country music, had hardly begun her career when it was inter-
rupted by two babies and the war. A native of Nashville, she married Johnny Wright in 1937. During the depression she ironed shirts in a clothing
factory for $9.00 a week. Muriel performed with her husband, his brother
Jack, and a few others known first as the Tennessee Hillbillies and later as
the Tennessee Mountain Boys. The gasoline rationing of World War II disrupted personal appearances for the struggling entertainers, but by 1943
Johnny had renamed his wife Kitty Wells, which he had taken from an old
folk song. Kitty Wells sometimes joined Johnny and Jack on radio station
WNOX's "Midday Merry-Go-Round" in Knoxville. The touring began in
earnest after the war, and by 1953 Kitty Wells hit the top of the chart with
"It Wasn't God Who Made Honky-Tonk Angels," a female perspective on
infidelity. She had been less than enthusiastic about the song but had
agreed to record it because, as she put it, "at least we can make union pay
scale out of the session."[3] Her success inspired countless numbers of would-
be female country-music entertainers throughout the South and paved the
way for such stars as Dottie West, Patsy Cline, Loretta Lynn, Tammy Wy-
nette, and Dolly Parton.[4] The "Queen of Country Music," known for her
signature song about wayward women, celebrated the fiftieth anniversary
of her marriage to Johnny Wright in 1987.[5]

Hearth and home, not honky-tonks, remained in the ascendancy, and
the family retained its firm grip on southerners just as it did on other Americans. When young adults no longer had to study war, they set about creating or reestablishing households. Making war gave way to making love;
making bombs, to making babies. Men who had experienced and survived
the barbarism of their times not infrequently became tender loving fathers;
those who had been called upon to destroy human life also found within
themselves the capacity to nurture their young. The rising birthrate of the
immediate postwar period, the "baby boom," produced a new generation—
a coddled and pampered one according to some. Yet life hardly spared them
the troubles of their times. They never knew a world without the nuclear
threat, and they had either reached or were rapidly approaching middle age
before the Cold War—the life-and-death struggle between capitalism and
communism, the East and the West—had seemingly waned. The generation of Americans that carried the nation through World War II produced

sons who would become all too familiar with the rice paddies of Vietnam and who might turn on the government that would send them into such a quagmire and daughters who ran the gamut from beauty queens to bra burners.

The women's liberation movement of the postwar decades fomented a quiet rebellion that gave new meaning to "the battle of the sexes" but ultimately failed in its bid to secure the ratification of the Equal Rights Amendment to the Constitution. Ironically, the United States had foisted such a measure on occupied Japan. After the Japanese had surrendered aboard the battleship Missouri, the reconstruction of their defeated country went forward under the auspices of an American general, Douglas MacArthur. He had been born on 26 January 1880 in Little Rock, Arkansas, which officially rendered him a southerner. His mother, Mary Pinkney Hardy, hailed from Virginia; his wife, Jean Marie Faircloth, was from Tennessee. Acting as plenipotentiary suited the general, whose fortunes had risen considerably since his ordered departure from the Philippines on 11 March 1942, when he had promised, "I shall return." Somewhat less well known is the fact that his wife and young son, Arthur, evacuated the islands with him. They had been living in tunnels on Corregidor, dodging incoming Japanese bombs and shells. Mrs. MacArthur joined her husband, their only child, a nursemaid, and a few officers aboard the four small PT boats that made the escape. They eluded "Japanese planes and destroyers, suffered seasickness and slept on a sodden mattress. Eventually, they were picked up on one of the southern islands and transferred to an American bomber for the long trip to Australia."[6] A few years later, MacArthur, acting on behalf of the United States government, imposed a liberal constitution on the defeated Japanese; it included Article 24, which guaranteed individual dignity and equality of the sexes within marriage.[7]

Meanwhile, back in America, southern families had been welcoming their war-weary sons. Some of the South's World War II veterans returned with foreign wives in tow or surprised their relatives with the news that the women would soon be arriving. Indeed, the British alone eventually exported some sixty thousand American war brides. Although Britons generally liked the Yanks, British males had complained during the war that the GIs were "overpaid, oversexed and over here."[8] As late as the 1980s the British Wives Club, a contingent of Trans-Atlantic Brides and Parents Association, was still holding monthly meetings in northeast Tennessee. A bride out of Maidenhead, Berkshire, England, remembered that "the hot weather, the accents of the people, and the food" had presented her with the greatest challenges. One from Nottingham recalled that when people she had visited called out to her, "'You all come back!,' she thought they meant right then and there. Not wanting to displease them, she did—right then!" Another one, who hailed from Mansfield in Nottinghamshire, declared: "I thought the USA was the land of milk and honey, but I found out there were poor people as well as rich. . . . At four in the morning the headlights of the cab shined on a little 'shack' that [her husband] had brought her home to." She confessed that she had cried when she arrived at her new home near Kingsport, Tennessee, and found "no inside plumbing, [it was] heated by a fireplace, and the walls were papered with newsprint!" Almost forty years after first setting foot on American soil, these women, according to one of their daughters, discussed "politics, England, music, England, flights, England, television, England, airfare, England, food, England, Queen Mother, England, England, and England."[9]

Even as newcomers like these war brides were feeling their way toward adjustment in Dixie, a significant number of natives of the region were abandoning it to pursue better lives elsewhere; among them were World War II veterans who had ventured far enough from home to recognize that possibilities existed outside the South. In a 1958 story published in *Look*, Hodding Carter, the Pulitzer Prize-winning editor of the Greenville, Mississippi, *Delta Democrat-Times*, lamented that "the ghosts of departed people are walking the dusty roads of the Deep South."[10] The shifting population of the Southern Appalachians alone from 1940 to 1970 rivaled the displacement of the Irish, Italians, and other immigrants who had abandoned the rural villages of Europe and relocated in urban America during the nineteenth and early twentieth centuries.[11] Such southerners as the fictional Nevels family and its mother, Gertie, in Harriette Arnow's *The Dollmaker*, which was first published in 1954 and dealt with transplanted Appalachians, had moved to such northern cities as Detroit during World War II.[12] Wags in the North had their fun with the aspiring southerners. In spite of the ridicule that was sometimes heaped upon them, the transplants, especially the white ones, made the adjustment and eventually settled into comfortable working-class or middle-class neighborhoods in the North and the Midwest. Plenty of real people—both white and black, men and women—had been making the trek since the late nineteenth century; the migration of the postwar era simply received more attention from the press.

The media's representation of women in American society during the 1950s, just as its treatment of the great southern diaspora, merits scrutiny. Yet, manipulation of the media to promote one viewpoint or another has not been without precedent. In 1963 Betty Friedan, experiencing her first but not last epiphany, published *The Feminine Mystique*, that clarion call of the women's liberation movement. She claimed that "in the postwar era . . . journalists, educators, advertisers, and social scientists had pulled women into the home with an ideological stranglehold, 'the feminine mystique.'" The model that she railed against "held that women could 'find fulfillment only in sexual passivity, male domination, and nurturing maternal love.' It denied 'women careers or any commitment outside the home.'" The villains, she alleged, were the editors and writers for mass-circulation women's magazines.[13] The historian Joanne Meyerowitz counters that "the feminine mystique" represented "only one piece of the postwar cultural puzzle." In contradiction to Friedan's contention, the popular literature that Meyerowitz sampled "advocated both the domestic and the nondomestic, sometimes in the same sentence . . . [and] domestic ideals coexisted in ongoing tension with an ethos of individual achievement that celebrated nondomestic activity, individual striving, public service, and public success."[14]

The Feminine Mystique, dedicated to Friedan's spouse and three children, may have provided a fairly accurate portrayal of the existence of some middle-class suburban women. In all likelihood it more nearly reflected the author's own experience and her awakening, rather than that of American women in general. The world did not know it at the time the book was published, but would later learn, that Betty Friedan, who became president of the National Organization for Women (NOW), had been a battered wife. Indeed, in 1969 her face was so bruised from a beating that a professional makeup artist had to be summoned at the last moment to prepare her for a public engagement. On 14 May 1969 she finally divorced her husband, Carl.[15] Meyerowitz's reassessment represents a much-needed breath of fresh air, for clearly the postwar era, despite the influence of the "feminine mystique" and the book by that title, hardly signaled the consignment of all American women to domestic dementia.

Still, domesticity and its more favorable attributes mattered a great deal to most adults of the 1950s. New housing construction could hardly keep pace with the demand as Americans transformed hastily built tract dwellings into private sanctuaries and their own personal showplaces. With the deprivation of the depression years and the shortages of wartime behind it, the country went on a decade-long shopping binge. The end of rationing and the reconversion to a consumer market meant that many housewives throughout Dixie could embrace the chrome-and-enamel world of the fifties and buy their Maytags, Frigidaires, and dinette sets. Plenty of good ole boys scrounged enough money for a down payment on their first Chevrolets and Fords and, in a great leap of faith, plunged headlong into installment buying. Enough of them had made the transition from farm to factory and a regular income to take the risk. The men prided themselves on their jobs and their homes (some of which were purchased with Veterans Administration assistance), mowed the lawns on Saturday, and played with the kids. The women gave birth to their babies in local hospitals, joined the PTA (Parent-Teacher Association) and book clubs, and taught vacation

Bible schools. The more socially assertive among them fought their way into the Junior League. Families attended church on Sunday mornings, visited the relatives on Sunday afternoons, and plastered themselves in front of televisions to watch the "Ed Sullivan Show" on Sunday evenings. As children, "baby boomers" thought only their parents were dull; but as they matured, they came to realize that the older generation had behaved in essentially the same way all across the United States. Having experienced both the depression and the war, which provided them with enough excitement to last a lifetime, and determined at long last to find stability in an uncertain world, adults "nested" with a vengeance.[16]

All over the region, families produced daughters as well as sons; and despite the relative prosperity of the fifties and the much-vaunted idea of the privileged younger generation, plenty of parents gave little enough thought to their offsprings' futures. Among a fair number of parents, prevailing wisdom held that what had been good enough for themselves would be good enough for their children. If fathers and mothers had little ambition for the males, they had even less for the females. At best they might endorse high-school typing and shorthand for their daughters—and home economics, of course. Then the same parents happily anticipated "their girls'" marriages to "good" men (that is, men who worked) and the arrival of grandbabies with all due speed.

Sweet dispositions and good looks hastened "girls" on this prescribed feminine odyssey. The novelist Walker Percy, speaking through a male character in The Moviegoer, tells about a secretary—Sharon Kincaid of Eufa[u]la, Alabama—whose "bottom is so beautiful that once as she crossed the room to the cooler [he] felt [his] eyes smart with tears of gratitude." Sharon was "one of those village beauties of which the South is so prodigal. From the sleaziest house in the sleaziest town, from the loins of redneck pa and rockface ma spring these lovelies, these rosy-cheeked Anglo-Saxon lovelies, by the million." Percy claimed they were "commoner than sparrows, and like sparrows they are at home in the streets, in the parks, on doorsteps. No one marvels at them; no one holds them dear."[17]

The admixture of dry humor and stark realism that is found in Percy's work also appears in the writings of such southern women authors as Flannery O'Connor and Carson McCullers of Georgia and Eudora Welty from Mississippi. The characters and circumstances in the stories that they spin remind readers that although the South is often considered an ultraconservative region, it retains a tremendous toleration for personal differences and peculiar behavior. In The Member of the Wedding, published in 1946 and adapted to the screen and stage during the early 1950s, McCullers employs the symbolism of alienated adolescence and a mill-town environment to examine individual emotions within the larger society. Welty's early characters seemed unable to overcome the blighting effects of isolation; later ones she cast in extremely complex familial relationships. Such works as *Delta Wedding* (1946) and *Losing Battles* (1970) reflect her interest in the southern family. Welty reportedly once said: "We always took care of our eccentrics. There was one fellow who used to run up and down the street, thinking he was a streetcar, and nobody bothered him." Someone supposedly asked O'Connor why southerners wrote about freaks, to which she responded that southerners were still able to recognize them when they saw them.[18]

Members of a younger generation of female writers that includes such practitioners as Gail Godwin, Lee Smith, and Bobbie Ann Mason have proved themselves as adept as some of their predecessors in dealing with southern characters, family, and society in more contemporary settings. Godwin, who was born in Alabama and grew up in North Carolina, exhibits her regional flair in the novels *A Mother and Two Daughters*, *A Southern Family*, and *Father Melancholy's Daughter*. Smith, a professor of English at North Carolina State University, hails from Grundy, Virginia, which is located in the heart of Appalachia. She exemplifies the finest in southern story-telling tradition in such fictional works as *Oral History*, *Fair and Tender Ladies*, *Family Linen*, and *The Devil's Dream*. Mason also negotiates familiar turf in the settings to be found in some of her short stories. From a dairy-farming family in Mayfield, Kentucky, she has come home to the Bluegrass State and established herself in rural Anderson County; Kentucky is the backdrop for her 1993 novel *Feather Crowns*.[19]

Although fiction with its make-believe characters has demonstrated the capacity to capture a wide range of southern characteristics and distinctive segments of society below the Mason-Dixon line, nonfiction has a potential for brutal realism that fiction simply cannot duplicate. In an autobiography that is both powerful and moving, Anne Moody, the daughter of tenant farmers, details her life as a black female in Mississippi during the fifties and sixties. Her parents had split, the father seemed to renounce his obligations to his children, and the mother struggled to eke out an existence for them. The mother subsequently remarried, but her new husband allowed his own family to mistreat his wife. Anne knew deprivation and cruelty within her mother's household and likewise suffered discrimination at the hands of whites for whom she worked while still a child. She also had to confront a sexually menacing stepfather when she discovered to her consternation the relative truth of a statement made by one of her friends: "Stepfathers ain't no damn good. Once my cousin remarried some no-good man and put him over her teen-age daughter. One day she came home and caught that fucker in bed with her child."[20] Finally, unable to tolerate the circumstances in which she found herself, Anne escaped (with some assistance from the local white sheriff), and in the face of almost overwhelming obstacles she managed to finish high school and attend college before becoming a participant in the civil rights movement.

Anne's mother had proved either unable or unwilling to lift herself and her children from abusive circumstances, and she did little for her prodigal daughter except to show up for her high-school graduation. Still, some women in the South, both white and black, having experienced enough hard times themselves, wanted better for their female offspring; but too many fathers of both races, whatever their class, because they had been indoctrinated so thoroughly in the proper relation between the sexes, anticipated few alternatives to traditional feminine roles. If a daughter showed a particular intellectual bent (made good grades in school), a blue-collar patriarch might be moved to speculate that she just "might make a teacher"; but that was about as far as most of them were willing to go.

Such an environment had the capacity to inspire ambition as well as acquiescence, rebellion as well as conformity.[21] The South not only spawned such black activists as Huey P. Newton, of the Black Panther party, and Angela Davis, a Communist; it also hatched a clutch of Miss America contenders. Armelia Newton, out of Louisiana, had named her last child for the infamous governor of that state, Huey P. Long. In A Taste of Power: A Black Woman's Story, Elaine Brown wrote that Armelia "had demanded that the world rejoice in the birth of her beautiful seventh son, whose hair she had brushed with sweet oils when he was a boy, whose face she had fanned in the intense humidity of Louisiana evenings, whose name she had made sacred to her entire world, especially her family."[22]

Angela Davis, just as Huey P. Newton, left the South and after several detours made her way to California. She had grown up in Birmingham, Alabama, the daughter of middle-class blacks. Her mother taught, and her father had also been an educator before opening his own gas station. Angela completed her junior and senior years at the progressive and private Elizabeth Irwin High School in Greenwich Village and then went to Brandeis University on a scholarship. She majored in French literature and subsequently studied at the Sorbonne in Paris. Already gravitating toward intellectual radicalism, she turned from the relatively comfortable world of abstract political philosophy to the dangerous arena of personal activism. Such incidents as the bombing of a Baptist Sunday school in Birmingham, which resulted in the deaths of four little girls, had made politics personal for Angela Davis. Ultimately she commanded nationwide attention as the Communist fired by the University of California at Los Angeles (UCLA). It was during Ronald Reagan's tenure as governor that UCLA's Board of Regents, on which he served, terminated Davis's employment. Her involvement with the Soledad brothers and charges against her for the Marin

County Courthouse kidnappings, for which she was acquitted, made her notorious during the early 1970s.[23]

The emerging militancy of a sprinkling of young blacks and whites in Dixie hardly affected the lifestyles of most of their contemporaries. While a relatively small number faced fire hoses and police dogs, participated in mass demonstrations, and squared off against White Citizens Councils, others engaged in more "wholesome" activities. At the 1960 Olympic Games in Rome, Wilma Rudolph from Tennessee Agricultural and Industrial State University won three gold medals. "Running," according to one account, "with the speed of the wind and the grace of a frightened doe," she took the 100-meter and 200-meter dashes and competed with the victorious 400-meter team. The success of La Gazella Negra, as the Italians called her, proved all the more remarkable because she had overcome crippling childhood illnesses.[24] Several months before Rudolph was born, Anna Mae Bullock, who is better known as the singer and dancer Tina Turner, came into the world on 26 November 1939 at Nutbush, Tennessee. "If she is famous for anything besides her enormous energy and talent," observes a columnist who devotes his time to celebrities, "it is those legs"—right up to her neck, to paraphrase the Rod Stewart song![25] The South also influenced the future poet Nikki Giovanni, born in Knoxville, Tennessee, and educated at Fisk University.[26]

The majority of youths, black and white, interested themselves in such matters as football games, Saturday nights at the drive-in, senior proms, and fraternity and sorority activities. The common denominator between the politicized and the nonpoliticized, the militants and the nonmilitants, may have been the throbbing rhythms of rock-'n'-roll and the plaintive wails of protest songs. After all, such lily-white good ole boys as Jerry Lee Lewis and Elvis Presley borrowed freely from black musical traditions. Even the songs, however, that the young shared meant different things to different people.

This contradictory and confusing milieu fostered at least as many beauty queens as bra burners. During the post-World War II era, contestants from Dixie have fared extremely well in the Miss America Pageant, where beauty, not sensuality, and accomplishment, not overt ambition, have traditionally been prime commodities. Susan Akin of Mississippi, who won the crown in 1985, transferred it to her successor at the September pageant the following year; she placed it on the head of a neighboring Tennessean. At that particular annual pageant, eight of the ten finalists hailed from former Confederate states.[27]

Akin had supposedly "entered at least 50 beauty pageants by the time she took the national crown. Her first big win was the Little Miss America pageant. She was 7." Mary Francis Flood, who for more than thirty years had coached beauty contenders, claimed that southern girls have a natural advantage. She declared: "We have an image to keep that we have inherited. The South stresses more beauty, more manners, more charisma, more charm . . . girls from other parts of the country do not have the class, the beauty, or the charm our girls have." After the September 1986 Miss America pageant, a northern contestant huffed: "There ought to be a different category for Southern girls. They've been doing this since they were born. They're *professionals*." [28] Even in the South, ideals of beauty have surely crossed the color line; Miss South Carolina, Kimberly Clarice Aiken, an African-American, took top honors in Atlantic City in September 1993. Pointing to the unseemliness of having Miss America appear at a welcoming rally with the Confederate flag waving in the background, a black state senator, Darrell Jackson, used her victory to renew the offensive against the controversial banner flying over the capitol of the Palmetto State. [29]

If such southern-born females of the postwar era as Angela Davis have proved to be blatantly at odds with mainstream America, some of their contemporaries became its very embodiment. Still, beneath the placid and wholesome domestic front so closely identified with post-World War II America, inside those ticky-tacky houses on the hillside about which the folk artist Malvina Reynolds sang, anxiety and unrest had unfolded during the 1950s and 1960s. More than a few baby boomers recall the older generation's construction of fallout shelters (high-school health classes sometimes toured them), the dog tags that they wore to elementary school in some districts (one assumes that such identification was expected to withstand a nuclear attack even if their little bodies vaporized), and the practice drills at school when they had to crawl under their desks to shelter themselves from impending incoming attacks.

In this milieu, ultra-right-wing organizations took root. During the 1940s a naturalized citizen, Suzanne Silvercruys Stevenson, the daughter of Baron Silvercruys, a former president of the Supreme Court of Belgium, became alarmed by what she believed to be the trend toward socialism in her adopted country. She subscribed to a variety of political feminism similar to that later advocated by Phyllis Schlafly. Stevenson organized the Minute Women of the U.S.A., Inc., to mobilize female combatants against threats to the American way of life—as defined by Stevenson and company. In short order during the early 1950s, local chapters of the Minute Women sprang up across the United States. Active groups existed in such southern locales as Houston, Texas, Baltimore, Maryland, St. Petersburg, Florida, Charleston and Wheeling, West Virginia, and Memphis, Tennessee. By early 1952 the chapter in Houston harbored some of the militant redbaiters in that city. [30]

On the national front the onset of the Cold War and the right-wing propaganda that accompanied it called into question the activities of almost anyone who had ever belonged to a liberal or radical organization or who had supported a left-of-center cause. Publicly the ranking officials of the National Board of the YWCA, for example, responded with timely coordinated defenses of staff members who became targets. Privately they phased out the Industrial Department, which had been the National Board's most radical and controversial experiment, and terminated some longtime employees, among them Eleanor Copenhaver Anderson. The Southern Summer School, which had been in decline, gave up the ghost.[31]

Even such relatively innocuous but reform-oriented groups as the American Association of University Women may have felt the pressure of the times. At the 1951 national convention, Hallie Farmer, a professor of history at Alabama State College for Women in Montevallo, who had a Ph.D. from the University of Wisconsin, delivered a stirring reminder of the AAUW's past. Along with her other accomplishments and contributions, she had served as president of the Alabama AAUW from 1937 to 1939. Speaking as chair of the association's Committee on Legislative Program, she responded to disparaging comments that had been made about lobbying and lobbyists: "I for one am getting tired of the way the term lobbyist is being hurled about in this convention as an insult. I am getting even more tired of watching our members and our branches cringe and apologize and try to explain when anybody mentions lobbying." The lobbyists, she reminded her cohorts, were "the heroines of this Association." As for "the laws . . . written on the statute books," they were more than "black letters on white paper." Instead "they represent[ed] long days of toil and sleepless nights . . . bitter disappointment and moments of triumph. . . . Those women in their day stood at Armageddon and they battled for the Lord . . . for there were giants in those days."[32]

Generations come and go, reform ebbs and flows, but ideas endure. Even when the institutions that nurture liberal and radical causes change course, deteriorate, or cease to exist, their orphaned causes may go on living. During the second half of the twentieth century a considerable amount of the public involvement of southern women continued to be channeled through reform efforts that focused on other oppressed or repressed groups. Campaigning for better working conditions and higher wages and building a sisterhood across class lines, which had been in the forefront during the 1920s and 1930s, took a back seat to civil rights. Lives of such liberals and radicals as Zilphia Johnson Horton and Virginia Foster Durr provided threads of continuity between the second and third generations of southern female activists. Zilphia served as Highlander's music director. Even before her marriage to Myles Horton, she had stood with others from the folk school on picket lines at Daisy, Tennessee, and had faced gun thugs who

fired on strikers and strike sympathizers.[33] Durr had helped found the
Southern Conference for Human Welfare at Birmingham, Alabama, in
1938, had opposed the poll tax, and had associated herself with numerous
liberal causes.

Senator James Eastland subpoenaed Mrs. Durr and her husband, Clif-
ford, along with several other southern liberals, to testify before his Sub-
committee on Internal Security at New Orleans in 1954. By her own account, delivered with all the condescension of a true southern blue blood,
she dismissed Eastland as being "from the hill country . . . no Southern
aristocrat at all. The nice girls wouldn't have anything to do with him, but
he married a very nice woman." According to Virginia Durr, "sweet Southern ladies" would only intone: "Poor Mrs. Eastland. Now, her sister's a lovely woman. You know, she's in the Women's Society for Christian Service.
And Mrs. Eastland is really a nice woman. I declare, she has such a hard
time." Virginia Foster Durr took Senator Eastland seriously enough, despite
his lowly pedigree, to telephone both Lyndon B. Johnson, a Texan and fellow southerner as well as Democratic majority leader of the United States
Senate, and George Bender, a Republican congressman from Ohio who was
a friend of hers. She solicited and secured their help in keeping U.S. senators and representatives of both parties out of New Orleans and away from
the hearings.[34]

Accompanied by her attorney, this "striking southern lady"—a native
of Birmingham, Justice Hugo Black's sister-in-law, First Lady Eleanor Roosevelt's friend, and a one-time candidate for the United States Senate on the
Progressive-party ticket—took the stand. She refused to answer Eastland's
questions "for a number of reasons, but specifically excluding the Fifth
Amendment." Obviously disconcerted, the senator still accused her of being
under Communist-party discipline. When finally excused, "she promptly
and ostentatiously began powdering her nose, to the delight of the press
photographers."[35]

Although strident females had not been wholly unknown in Dixie, the
appearance of such activist women as Anne Gambriel McCarty Braden
during the post-World War II era signified the dynamism that typified an
important aspect of third-generation feminism in Dixie. In 1954, Anne, a
native of Anniston, Alabama, along with her husband, Carl, flouted the
social mores of his hometown of Louisville, Kentucky. Purchasing a house
in a white neighborhood and transferring ownership of it to a black family
temporarily landed her in jail and garnered a conviction and prison sentence for her husband.[36]

Nor was the more militant stance that characterized third-generation
southern feminists a lily-white phenomenon. Strong and courageous black
women seemed especially motivated by a new sense of urgency. Whereas

such names as Mary McLeod Bethune and Charlotte Hawkins Brown figured prominently during the interwar years, those of Rosa Louise Parks,
Fannie Lou Hamer, Septima Poinsette Clark, and Bernice V. Robinson
came to the fore with the civil rights movement of the 1950s and 1960s.
Bethune, a native of Mayesville, South Carolina, had founded a school for
black girls at Daytona Beach, Florida, in 1904, which merged with a boys'
school in 1923 to form Bethune-Cookman College. Appointed to various
federal posts by Presidents Coolidge, Hoover, and Roosevelt, she became
the first black woman to head a federal agency when she served from 1936
to 1944 as director of the Division of Negro Affairs of the National Youth
Administration.[37] Charlotte Hawkins Brown's career, like Bethune's, began
with teaching. Born in Henderson, North Carolina, she first worked in a
one-room school at Sedalia in her native state that became Palmer Memorial Institute. Active in the National Council of Negro Women, which Bethune had founded, Brown became the first black woman to serve on the
National Board of the Young Women's Christian Association.[38]

In 1954 the United States Supreme Court rendered its decision in
Brown et al. v. *The Board of Education of Topeka, Kansas,* et al. (347 U.S.
483), which paved the way for the desegregation of public schools. The
next year, on 1 December 1955, Rosa Louise Parks refused to give up her
seat to a white man on a bus in Montgomery, Alabama. Since that incident, race relations in the United States have never been quite the same.
Mrs. Parks, a tailor's assistant at a department store and a member of the
local chapter of the National Association for the Advancement of Colored
People (NAACP), deliberately violated a segregation law. Duly arrested,
she became a catalyst for a wave of nonviolent protests against racial segregation across the South and the nation. The subsequent bus boycott took
black protest out of the courts, where it had been conducted by NAACP
attorneys, and transformed it into a mass movement that exerted pressure
in public places.[39] Rightfully known as the "mother of the modern freedom
movement," Rosa Louise Parks had been a student in a desegregation workshop at Highlander Folk School in Monteagle, Tennessee, during August
1955.[40]

Evidence clearly indicates that what appeared to be a spontaneous out-
pouring was in fact the product of careful, difficult, and dangerous ground-
work of the 1920s, 1930s, and 1940s.[41] During the first half of the twentieth
century even as bigotry held full sway and racism ran rampant, foundations were being laid for the reformation of Dixie. With a vision of equality of opportunity for blacks and females and a nonoppressive economic
system, a few native-born southern whites, in league with some of their
Yankee brethren, prodded the South toward a new social order. Various
Old Left activists, as individuals and within organizations, had forged a

loose network that transcended race and class and shared the notion—although not always a common vision—of a more humane society. The more radical among them—who not only established ties with like-minded northerners but also maintained political contacts with leftists in the international community—solicited financing from within the South and without. Nevertheless, their peculiar regional heritage still shaped their initiatives and responses.[42]

Although Rosa Louise Parks became a powerful symbol of the civil rights movement, she was hardly the only black woman—or white one for that matter—who was prepared to oppose racism and bigotry in the South. Indeed, in Montgomery, Alabama, itself, writes the historian David J. Garrow, "the most active and assertive black civic group . . . had been the Women's Political Council (WPC) headed by Mrs. Jo Ann Robinson, then a professor of English at Alabama State College." On 21 May 1954, a year and a half before Parks captured the national limelight, Robinson had written to the mayor, urging him to either improve conditions or expect a boycott.[43]

By one way of reckoning, another black woman, Septima Poinsette Clark of South Carolina, served the civil rights movement as well as Rosa Louise Parks or Jo Ann Robinson. Less well known and even more closely associated with Highlander Folk School than Parks had been, Clark at the age of eighteen had begun her teaching career at Johns Island, which was under the auspices of the Charleston school board. Years later she observed that she had "spent nearly all [her] adult life teaching citizenship to children who really aren't citizens. They have fulfilled all the requirements for citizenship; many of their fathers and brothers have died for their country—bullets and bombs tear black skin as easily as white, and all men bleed red."[44]

In 1955 Clark lost her job in South Carolina because she had encouraged blacks to vote and because she herself had accepted social invitations to visit in the home of a white judge and his wife in Charleston. Having earlier been a student at Highlander, she then became the school's director of education. Operating under the terms of a three-year grant from the Schwartzhaupt Foundation to fund experimentation in adult education, she developed the citizenship-school concept and established the first such school on Johns Island. The fledgling experiment became the prototype for scores of similar efforts throughout the South which through consciousness-raising and literacy education cleared some of the obstacles to voter registration for blacks. In 1963 the Southern Christian Leadership Conference (SCLC), having directed the program since 1960, revealed that during the preceding three years nearly twenty-six thousand blacks in twelve states had learned to read enough so that they could register. At the time these figures were released, more than four hundred volunteers were conducting citizenship schools across the South for more than sixty-five hundred adults. Clark estimated that nearly one hundred thousand learned to read and write as a result of the program.[45]

In the midst of Clark's important work with citizenship schools she had become embroiled in the whirlwind of controversy that led to the confiscation of Highlander's property and the revocation of its charter by the state of Tennessee. Indeed, Clark was arrested when the school was raided in 1959, ostensibly because of allegations that it sold intoxicants but really because of its desegregation activities.[46] During the months that followed, Highlander's staff attempted to salvage what they could and to recharter as Highlander Research and Education Center, which was located briefly at Knoxville and later at New Market, Tennessee. Clark's work and the Field Foundation grant under which it was then being conducted were transferred to the SCLC.

Obviously disconcerted by unfolding developments, Clark expressed her not-inconsiderable dissatisfaction, which led Myles Horton, Highlander's director, to observe that "Septima sometimes assumes that she is a victim of white prejudice and chicanery, even though everything possible is being done by all of us." He pointed out that she was "to be provided with a salary and program expenses for a year as a result of the grant"; but Clark found "it difficult to believe that the situation [would] ever be cleaned up . . . the delays inevitably seem[ed] to be the result of either a lack of interest in the Citizenship Training Program or in her."[47]

When criticized for her inability to "grasp the overview . . . [and] codify her procedure so as to make for mass replication," Clark responded: "I was not supposed to be professional. The idea and dream was in Myles Horton's mind." She claimed that "the procedure and technique" varied from one community to another and that "there was no general academic pattern."[48] Earlier, in a letter to Dorothy Cotton of the SCLC in Atlanta, Clark had written: "You are troubled as I was many years ago about broken verbs. Now I am deeply concerned about broken promises and in all my work and participation with civic organizations the broken verb participant never becomes the broken promise participant."[49]

After the citizenship program had been officially transferred to SCLC, Highlander's extension director, Bernice V. Robinson, a young black woman who did field work in Louisiana and Mississippi during the 1960s, employed methodology similar to Clark's. Individuals like Clark and Robinson had moved well beyond accepted southern norms for females and blacks. They risked their lives, not just their reputations. In July 1962 Robinson reported from Mount Beulah at Edwards, Mississippi, that "all the white people were sent away from our first night session because threats had been made to blow up the meeting place."[50] Later the local sheriff and members of the White Citizens Council of Edwards subjected the director of Mount Beulah to a four-hour "conference." From Greenwood, Mississippi, Robinson wrote on 15 June 1963 that the workshop had closed "last night because everybody wanted to go down to Jackson to Medgar Evers funeral." Evers, the field secretary for the NAACP in Mississippi, had been shot to death outside his home in Jackson on 12 June .[51]

In 1964 the daughter of black tenant farmers, Fannie Lou Hamer, "poor and unlettered," challenged the National Democratic party, the president of the United States, congressmen, and the American citizenry. Out of the Delta, she spoke on behalf of the Freedom party, which was attempting to unseat the all-white Mississippi delegation at the convention in Atlantic City. According to one writer, "her health and formal education were severely stunted by her surroundings; her penetrating analysis of society was at times dismissed by those who picked apart her unlettered grammar or could hear only her Delta dialect." Still, she dared face television cameras and convention delegates and to reject President Lyndon B. Johnson's offer of two token seats instead of the full representation that the Freedom party had demanded.[52]

Along with an assortment of black women of all ages, a few young white women, sometimes out of strong religious convictions, also moved into the civil rights movement which was beginning to shake the racist foundations of southern society.[53] Role models for them were scarce. According to one source, Anne Braden "was perhaps the most important adult white woman to young southern activists throughout the sixties"; nevertheless "the dearth of models was an indication of the unprecedented nature of this revolt led by black youth and of the sparseness of southern white women's participation in it." Young activists included Sandra ("Casey") Cason, Dorothy Dawson, Jane Stembridge, Mary King, and Sue Thrasher, who involved themselves deeply with the Southern Students Organizing Committee and the Student Non-Violent Coordinating Committee (SNCC). "The daring of younger women, the strength and perseverance of 'mamas' in local communities, the unwavering vision, energy, and resourcefulness of an Ella Baker [SCLC], opened new possibilities in vivid contrast to the tradition of the 'southern lady,'" Sara Evans explained. "Having broken with traditional culture, young white women welcomed the alternative they represented."[54]

Not unlike their abolitionist sisters of the preceding century, New Left women, products of the civil rights movement, eventually realized that they too were oppressed. For indigenous females as well as the scores of non-southerners who worked for racial equality, the South cradled an important wing of women's liberation and may have contributed to subsequent New Left activism on northern college campuses. Separating myth from reality here is fraught with obstacles. Whether accurate or apocryphal, Stokely Carmichael's rebuttal to "SNCC Position Paper (Women in the Movement)" proved to be galvanizing; Carmichael's alleged comment was "The only position for women in SNCC is prone."

Robin Morgan, the author of *Sisterhood Is Powerful*, claimed that a black woman, Ruby Doris Smith Robinson, had presented the paper during an SNCC retreat at Waveland, Mississippi, in November 1964; and others have used this explanation. Mary King denies it. Ruby Doris, according to King, considered the rising consciousness among women within the SNCC as "disruptive and divisive." Furthermore, "she often bristled with antagonism toward white women, perhaps because they represented a standard different from the ideal cherished by black women." In consultation with such individuals as Casey Hayden (Sandra Cason at one time was married to Tom Hayden) and Mary Varela, King actually wrote the statement. Circulated anonymously at the retreat, it was met for the most part with ridicule, scorn, or plain disinterest. King also claims that Carmichael's statement had been made in jest among friends who had been enjoying a bottle of wine. Carmichael's statement, as subsequently reported, focused attention on the sexual activity of the preceding summer and the rivalry between young black and young white women for the attentions of black men.[55]

Still, young, fairly affluent white women often empathized with the plight of poverty-stricken black women and put their lives on the line in an effort to change the circumstances that blighted the latter's existence. In *Freedom Song: A Personal Story of the 1960s Civil Rights Movement*, Mary King, one of the young whites, insightfully describes Hannah, a black tenant farmer in Mississippi, the mother of twelve children. Hannah was so tired at the end of the day that she sometimes forgot their names and just called them "Peaches" and "Cupcakes." Hannah "innocently explained . . . that after she and her husband finished a day's work in the field . . . she would urge him to make love." This was a dimension in an otherwise dreary life over which she had control and from which she obviously derived pleasure.[56]

Black men's attitudes toward women who were involved in the civil rights movement differed little from the attitudes of their white counterparts in all other segments of American society. It was rare for most black and white men to treat females as equals, and they often failed to accord women the recognition and respect that the women's efforts merited.[57] Even Fannie Lou Hamer—who adamantly opposed such feminist ideas as a woman's right to abortion and declared herself to be interested in liberating all people, not just women—sometimes complained about the black male's reluctance to become involved in the movement.[58] Septima Poinsette Clark pulled no punches when she remembered that "those men [on the executive staff of the SCLC] didn't have any faith in women, none whatsoever. They just thought that women were sex symbols and had no contribution to make. That's why Rev. Abernathy would say continuously, 'Why is Mrs. Clark on this staff?'"[59] Rosa Louise Parks recalled that E.D. Nixon, president of the Montgomery NAACP, had said, "Women don't need to be nowhere but in the kitchen."[60]

Parks also pointed out that when the historic March on Washington was staged in 1963, "women were not allowed to play much of a role." Indeed, the committee that planned the event "didn't want Coretta Scott King and the other wives of the male leaders to march with their husbands. Instead, there was a separate procession for them." The main program, which featured Dr. Martin Luther King's now-famous "I Have a Dream" speech, included no females. Again the men distanced themselves from the women, captured the limelight, and assigned the "sisters" a diminutive billing in a separate and less significant "Tribute to Women." One of the march's organizers, A. Philip Randolph, who founded the Brotherhood of Sleeping Car Porters, presented "some of the women who had participated in the struggle," and Parks remembered being among them.[61]

The younger generation—the New Left males, both black and white—seemed to differ little from southern good ole boys in how they viewed females; that is, as "workers" or "wives," valued for cooking and stenographic skills or for sexual favors. This proved a staggering realization for New Left females. After their movement days in the Deep South, some southerners as well as non-southerners of both sexes forsook Dixie. Disenchanted, burned out, or just tired, some women parted company with former colleagues; others reflected on what work in the South and with subsequent radical activities had meant to them as females.[62] While some female activists who had been civil-rights workers in the South protested the war in Vietnam, other southern women, like Lynda Van Devanter, a nurse from Arlington, Virginia, joined the forces in the field. In *Home before Morning*, she recounts her experience as an army nurse in Vietnam.[63]

With women's groups enjoying a subordinate but nonetheless symbiotic relationship with the civil rights movement and riding the crest of a somewhat liberal wave of the times, females realized some important gains. Indeed, a significant portion of the protective legislation that has expanded opportunities for women dates from the 1960s, particularly the Equal Pay Act of 1963 and the Civil Rights Act of 1964. As amended, the Equal Pay Act prohibits those firms which have more than twenty employees and which are engaged in interstate commerce from paying men and women differently if they work for the same company and if they perform jobs requiring equal skill and responsibility under similar conditions. Title VII of the Civil Rights Act prohibits sex discrimination by private and public employers with fifteen or more workers. Congressman Howard W. Smith of

Virginia initiated the addition of the word "sex," believing that it would make the bill seem ridiculous and that it would divide liberals, thereby preventing passage of the legislation. Congresswoman Martha Griffiths of Michigan, the leading feminist in the House at the time, considered it a serious matter and realized that Smith probably carried a hundred votes with him. Smith and his followers had their day; the uproar that ensued went down as "Ladies Day in the House."[64]

Since Title VII was written into law, a few women have been "laughing" all the way to the Equal Employment Opportunity Commission (EEOC) or to the federal courts to file individual and class actions dealing with sex discrimination. Other milestones in "expansive" legislation for women included Executive Order 11246, as amended in 1967, from the Johnson administration and Executive Order 11478 from the Nixon years. These require that equal employment opportunity be provided by both the federal government and firms that contract with the federal government. In tandem with Title VII of the Civil Rights Act of 1964, they provide the legal basis for "affirmative action," the idea that discrimination can be eliminated when employers take positive steps to identify and change policies and practices and to alter institutional barriers that cause or perpetuate inequality. The Women's Educational Equity Act (WEEA) of 1974 and Title IX of the Education Amendments of 1972, as well as the Civil Rights Restoration Act of 1988 (passed over President Ronald Reagan's veto) and the earlier Equal Credit Opportunity Act, have likewise benefited women.[65]

Third-generation southern female activists, those of the post-World World II era, ranged farther afield of regional culture than did their predecessors. To a greater degree than either the first or second generation, they parted company with tradition. They alienated a goodly number of Dixie's mainstream females and aroused the ire of extremists. Irritated by outside agitators and federal interference, two Mississippi journalists, Mary Dawson Cain and Florence Sillers Ogden, organized Women for Constitutional Government (WCG) in September 1962. Cain was "the fiery editor of the *Summit Sun*," and Ogden was "'Dis 'n Dat' reporter from the Delta to the Jackson *Clarion Ledger*." Ogden described the organization as "no place for moderates, liberals, publicans, or sinners." It served "just conservative women who believe in standing up for their constitutional rights." The WCG resoundingly opposed the Equal Rights Amendment and looked with disdain on the entire feminist movement and females who disavowed the politics of their male counterparts. Although this extremist group may have been an anomaly, it expressed the opinions that a small silent minority shared.[66]

The failure of the Equal Rights Amendment, a watershed of women's liberation, had particular significance in the South. Of the fifteen legislatures that failed to ratify ERA, nine were in former Confederate states.[67] Assuming a position of disregard for mainstream culture and imagining themselves morally and ethically superior, feminists cut the ground from beneath themselves. Gloria Steinem, for example, was invited to lead an ERA march on the Georgia capitol in Atlanta. Rosalynn Carter, later characterized during her husband's presidency as the "Iron Magnolia" but an enlightened and politically astute southern woman, told her husband Jimmy, then governor of the state, that she thought it was the worst possible thing to do. "The television news had been full of bra-burnings and strong statements by ERA supporters such as Bella Abzug and Gloria Steinem," Mrs. Carter recalled. Georgians considered Steinem radical and threatening, and her presence was likely to have an adverse effect on the legislature. The Georgia lawmakers soundly defeated ERA, so Governor Carter never had the opportunity to give it his stamp of approval.[68]

Across the nation as well as in the South, the younger generation of feminists alienated well-placed, respected, and accomplished business and professional women. Still, the opposition to ERA in Dixie bore a striking similarity to that confronted by the earlier Woman's Suffrage Amendment and seemed to suggest that the mind-set of state lawmakers had altered little during the half century that had elapsed. Swirling side issues that included gay rights, common restrooms, abortion, and the draft clouded the legislative horizon and conveniently confused male politicians who were already highly susceptible to the likes of Phyllis Schlafly, Marabel Morgan, and vocal female opponents within the southern states.

Although *liberating* legislation remained on the statute books, the *liberal* fling of the 1960s and 1970s quietly receded into the past. During the Reagan and Bush administrations and in the late 1970s and 1980s, conservatism again became fashionable. In their own communities, however, women like Eula Hall persevered and sometimes triumphed. A Kentuckian who grew up poor in Joe Boner Hollow off Greasy Creek, she established the Mud Creek Clinic in eastern Kentucky.[69] All the same, females have rarely fared well when prevailing social conditions have encouraged Americans to feel good about their prejudices. The failure of ERA, on which the women's liberation movement essentially made its last stand, left American feminism in shock and disarray. Betty Friedan, however, experienced a second epiphany in 1981, the revelation that the leaders of women's liberation had ignored women as mothers. It garnered her another book, *The Second Stage*. The economist Sylvia Ann Hewlett called the movement to task in *A Lesser Life: The Myth of Women's Liberation in America*, published in 1986; and Susan Faludi in 1991, detailed the reactionary response to women's gains in *Backlash: The Undeclared War against American Women*.[70]

In February 1988, former first ladies Lady Bird Johnson and Rosalynn

Carter, with the endorsement but without the presence of Pat Nixon and Betty Ford, had hosted a symposium known as "Women and the Constitution: A Bicentennial Perspective." Literally and figuratively it had been a long road from the first women's-rights convention in 1848 at Seneca Falls, an isolated rural village in upstate New York, to Atlanta, the pulsating self-proclaimed capital of the New South. With the heroines of the civil rights movement and women's liberation in attendance, it was a heady, exhilarating experience, a giant feminist pep rally. It occurred in the South, it was hosted by southern-born wives of presidents, and southern women (mostly business and professional types and political activists) attended. Many others from around the country and some from the international community were also present. Still, the distance between the overwhelming majority of southern women and those who went as delegates to this event remained great. Those in attendance signed petitions for the reintroduction of the ERA in the United States Congress and volunteered their time and money. In the closing moments, Lady Bird Johnson pronounced the symposium "a feast of the mind and spirit."[71] Exciting as it was, it seems to have had no lasting political consequences.

The nomenclature of the American women's-rights movement—such words as "feminist" and "feminism"—has been especially problematic in the South, where it has not been unusual for females to say, "Well, I believe in equal rights but I'm no feminist." For the common run of southern women as well as men, "feminism" has often been associated with gynecological self-examination, lesbianism, unisex toilets, and forced military service for the "fairer sex." Just mentioning the Equal Rights Amendment in certain quarters below the Mason-Dixon line has often conjured up images of dainty females in full battle regalia squaring off against "the enemy" on the "front lines." Reproductive freedom seems to have provided the single issue on which significant groups of American women of all ages, ethnicities, colors, and regional origins have been able to focus since the defeat of the Equal Rights Amendment. Indeed, even many southern good ole boys and good ole girls, with their well-earned reputations as conservatives, have resented interference with their sex lives and have privately expressed doubt about having self-proclaimed moralists monitor their bedroom antics. The availability of reliable birth-control devices, the advent and widespread use of "the pill" during the 1960s, and the freedom to disseminate reliable information for limiting or restricting pregnancies serve to separate women of the post-World War II era from their predecessors.[72] This may have done more for southern women, indeed for all American women, than all the laws ever written and enacted by male legislators. Even on this issue, however, which is so fundamental to the lives of mature females, women have hardly been united.

A woman's right to have an abortion, which was established in the critical 1973 decision *Roe* v. *Wade*, has come under strong attack from the extreme Right. This landmark case originated in Texas and made its way to the United States Supreme Court, where it was argued by attorney Sarah Weddington. A minister's daughter who had grown up in small West Texas towns and had attended a Methodist college, Weddington also knew the dilemma of an unwanted pregnancy. In 1967, according to her own account, she had been "a scared graduate student . . . in a dirty, dusty Mexican border town," where she had gone because abortion on demand was still illegal in the Lone Star State. Some six years later, Weddington, who had never argued a case in court before, persuaded a majority of the nation's highest legal authorities that females should have the right to choose.[73]

During the 1988 presidential campaign, the Republican candidate, George Herbert Walker Bush, spoke about "a gentler, kinder America"; but as he was preparing to assume the nation's highest office, the United States Supreme Court—bearing the heavy stamp of Ronald Reagan— agreed to hear a case arising from a Missouri law that restricted abortions and declared that human life begins at conception. During the Reagan administration, opposition to abortion became a kind of litmus test for his Supreme Court nominees, and Bush did not separate himself from the Reagan position. In 1973, in the cases of *Roe* v. *Wade* and *Doe* v. *Bolton*, the tribunal had ruled on the constitutionality of a woman's right to have an abortion under certain conditions during the first six months of pregnancy. In 1986, after thirteen years of repeated attempts to narrow or overturn the *Roe* decision, the Supreme Court reaffirmed women's right to reproductive freedom in *Thornburgh* v. *American College of Obstetricians and Gynecologists*.[74]

After the November 1988 presidential election but not until the outcome of the fall campaign had been decided, the United States Department of Justice took the unusual step of asking the Supreme Court to review the *Roe* v. *Wade* decision; it also intervened in a Missouri case that the Court had not at that time agreed to hear. With the conservative William H. Rehnquist at the helm and with Reagan appointees Sandra Day O'Connor, Antonin Scalia, and Anthony M. Kennedy on board, Associate Justice Harry A. Blackmun, the author of the *Roe* decision, warned publicly that it might not stand through the term.[75] In July 1989, in *Webster* v. *Reproductive Health Services*, the United States Supreme Court undermined but did not reverse *Roe* v. *Wade*. State legislators, overwhelmingly male and at least as susceptible to pressure from vocal minorities as the United States Congress is, gained more latitude to cut deals over women's bodies.[76]

With the passing of the Bush presidency and the advent of the Clinton administration, the nation's highest tribunal seemed to be moving toward a more sympathetic stance on issues of particular interest to women. In a 9-0 decision out of the November 1993 session, the justices eased the burden of proof in sexual-harassment suits. The case had arisen when Teresa Harris of Nashville, Tennessee, turned to the courts for legal remedy. She targeted her former employer, Charles Hardy, president of Forklift Systems, Incorporated. Harris received no satisfaction at the lower and appellate levels, but her persistence paid off when she managed to persuade the United States Supreme Court to hear her case. In an opinion drafted by Justice Sandra Day O'Connor the Court rejected a standard, which had been adopted by several lower federal courts, requiring plaintiffs to show that sexual harassment made the environment of the workplace so hostile as to cause them "severe psychological injury." O'Connor pointed out that psychologcial harm is but one factor among many that courts may consider but that federal law "comes into play before the harassing conduct leads to a nervous breakdown."[77] On 24 January 1994, in *National Organization for Women* v. *Scheidler*, the nation's highest court held unanimously that anti-racketeering (RICO) laws might be used to combat the extremist tactics of certain "pro-lifers," which have been aimed at women seeking abortions and also at clinics and physicians that perform them.[78]

Only a few southern women, among them Sarah Weddington and Teresa Harris, have possessed the courage to carry private matters into the public arena and to employ statutory law and constitutional provisions in order to seek redress in the nation's courts. The battles they have waged and the victories they have won, however, have in turn affected the lives of all of their sisters. A tendency exists in both the country and the region to point to a few highly visible women and then to suggest that females have finally "made it" in American society. Encouraging as the increasing numbers of success stories have been, the millennium has hardly arrived. Public female profiles—even such distinguished ones as those of Dr. Rhea Seddon, an astronaut from Murfreesboro, Tennessee, and United States Attorney General Janet Reno of Miami, Florida—hardly signal an end to sexual discrimination. Neither does the random sprinkling of women in state legislatures, the national congress, or the governorships. The mere presence of female lawmakers hardly guarantees significant and serious attention to women's issues, and gratifying as it may have been to have Martha Layne Collins of Kentucky or Ann Richards of Texas in a governor's mansion, women do not automatically think alike or vote alike. Collins and Richards secured election in their own right, but Lurleen B. Wallace, who became governor of Alabama, was merely the political pawn of her husband, George; she died of cancer in 1970 while still in office. Moreover, some of the high-visibility positions have proved to be only brief cameo roles.

Demographics and empirical evidence suggest that the underpinnings of patriarchy in Dixie have become much less secure than they once were, but the news is ambiguous. Whatever the overriding factors may be, the South has registered the highest rate of hysterectomies in the country; the same is true of tubal sterilizations. Tennessee, Mississippi, Alabama, and Georgia have on occasion recorded the largest number of reported cases of syphilis and gonorrhea among females in the contiguous forty-eight states. Females outnumbered males in every southern state by the mid-1980s and, except in Kentucky and West Virginia, approximately one-half or more of the females lived in urban areas. More women than men between the ages of eighteen and twenty-four possessed high-school diplomas. Females constituted 49 percent or more of the enrollment in southern colleges and universities. The highest percentage of women with children under six years of age who worked outside the home, 52 percent or so, clustered in the Deep South; but the "feminization" of poverty manifested itself especially in Kentucky and the Deep South, where it coexisted alongside amazing individual success stories. Except in Florida, Louisiana, and West Virginia, where fewer than 44 percent of married women claimed employment outside the home, the range fell around 50 percent. Likewise, females made up about half of the practicing professionals throughout the region.[79]

In general, educational opportunities, earning power, and urban environments coalesce to raise women's personal expectations and the realization of their human potential. With a changing southern landscape, suburbs and urban villages have concentrated populations and have engendered a cohesiveness among women as well as other groups, which the isolation of farms and plantations precluded. Female professors, engineers, lawyers, business executives, and physicians, as well as waitresses, secretaries, factory workers, and even coal miners, can be found in the contemporary South.[80] They maneuver their four-wheel-drive vehicles, economy models, or family luxury cars into crowded day-care parking lots to retrieve their offspring.[81] The advent of large-scale public employment for females has brought earning power. Be it blessing or bane, choice or necessity, work outside the home has enhanced a woman's economic value and offered the possibility for some degree of personal independence. Still, the female sex bears a disproportionate share of housework and caregiving for the elderly and the young; women also function in both national and regional social settings that are less than sympathetic to their needs and the conditions of their lives.[82] Victimization is an ever-present possibility, and the perpetrators are more likely to be family members or acquaintances than strangers, for date rape, wife battering, and child abuse have not been strangers to Dixie.

The South and all of American society have experienced profound social, economic, political, and demographic transformations in the course of the twentieth century. In the forefront has been the fundamental alteration in ethnic and race relations, but within respective groups, the reassessment of gender has been almost a foregone conclusion. In 1989, Kim and Cam Cook, Native Americans, faced expulsion from the small Pamunkey Indian reservation in King William County, Virginia, because they had married white men. Crusading to win for Indian women the same right as that of men to remain on the reservation if they married outside the tribe, Kim Cook explained: "They want you to marry a Pamunkey Indian. That's impossible. They're all girls or they're my cousins."[83] In 1985, Wilma Mankiller had become the first female chief of the Cherokee Nation. When her predecessor landed an appointment in the Reagan administration, Mankiller, who had been deputy chief, moved into her people's most exalted position. Apparently there was little grumbling about her gender, and Mankiller herself explained: "We are a revitalized tribe. We have kept the best of our old way of life and incorporated the sounder elements of today's non-Indian world."[84]

The South's population has always been more diverse than its reputation as a "WASP" nest might suggest. In recent decades, immigration and internal migration have given rise to an even more heterogeneous population; Hispanic and Oriental refugees, attracted by the climate and the economic possibilities of the Sunbelt, have contributed to the changing complexion of the region. In September 1993, *Lear's* designated Maria Elena Torano of Miami as the magazine's woman of the month. A refugee from Castro's Cuba, Torano founded META and subsequently served as its chief executive officer. META is an acronymn for Maria Elena Torano Associates, and "meta" is a Spanish word that means "goal." META, which had been certified as a minority business, handled federal contracts dealing with environmental services and information technology.[85]

In the long run, historians must guard against the tendency to overestimate isolated individual accomplishments and such watersheds or milestones as the opportunities that came for southern women after their men were defeated in the Civil War, after the advent of suffrage, or out of the civil rights movement. As recently as 1963 an Arkansas legislator proclaimed, "We don't have any of those University Women [American Association of University Women] in Perry County." He then unabashedly explained how he and his cohorts dealt with their women "when one . . . starts poking around in something she doesn't know anything about": "We get her an extra milk cow. It that don't work, we give her a little more garden to tend. And if that's not enough, we get her pregnant and keep her barefoot."[86]

In some respects, America and the South have experienced more progress in race relations than in sex equity. Most public figures, for example, dare not make the denigrating remarks about blacks or show the conde- scension toward them that some still seem to think is appropriate for fe- males. First Lady Hillary Rodham Clinton, from Arkansas by way of Chi- cago, appeared on Capitol Hill in 1993 to promote the Clinton admini- stration's health-care plan, and rather than moving immediately to the business at hand, one pompous solon took time to banter gratuitously about her "charm" and "wit." One finds it hard to imagine his engaging in comparable rhetoric with an accomplished African-American.

Southern women, indeed many southern feminists, have never re- nounced their femininity. Radical feminists are hard to find in the South; the great majority of females are not in sympathy with lesbianism; they do not generally dispense with their undergarments or go out in public without their makeup. Furthermore, they reject the notion of an all-encompassing cross-cultural and historical patriarchal plot to subjugate women. If in fact such a plot ever existed, many southern women have been all-too-willing accomplices. All those things that have been regarded as radical feminist rites of passage have never been embraced warmly below the Mason-Dixon line. Southern women know that males and females are biologically and psychologically different and that females, on whom both sexes depend to promulgate the species, require some special consideration; at the same time, as human beings, women deserve legal equity. "Southerners, like the ancient Hebrews," writes the historian David R. Goldfield, "fought among themselves and engaged in a battle of will against their God, but like the Israelites they forged a land of promise out of the conflict itself, and the South may yet be that redemptive region foretold as the first settlers en- countered its incomparable beauty and promise."[87] For the women of Dixie, the exodus is not yet concluded, the dream not yet realized.

Epilogue

For some four hundred years, women of the American South have been engaged in a great trek through time. Their travels for the most part represent a chronicle of ordinary people suspended in the rather monotonous, predictable routine of day-to-day existence and rushed along by myriad developments over which they have had little control. Once in a great while, when confronted with extraordinary circumstances and unusual challenges, they have risen to heroic heights. The recorded pages of that historical human passage reveal a story of epic proportions, a saga of surprising strength. Yet southern women, past and present, were and are real people. Of flesh and blood, they exhibit the usual failings and foibles. Nevertheless, the resemblance that some of them have borne and still bear to the ethereal southern lady of myth and legend is not entirely coincidental. When the daughters of Dixie were still in their infancy, their elders immersed them in the baptismal font of that uniquely southern goddess; and she, like their ancestors, has watched over them from cradle to grave. The more daring have sometimes managed to invoke her name or conjure up her image to uplift mere mortals; some have eluded her cautionary presence altogether.

The general run of southern men and women have tolerated each other extraordinarily well, and most females below the Mason-Dixon line have adjusted themselves to the prescribed feminine roles of service and sacrifice. Friendship, genuine affection, and love have eased the way. Still, Dixie renders up some enigmatic examples of male-female relationships that defy simple explanations. In 1989, for example, a Sullivan County, Tennessee, man pleaded guilty to second-degree murder for gunning down his spouse while she was conversing by telephone with her parish priest. Some eighteen years earlier in Alabama, his first wife had died when he had fired twelve shotgun blasts into her back. The prosecutor in Sullivan County opted for a plea bargain of twelve-years' incarceration rather than risk a jury verdict of not guilty by reason of insanity. In the Alabama killing the perpetrator had escaped indictment altogether because local law-enforcement officials had found a gun in the woman's hand; he had claimed the shooting was in self-defense.[1]

The syndicated columnist Mike Royko recounted the story of a middle-aged Edwards, Mississippi, nurse who saved herself from an assailant intent upon robbing and raping her. He peeled off most of his clothing and jumped into her bed. As reported by the "victim," this is what happened next: "I got it. I grabbed it by my right hand. And when I grabbed it, I gave it a yank. And when I yanked it, I twisted all at the same time." The assailant then struck her a hard blow across her head. "When he hit me," the woman explained, "I grabbed hold to his scrotum with my left hand and I was twisting it the opposite way. He started to yell and we fell to the floor and he hit me a couple of more licks, but they were light licks. He was weakening some then." Finally, the attacker surrendered, saying: "You've got me, you've got me, please, you've got me. . . . Please, please, you're killing me, you're killing me. . . . I can't do nothing. Call the police, call the police." She finally turned him loose and allowed him to get away, firing two shots at him to speed him along. When the police came, they found his trousers with his name written on them; then they found him "at home, in considerable pain and wondering if he could ever be a daddy."[2]

The case of the severed penis gave rise to the media event of 1993-94, the "Third Battle of Manassas," the thrilling adventures of John Wayne Bobbitt and Lorena Bobbitt. Whether the mutilation represented a vindictive act of a spiteful woman, as John Wayne might have one believe, or the logical consequence of years of spousal abuse—Lorena's defense—remains undecided. Both John Wayne and Lorena were charged, indicted, and tried in separate cases. Verdicts rendered by different juries set him free and detained her for psychological evaluation and possible treatment. Although Manassas, Virginia, figured prominently in the legal maneuverings, neither John Wayne nor Lorena hailed from there. The press often identified her as an Ecuadorian manicurist and mentioned his connections to New York.

Although the overwhelming majority of men and women in Dixie have shrunk from such approaches to their differences as those just mentioned, much of southern history has been sexually polarized. Long-standing assumptions about woman's place have relegated her to a private world where she was constantly reminded of her duties and responsibilities. When she entered the public arena as a male accessory or to support a masculine cause, she did so at the pleasure of the dominant power structure. If she found an alternate route into southern public society, she challenged the prevailing order and risked censure. Gradually, for complex and far-ranging reasons, the patriarchy has been eroded; it has not been eliminated. Southern women's past must be told, for their legacy matters to present and future generations. I only hope that I have done them no serious injustice in recounting it.

One presumes that the future has the potential to bring ever-expanding opportunities for women, but that should not be taken for granted. Margaret Atwood's novel *The Handmaid's Tale*, which, incidentally, she completed in Alabama, is a chilling vision of a postmodern utopia set in an age of dramatically declining births occasioned by environmental disasters. Atwood's principal character, Offred, and the other handmaids are valued only for viable ovaries.[3] On a more optimistic note, a prominent black female from Texas, the former congresswoman Barbara Jordan, has given great odds for the future; she anticipates "men and women working together—in our common humanity—trying to assure at every turn that we live in peace and freedom with civility and order."[4] Barring cataclysmic reversals, the lines of an old Baptist preacher may be a fitting tribute to southern women: "We ain't what we want to be. We ain't what we gonna be. But, thank God, we ain't what we was." Finally, after a long sermon, a short benediction: "Hallelujah, Ah Women, Ah Men!"

Notes

Prologue

1. Joan Hoff, "The Pernicious Effects of Poststructuralism on Women's History," *Chronicle of Higher Education*, 20 October 1993, B1-2.

2. Hubert Shuptrine and James Dickey, *Jericho: The South Beheld* (Birmingham, Ala.: Oxmoor House, Inc., 1974), with illustration no. 23 (n.p.) and also on 120.

3. Gerda Lerner, *The Creation of Patriarchy* (New York: Oxford University Press, 1986), 239.

4. Julia Cherry Spruill, *Women's Life and Work in the Southern Colonies* (Chapel Hill: University of North Carolina Press, 1938), 44.

5. Quoted in David Hackett Fischer, *Albion's Seed: Four British Folkways in America* (New York: Oxford University Press, 1989), 280.

6. Arthur M. Schlesinger, *Learning How to Behave: A Historical Study of American Etiquette Books* (New York: Macmillan Co., 1947), 6-10.

7. Bertram Wyatt-Brown, *Southern Honor: Ethics and Behavior in the Old South* (New York: Oxford University Press, 1982; paperback ed., 1983), 54.

8. W.J. Cash, *The Mind of the South* (New York: Alfred A. Knopf, 1941; Vintage Books, 1969), 52.

9. Florence King, *Southern Ladies and Gentlemen* (Briarcliff Manor, N.Y.: Stein & Day, 1975); Sharon McKern, *Redneck Mothers, Good Ol' Girls, and Other Southern Belles: A Celebration of the Women of Dixie* (New York: Viking Press, 1979); Marlyn Schwartz, *A Southern Belle Primer: Or, Why Princess Margaret Will Never Be a Kappa Kappa Gamma* (New York: Doubleday, 1991), and *New Times in the Old South; Or, Why Scarlett's in Therapy and Tara's Going Condo* (New York: Harmony Books, 1993).

10. Anne Firor Scott, *The Southern Lady: From Pedestal to Politics, 1830-1930* (Chicago: University of Chicago Press, 1970).

11. See Spruill, *Women's Life and Work in the Southern Colonies*, cited in note 4 above; A. Elizabeth Taylor is the author of numerous articles on the subject of female suffrage in various southern states and the book *The Woman Suffrage Movement in Tennessee* (New York: Bookman Associates, 1957).

12. The historiography of southern women has become considerably more sophisticated than it was when I published my first article on them: see Margaret Ripley Wolfe,

"The Southern Lady: Long Suffering Counterpart of the Good Ole Boy," *Journal of Popular Culture* 11 (Summer 1977): 18-27.

13. Quoted in Henry Steele Commager, *The Nature and Study of History* (Columbus, Ohio: Charles E. Merrill, 1966), 43.

14. Nancy Woloch, *Women and the American Experience* (New York: Alfred A. Knopf, 1984); and Sara M. Evans, *Born for Liberty: A History of Women in America* (New York and London: Free Press and Collier Macmillan Publishers, 1989).

15. For a discussion of the status of southern women's history and the writing of it see Catherine Clinton, "In Search of Southern Women's History: The Current State of Academic Publishing," *Georgia Historical Quarterly* 76 (Summer 1992): 420-27; Jacquelyn Dowd Hall, "Partial Truths: Writing Southern Women's History," in *Southern Women: Histories and Identities*, ed. Virginia Bernhard et al. (Columbia: University of Missouri Press, 1992), 11-29; Anne Firor Scott, "A Different View of Southern History," in *Unheard Voices: The First Historians of Southern Women*, ed. Anne Firor Scott (Charlottesville: University Press of Virginia, 1993), 1-71 (this book appears in the series Feminist Issues: Practice, Politics, Theory, ed. Alison Booth and Anne Lane); and idem, "Historians Construct the Southern Woman," in *Sex, Race, and the Role of Women in the South*, ed. Joanne V. Hawks and Sheila L. Skemp (Jackson: University Press of Mississippi, 1983), 95-110; see also Jacquelyn Dowd Hall and Anne Firor Scott, "Women in the South," in *Interpreting Southern History: Historiographical Essays in Honor of Sanford W. Higginbotham*, ed. John B. Boles and Evelyn Thomas Nolen (Baton Rouge: Louisiana State University Press, 1987), 545-609; and Carol Ruth Berkin, "'Of Course, It May Be Different in the South': A Critical Review of the Historiography of Southern Colonial Women," unpublished manuscript in my possession. Catherine Clinton's edited collection *Half Sisters of History: Southern Women and the American Past* (Durham, N.C.: Duke University Press, 1994) contains essays by pioneering scholars in the specialty of southern women's history that cut across the full range of the feminine experience in Dixie.

16. As a specialty, women's history in the United States has all too often placed heavy emphasis on northern women in general and New England women in particular. Catherine Clinton was among the first to call attention in print to the "New Englandization" of women's studies: see her *The Plantation Mistress: Woman's World in the Old South* (New York: Pantheon Books, 1982), xiii, xv, which she offered as a southern counterpoint to Nancy F. Cott, *The Bonds of Womanhood: "Woman's Sphere" in New England, 1780-1835* (New Haven, Conn.: Yale University Press, 1977).

17. See James C. Cobb, *The Most Southern Place on Earth: The Mississippi Delta and the Roots of Regional Identity* (New York: Oxford University Press, 1992).

18. George B. Tindall, "Beyond the Mainstream: The Ethnic Southerners," *Journal of Southern History* 40 (February 1974): 8.

19. Edward D.C. Campbell, Jr., *The Celluloid South: Hollywood and the Southern Myth* (Knoxville: University of Tennessee Press, 1981); and Jack Temple Kirby, *Media-Made Dixie: The South in the American Imagination* (Baton Rouge: Louisiana State University Press, 1978); see also Robert Sklar, *Movie-Made America: A Social History of American Movies* (New York: Random House, 1975), 3-17 et passim.

20. Shirley Abbott, *Womenfolks: Growing Up down South* (New Haven, Conn.: Ticknor & Fields, 1983), 6.

21. C. Vann Woodward, "Slaves and Mistresses," a review of Elizabeth Fox-Genovese, *Within the Plantation Household: Black and White Women of the Old South*, in *New York Review of Books*, 8 December 1988, 3-4.

Chapter 1. In the Beginning

1. See David E. Stannard, *American Holocaust: The Conquest of the New World* (New York: Oxford University Press, 1992).

2. Quoted in Theda Perdue, "Columbus Meets Pocahontas in the American South," an address before the Southern Association for Women Historians, 6 November 1992, 1-5, copy in my possession, graciously provided by Dr. Perdue. See Philip Young, "Pocahontas," in *Portraits of American Women: From Settlement to the Present*, ed. G.J. Barker-Benfield and Catherine Clinton (New York: St. Martin's Press, 1991), 15-33. Gary B. Nash, in *Red, White, and Black: The Peoples of Early America*, History of the American People Series, ed. Leon Litwack (Englewood Cliffs, N.J.: Prentice-Hall, Inc., 1974), provides an interesting and useful treatment of colonial America's diverse population; see also James S. Wamsley with Anne M. Cooper, *Idols, Victims, Pioneers: Virginia's Women from 1607* (n.p.: Virginia Chamber of Commerce, 1976), a Bicentennial Project of the Virginia State Chamber of Commerce and the Virginia Commission on the Status of Women.

3. Edmund S. Morgan, *American Slavery—American Freedom: The Ordeal of Colonial Virginia* (New York: W.W. Norton, Inc., 1975), 52

4. Quoted in Conway Whittle Sams, *The Conquest of Virginia: The First Attempt* (Norfolk, Va.: Keyser-Doherty Printing Corp., 1924; reprint ed., Spartanburg, S.C.: Reprint Co., 1973), 68.

5. Ibid., 69.

6. Perdue, "Columbus Meets Pocahontas," 5-12; quotation from Stephanie Coontz, *The Social Origins of Private Life: A History of American Families, 1600-1900* (London: Verso, 1988), 57-58.

7. Perdue, "Columbus Meets Pocahontas," 10-11.

8. Ibid., 8-9; see also Theda Perdue, "Southern Indians and the Cult of True Womanhood," in *The Web of Southern Social Relations: Women, Family, and Education*, ed. Walter J. Fraser, Jr., R. Frank Saunders, Jr., and Jon L. Wakelyn (Athens: University of Georgia Press, 1985), 35-51, especially 36-37; and Jon A. Schlenker, "An Historical Analysis of the Family Life of the Choctaw Indians," *Southern Quarterly* 13 (July 1975): 323-34.

9. Perdue, "Columbus Meets Pocahontas," 8.

10. John Spencer Bassett, ed., *The Writings of William Byrd of Westover in Virginia Esqr.* (New York: Burt Franklin, 1901; reprint by same, 1970), 244-45; see also Kenneth A. Lockridge, *The Diary, and Life, of William Byrd II of Virginia, 1674-1744* (Chapel Hill: University of North Carolina Press for the Institute of Early American History and Culture in Williamsburg, Va., 1987).

11. Louis Philippe, king of France, 1830-1848, *Diary of My Travels in America*, trans. Stephen Becker with preface by Henry Steele Commager (New York: Delacorte Press, 1977), 72, 85 et passim.

12. Morgan, *American Slavery—American Freedom*, 35.

13. Quoted in ibid., 74.

14. Bernard Bailyn et al., *The Great Republic: A History of the American People*, 4th ed. (Lexington, Mass.: D.C. Heath, 1992), 40-41.

15. Quoted in Sams, *Conquest of Virginia*, 259; the women are listed on 508.

16. Quoted in Spruill, *Women's Life and Work in the Southern Colonies*, 3.

17. Ibid., 3-5; see also Carl Bridenbaugh, *Jamestown, 1544-1699* (New York: Oxford University Press, 1989), 43, 53, 125-26; and Virginia Bernhard, "'Men, Women and

Children' at Jamestown: Population and Gender in Early Virginia, 1607-1610," *Journal of Southern History* 58 (November 1992): 599-618.

18. Spruill, *Women's Life and Work in the Southern Colonies*, 5; see also Arthur Frederick Ide, *Woman in the American Colonial South* (Mesquite, Tex.: Ide House, 1980), 5.

19. Spruill, *Women's Life and Work in the Southern Colonies*, 8-10; and quotation from Richard L. Morton, *The Tidewater Period, 1607-1710*, vol. 1 of *Colonial Virginia* (Chapel Hill: University of North Carolina Press for the Virginia Historical Society, 1960), 71-72.

20. David R. Ransome, "Wives for Virginia, 1621," *William and Mary Quarterly*, 3d ser., 48 (January 1991): 3, 12; Bernard Bailyn with the assistance of Barbara DeWolfe, *Voyagers to the West: A Passage in the Peopling of America on the Eve of the Revolution* (New York: Alfred A. Knopf, 1986), 105-6, 122-24, 274-75; and the chapter entitled "A Horse Foaled by an Acorn" in Robert Hughes, *The Fatal Shore* (New York: Alfred A. Knopf, 1987), 19-42. The last-named tends to disabuse one of any nostalgia for Georgian England.

21. Suzanne Lebsock, *"A Share of Honour": Virginia Women, 1600-1945* (Richmond: Virginia Women's Cultural History Project, 1984), 18.

22. Walter Hart Blumenthal, *Brides from Bridewell: Female Felons Sent to Colonial America* (Rutland, Vt.: Charles E. Tuttle, 1962; reprint, Westport, Conn.: Greenwood Press, 1973), 54 et passim; Faulkner is quoted on 53; see also James Curtis Ballagh, *White Servitude in the Colony of Virginia: A Study of the System of Indentured Labor in the American Colonies* (New York: Burt Franklin, 1969), passim.

23. Bailyn, *Voyagers to the West*, 463-64, quotation on 463.

24. Blumenthal, *Brides from Bridewell*, 64-78; and Morgan, *American Slavery— American Freedom*, 117.

25. Morgan, *American Slavery—American Freedom*, 127-28; see also Lebsock, "A Share of Honour," 18-21.

26. Lebsock, "A Share of Honour," 18-21; and Lois Green Carr and Lorena S. Walsh, "From Indentured Servant to Planter's Wife: White Women in Seventeenth-Century Maryland," in *The Underside of American History*, ed. Thomas R. Frazier, 5th ed. (San Diego: Harcourt Brace Jovanovich, 1987), 36-55, particularly 42; see also idem, "The Planter's Wife: The Experience of White Women in Seventeenth-Century Maryland," in *Women and Power in American History: A Reader*, ed. Kathryn Kish Sklar and Thomas Dublin, vol. 1 (Englewood Cliffs, N.J.: Prentice-Hall, 1991), 51-71.

27. Lebsock, "A Share of Honour," 21.

28. Lorena S. Walsh, "The Experience and Status of Women in the Chesapeake, 1750-1755," in *Web of Southern Social Relations*, 1-4.

29. Ibid., 4-5.

30. Ibid., 5; and Gwen Victor Gampel, "The Planter's Wife Revisited: Women, Equity Law, and the Chancery Court in Seventeenth-Century Maryland," in *Women and the Structure of Society*, ed. Barbara J. Harris and JoAnn K. McNamara (Durham, N.C.: Duke University Press, 1984), 20-35, particularly 34 and 35; see also Joan Hoff, *Law, Gender, and Injustice: A Legal History of U.S. Women* (New York: New York University Press, 1991), 21-26.

31. Walsh, "The Experience and Status of Women in the Chesapeake," 4.

32. Lebsock, "A Share of Honour," 23.

33. Allan Kulikoff, *Tobacco and Slaves: The Development of Southern Cultures in*

the *Chesapeake, 1680-1800* (Chapel Hill: University of North Carolina Press for the Institute of Early American History and Culture, Williamsburg, Va., 1986), 24 and 180; idem, "The Colonial Chesapeake: Seedbed of Antebellum Southern Culture?" *Journal of Southern History* 45 (November 1979): 513-40; see also Anne Elizabeth Yentsch, *A Chesapeake Family and Their Slaves: A Study in Historical Archaeology*, New Studies in Archaeology (New York: Cambridge University Press, 1994).

34. Walsh, "Experience and Status of Women in the Chesapeake," 5.

35. Kulikoff, *Tobacco and Slaves*, 12.

36. Ibid., 7, 13, 421-22; see also Michael Mullin, *Africa in America: Slave Accultur-ation and Resistance in the American South and the British Caribbean, 1736-1831* (Urbana: University of Illinois Press, 1991), passim.

37. Winthrop D. Jordan, *White over Black: American Attitudes toward the Negro, 1550-1812* (Chapel Hill: University of North Carolina Press, 1968; reprint ed., New York: W.W. Norton, 1977), 73, 74.

38. Coontz, *Social Origins of Private Life*, 91.

39. Lebsock, "A Share of Honour," 27, 28.

40. Walsh, "Experience and Status of Women in the Chesapeake," 2, 14-15; see Allan Kulikoff, "The Beginnings of the Afro-American Family in Maryland," in *Women and Power in American History*, 1:72-89; and Jean Butenhoff Lee, "The Problem of Slave Community in the Eighteenth-Century Chesapeake," *William and Mary Quarterly*, 3d ser., 53 (January 1986): 333-61; see also Coontz, *Social Origins of Private Life*, 91-92.

41. Lebsock, "A Share of Honour," 37-41.

42. Ibid., 23-25; see also Mary Beth Norton, "Gender and Defamation in Seventeenth-Century Maryland," *William and Mary Quarterly*, 3d ser., 44 (January 1987): 3-39.

43. Morgan, *American Slavery—American Freedom*, 333-37, quotation on 335; see also Jordan, *White over Black*, 78-80; and Warren M. Billings, *The Old Dominion in the Seventeenth Century: A Documentary History of Virginia, 1606-1689* (Chapel Hill: University of North Carolina Press for the Institute of Early American History and Culture, Williamsburg, Va., 1975), 160-63.

44. Fischer, *Albion's Seed*, 300-304.

45. Ibid., 304-5.

46. Quoted in ibid., 305; and Spruill, *Women's Life and Work in the Southern Colonies*, 71.

47. Spruill, *Women's Life and Work in the Southern Colonies*, 45-48.

48. Ibid., 49-51.

49. Fischer, *Albion's Seed*, 220-21.

50. Lebsock, "A Share of Honour," 23, 25-26; see also Richard Beale Davis, *Literature and Society in Early Virginia, 1608-1840* (Baton Rouge: Louisiana State University Press, 1973), 43-62. There is some difference of opinion as to whether the history of the rebellion was written by Anne Cotton or her husband, John: see, e.g., Richard Beale Davis, C. Hugh Holman, and Louis D. Rubin, Jr., eds., *Southern Writing, 1585-1920* (New York: Odyssey Press, 1970), 69; see also Coontz, *Social Origins of Private Life*, 101; and Susan Westbury, "Women in Bacon's Rebellion," in *Southern Women: Histories and Identities*, 30-46.

51. Fischer, *Albion's Seed*, 287-92, quotation on 292.

52. Ibid., 293-97.

53. Stephanie Grauman Wolf, *As Various as Their Land: The Everyday Lives of Eighteenth-Century Americans* (New York: HarperCollins, 1993), 98.

54. Elisabeth Anthony Dexter, *Career Women of America, 1776-1840* (Boston: Houghton Mifflin, 1950; reprint, Clifton, N.J.: Augustus M. Kelley, 1972), xi-xii.

55. Elisabeth Anthony Dexter, *Colonial Women of Affairs: Women in Business and the Professions before 1776* (Boston: Houghton Mifflin, 1931; reprint, Clifton, N.J.: Augustus M. Kelley, 1972), 12, 83, 99, 119-25, 147, 157, 166-67, 172-76, et passim.

56. Susan C. Boyle, "Did She Generally Decide? Women in Ste. Genevieve, 1750-1805," *William and Mary Quarterly*, 3d ser., 44 (October 1987): 775-79.

57. Ibid., 779-89; see also Morris S. Arnold, *Colonial Arkansas, 1686-1804* (Fayetteville: University of Arkansas Press, 1991), 94-97 et passim.

58. Thomas N. Ingersoll, "Free Blacks in a Slave Society: New Orleans, 1718-1812," *William and Mary Quarterly*, 3d ser., 48 (April 1991): 187-88; Mary Gehman and Nancy Ries, *Women of New Orleans* (New Orleans: Margaret Media, 1985), 6; see also Gwendolyn Midlo Hall, *Africans in Colonial Louisiana: The Development of an Afro-American Culture in the Eighteenth Century* (Baton Rouge: Louisiana State University Press, 1992).

59. Gehman and Ries, *Women of New Orleans*, 5.

60. Ibid., 6.

61. Ibid., 7-8.

62. Louis B. Wright, *The Cultural Life of the American Colonies, 1607-1763*, New American Nation Series, ed. Henry Steele Commager and Richard B. Morris (New York: Harper & Row, 1957), 45-71; idem, *South Carolina: A Bicentennial History*, The State and the Nation Series, ed. James Morton Smith (New York: W.W. Norton for the American Association for State and Local History in Nashville, 1976), 30-62; Hugh T. Lefler and William S. Powell, *Colonial North Carolina: A History*, A History of the American Colonies in Thirteen Volumes, ed. Milton M. Klein and Jacob E. Cooke (New York: Charles Scribner's Sons, 1973), 81-112; Kenneth Coleman, *Colonial Georgia: A History*, A History of the American Colonies in Thirteen Volumes, ed. Milton M. Klein and Jacob E. Cooke (New York: Charles Scribner's Sons, 1976), 36-54; Harold H. Martin, *Georgia: A Bicentennial History*, The State and the Nation Series, ed. James Morton Smith (New York: W.W. Norton for the American Association for State and Local History in Nashville, 1977), 24-26; Carol E. Hoffecker, *Delaware: A Bicentennial History* (New York: W.W. Norton for the American Association for State and Local History in Nashville, 1977), 69-93; and Sydney G. Fisher, *The Quaker Colonies: A Chronicle of the Proprietors of the Delaware*, Chronicles of America Series, ed. Allen Johnson (New Haven, Conn.: Yale University Press, 1919), 197-214; see also K.G. Davies, *The North Atlantic World in the Seventeenth Century*, Europe and the World in the Age of Expansion Series, ed. Boyd C. Shafer (Minneapolis: University of Minnesota Press, 1974), 63-140; and Oliver Perry Chitwood, *A History of Colonial America*, 3rd ed. (New York: Harper & Row, 1961), 185-86, 188.

Chapter 2. And Another Generation Cometh

1. Quoted in Coontz, *Social Origins of Private Life*, 146.

2. Mary Beth Norton, "'What an Alarming Crisis Is This': Southern Women and the American Revolution," in *The Southern Experience in the American Revolution*, ed. Jeffrey J. Crow and Larry E. Tise (Chapel Hill: University of North Carolina Press,

1979), 203-34; quoted material from idem, *Liberty's Daughters: The Revolutionary Experience of American Women, 1750-1800* (Boston: Little, Brown, 1980), 202, 204.

3. Evans, *Born for Liberty*, 41-42, 57-58; see also Harvey H. Jackson, "Hugh Bryan and the Evangelical Movement in Colonial South Carolina," *William and Mary Quarterly*, 3d ser., 53 (October 1986): 594-614.

4. Jean E. Friedman, *The Enclosed Garden: Women and Community in the Evangelical South, 1830-1930* (Chapel Hill: University of North Carolina Press), 110-27; Scott, *Southern Lady*, 135-63.

5. Norton, *Liberty's Daughters*; Mary Beth Norton, "The Myth of the Golden Age," in *Women of America: A History*, ed. Carol Ruth Berkin and Mary Beth Norton (Boston: Houghton Mifflin, 1979), 37-47; Claudia Goldin, "The Economic Status of Women in the Early Republic: Quantitative Evidence," *Journal of Interdisciplinary History* 16 (Winter 1986): 375-404; Mary Sumner Benson, *Women in Eighteenth-Century America: A Study of Opinion and Social Usage* (Port Washington, N.Y.: Kennikat Press, 1935; reprint ed. by same, 1966); Cott, *Bonds of Womanhood*; Laurel Thatcher Ulrich, *Good Wives: Image and Reality in the Lives of Women in Northern New England, 1650-1750* (New York: Alfred A. Knopf, 1982); Linda Kerber, *Women of the Republic: Intellect and Ideology in Revolutionary America* (Chapel Hill: University of North Carolina Press for the Institute of Early American History and Culture, Williamsburg, Va., 1980); Linda Grant DePauw, *Founding Mothers: Women in America in the Revolutionary Era* (Boston: Houghton Mifflin, 1975); Linda Grant DePauw and Conover Hunt with the assistance of Miriam Schneir, *Remember the Ladies: Women in America, 1750-1815* (New York: Viking Press, 1976); Sally Smith Booth, *The Women of '76* (New York: Hastings House, 1973); Ronald Hoffman and Peter J. Albert, eds., *Women in the Age of the American Revolution* (Charlottesville: University Press of Virginia, 1989); Ruth H. Bloch, "The Gendered Meanings of Virtue in Revolutionary America," *Signs* 13 (Autumn 1987): 37-58; Jan Lewis, "The Republican Wife: Virtue and Seduction in the Early Republic," in *American Vistas, 1607-1877*, ed. Leonard Dinnerstein and Kenneth T. Jackson, 6th ed. (New York: Oxford University Press, 1991), 147-76. For a study of the "other women" see Mary Beth Norton, "Eighteenth-Century American Women: The Case of the Loyalists," in *A Heritage of Our Own: Toward a New Social History of American Women*, ed. Nancy F. Cott and Elizabeth H. Pleck (New York: Simon & Schuster, 1979), 136-61; see also Joan Hoff-Wilson, "The Negative Impact of the American Revolution," and Mary Beth Norton, "The Positive Impact of the American Revolution," in *Major Problems in American Women's History: Documents and Essays*, ed. Mary Beth Norton (Lexington, Mass.: D.C. Heath, 1989), 90-101 and 101-11 respectively; and Mary Beth Norton, "The Evolution of White Women's Experience in Early America," *American Historical Review* 89 (June 1984): 593-619.

6. Coontz, *Social Origins of Private Life*, 151.

7. Marylynn Salmon, *Women and the Law of Property in Early America* (Chapel Hill: University of North Carolina Press, 1986), xv.

8. Rhys Isaac, *The Transformation of Virginia, 1740-1790* (Chapel Hill: University of North Carolina Press for the Institute of Early American History and Culture, Williamsburg, Va., 1982), 309.

9. Gordon S. Wood, *The Radicalism of the American Revolution* (New York: Alfred A. Knopf, 1992), 7.

10. Coontz, *Social Origins of Private Life*, 2-3, 79, 97.

11. Ibid., 80, 98.

12. Ibid., 77-78.

13. Carl Bridenbaugh, *Myths and Realities: Societies of the Old South* (Baton Rouge: Louisiana State University Press, 1952), vii.

14. John Richard Alden, "The First South," in *Myth and Southern History*, vol. 1: *The Old South*, ed. Patrick Gerster and Nicholas Cords, 2d ed. (Urbana: University of Illinois Press, 1989), 68.

15. Salmon, *Women and the Law of Property in Early America*, 37-38.

16. Ibid., 39.

17. Woloch, *Women and the American Experience*, 67-68.

18. Deposition of Peter Williams before the Clerk and master in equity for the district of Washington, Tenn., 9 February 1799, in *Agnes Tarbet* v. *Alexander Tarbet*, Jonesborough, Tenn., private collection of Tony Marion, Blountville, Tenn.

19. Elizabeth Crawley's petition for divorce in the superior court, state of Tennessee, Washington district, 2 September 1806, private collection of Tony Marion, Blountville, Tenn.

20. Max Savelle and Darold D. Wax, *A History of Colonial America*, 3d ed. (Hinsdale, Ill.: Dryden Press, 1973), 741-42; DePauw and Hunt, *Remember the Ladies*, 101; and Christine Ladd Franklin, "The Education of Woman in the Southern States," in *Woman's Work in America*, ed. Annie Nathan Meyer (New York: Henry Holt, 1891; reprint ed., New York: Arno Press, 1972), 93. Franklin claims that 1804 marked the opening of the boarding school at Salem. Another source notes that "in 1802 they [the Moravians] founded Salem Academy, a school for girls": see Mrs. I.M.E. Blandin, *History of Higher Education of Women in the South Prior to 1860* (New York: Neale Publishing Co., n.d.; reprint ed., Washington, D.C.: Zenger Publishing Co., 1975), 31. Sally G. McMillen cites 1802 in *Southern Women: Black and White in the Old South* (Arlington Heights, Ill.: Harlan Davidson, 1992), 82.

21. Blandin, *History of Higher Education of Women in the South Prior to 1860*, 33.

22. Quoted in Dexter, *Career Women of America, 1776-1840*, 220-21.

23. Jack P. Greene, *Landon Carter: An Inquiry into the Personal Values and Social Imperatives of the Eighteenth-Century Gentry* (Charlottesville: Dominion Books, a division of University Press of Virginia, 1967), 80-81.

24. Kenneth A. Lockridge, *On the Sources of Patriarchal Rage: The Commonplace Books of William Byrd and Thomas Jefferson and the Gendering of Power in the Eighteenth Century* (New York: New York University, 1992), 81-82, 112-13, et passim.

25. Ibid., 113.

26. Spruill, *Women's Life and Work in the Southern Colonies*, 60-61.

27. Lockridge, *On the Sources of Patriarchal Rage*, 70.

28. Ibid., 70-73 et passim.

29. Robert Wernick, "At Monticello, a Big Birthday for the Former Owner," *Smithsonian*, May 1993, 83-84; see also Dumas Malone, *Jefferson the Virginian*, vol. 1 of *Jefferson and His Time* (Boston: Little, Brown, 1948), 159-60.

30. Malone, *Jefferson the Virginian*, 153.

31. Fawn M. Brodie, *Thomas Jefferson: An Intimate History* (New York: W.W. Norton, 1974); see also Jan Lewis, *The Pursuit of Happiness: Family and Values in Jefferson's Virginia* (New York: Cambridge University Press, 1985).

32. Woloch, *Women and the American Experience*, 67, 91. For a discussion of the contribution of Scottish theorists to the concept of "republican mother" see Rosemarie Zagarri, "Morals, Manners, and the Republican Mother," *American Quarterly* 44 (June 1992): 192-215.

33. Evans, *Born for Liberty*, 63.

34. Quoted in Phillip Greven, *The Protestant Temperament: Patterns of Child-Rearing, Religious Experience, and the Self in Early America* (New York: Alfred A. Knopf, 1977), 289.

35. Benson, *Women in Eighteenth-Century America*, 160.

36. Quoted in Lebsock, "A Share of Honour," 49.

37. Quoted in Norton, *Liberty's Daughters*, 61.

38. Quoted in Greven, *Protestant Temperament*, 290.

39. Quoted in Norton, *Liberty's Daughters*, 53.

40. Ibid., 55.

41. Norton, "'What an Alarming Crisis Is This,'" 210.

42. Ibid., 211; see also Donald R. Wright, *African Americans in the Early Republic, 1789-1831*, American History Series, ed. John Hope Franklin and Abraham S. Eisenstadt (Arlington Heights, Ill.: Harlan Davidson, 1993).

43. Quoted in DePauw and Hunt, *Remember the Ladies*, 68.

44. Norton, "'What an Alarming Crisis Is This,'" 209-10.

45. Ibid., 212-13, 222-24; Norton, *Liberty's Daughters*, 164; see also Michael Mullin, "British Caribbean and North American Slaves in an Era of War and Revolution, 1775-1807," in *Southern Experience in the American Revolution*, 259-62.

46. Woloch, *Women and the American Experience*, 51-64.

47. Joanna Bowen Gillespie, "1795: Martha Laurens Ramsay's 'Dark Night of the Soul,'" *William and Mary Quarterly*, 3d ser., 48 (January 1991): 68-72.

48. Ibid., 73-77.

49. Ibid., 72-84.

50. Ibid., 70, 72, 80, 91.

51. Bridenbaugh, *Myths and Realities*, 66-99, particularly 76, 84; the David Ramsay quotation is from 84.

52. Ibid., 66-99; and Ide, *Woman in the American Colonial South*, 80. The contemporary commentary on the St. Cecilia Ball is from Schwartz, *Southern Belle Primer*, vii; see also Wright, *Cultural Life of the American Colonies*, 176-215, for a general discussion of architecture, music, and decorative arts with occasional references to the South.

53. Carl Bridenbaugh, *Cities in the Wilderness: The First Century of Urban Life in America, 1625-1742* (New York: Alfred A. Knopf, 1964), 279; quotation from ibid.

54. Depauw and Hunt, *Remember the Ladies*, 127; and Jessie Poesch, *The Art of the Old South: Painting, Sculpture, Architecture and the Products of Craftsmen, 1560-1860* (New York: Knopf, 1983; reprint, New York: Harrison House, 1989), 29-31.

55. Quoted in Benson, *Women in Eighteenth-Century America*, 287.

56. Ibid., 286, 289.

57. Dexter, *Career Women of America, 1776-1840*, 185-86, quotation from 186.

58. Daniel J. Boorstin, *The Americans: The Colonial Experience* (New York: Random House, 1958), 349-50; the material quoted by Boorstin is from 350.

59. Quoted in Page Smith, *Daughters of the Promised Land: Women in American History* (Boston: Little, Brown, 1970), 54.

60. Quoted in Abbott, *Womenfolks*, 41.

61. Benson, *Women in Eighteenth-Century America*, 285.

62. Abbott, *Womenfolks*, 32-33; and William Chauncy Langdon, *Everyday Things in American Life, 1606-1776* (New York: Charles Scribner's Sons, 1937; reprint ed. by same, 1965), 110-24; see also James G. Leyburn, "The Scotch-Irish in America," in *His-*

torical Viewpoints: Notable Articles from "American Heritage," vol. 1, *To 1877*, 6th ed., ed. John A. Garraty (New York: HarperCollins, 1991), 99-108.

63. Stanley J. Folmsbee, Robert E. Corlew, and Enoch L. Mitchell, *Tennessee: A Short History* (Knoxville: University of Tennessee Press, 1969), 39-46; Stuart O. Stumpf, "Fort Loudoun, Tennessee," in *Tennessee in American History*, ed. Larry H. Whiteaker and W. Calvin Dickinson (Needham Heights, Mass.: Ginn Press, 1991), 1-6; and J.G.M. Ramsey, *The Annals of Tennessee to the End of the Eighteenth Century* (Charleston, S.C.: Walker & Jones, 1853; reprint ed., Knoxville: East Tennessee Historical Society, 1967), 51-61.

64. All sources cited in preceding note; and Theda Perdue, "Nancy Ward (1738?-1822)," in *Portraits of American Women*, 92-93.

65. Perdue, "Nancy Ward," 85-90.

66. Ibid., 90-97; Timberlake's statement appears on 90. A highly romanticized version of Nancy Ward's life appears in E. Sterling King, *The Wild Rose of Cherokee; . . . Or, Nancy Ward, the Pocahontas of the West* (Nashville: Nashville University Press, 1895; reprint ed., Kingsport, Tenn.: Kingsport Press, for Reba Frazier Durham, n.d.).

67. Quoted in Evans, *Born for Liberty*, 50-51.

68. Mary Beth Norton, "Women in the American Revolution," in *Historical Viewpoints: Notable Articles from "American Heritage,"* 1:138-41; and Kerber, *Women of the Republic*, 99, 102-3. Norton claims that Mrs. Jefferson wrote to Eleanor Madison, but Kerber says it was Sarah Tate Madison. The footnote, however, cites Mrs. Jefferson to a Mrs. James Madison, 9 August 1780. It is safe to assume that Martha Jefferson wrote to a female Madison; any other conclusion would only add to the confusion.

69. David J. Harkness, comp., *Southern Heroines of the American Revolution* (Knoxville: University of Tennessee Continuing Education Series, June 1973), 1-2.

70. Norton, "Women in the American Revolution," 141; Kerber, *Women of the Republic*, 58.

71. Harkness, *Southern Heroines of the American Revolution*, 1; DePauw and Hunt, *Remember the Ladies*, 147; Martha Washington's financial worth is from an article in the *Richmond Times-Dispatch*, 21 April 1985.

72. Mary Beth Norton, "Southern Women and the Revolution," in *Major Problems in the American South*, vol. 1: *The Old South: Documents and Essays*, ed. Paul D. Escott and David R. Goldfield (Lexington, Mass.: D.C. Heath & Co., 1990), 181.

73. Ibid.

74. "Eliza Wilkinson's Thoughts on Women and War, 1779," in *Major Problems in the History of the American South*, vol. 1:156, 158.

75. "A Carolina Patriot: Eliza Wilkinson, 1782, Letter 6," in *Early American Women: A Documentary History, 1600-1900*, ed. Nancy Woloch (Belmont, Calif.: Wadsworth Publishing Co., 1992), 169.

76. Sandra Gioia Treadway, "Anna Maria Lane: An Uncommon Soldier of the American Revolution," *Virginia Cavalcade* 37 (Winter 1988): 142-43.

77. Ibid., 134.

78. Ibid., 143; and Harkness, *Southern Heroines of the American Revolution*, passim.

79. Harkness, *Southern Heroines of the American Revolution*, 12.

80. Quoted in Norton, "'What an Alarming Crisis Is This,'" 219, 223.

81. Ibid., 220-21; and Norton, "Eighteenth-Century American Women," 136-61; see also Kathy Roe Coker, "The Calamities of War: Loyalism and Women in South

Carolina," in *Southern Women: Histories and Identities*, 47-70. Coker writes on p. 70: "South Carolina courts evidently had no intention of punishing a woman for the conduct of her husband, father, brother, or other male relative. But sometimes, when the best interest of a woman was at odds with the best interest of the early Carolina republic, the woman lost."

82. Kerber, *Women of the Republic*, 98-99.

83. Treadway, "Anna Maria Lane," 134-43.

84. Depauw and Hunt, *Remember the Ladies*, 14; see also Norton, *Liberty's Daughters*, 138-39.

85. DePauw and Hunt, *Remember the Ladies*, 118.

86. The quoted material is from Norton, "'What an Alarming Crisis Is This,'" 224-26; see also Hoff-Wilson, "Negative Impact of the American Revolution," 98-101, who argues that the egalitarian ideals of the revolutionary era failed to have much impact on women's lives, North or South.

87. Glenna Matthews, *The Rise of Public Woman: Woman's Power and Woman's Place in the United States, 1630-1970* (New York: Oxford University Press, 1992), 46.

88. Norton, "'What an Alarming Crisis Is This,'" 226-27; and Gerda Lerner, *The Grimké Sisters from South Carolina* (Boston: Houghton Mifflin, 1967), 13; see also Patricia Jewell McAlexander, "The Creation of the American Eve: The Cultural Dialogue on the Nature and Role of Women in Late Eighteenth-Century America," *Early American Literature* 9 (Winter 1975): 252-66.

Chapter 3. A Garden Encosed Is My Sister, My Spouse

1. For a discussion of American women and the nineteenth-century political situation and the meaning of "politics" see Paula Baker, "The Domestication of Politics: Women and American Political Society, 1780-1920," *American Historical Review* 89 (June 1984): 620-47; a useful concise treatment of antebellum southern women appears in William J. Cooper, Jr., and Thomas E. Terrill, *The American South: A History* (New York: McGraw-Hill, 1991), 278-87.

2. Stephanie McCurry, "The Two Faces of Republicanism: Gender and Proslavery Politics in Antebellum South Carolina," *Journal of American History* 78 (March 1992): 1258; see also Bill Cecil-Fronsman, *Common Whites: Class and Culture in Antebellum North Carolina* (Lexington: University Press of Kentucky, 1992).

3. Woloch, *Women and the American Experience*, 145.

4. Edward Pessen, "How Different from Each Other Were the Antebellum North and South?" *American Historical Review* 85 (December 1980): 1123; see also Bruce Collins, *White Society in the Antebellum South*, Studies in Modern History, ed. John Morrill and David Cannadine (London: Longman, 1985), which offers some perspective on the complexities of the South; and Carl N. Degler, *Place over Time: The Continuity of Southern Distinctiveness* (Baton Rouge: Louisiana State University Press, 1977).

5. Franklin, "Education of Woman in the Southern States," 89.

6. Christie Anne Farnham, *The Education of the Southern Belle: Higher Education and Student Socialization in the Antebellum South* (New York: New York University Press, 1994), 11.

7. Franklin, "Education of Woman in the Southern States," 89.

8. The spelling of O'Neal varies, sometimes appearing as O'Neale and O'Neill. Pauline Wilcox Burke, *Emily Donelson of Tennessee* (Richmond, Va.: Garrett & Massie,

1941), 1:8, 15-18, 104, 121, 122, 125, 165; Woloch, *Women and the American Experience*, 151-66; Betty Boyd Caroli, *First Ladies* (New York: Oxford University Press, 1987; paperback ed., 1988), 12-17; and DePauw and Hunt, *Remember the Ladies*, 148-49. Frances Wright's experiment has been the subject of at least one novel: see Edd Winfield Parks, *Nashoba* (New York: Twayne Publishers, 1963); see also Celia M. Eckhardt, *Fanny Wright: Rebel in America* (Cambridge, Mass.: Harvard University Press, 1984); and Susan Kissel, *By Common Cause: The "Conservative" Frances Trollope and the "Radical" Frances Wright* (Bowling Green, Ohio: Bowling Green State University Popular Press, 1993).

9. Olive Gilbert, comp., *Narrative of Sojourner Truth, A Bondswoman of Olden Time* ([1878]; reprint ed., New York: Arno Press, 1968), 133-34. Truth was born into slavery as Isabella Baumfree around 1797 in Ulster, N.Y., and was freed in 1828 by legislation in that state.

10. A substantial body of data pertaining to nineteenth-century southern women exists in the form of diaries and manuscript collections, some of which have been made accessible to scholars in the form of edited publications and microforms. Such valuable contributions include works contained in Carol K. Bleser's series Women's Diaries and Letters of the Nineteenth-Century South, University of South Carolina Press, Columbia; and Southern Women and Their Families in the Nineteenth Century: Papers and Diaries, ed. Anne Firor Scott and William H. Chafe; the latter is a vast microfilm collection released by University Publications of America, Bethesda, Md. Joan E. Cashin, *Our Common Affairs: Documents in the History of Southern Women* (Athens: University of Georgia Press, c. 1995) is forthcoming.

11. Guion Griffis Johnson, "The Changing Status of the Southern Woman," in *The South in Continuity and Change*, ed. John C. McKinney and Edgar T. Thompson (Durham, N.C.: Duke University Press, 1965), 419; see also D. Harland Hagler, "The Ideal Woman in the Antebellum South: Lady or Farmwife," *Journal of Southern History* 46 (August 1980): 405-18.

12. Eugene D. Genovese, *Roll, Jordan, Roll: The World the Slaves Made* (New York: Pantheon Books, 1974), 81; see also Kathryn L. Seidell, "The Southern Belle as an Antebellum Ideal," *Southern Quarterly* 15 (July 1977): 387-401.

13. Norton, *Liberty's Daughters*, 26-27.

14. Carl N. Degler, *At Odds: Women and the Family in America from the Revolution to the Present* (New York: Oxford University Press, 1980), 28-29.

15. McMillen, *Southern Women*, 1.

16. Woloch, *Women and the American Experience*, 145.

17. Friedman, *Enclosed Garden*, xi-xii.

18. Virginia Gearhart Gray, "Activities of Southern Women, 1840-1860," in *Unheard Voices*, 75-91.

19. The full citation for Dexter's *Career Women* appears in note 54 of chap. 1.

20. Suzanne Lebsock, *The Free Women of Petersburg: Status and Culture in a Southern Town, 1784-1860* (New York: W.W. Norton, 1984), 240; Lebsock writes in a similar vein in "A Share of Honour," 59 et passim.

21. Nancy Ann White, "Idol, Equal, and Slave: White Female Identity and White Male Guilt: A Study of Female Role Definition in the Antebellum South" (Ph.D. diss., American University, 1980), iv, 177, 178.

22. Pessen, "How Different from Each Other Were the Antebellum North and South?" 1147, 1149.

23. Michael P. Johnson, "Planters and Patriarchy: Charleston, 1800-1860," *Journal of Southern History* 46 (February 1980): 72.

24. Ann Douglas, *The Feminization of American Culture* (New York: Alfred A. Knopf, 1977), 11.

25. Carroll Smith-Rosenberg, "The Female World of Love and Ritual: Relations Between Women in Nineteenth-Century America," *Signs* 1 (Autumn 1975): 1-30, quotations from 10, 14.

26. Barbara Welter, "The Cult of True Womanhood: 1820-1860," *American Quarterly* 18 (Summer 1966): 151-74, specifically 151.

27. Clinton, *Plantation Mistress*, 8.

28. Spruill, *Women's Life and Work in the Southern Colonies*, 105.

29. Clinton, *Plantation Mistress*, 102.

30. Fischer, *Albion's Seed*, 635, 638, 642-50.

31. Ibid., 676; see also Grady McWhiney, *Cracker Culture: Celtic Ways in the Old South* (Tuscaloosa: University of Alabama Press, 1988), passim.

32. Featherstonhaugh is quoted in Michael B. Dougan, "The Arkansas Married Woman's Property Law," *Arkansas Historical Quarterly* 46 (Spring 1987): 4; Dougan continues the description of Mrs. Barkman on the next page. For an overview of Arkansas women see Elizabeth Jacoway, ed., *Behold, Our Works Were Good: A Handbook of Arkansas Women's History* (Little Rock: Arkansas Women's History Institute in association with August House Publishers, 1988).

33. Quoted in James C. Klotter, *The Breckinridges of Kentucky, 1760-1981* (Lexington: University Press of Kentucky, 1986), 33.

34. Melinda S. Buza, "'Pledges of Our Love': Friendship, Love, and Marriage among the Virginia Gentry, 1800-1825," in *The Edge of the South: Life in Nineteenth-Century Virginia*, ed. Edward L. Ayers and John C. Willis (Charlottesville: University Press of Virginia, 1991), 18.

35. Joan E. Cashin, *A Family Venture: Men and Women on the Southern Frontier* (New York: Oxford University Press, 1991), 6; and idem, "The Structure of Antebellum Planter Families: 'The Ties that Bound Us Was Strong,'" *Journal of Southern History* 56 (February 1990): 55-70; see also Goodloe Stuck, *End of the Land: A South Carolina Family on the Louisiana Frontier* (Rustin: Louisiana Tech University, 1992).

36. Durwood Dunn, *Cades Code: The Life and Death of a Southern Appalachian Community, 1818-1937* (Knoxville: University of Tennessee Press, 1988), 2-3.

37. John Mack Faragher, *Daniel Boone: The Life and Legend of an American Pioneer* (New York: Henry Holt, 1992), 58-62.

38. Paul M. Fink, "Russell Bean, Tennessee's First Native Son," East Tennessee Historical Society *Publications* 37 (1965): 37.

39. Ibid., 37-39.

40. Ibid., 43-44.

41. Thomas D. Clark, *Kentucky: Land of Contrast* (New York: Harper & Row, 1968), 9-10. Suzanne Lebsock recounts the Mary Ingles story in "A Share of Honour," 34-35, but she mentions only Mary's two sons whom the captors sent off for adoption by other Indians.

42. Helen Deiss Irvin, *Women in Kentucky* (Lexington: University Press of Kentucky, 1979), 2.

43. Burke, *Emily Donelson of Tennessee*, 1:9-10.

44. Ibid., 10; and Irvin, *Women in Kentucky*, 5-8.

45. Irvin, *Women in Kentucky*, 9-10; Irvin gives the name as Merril; other sources use Merrill.

46. George Morgan Chinn, *Kentucky: Settlement and Statehood, 1750-1800* (Frankfort: Kentucky Historical Society, 1975), 266-75, quote from 275.

47. Clark, *Kentucky*, 27.

48. Irvin, *Women in Kentucky*, 10-15; see also Thurman B. Rice, "The Shanks (Scraggs, Skaggs, Skeggs, Scraggs) Family Massacre," *Register of the Kentucky Historical Society* 49 (1951): 83-92.

49. Chinn, *Kentucky*, 110.

50. Irvin, *Women in Kentucky*, 15-17.

51. Elizabeth A. Perkins, "The Consumer Frontier: Household Consumption in Early Kentucky," *Journal of American History* 78 (September 1991): 488, 489, 506-7; see also Daniel B. Thorp, "Doing Business in the Backcountry: Retail Trade in Colonial Rowan County, North Carolina," *William and Mary Quarterly*, 3d ser., 48 (July 1991): 397-98; Daniel H. Usner, Jr., "The Frontier Exchange Economy of the Lower Mississippi Valley in the Eighteenth Century," ibid. 44 (April 1987): 176; and Usner, *Indians, Settlers, and Slaves in a Frontier Exchange Economy* (Chapel Hill: University of North Carolina Press, 1992).

52. William L. Hiemstra, "Early Frontier Revivalism in Kentucky," *Register of the Kentucky Historical Society* 59 (April 1961): 137-38.

53. Anita Shafer Goodstein, *Nashville, 1780-1860: From Frontier to City* (Gainesville: University Press of Florida, 1989), 14.

54. Cashin, *Family Venture*, 4, 119, 120.

55. Wyatt-Brown, *Southern Honor*, 54-55; see also Ted Ownby, *Subduing Satan: Religion, Recreation, and Manhood in the Rural South, 1865-1920* (Chapel Hill: University of North Carolina Press, 1990).

56. Cash, *Mind of the South*, 52.

57. Brian Steel Wills, *A Battle from the Start: The Life of Nathan Bedford Forrest* (New York: HarperCollins, 1992), 25, 26.

58. John Hoyt Williams, *Sam Houston: A Biography of the Father of Texas* (New York: Simon & Schuster, 1993), 63-71, 77, 86-87, 99, 112-13, 171, 180, 184, 198-99, 361, 366, et passim.

59. Statement of John Hokem [?] before William Gilleyland, justice of the peace, probably in Washington County, Tennessee, 1 April 1842, private collection of Tony Marion, Blountville, Tenn.

60. Quoted in Norton, *Liberty's Daughters*, 94-95; see also Joel W. Martin, *Sacred Revolt: The Muskogees' Struggle for a New World* (Boston: Beacon Press, 1991), 20-21, 30, 77, 99-101.

61. Perdue, "Southern Indians and the Cult of True Womanhood," 47-48; see Thomas Hatley, "Cherokee Women Farmers Hold Their Ground," in *Appalachian Frontiers: Settlement, Society, and Development in the Preindustrial Era*, ed. Robert D. Mitchell (Lexington: University Press of Kentucky, 1991), 37-51. Hatley is particularly concerned with the eighteenth century, during which time, according to him, farming remained largely the province of Cherokee women, at least among the full bloods; see also Thomas Hatley, *The Dividing Paths: Cherokees and South Carolinians through the Era of Revolution* (New York: Oxford University Press, 1993).

62. Joan M. Jensen, *With These Hands: Women Working on the Land*, Women's Lives Women's Work Series, ed. Sue Davidson (Old Westbury, N.Y., and New York: Feminist Press and McGraw-Hill respectively, 1981), 27.

63. Wood, *Radicalism of the American Revolution*, 357-58.

64. Quotations from Jensen, *With These Hands*, 28-29.

65. Michael Paul Rogin, "Indian Removal," in *The Underside of American History*, 1:218-19; see also Grant Foreman, *Indian Removal: The Emigration of the Five Civilized Tribes of Indians* (Norman: University of Oklahoma Press, 1953); Grace S. Woodward, *The Cherokees* (Norman: University of Oklahoma Press, 1963); Arthur H. DeRosier, Jr., *The Removal of the Choctaw Indians* (Knoxville: University of Tennessee Press, 1970); John R. Finger, "The Abortive Second Cherokee Removal, 1841-1844," *Journal of Southern History* 47 (May 1981): 207-26; and Ray G. Lillard, "Rattlesnake Springs," *An Encyclopedia of East Tennessee History*, ed. Jim Stokely and Jeff D. Johnson (Oak Ridge, Tenn.: Children's Museum of Oak Ridge, 1981), 408-9.

66. Virginia Dean, *Naples on the Gulf: An Illustrated History* (Chatsworth, Calif.: Windsor Publications, 1991), 14-16; and Records of the Bureau of Indian Affairs, RG 75-N (Prints: General Photographs of Indians, ser. N, box 35), National Archives and Records Administration, Washington, D.C.; see also James W. Covington, *The Seminoles of Florida* (Gainesville: University Press of Florida, 1993); and Harry A. Kersey, Jr., *The Florida Seminoles and the New Deal, 1933-1942* (Gainesville: University Press of Florida, 1989).

67. For a discussion of antebellum American family life see Coontz, *Social Origins of Private Life*, 161-250; for detailed studies of family life in the antebellum South see Steven M. Stowe, *Intimacy and Power in the Old South: Ritual in the Lives of the Planters*, New Studies in American Intellectual and Cultural History, ed. Thomas Bender (Baltimore: Johns Hopkins University Press, 1987); idem, "All the Relations of Life: A Study in Sexuality, Family, and Social Values in the Southern Planter Class" (Ph.D. diss., State University of New York at Stony Brook, 1979); Orville Vernon Burton, *In My Father's House Are Many Mansions: Family and Community in Edgefield, South Carolina*, Fred W. Morrison Series in Southern Studies (Chapel Hill: University of North Carolina Press, 1985); Jane Turner Censer, *North Carolina Planters and Their Children, 1800-1860* (Baton Rouge: Louisiana State University Press, 1984); and Robert C. Kenser, *Kinship and Neighborhood in a Southern Community: Orange County, North Carolina, 1849-1881* (Knoxville: University of Tennessee Press, 1987).

68. William R. Taylor, *Cavalier and Yankee: The Old South and American National Character* (New York: George Braziller, 1961), 162.

69. Carol K. Bleser, "The Perrys of Greenville: A Nineteenth-Century Marriage," in *Web of Southern Social Relations*, 77; and quotation from Nancy Vance Ashmore, *Greenville: Woven from the Past, An Illustrated History* (Northridge, Calif.: Windsor Publications, 1986), 76.

70. Sally G. McMillen, *Motherhood in the Old South: Pregnancy, Childbirth, and Infant Rearing* (Baton Rouge: Louisiana State University Press, 1990), 7, 35; for an example of medical-advice books available in the South see [John Gunn], *Gunn's Domestic Medicine: A Facsimile of the First Edition*, with an introduction by Charles E. Rosenberg (Knoxville: University of Tennessee Press, 1986), which was first published in 1830. See also Janet Farrell Brodie, *Contraception and Abortion in Nineteenth-Century America* (Ithaca, N.Y.: Cornell University Press, 1994).

71. Quoted in Barbara L. Bellows, "'My Children, Gentleman, Are My Own': Poor Women, the Urban Elite, and the Bonds of Obligation in Antebellum Charleston," in *Web of Southern Social Relations*, 77; see also idem, *Benevolence among Slaveholders: Assisting the Poor in Charleston, 1670-1860* (Baton Rouge: Louisiana State University Press, 1993), in which Bellows argues that the southern urban elite engaged in relief in

order to engender in lower-class whites a sense of obligation to them, thus preventing lower-class whites from identifying with the free blacks who shared their economic plight.

72. Wyatt-Brown, *Southern Honor*, 296.

73. Clinton, *Plantation Mistress*, 103.

74. In addition to works cited elsewhere in this chapter, the following are helpful in attempting to understand slavery and its impact on women's lives: Elizabeth Fox-Genovese, *Within the Plantation Household: Black and White Women of the Old South*, Gender and American Culture, ed. Linda K. Kerber and Nell Irvin Painter (Chapel Hill: University of North Carolina Press, 1988); Jacqueline Jones, *Labor of Love, Labor of Sorrow: Black Women, Work, and the Family from Slavery to the Present* (New York: Basic Books, 1985); Edward D.C. Campbell and Kym S. Rice, eds., *Before Freedom Came: African-American Life in the Antebellum South* (Richmond and Charlottesville: Museum of the Confederacy and the University of Virginia Press, 1991); Marie Tyler-McGraw and Gregg D. Kimball, *In Bondage and Freedom: Antebellum Black Life in Richmond, Virginia* (Richmond: Valentine Museum, 1988); Charles Joyner, *Down by the Riverside: A South Carolina Slave Community* (Urbana: University of Illinois Press, 1984); Janet Duitsman Cornelius, *"When I Can Read My Title Clear": Literacy, Slavery, and Religion in the Antebellum South* (Columbia: University of South Carolina Press, 1991); Herbert G. Gutman, *The Black Family in Slavery and Freedom, 1750-1925* (New York: Pantheon Books, 1976); Carol Bleser, ed., *Secret and Sacred: The Diaries of James Henry Hammond, a Southern Slaveholder* (New York: Oxford University Press, 1988); and Ann Patton Malone, *Sweet Chariot: Slave Family and Household Structure in Nineteenth-Century Louisiana*, Fred W. Morrison Series in Southern Studies (Chapel Hill: University of North Carolina Press, 1992); see also Gwin Minrose, *Black and White Women of the Old South: The Peculiar Sisterhood in American Literature* (Knoxville: University of Tennessee Press, 1985).

75. "Mary Boykin Chesnut on Women and Slavery, 1861," in *Major Problems in the History of the American South*, 1:384; see also C. Vann Woodward and Elisabeth Muhlenfeld, *The Private Mary Chesnut: The Unpublished Civil War Diaries* (New York: Oxford University Press, 1984); C. Vann Woodward, ed., *Mary Chesnut's Civil War* (New Haven, Conn.: Yale University Press, 1981); and Elisabeth Muhlenfeld, *Mary Boykin Chesnut: A Biography* (Baton Rouge: Louisiana State University Press, 1981).

76. Quoted in Catherine Clinton, "Caught in the Web of the Big House," in *Web of Southern Social Relations*, 22.

77. "Fanny Kemble on Slave Women, 1839," in *Major Problems in the History of the American South*, 1:393; see also Frances A. Kemble, *Journal of a Residence on a Georgian Plantation in 1838-1839*, ed. John A. Scott (New York: NAL-Dutton, c. 1993).

78. Nell Irvin Painter, "Of *Lily*, Linda Brent, and Freud: A Non-Exceptionalist Approach to Race, Class, and Gender in the Slave South," *Georgia Historical Quarterly* 76 (Summer 1992): 243; Joyce D. Goodfriend and Claudia M. Christie, *Lives of American Women: A History with Documents* (Boston: Little, Brown, 1981), 100-110; and Harriet A. Jacobs, *Incidents in the Life of a Slave Girl, Written by Herself*, ed. Jean Fagan Yellin (Cambridge, Mass.: Harvard University Press, 1987); see also David Thomas Bailey, "A Divided Prism: Two Sources of Black Testimony on Slavery," *Journal of Southern History* 46 (August 1980): 380-404.

79. "Harriet Jacobs's Trials as a Slave Girl (1828), 1861," in *Major Problems in the History of the American South*, 1:394.

80. Melton A. McLaurin, *Celia, a Slave* (Athens: University of Georgia Press, 1991).

81. Clinton, "Caught in the Web of the Big House," 21-22.

82. Ibid., 25-26; for a discussion of free black women and their struggle for economic existence see Whittington Johnson, "Free African-American Women in Savannah, 1800-1860," *Georgia Historical Quarterly* 76 (Summer 1992): 260-83.

83. Adele Logan Alexander, *Ambiguous Lives: Free Women of Color in Rural Georgia, 1789-1879* (Fayetteville: University of Arkansas Press, 1991); see also James L. Roark, "Hidden Lives: Georgia's Free Women of Color," *Georgia Historical Quarterly* 76 (Summer 1992): 410-19; and Kent Anderson Leslie, "Amanda America Dickson: An Elite Mulatto Lady in Nineteenth-Century Georgia," in *Southern Women: Histories and Identities*, 71-86.

84. Deborah Gray White, *Ar'n't I A Woman? Female Slaves in the Antebellum South* (New York: W.W. Norton, 1985), 37; see also Judith Kelleher Schafer, "New Orleans Slavery in 1850 as Seen in Advertisements," *Journal of Southern History* 47 (February 1981): 33-56.

85. Gregory Cerio, "Between Two Worlds: From an Attic Trunk, One Black Family's Story," *Newsweek*, 17 August 1992, 54; T.O. Madden, Jr., with Ann L. Miller, *We Were Always Free: The Maddens of Culpeper County, Virginia: A 200-Year Family History*, foreword by Nell Irvin Painter (New York: W.W. Norton, 1992).

86. Stephen Ward Angell, *Bishop Henry McNeal Turner and African-American Religion in the South* (Knoxville: University of Tennessee Press, 1992), 7.

87. *Turning the World Upside Down: The Anti-Slavery Convention of American Women Held in New York City, May 9-12, 1837*, containing minutes of the convention, with an introduction by Dorothy Sterling (New York: Feminist Press at the City University of New York, 1987); see Dickson D. Bruce, Jr., *Archibald Grimké: Portrait of a Black Independent* (Baton Rouge: Louisiana State University Press, 1993). Archibald Grimké was the nephew of Angelina and Sarah Grimké. After emancipation they helped him attend college. He became one of Harvard Law School's first black graduates and subsequently actively involved himself in the founding of the National Association for the Advancement of Colored People and its work with the District of Columbia branch; see also Jean Fagan Yellin, *Women and Sisters: Antislavery Feminists in American Culture* (New Haven, Conn.: Yale University Press, 1990).

88. From the Frederick Douglass and Harriet Tubman Series of Narrative Paintings, Jacob Lawrence Exhibit, Joslyn Museum, Omaha, Neb., March 1993.

89. Hoffecker, *Delaware*, 99.

90. White, *Ar'n't I a Woman?* 159-60, 162; see also Cheryl Thurber, "The Development of the Mammy Image and Mythology," in *Southern Women: Histories and Identities*, 87-108; and K. Sue Jewell, *From Mammy to Miss America and Beyond: Cultural Images and the Shaping of U.S. Social Policy* (New York: Routledge, 1992). Quaker Oats has updated Aunt Jemima's image from that of "a fat cheerful cook wearing starched clothes and a red bandana around her head" to that of "a young, working grandmother." She now "sports earrings, neatly permed hair and what looks suspiciously like a suit jacket over her white blouse." See *Economist*, 6 May 1989.

Chapter 4. And If a House Be Divided Against Itself

1. Campbell, *Celluloid South*, 3-4, 15-16, et passim; Kirby, *Media-Made Dixie*, 72-74, 166-67, 169, et passim; and Darden Asbury Pyron, *Southern Daughter: The Life of Margaret Mitchell* (New York: Oxford University Press, 1991).

2. Maxine P. Atkinson and Jacqueline Boles, "The Shaky Pedestal: Southern

Ladies Yesterday and Today," *Southern Studies: An Interdisciplinary Journal of the South* 23 (Winter 1985): 398.

3. Allan Gurganus, *Oldest Living Confederate Widow Tells All* (New York: Alfred A. Knopf, 1989), 12-13.

4. Michael O'Brien, *The Idea of the South, 1920-1941* (Baltimore: Johns Hopkins University Press, 1979), 5-6; see also Thomas B. Alexander, "The Civil War as Institutional Fulfillment," *Journal of Southern History* 47 (February 1981): 3-32; and Edward R. Crowther, "Holy Honor: Sacred and Secular in the Old South," ibid., 58 (November 1992): 619-36.

5. Cash, *Mind of the South*, 130.

6. Wyatt-Brown, *Southern Honor*, 454.

7. Cash, *Mind of the South*, 131.

8. Atkinson and Boles, "Shaky Pedestal," 405-6.

9. Mary Elizabeth Massey, *Bonnet Brigades: American Women and the Civil War*, The Impact of the Civil War (Civil War Centennial Commission Series), ed. Allan Nevins (New York: Alfred A. Knopf, 1966), 367; see also Marjorie Stratford Mendenhall, "Southern Women of a 'Lost Generation,'" in *Unheard Voices*, 92-110.

10. Bell Irvin Wiley, *Confederate Women*, Contributions in American History, ed. Jon L. Wakelyn (Westport, Conn.: Greenwood Press, 1975), 178.

11. Scott, *Southern Lady*, 81 and 102.

12. Catherine Clinton, *The Other Civil War: American Women in the Nineteenth Century*, American Century Series, ed. Eric Foner (New York: Hill & Wang, 1984), 89.

13. George C. Rable, *Civil Wars: Women and the Crisis of Southern Nationalism*, Women in American History (Urbana: University of Illinois Press, 1989), x, 288, which provides an extraordinarily fine listing of sources. Such works as the following are also helpful: Katharine M. Jones, *Heroines of Dixie: Confederate Women Tell Their Story of the War*, Stars and Bars ed. (Indianapolis, Ind.: Bobbs-Merrill, 1955), which is an anthology; and Elizabeth Avery Meriwether, *Recollections of Ninety-two Years, 1824-1916* (Nashville: Tennessee Historical Commission, 1958); see also Matthew Page Andrews, *The Women of the South in War Times* (Baltimore: Norman, Remington, 1920). A treatment of both northern and southern women appears in Marilyn Mayer Culpepper, *Trials and Triumphs: The Women of the American Civil War* (East Lansing: Michigan State University Press, 1991).

14. LeeAnn Whites, "The Civil War as a Crisis in Gender," in *Divided Houses: Gender and the Civil War*, ed. Catherine Clinton and Nina Silber (New York: Oxford University Press, 1992), 21.

15. Drew Gilpin Faust, "Altars of Sacrifice: Confederate Women and the Narratives of War," *Journal of American History* 76 (March 1990): 1228.

16. Mary Elizabeth Massey, *Ersatz in the Confederacy* (Columbia: University of South Carolina Press, 1952), 171.

17. Wiley, *Confederate Women*, 177.

18. Arnoldo DeLeon, *Mexican Americans in Texas: A Brief History* (Arlington Heights, Ill.: Harlan Davidson, 1993), 60-61.

19. McMillen, *Motherhood in the Old South*, 3.

20. From vertical file material at the Kentucky Historical Society, Frankfort.

21. Quotation from John R. Kemp et al., *New Orleans* (Woodland Hills, Calif.: Windsor Publications for the Preservation Resource Center of New Orleans, 1981), 87-88; see also McMillen, *Motherhood in the Old South*, 47-52; Ronald L. Numbers and

Todd L. Savitt, eds., *Science and Medicine in the Old South* (Baton Rouge: Louisiana State University Press, 1989), 171, 281, 285, 289, 290, 335, 344-46, 355; Jo Ann Carrigan, "Yellow Fever in New Orleans, 1853: Abstractions and Realities," *Journal of Southern History* 25 (August 1959): 339-55; idem, "Privilege, Prejudice, and the Strangers' Disease in Nineteenth-Century New Orleans," ibid. 36 (November 1970): 568-78; and idem, "Yellow Fever: Scourge of the South," in *Disease and Distinctiveness in the American South*, ed. Todd L. Savitt and James Harvey Young (Knoxville: University of Tennessee Press, 1988), 55-78.

22. Charles P. Roland, *An American Iliad: The Story of the Civil War* (New York and Lexington: McGraw Hill and University Press of Kentucky respectively, 1991), 237; see also idem, *The Confederacy*, Chicago History of American Civilization, ed. Daniel J. Boorstin (Chicago: University of Chicago Press, 1960), 167-70.

23. Clinton, *Other Civil War*, 89.

24. Robert E. Riegel, *Young America, 1830-1840* (Norman: University of Oklahoma Press, 1949), 212; see also Michael O'Brien, ed., *An Evening When Alone: Four Journals of Single Women in the South, 1827-67* (Charlottesville: University of Virginia Press, 1993).

25. Irvin, *Women in Kentucky*, 45-46; see also Lawrence Foster, *Women, Family, and Utopia: Communal Experiments of the Shakers, the Oneida Community, and the Mormons* (Syracuse, N.Y.: Syracuse University Press, 1991), 7-8, 20-21, 24-25, 61-62.

26. Sister Aloysium Mackin, ed., "Wartime Scenes from Convent Windows: St. Cecilia, 1860 through 1865," *Tennessee Historical Quarterly* 39 (Winter 1980): 401-22, quotation from 407; see also n.a. (a member of the congregation), *A Brief History of the Origin and Development of the St. Cecilia Congregation of Dominican Sisters* (Nashville: n.p., 1935).

27. Rable, *Civil Wars*, 51.

28. Ibid., 133-34.

29. Ibid., 27-28.

30. Coontz, *Social Origins of Private Life*, 198.

31. Ira Berlin, *Slaves without Masters: The Free Negro in the Antebellum South* (New York: Pantheon Books, 1974), 221.

32. Rable, *Civil Wars*, 2-3; see also the chapter entitled "Idle Womanhood: Feminist Versions of the Work Ethic," in Daniel T. Rodgers, *The Work Ethic in Industrial America, 1850-1920* (Chicago: University of Chicago Press, 1978), 182-209.

33. Marsha Wedell, *Elite Women and the Reform Impulse in Memphis, 1875-1915* (Knoxville: University of Tennessee Press, 1991), 9-10; see also Richard Rankin, *Ambivalent Churchmen and Evangelical Churchwomen: The Religion of the Episcopal Elite in North Carolina, 1800-1860* (Columbia: University of South Carolina Press, 1993).

34. Harriet E. Amos, *Cotton City: Urban Development in Antebellum Mobile* (Tuscaloosa: University of Alabama Press, 1985), 179; see also Lori D. Ginzberg, *Women and the Work of Benevolence: Morality, Politics, and Class in the Nineteenth-Century United States* (New Haven, Conn.: Yale University Press, 1990).

35. Page Putnam Miller, "Women in the Vanguard of the Sunday School Movement," *Journal of Presbyterian History* 58 (Winter 1980): 316-20; and Bayless Hardin, "The Brown Family of Liberty Hall," *Filson Club History Quarterly* 16 (April 1941): 75-87; see also Mary P. Ryan, "Women, Revival, and Reform," in *Underside of American History*, 1:173-212; and Anne M. Boylan, *Sunday School: The Formation of an American Institution, 1790-1880* (New Haven, Conn.: Yale University Press, 1988).

36. Miller, "Women in the Vanguard of the Sunday School Movement," 320-23.

37. Quoted in Jayne Crumpler DeFiore, "COME, and Bring the Ladies: Tennessee Women and the Politics of Opportunity during the Presidential Campaigns of 1840 and 1844," *Tennessee Historical Quarterly* 51 (Winter 1992): 199; see also the chapter entitled "Ceremonial Space: Public Celebration and Private Woman," in Mary P. Ryan, *Women in Public: Between Banners and Ballots, 1825-1880* (Baltimore: Johns Hopkins University Press, 1990), 19-57.

38. Joe L. Kincheloe, Jr., "Transcending Role Restrictions: Women at Camp Meetings and Political Rallies," *Tennessee Historical Quarterly* 40 (Summer 1981): 169; see also Barbara Leslie Epstein, *The Politics of Domesticity: Women, Evangelism, and Temperance in Nineteenth-Century America* (Middletown, Conn.: Wesleyan University Press, 1981); and Cott, *Bonds of Womanhood*.

39. Rable, *Civil Wars*, 13-14.

40. DeFiore, "COME, and Bring the Ladies," 197, 204.

41. Ibid., 207.

42. Quoted in Robert V. Remini, *Henry Clay: Statesman for the Union* (New York: W.W. Norton, 1991), 29-31, quotation on 30.

43. DeFiore, "COME, and Bring the Ladies," 200.

44. Caroli, *First Ladies*, 65-67.

45. Jennifer K. Boone, "'Mingling Freely': Tennessee Society on the Eve of the Civil War," *Tennessee Historical Quarterly* 51 (Fall 1992): 144-45. Fred A. Bailey's conclusions appear to be almost diametrically opposed to Boone's perspective on antebellum southern males: See Bailey's "Class and Tennessee's Confederate Generation," *Journal of Southern History* 51 (February 1985): 30-60; Bailey declares on p. 60 that "the South was more a land of social seams than social seamlessness." See also Fred A. Bailey, *Class and Tennessee's Confederate Generation* (Chapel Hill: University of North Carolina Press, 1987).

46. Gray, "Activities of Southern Women, 1840-1860," 78-79; see also Ruth E. Finley, *The Lady of Godey's: Sarah Josepha Hale* (Philadelphia: J.B. Lippincott, 1931), 187.

47. Eleanor M. Boatwright, "The Political and Civil Status of Women in Georgia, 1783-1860," in *Unheard Voices*, 173-74.

48. Rable, *Civil Wars*, 11-12; see also Glenda Riley, *Divorce: An American Tradition* (New York: Oxford University Press, 1991), 34-84.

49. Boatwright, "Political and Civil Status of Women in Georgia, 1783-1860," 183.

50. Rable, *Civil Wars*, 24.

51. Hoff, *Law, Gender, and Injustice*, 127-28.

52. Ibid., 127-29; and Dougan, "Arkansas Married Woman's Property Law," 5.

53. Sandra Moncrief, "The Mississippi Married Women's Property Act of 1839," *Journal of Mississippi History* 47 (May 1985): 113-19.

54. Victoria E. Bynum, *Unruly Women: The Politics of Social and Sexual Control in the Old South*, Gender and American Culture, ed. Linda K. Kerber and Nell Irvin Painter (Chapel Hill: University of North Carolina Press, 1992), 14 et passim.

55. Suzanne Lebsock, "Radical Reconstruction and the Property Rights of Southern Women," *Journal of Southern History* 43 (May 1977), 195-216, quotation from 197; see also Mary Frances Berry, "Judging Morality: Sexual Behavior and Legal Consequences in the Late Nineteenth-Century South," *Journal of American History* 78 (December 1991): 835-56; and Israel Kugler, *From Ladies to Women: The Organized Struggle for Woman's Rights in the Reconstruction Era*, Contributions in Women's Studies no. 77 (New York: Greenwood Press, 1987).

56. Paul Goodman, "The Emergence of Homestead Exemption in the United States: Accommodation and Resistance to the Market Revolution, 1840-1880," *Journal of American History* 80 (September 1993): 470, 497.

57. Rable, *Civil Wars*, 18.

58. Quoted in Blandin, *History of Higher Education of Women in the South Prior to 1860*, 16; see also Steven M. Stowe, "The Not-So-Cloistered Academy: Elite Women's Education and Family Feeling in the Old South," in *Web of Southern Social Relations*, 90-106; and Jon L. Wakelyn, "Antebellum College Life and the Relations between Fathers and Sons," ibid., 107-26.

59. Eleanor Flexner, *Century of Struggle: The Woman's Rights Movement in the United States* (Cambridge, Mass.: Belknap Press of Harvard University Press, 1975), 179.

60. Farnham, *Education of the Southern Belle*, 2.

61. Robert E. Corlew, *Tennessee: A Short History*, 2d paperback ed. (Knoxville: University of Tennessee Press, 1987), 120.

62. Farnham, *Education of the Southern Belle*, 151-54 et passim, quoted material from 11.

63. J. Winston Coleman, Jr., "Delia Webster and Calvin Fairbank—Underground Railroad Agents," *Filson Club History Quarterly* 17 (July 1943): 129-42.

64. Anne Firor Scott, "Almira Lincoln Phelps: The Self-Made Woman in the Nineteenth Century," *Maryland Historical Magazine* 75 (September 1980): 203, 213; see also Elizabeth Brown Pryor, "An Anomalous Person: The Northern Tutor in Plantation Society, 1773-1860," *Journal of Southern History* 47 (August 1981): 363-92; and Wilma King, ed., *A Northern Woman in the Plantation South: Letters of Tryphena Blanche Holder Fox, 1856-1876* (Columbia: University of South Carolina Press, 1993). A tutor on a Mississippi plantation, Tryphena Blanche Holder Fox subsequently wed a Louisiana physician.

65. Devon A. Mihesuah, *Cultivating the Rosebuds: The Education of Women at the Cherokee Female Seminary, 1851-1909* (Urbana: University of Illinois Press, 1993), 1, 31, 36, et passim.

66. Jean H. Baker, "Mary Todd Lincoln: Biography as Social History," *Register of the Kentucky Historical Society* 86 (Summer 1988): 206-7; see also C.W. Hackensmith, "Family Background and Education of Mary Todd," ibid. 69 (July 1971): 187-96; Jean H. Baker, *Mary Todd Lincoln: A Biography* (New York: W.W. Norton, 1989); and Edna Talbott Whitley, "Mary Beck and the Female Mind," *Register of the Kentucky Historical Society* 77 (Winter 1979): 15-24.

67. Joan Cashin, "Varina Howell Davis (1826-1906)," in *Portraits of American Women*, 1:260-61.

68. Ibid., 260-62, 270-71.

69. Mary Forrest, *Women of the South: Distinguished in Literature* (New York: Derby & Jackson, 1861).

70. *The Living Female Writers of the South*, ed. by the author (not identified by name) of "Southland Writers" (Philadelphia: Claxton, Remsen & Haffelfinger, 1872), 1.

71. Anne Goodwyn Jones, "Southern Literary Women as Chroniclers of Southern Life: 'Something Else to Be': Race, Language, and Identity in the Texts of Harriet Jacobs, Mary Chesnut, and Zora Neale Hurston," in *Sex, Race, and the Role of Women in the South*, 75, 76. There is a steadily expanding body of published Civil War era and nineteenth-century diaries that provide private feminine perspectives on public events: see, e.g., Mary D. Robertson, ed., *A Confederate Lady Comes of Age: The Journal of*

Pauline DeCaradeuc Heyward, 1863-1888, Women's Diaries and Letters in the Nineteenth Century South Series, ed. Carol K. Bleser (Columbia: University of South Carolina Press, 1992); Cornelia Peake McDonald, *A Woman's Civil War: A Diary, with Reminiscences of the War, from March 1862,* ed. Minrose C. Gwin (Madison: University of Wisconsin Press, 1992); and Charles East, ed., *The Civil War Diary of Sarah Morgan* (Athens: University of Georgia Press, 1991).

72. Matthews, *Rise of Public Woman,* 83-84; see also Elizabeth Moss, *Domestic Novelists in the Old South: Defenders of Southern Culture* (Baton Rouge: Louisiana State University Press, 1992).

73. *Living Female Writers of the South,* 468-72; and Forrest, *Women of the South,* 68-79.

74. Fox-Genovese, *Within the Plantation Household,* 242-89 et passim.

75. Anne Goodwyn Jones, *Tomorrow Is Another Day: The Woman Writer in the South, 1859-1936* (Baton Rouge: Louisiana State University Press, 1981), 362; see also Helen Taylor, *Gender, Race, and Region in the Writings of Grace King, Ruth McEnery Stuart, and Kate Chopin* (Baton Rouge: Louisiana State University Press, 1989); and Carol S. Manning, ed., *The Female Tradition in Southern Literature* (Champaign: University of Illinois Press, 1993).

76. Harriet Beecher Stowe, *Uncle Tom's Cabin: Or, Life among the Lowly,* introduction by Raymond Weaver (New York: Modern Library [Random House], 1938), xi; see also Joan D. Hedrick, "'Peaceable Fruits': The Ministry of Harriet Beecher Stowe," *American Quarterly* 40 (Spring 1988): 307-32.

77. Whites, "Civil War as a Crisis in Gender," 8.

78. Mary Elizabeth Massey, *Refugee Life in the Confederacy* (Baton Rouge: Louisiana State University Press, 1964), 4.

79. Rable, *Civil Wars,* 108-10.

80. Whites, "Civil War as a Crisis in Gender," 13-14.

81. Rable, *Civil Wars,* 48-49.

82. Irvin, *Women in Kentucky,* 61-66; see also Mary E. Wharton and Ellen F. Williams, *Peach Leather and Rebel Gray: Bluegrass Life and the War, 1860-1865: Diary and Letters of a Confederate Wife* (Lexington: Helicon, 1986); Aloma Williams Dew, "From Cramps to Consumption: Women's Health in Owensboro, Ky. during the Civil War," *Register of the Kentucky Historical Society* 74 (April 1976): 85-98; idem, "'Between the Hawk and the Buzzard': Owensboro during the Civil War," ibid. 77 (Winter 1979): 12, from which the Margaret Ray quotation is drawn.

83. Wiley, *Confederate Women,* 142; see also Rable, *Civil Wars,* 151-53, 339 n. 53. Massey, *Bonnet Brigades,* 81-84, is also particularly helpful; and Janet E. Kaufman, "'Under the Petticoat Flag': Women Soldiers in the Confederate Army," *Southern Studies* 23 (Winter 1984): 363-75. Neither Massey nor Kaufman attaches much credibility to the story of Madame Loreta Janeta Velasquez, who claimed to have been Lieutenant Harry T. Buford; Velasquez's story resembles that of Mrs. Laura J. Williams of Arkansas, who adopted the name Henry Buford, recruited an independent company which she took to Virginia, and fought in several engagements before it was discovered that she was a woman. For a compilation of women, both northern and southern, who went to war disguised as men, see Lee Middleton, comp. and ed., *Hearts of Fire . . . Soldier Women of the Civil War: With an Addendum on Female Reenactors* (Franklin, N.C.: Genealogy Publishing Service, 1993); see also Eugene L. Meyer, "The Soldier Left a Portrait and Her Eyewitness Account," *Smithsonian,* January 1994, 96-104, which details the soldiering experience of a northern woman, Rosetta Wakeman.

84. Carolyn Brackett, "Belmont Mistress Makes Scarlett Look Meek," from *Tennessee Traveler*, reprinted in *Kingsport Times-News*, 24 September 1989; see also James A. Hoobler, "Adelicia Hayes Franklin Acklen Cheatham," *Distinctive Women of Tennessee* (Nashville: Tennessee Historical Society, n.d.—an exhibition guide), 9.

85. O.S. Barton, *Three Years with Quantrill: A True Story Told by His Scout John McCorkle*, with notes by Albert Castel and commentary by Herman Hattaway, Western Frontier Library (Armstrong, Mo.: Armstrong Herald Print, 1914; reprint, Norman: University of Oklahoma Press, 1992), 14-15. Civilians also suffered tremendously in areas where loyalties were divided: see William C. Harris, "East Tennessee's Civil War Refugees and the Impact of the War on Civilians," *East Tennessee Historical Society Publications*, no. 64 (1992): 3-19.

86. Quoted from "General Forrest's Account of Miss Emma Sansom as a Pilot," *Register of the Kentucky Historical Society* 2 (September 1904): 25-28; see also Wills, *A Battle from the Start*, 115-16.

87. Quoted in James M. McPherson, *Battle Cry of Freedom: The Civil War Era* (New York: Oxford University Press, 1988), 477.

88. Ibid., 478-79; and Wiley, *Confederate Women*, 145, 157; see also Frank R. Freemon, "The Medical Support System for the Confederate Army of Tennessee during the Georgia Campaign, May-September 1864," *Tennessee Historical Quarterly* 52 (Spring 1993): 44-55. Fannie A. Beers, a volunteer nurse during the Georgia Campaign, subsequently published her recollections as *Memories: A Record of Personal Experience and Adventure during the Four Years of War* (Philadelphia: n.p., 1889).

89. Details from the exhibit "They Also Served" at the Museum in Jackson Chapel, Virginia Military Institute, Lexington, Va.

90. Wiley, *Confederate Women*, 143; some of the details on Pauline Cushman are from the exhibit "Unconventional Warfare," Tennessee State Museum, Nashville; see also Oscar A. Kinchen, *Women Who Spied for the Blue and the Gray* (Philadelphia: Dorrance, 1972).

91. James D. Horan, *The Pinkertons: The Detective Dynasty That Made History* (New York: Crown Publishers, 1967), 81-97.

92. Quoted in Degler, *At Odds*, 223.

93. James A. Ramage, *Rebel Raider: The Life of General John Hunt Morgan* (Lexington: University Press of Kentucky, 1986), passim; and Alice Hooker Buchtel, "Martha Ready Morgan Williamson," *Distinctive Women of Tennessee*, 9.

94. Ramage, *Rebel Raider*, 80, 226-44; see also Patricia C. Click, *The Spirit of the Times: Amusements in Nineteenth-Century Baltimore, Norfolk, and Richmond* (Charlottesville: University Press of Virginia, 1989).

95. Harriet E. Amos, "'City Belles': Images and Realities of the Lives of White Women in Antebellum Mobile," *Alabama Review* 24 (January 1981): 12; and David Kaser, "Nashville's Women of Pleasure in 1860," *Tennessee Historical Quarterly* 23 (December 1964): 379-82.

96. Quoted in Kemp et al., *New Orleans*, 102.

97. James Lee McDonough and Thomas L. Connelly, *Five Tragic Hours: The Battle of Franklin* (Knoxville: University of Tennessee Press, 1983), 36, 57-58.

98. Ibid.; Stone is quoted on 58.

99. Rable, *Civil Wars*, 160-62; Gutman, *Black Family in Slavery and Freedom*, 385-88; see also Darlene Clark Hine, "Rape and the Inner Lives of Southern Black Women: Thoughts on the Culture of Dissemblance," in *Southern Women: Histories and Identities*, 177-89.

100. Quoted in Timothy Roberts, "Lest We Forget: The Battle over the Civil War and Its Symbols Rages On," *Nashville Scene*, 25 February 1993, 8.

Chapter 5. Set Thine House in Order

1. Jim Crow, as applied to separate public accommodations—in this instance, railroad cars—originated in Massachusetts: see Leon Litwack, *North of Slavery: The Negro in the Free States, 1790-1860* (Chicago: University of Chicago Press, 1961), 106; and idem, *Been in the Storm So Long: The Aftermath of Slavery* (New York: Alfred A. Knopf, 1980); see also C. Vann Woodward, *The Strange Career of Jim Crow*, 2d rev. ed. (New York: Oxford University Press, 1966); V. Jacque Voegeli, *Free But Not Equal: The Midwest and the Negro during the Civil War* (Chicago: University of Chicago Press, 1967); George M. Fredrickson, *The Black Image in the White Mind: The Debate on Afro-American Character and Destiny, 1817-1914* (New York: Harper & Row, 1971); Forrest G. Wood, *Black Scare: The Racist Response to Emancipation and Reconstruction* (Ann Arbor, Mich.: Books on Demand/University Microfilms International, 1967).

2. Meriwether, *Recollections of Ninety-two Years*, v; the most useful account of the Ku Klux Klan of this era can be found in Stanley F. Horn, *Invisible Empire: The Story of the Ku Klux Klan, 1866-1871*, 2d ed. (Montclair, N.J.: Patterson Smith, 1969).

3. Meriwether, *Recollections of Ninety-two Years*, vi.

4. Charles Reagan Wilson, *Baptized in Blood: The Religion of the Lost Cause, 1865-1920* (Athens: University of Georgia Press, 1980), 1; see also Bertram Wyatt-Brown, *Yankee Saints and Southern Sinners* (Baton Rouge: Louisiana State University Press, 1990).

5. David Joseph Singal, *The War Within: From Victorian to Modernist Thought in the South, 1919-1945*, Fred W. Morrison Series in Southern Studies (Chapel Hill: University of North Carolina Press, 1982), 21.

6. John Hope Franklin, *Reconstruction after the Civil War*, Chicago History of American Civilization, ed. Daniel J. Boorstin (Chicago: University of Chicago Press, 1961), 4-5.

7. Meriwether, *Recollections of Ninety-two Years*, 80-81.

8. Quoted in Noel C. Fisher, "'Prepare Them for My Coming': General William T. Sherman, Total War, and Pacification in West Tennessee," *Tennessee Historical Quarterly* 51 (Summer 1992): 76; see also James M. Merrill, *William Tecumseh Sherman* (Chicago: Rand McNally, 1971), 57-58.

9. Susan Brownmiller, *Against Our Will: Men, Women and Rape* (New York: Simon & Schuster, 1975), 88. For a discussion of attitudes of Union soldiers toward southern women, including the abuse of them, see the chapter entitled "She Devils" in Reid Mitchell, *The Vacant Chair: The Northern Soldier Leaves Home* (New York: Oxford University Press, 1993), 89-113.

10. Wilson, *Baptized in Blood*, 47; see also Marjorie Spruill Wheeler, *New Women of the New South: The Leaders of the Woman Suffrage Movement in the Southern States* (New York: Oxford University Press, 1993), 190; and Catherine Clinton, "Bloody Terrain: Freedwomen, Sexuality and Violence during Reconstruction," *Georgia Historical Quarterly* 76 (Summer 1992): 313-32.

11. Quoted in Jim Miles, *To the Sea: A History and Tour Guide of Sherman's March* (Nashville, Tenn.: Rutledge Hill Press, 1989), 255-58; see also Marion B. Lucas, *Sherman and the Burning of Columbia* (College Station: Texas A & M Press, 1976); and

Katharine M. Jones, *When Sherman Came: Southern Women and the "Great March"* (Indianapolis: Bobbs-Merrill, 1964).

12. Nina Silber, "Intemperate Men, Spiteful Women, and Jefferson Davis: Northern Views of the Defeated South," *American Quarterly* 41 (December 1989): 614-35, especially 624-27; see also Whites, "Civil War as a Crisis in Gender," 14-15; and idem, *The Romance of Reunion: Northerners and the South, 1865-1900* (Chapel Hill: University of North Carolina Press, 1993).

13. C. Vann Woodward, *The Burden of Southern History*, rev. ed. (Baton Rouge: Louisiana State University Press, 1968), 109.

14. Quoted from ibid., 133-34.

15. Douglas, *Feminization of American Culture*, passim, presents a rather negative view of nineteenth-century feminine influence; for a more sympathetic treatment see Kathleen D. McCarthy, *Women's Culture: American Philanthropy and Art, 1830-1930* (Chicago: University of Chicago Press, 1991); see also Carroll Smith-Rosenberg, *Disorderly Conduct: Visions of Gender in Victorian America* (New York: Alfred A. Knopf, 1985); and Lewis O. Saum, *The Popular Mood of America, 1860-1890* (Lincoln: University of Nebraska Press, 1990).

16. Woodward, *Burden of Southern History*, 139, 140.

17. Wilson, *Baptized in Blood*, 40-46.

18. Whites, "Civil War as a Crisis in Gender," 16, 17.

19. Ownby, *Subduing Satan*, 1, 11.

20. Quoted in ibid., 139-40; see also Karen Lystra, *Searching the Heart: Women, Men, and Romantic Love in Nineteenth-Century America* (New York: Oxford University Press, 1989; paperback ed., 1992); John D'Emilio and Estelle B. Freedman, *Intimate Matters: A History of Sexuality in America* (New York: Harper & Row, 1988); Peter Gay, *The Bourgeois Experience: Victoria to Freud*, vol. 1 of *Education of the Senses* (New York: Oxford University Press, 1984); and Jane H. Hunter, "Inscribing the Self in the Heart of the Family: Diaries and Girlhood in Late-Victorian America," *American Quarterly* 44 (March 1992): 51-81.

21. Jones, *Labor of Love, Labor of Sorrow*, 45.

22. Franklin, *Reconstruction after the Civil War*, 6.

23. For a study of the black experience in southern cities during the late nineteenth century see Howard N. Rabinowitz, *Race Relations in the Urban South, 1865-1890*, Urban Life in America Series, ed. Richard C. Wade (New York: Oxford University Press, 1978).

24. "Anonymous Negro Nurse," in *Lives of American Women*, 296.

25. Thurber, "Development of the Mammy Image and Mythology," 98-99.

26. Alex Haley, "The 'Roots' of Queen," and Michael Logan, "A Hundred Years Ago . . . ' I Could Have Been Queen,'" *TV Guide*, 13 February 1993, 9-10 and 12-14 respectively.

27. Ernest J. Gaines, *The Autobiography of Miss Jane Pittman* (New York: Dial Press, 1971; Bantam Books, 1972).

28. Jones, *Labor of Love, Labor of Sorrow*, 49-51, 62, 103.

29. Meriwether, *Recollections of Ninety-two Years*, 178-80; Susan Brownmiller quotes the testimony of Frances Thompson and Lucy Smith as fact in *Against Our Will*, 126-28; see also Bobby L. Lovett, "Memphis Riots: White Reaction to Blacks in Memphis, May 1865-July 1866," *Tennessee Historical Quarterly* 38 (Spring 1979): 9-33.

30. Catherine Clinton, "Reconstructing Freedwomen," in *Divided Houses*, 310.

31. Jones, *Labor of Love, Labor of Sorrow*, 108.

32. Meriwether, *Recollections of Ninety-two Years*, 206; and John Hope Franklin, *From Slavery to Freedom: A History of Negro Americans*, 5th ed. (New York: Alfred A. Knopf, 1980), 288; see Kathleen C. Berkeley, "'Colored Ladies Also Contributed': Black Women's Activities from Benevolence to Social Welfare, 1866-1896," in *The Web of Southern Social Relations*, 181-203; see also William E. Montgomery, *Under Their Own Vine and Fig Tree: The African-American Church in the South, 1865-1900* (Baton Rouge: Louisiana State University Press, 1993), 95, 114, 139, 320-22.

33. Berlin, *Slaves without Masters*, 179.

34. Willard B. Gatewood, *Aristocrats of Color: The Black Elite, 1880-1920* (Bloomington: Indiana University Press, 1990), ix, 237-38; Loren Schweninger, *Black Property Owners in the South, 1790-1915*, Blacks in the New World, ed. August Meier (Urbana: University of Illinois Press, 1990), 84-87, 173, 197, 219; see also William Cohen, *At Freedom's Edge: Black Mobility and the Southern White Quest for Racial Control, 1861-1915* (Baton Rouge: Louisiana State University Press, 1991).

35. Glenn T. Eskew, "Black Elitism and the Failure of Paternalism in Postbellum Georgia: The Case of Bishop Lucius Henry Holsey," *Journal of Southern History* 58 (November 1992): 637-66, quotation from 642.

36. Clinton, "Reconstructing Freedwomen," 310-11.

37. Martha Hodes, "Wartime Dialogues on Illicit Sex," in *Divided Houses*, 240-41.

38. Howard A. White, *The Freedmen's Bureau in Louisiana* (Baton Rouge: Louisiana State University Press, 1970), 79-81; see also Jacqueline Jones, *Soldiers of Light and Love: Northern Teachers and Georgia Blacks, 1865-1873* (Chapel Hill: University of North Carolina Press, 1980); Ruth Currie-McDaniel, "Northern Women in the South, 1860-1880," *Georgia Historical Quarterly* 76 (Summer 1992): 284-312; Mary Ames, *She Came to the Island: From Mary Ames' "A New England Woman's Diary in Dixie in 1865"* (3d reprinting; Edisto Beach, S.C.: Sea Side Services, 1985); and Wayne E. Reilly, *Sarah Jane Foster, Teacher of the Freedmen*, foreword by Jacqueline Jones (Charlottesville: University Press of Virginia, 1990).

39. Quoted in Meriwether, *Recollections of Ninety-two Years*, 181.

40. Clinton, "Reconstructing Freedwomen," 313.

41. Paula Giddings, "Ida Wells-Barnett (1862-1931)," in *Portraits of American Women*, 367-75.

42. Ibid., 378; and Linda T. Wynn, "Ida B. Wells: The Kindling Voice of America's Conscience," *Tennessee Conservationist*, January-February 1992, 15-17; see also Rodger Streitmatter, *Raising Her Voice: African-American Women Journalists Who Changed History* (Lexington: University Press of Kentucky, 1994), a study of black women, including Ida B. Wells, who have written for American newspapers or television news; and for an analysis of the life stories of early-twentieth-century black women in the professions of law, medicine, and higher education see Gwendolyn Etter-Lewis, *My Soul Is My Own: Oral Narratives of African American Women in the Professions* (New York: Routledge, 1993).

43. Woodrow W. Long, interview by Randall Wells, 8 May 1991, Horry County Oral History Project, Coastal Carolina University Library, Conway, S.C; Long's account is reminiscent of a short story "The Old Order" by the Texas-born writer Katherine Anne Porter. The story appeared in *The Leaning Tower and Other Stories* (New York: Harcourt, Brace, 1944); see Robert H. Brinkmeyer, Jr., *Katherine Anne Porter's Artistic Development: Primitivism, Traditionalism and Totalitarianism*, Southern Liter-

ary Studies, ed. Louis D. Rubin, Jr. (Baton Rouge: Louisiana State University Press, 1993); see also Jacqueline Jones, "Encounters, Likely and Unlikely, between Black and Poor White Women in the Rural South, 1865-1940," *Georgia Historical Quarterly* 76 (Summer 1992): 333-53; and Elizabeth Allston Pringle (Patience Pennington), *A Woman Rice Planter*, introduction by Charles Joyner (New York: Macmillan, 1913; Cambridge: The President and Fellows of Harvard College, 1961; reprint, Columbia: University of South Carolina Press, 1992), xxiii et passim.

44. Woodward, *Burden of Southern History*, 21.

45. Nicholas Fischer Hahn, "Female State Prisoners in Tennessee: 1831-1979," *Tennessee Historical Quarterly* 39 (Winter 1980): 485-97.

46. Ibid., quotation from 491-92; see also Folmsbee, Corlew, and Mitchell, *Tennesse: A Short History*, 404-10; A.C. Hutson, Jr., "The Coal Miners' Insurrection of 1891 in Anderson County, Tennessee," *East Tennessee Historical Society Publications* no. 7 (1935): 103-121; and idem, "The Overthrow of the Convict Lease System in Tennessee," ibid., no. 8 (1936): 82-103.

47. Robert Gunn Crawford, "A History of the Kentucky Penitentiary System, 1865-1937" (Ph.D. diss., University of Kentucky, 1955), 108-10, 136, copy provided courtesy of Mrs. Robert Gunn (Anita Roddey) Crawford, Johnson City, Tenn.

48. Ibid., 255.

49. John S. Hughes, ed., *The Letters of a Victorian Madwoman*, Women's Diaries and Letters of the Nineteenth-Century South, ed. Carol K. Bleser (Columbia: University of South Carolina Press, 1993), 1-46, quotation from 12.

50. Ibid., 20, 242; see also John S. Hughes, "Labeling and Treating Black Mental Illness in Alabama, 1861-1910," *Journal of Southern History* 58 (August 1993): 435-60.

51. Buddy Thompson, *Madam Belle Brezing* (Lexington, Ky.: Buggy Whip Press, 1983), passim.

52. Howard B. Woolston, *Prostitution in the United States: Prior to the Entrance of the United States into the World War*, publication no. 29 in the Patterson Smith Reprint Series in Criminology, Law Enforcement, and Social Problems (Montclair, N.J.: Patterson Smith, 1969), vii.

53. Kemp, *New Orleans*, 134-35, 164-65. Photographs of prostitutes from the Storyville district can be found in Jeffrey Simpson, comp., *The Way Life Was: A Photographic Treasury from the American Past* (New York: Praeger Publishers, 1975), 98-102; see Lois Battle's novel *Storyville* (New York: Viking, 1993). The Iberville Federal Housing Project, constructed during the New Deal era, subsequently occupied the site where Storyville had once stood. See also Al Rose, *Storyville, New Orleans: Being an Authentic Illustrated Account of the Notorious Red-Light District* (Tuscaloosa: University of Alabama Press, 1974).

54. Woolston, *Prostitution in the United States*, 336-37, 341; see also Richard F. Selcer, *Hell's Half Acre: The Life and Legend of a Red-Light District*, Chisholm Trail Series no. 9 (Fort Worth: Texas Christian University Press, 1991), 151 et passim.

55. M.J. Exner, "Prostitution in Its Relation to the Army on the Mexican Border," *Social Hygiene* 3 (April 1917): 205-20, quoted material on 210; see also Ruth Rosen, *The Lost Sisterhood: Prostitution in America, 1900-1918*, paperback ed. (Baltimore: Johns Hopkins University Press, 1983); and Regina G. Kunzel, *Fallen Women, Problem Girls: Unmarried Mothers and the Professionalization of Social Work, 1890-1945* (New Haven, Conn.: Yale University Press, 1993). For a discussion of the undesirable aspects of American life in the era since World War I see John C. Burnham, *Bad Habits: Drinking*,

Smoking, Taking Drugs, Gambling, Sexual Misbehavior, and Swearing in American History, American Social Experience Series, ed. James Kirby Martin et al. (New York: New York University Press, 1993).

56. Elizabeth Boies, "The Girls on the Border and What They Did for the Militia," *Social Hygiene* 3 (April 1917): 221-28.

57. William A. Link, *The Paradox of Southern Progressivism, 1880-1930*, Fred W. Morrison Series in Southern Studies (Chapel Hill: University of North Carolina Press, 1993).

58. These books are useful in attempting to understand southern lifestyles of this era: Ownby, *Subduing Satan*, passim; Edward L. Ayers, *The Promise of the New South: Life after Reconstruction* (New York: Oxford University Press, 1992); William A. Link, *A Hard Country and a Lonely Place: Schooling, Society, and Reform in Rural Virginia, 1870-1920* (Chapel Hill: University of North Carolina Press, 1986); and idem, *Paradox of Southern Progressivism*; see also Rebecca Sharpless, "Southern Women and the Land," *Agricultural History* 67 (Spring 1993): 30-42.

59. Ayers, *Promise of the New South*, 233-34; Julie Roy Jeffrey, "Women in the Southern Farmers' Alliance: A Reconsideration of the Role and Status of Women in the Late Nineteenth-Century South," *Feminist Studies* 3 (Fall 1975): 348-71; see also Marilyn P. Watkins, "Political Activism and Community-Building among Alliance and Grange Women in Western Washington, 1892-1925," *Agricultural History* (Spring 1993): 197-214.

60. Quoted in LeeAnn Whites, "Rebecca Latimer Felton and the Wife's Farm: The Class and Racial Politics of Gender Reform," *Georgia Historical Quarterly* 76 (Summer 1992): 359.

61. Elizabeth Madox Roberts, *The Time of Man: A Novel*, introduction by William H. Slavick and Robert Penn Warren (New York: Viking Press, 1926; reprint ed., Lexington: University Press of Kentucky, 1982).

62. Charles A. Le Guin, ed., *A Home-Concealed Woman: The Diaries of Magnolia Wynn Le Guin, 1901-1913*, foreword by Ursula K. Le Guin (Athens: University of Georgia Press, 1990); see also Margaret Jones Bosterli, ed., *Vinegar Pie and Chicken Bread: A Woman's Diary of Life in the Rural South, 1890-1891 [Nannie Stillwell Jackson]* (Fayetteville: University of Arkansas Press, 1983).

63. Le Guin, *Home-Concealed Woman*; see also Thomas D. Clark, *Pills, Petticoats, and Plows: The Southern Country Store* (Indianapolis, Ind.: Bobbs-Merrill, 1944), which offers insights into an important social institution—the crossroads mercantile establishments—in the late-nineteenth- and early-twentieth-century South.

64. Ayers, *Promise of the New South*, 3.

65. From an exhibit panel, Tennessee State Museum, Nashville. For treatment of New South philosophy and its effects on the South see C. Vann Woodward, *Origins of the New South, 1877-1913*, A History of the South, ed. Wendell Holmes Stephenson and E. Merton Coulter (Baton Rouge: Louisiana State University Press, 1951); Paul M. Gaston, *The New South Creed: A Study in Southern Myth-Making* (New York: Knopf, 1970); and Harold E. Davis, *Henry Grady's New South: Atlanta, a Brave and Beautiful City* (Tuscaloosa: University of Alabama Press, 1990). On southern industrialization see James C. Cobb, *Industrialization and Southern Society, 1877-1984* (Lexington: University Press of Kentucky, 1984); and idem, *The Selling of the South: The Southern Crusade for Industrial Development, 1936-1980* (Baton Rouge: Louisiana State University Press, 1982). Also useful is David R. Goldfield, *Cotton Fields and Skyscrapers: Southern City and Region, 1607-1980* (Baton Rouge: Louisiana State University Press, 1982).

66. Jacquelyn Dowd Hall, Robert Korstad, and James Leloudis, "Cotton Mill People: Work, Community, and Protest in the Textile South, 1880-1940," *American Historical Review* 91 (April 1986): 245; see also Jacquelyn Dowd Hall et al., *Like a Family: The Making of A Southern Cotton Mill World*, Fred W. Morrison Series in Southern Studies (Chapel Hill: University of North Carolina Press, 1987).

67. Ayers, *Promise of the New South*, 113.

68. J. Wayne Flynt, *Dixie's Forgotten People: The South's Poor Whites*, Minorities in Modern America, ed. Warren F. Kimball and David Edwin Harrell, Jr. (Bloomington: Indiana University Press, 1979), 51.

69. Ayers, *Promise of the New South*, 114; see also Crandall A. Shifflett, *Coal Towns: Life, Work, and Culture in Company Towns of Southern Appalachia, 1880-1960* (Knoxville: University of Tennessee Press, 1991). Shifflett finds some redeeming qualities in coal towns, as Jacquelyn Dowd Hall and others have in mill villages.

70. Ayers, *Promise of the New South*, 113; see also Leslie Woodcock Tentler, *Wage-Earning Women: Industrial Work and Family Life in the United States, 1900-1930* (New York: Oxford University Press, 1979).

71. Andy Edmonds, *Bugsy's Baby: The Secret Life of Mob Queen Virginia Hill* (New York: Birch Lane Press, 1993), 6-9.

72. "Alice Caudle," in *First-Person America*, ed. Ann Banks (New York: W.W. Norton, 1980; Norton paperback, 1991), 163-65, quotation on 163.

73. "The 1935 Scrap Book," 13, Southern Summer School, Little Switzerland, N.C., from the Southern Summer School Papers, American Labor Education Service Records, Labor-Management Documentation Center, Cornell University, Ithaca, N.Y.; hereinafter referred to as SSS Papers and ALES Records.

74. "Scrapbook" of the 1934 Southern Summer School, 9-10, SSS Papers, ALES Records.

75. Dolores Janiewski, "Sisters under Their Skins: Southern Working Women, 1880-1950," in *Sex, Race, and the Role of Women in the South*, 34-35.

76. Sharon Harley, "Black Women in a Southern City: Washington, D.C., 1890-1920," in *Sex, Race, and the Role of Women in the South*, 60, 63, 64; see also Bettina Aptheker, "Quest for Dignity: Black Women in the Professions, 1865-1900," in *Woman's Legacy: Essays on Race, Sex, and Class in American History*, comp. Bettina Aptheker (Amherst: University of Massachusetts Press, 1982), 89-110; and Darlene Clark Hine, *Black Women in White: Racial Conflict and Cooperation in the Nursing Profession, 1860-1950* (Bloomington: Indiana University Press, 1989).

77. Margaret Ripley Wolfe, "Aliens in Southern Appalachia: Catholics in the Coal Camps, 1900-1940," *Appalachian Heritage* 6 (Winter 1978): 43-56; idem, "Aliens in Southern Appalachia, 1900-1920: The Italian Experience in Wise County, Virginia," *Virginia Magazine of History and Biography* 87 (October 1979): 455-72; and idem, "The Appalachian Reality: Ethnic and Class Diversity," *East Tennessee Historical Society Publications*, nos. 52 and 53 (1981-82): 40-60; see also Ronald D. Eller, *Miners, Millhands, and Mountaineers: Industrialization of the Appalachian South, 1880-1930*, Twentieth-Century America Series, ed. Dewey W. Grantham (Knoxville: University of Tennessee Press, 1982); and Shifflett's *Coal Towns*.

78. Robert J. Higgs, "Mary N. Murfree and the Third Tradition of Tennessee Literature," unpublished manuscript which Dr. Higgs, professor of English at East Tennessee State University, graciously shared with me; and Maria Juliana Kirby-Smith, "Mary Noailles Murfree," *Distinctive Women of Tennessee*, 23.

79. Ownby, *Subduing Satan*, 70.

80. John Hawkins Napier III, "Patriotic Societies," in *Encyclopedia of Southern Culture*, ed. Charles Reagan Wilson and William Ferris with assoc. ed. Ann J. Abadie and Mary L. Hart (Chapel Hill: University of North Carolina Press, 1989, sponsored by the Center for the Study of Southern Culture, University of Mississippi), 698; and cataloguing worksheet for framed portrait of Mrs. Caroline Meriwether Goodlett and label copy for the United Daughters of the Confederacy, Tennessee State Museum, Nashville.

81. Helen Dortch Longstreet to Mrs. J.F. Howell, 9 May 1941, from the private collection of Tony Marion, Blountville, Tenn., copies in my possession. All subsequent citations from this correspondence are likewise from the privately held Marion collection.

82. H.D. Longstreet to Gen. J.F. Howell, 12 October 1942.

83. H.D. Longstreet to Gen. J.F. Howell, 22 November 1942; see also Jeffry D. Wert, *General James Longstreet: The Confederacy's Most Controversial Soldier—a Biography* (New York: Simon & Schuster, 1993), 425-26.

84. H.D. Longstreet to Mrs. J.F. Howell, 24 November 1943; see also "Confederate General Enjoys 102nd Birthday: War Veteran Weathers Kisses, Cake and Virginia Reel," *Life*, 16 February 1948, 128-30, 133. A photograph of Mrs. Longstreet with General Howell appears on p. 129. Howell had actually served as a corporal under General James Longstreet's command but had advanced to the rank of "general" in the United Confederate Veterans.

85. Edmund Vincent Gillon, Jr., and Henry G. Pitz, *The Gibson Girl and Her America: The Best Drawing of Charles Dana Gibson* (New York: Dover Publications, 1969), xi. See Carroll Smith-Rosenberg and Charles E. Rosenberg, "The Female Animal: Medical and Biological Views of Woman and Her Role in Nineteenth-Century America," *Journal of American History* 60 (September 1973): 332-56; Charles E. Rosenberg, "Sexuality, Class and Role in Nineteenth-Century America," *American Quarterly* 25 (May 1973): 131-53; Carroll Smith-Rosenberg, "The Hysterical Woman: Sex Roles and Role Conflict in Nineteenth-Century America," *Social Research* 39 (Winter 1972): 652-78; Carl N. Degler, "What Ought to Be and What Was: Women's Sexuality in the Nineteenth Century," *American Historical Review* 79 (October 1974): 1467-90; Sidney H. Bremer, "Invalids and Actresses: Howell's Duplex Imagery for American Women," *American Literature* 47 (January 1976): 599-614; John C. Ruoff, "Frivolity to Consumption: Or, Southern Womanhood in Antebellum Literature," *Civil War History* 18 (September 1972): 213-29; Barbara Ehrenreich and Deirdre English, *Complaints and Disorders: The Sexual Politics of Sickness*, Glass Mountain Pamphlet no. 2 (Old Westbury, N.Y.: Feminist Press, 1973).

86. Woody Gelman, ed., *The Best of Charles Dana Gibson* (n.p.: Bounty Books, 1969), vii; see also Lois W. Banner, *American Beauty* (New York: Alfred A. Knopf, 1983), 159-74.

87. Elizabeth Langhorne, "Nancy Langhorne Astor: A Virginian in England," *Virginia Cavalcade* 23 (Winter 1974): 38-47.

88. Ralph G. Martin, *The Woman He Loved: The Story of the Duke and Duchess of Windsor* (New York: a Signet Book, New American Library, 1974), 197-98.

89. John Jakes, *Homeland* (New York: Doubleday, 1993), 324. See Linda W. Rosenzweig, *The Anchor of My Life: Middle-Class American Mothers and Daughters, 1880-1920* (New York: New York University Press, 1993), which explores the mother-daughter relationship during the era of the "New American Woman"; see also Harvey Green, *The*

Light of the Home: An Intimate View of the Lives of Women in Victorian America (New York: Pantheon Books, 1983).

90. *Courier-Journal* (Louisville, Ky.), 11 January 1890; see also Josephine K. Henry, *Marriage and Divorce* (Lexington, Ky.: James E. Hughers, 1905). Aloma Williams Dew, a historian from Owensboro, Ky., kindly shared her research on Josephine K. Henry.

91. Baker, "Domestication of Politics," 625.

92. Whites, "Rebecca Latimer Felton and the Wife's Farm," 372.

93. Margaret Ripley Wolfe, "Feminizing Dixie: Toward a Public Role for Women in the American South," in *Research in Social Policy: Historical and Contemporary Perspectives*, ed. John H. Stanfield II (Greenwich, Conn.: JAI Press, 1987); 1:179-211; see also idem, "Twentieth-Century Feminism, Southern Style," *Helicon Nine: The Journal of Women's Arts and Letters*, special edition devoted to southern womanhood, nos. 17-18 (Spring 1987): 148-57.

94. Anne Firor Scott, "Women, Religion and Social Change in the South, 1830-1930," in Samuel S. Hill, Jr., et al., *Religion and the Solid South* (Nashville: Abingdon Press, 1972), 92-121, quotation on 93; see John Patrick McDowell III, "A Social Gospel in the South: The Woman's Home Mission Movement in the Methodist Episcopal Church, South, 1886-1939" (Ph.D. diss., Duke University, 1979); idem, *The Social Gospel in the South: The Woman's Home Mission Movement in the Methodist Episcopal Church, 1886-1939* (Baton Rouge: Louisiana State University Press, 1982); and Friedman, *Enclosed Garden*, 110-27; see also Virginia Lieson Brereton, *Training God's Army: The American Bible School, 1880-1940* (Bloomington: Indiana University Press, 1990).

95. Dewey W. Grantham, *Southern Progressivism: The Reconciliation of Progress and Tradition*, Twentieth-Century America Series, ed. Dewey W. Grantham (Knoxville: University of Tennessee Press, 1983; paperback ed., 1983), 23-24; and Anastatia Sims, "Feminism and Femininity: Women's Organizations in North Carolina, 1890-1930," a paper presented at the fiftieth meeting of the Southern Historical Association, Louisville, Ky., 1 November 1984 (copy in my possession); see also Wedell, *Elite Women and the Reform Impulse in Memphis*, 31-107.

96. LeeAnn Whites, "Southern Ladies and Millhands: The Domestic Economy and Class Politics: Augusta, Georgia, 1870-1890" (Ph.D. diss., University of California, Irvine, 1982), v, vi, 373, 374; see also Wendy Kaminer, *Women Volunteering: The Pleasure, Pain, and Politics of Unpaid Work from 1830 to the Present* (Garden City, N.Y.: Anchor Press, Doubleday, 1984); Linda Gordon, "Black and White Visions of Welfare: Women's Welfare Activism, 1890-1945," *Journal of American History* 78 (September 1991): 559-90; idem, "Social Insurance and Public Assistance: The Influence of Gender in Welfare in the United States, 1890-1935," *American Historical Review* 97 (February 1992): 19-54; Mary Jean Houde, *Reaching Out: A Story of the General Federation of Women's Clubs* (Chicago: Mobium Press, 1989); Anne Firor Scott, *Natural Allies: Women's Associations in American History* (Champaign: University of Illinois Press, 1992); and Mary S. Sims, *The Natural History of a Social Institution—the Young Women's Christian Association* (New York: Womans Press, 1936). Southern women were involved with service clubs and such organizations as the Young Women's Christian Association at all levels, local, state, and national, during the late nineteenth and early twentieth centuries.

97. *World Book Encyclopedia*, 1982 ed., s.v. "Girl Scouts" and "Juliette Gordon Low"; see also Elisabeth Israels Perry, "'The Very Best Influence': Josephine Holloway

and Girl Scouting in Nashville's African-American Community," *Tennessee Historical Quarterly* 52 (Summer 1993): 73-85.

98. Martha H. Swain, "Clubs and Voluntary Organizations," *Encyclopedia of Southern Culture*, 1536.

99. Ibid.; see Dorothy D. DeMoss, "A 'Fearless Stand': The Southern Association of College Women, 1903-1921," *Southern Studies* 26 (Winter 1987): 249-60.

100. Houde, *Reaching Out*, 11, 19, 25, 31, 78, 88; all specific material in the text of this paragraph and the preceding one related to the General Federation of Women's Clubs is drawn from this source.

101. Allen F. Davis, *Spearheads for Reform: The Social Settlements and the Progressive Movement, 1890-1941*, Urban Life in America, ed. Richard Wade (New York: Oxford University Press, 1968; paperback ed., 1970), 37; see also Ellen S. More, "'A Certain Restless Ambition': Women Physicians and World War I," *American Quarterly* 41 (December 1989): 636-60, which contains a discussion of the career of Dr. Rosalie Slaughter Morton, a native of Virginia and a graduate of the Woman's Medical College of Pennsylvania. When she completed her course of study there in 1897, she received the awards for not only inventing the best surgical equipment but also submitting the best clinical case report, which dealt with pernicious anemia.

102. Amy Thompson McCandless, "The Distinctiveness of Higher Education for Women in the Southern United States," in *The United States South: Regionalism and Identity*, ed. Valeria Gennaro Lerda and Tjebbe Westendorp (Rome: Biblioteca di Cultura, 1991), 202.

103. Martha H. Swain, "Organized Women in Mississippi: The Clash over Legal Disabilities in the 1920's," *Southern Studies* 23 (Spring 1984): 91; and Bridget Smith Pieschel and Stephen Robert Pieschel, *Loyal Daughters: One Hundred Years at Mississippi University for Women, 1884-1984* (Jackson: University Press of Mississippi, 1984), 4-6; see also Joyce Thompson, *Marking a Trail: A History of the Texas Woman's University* (Denton: Texas Woman's University Press, 1982), 1-5 et passim; and Barbara Miller Solomon, *In the Company of Educated Women: A History of Women and Higher Education in the United States* (New Haven, Conn.: Yale University Press, 1985), 54, which deals almost exclusively with non-southern women.

104. Peter Wallenstein, *From Slave South to New South: Public Policy in Nineteenth-Century Georgia*, Fred W. Morrison Series in Southern Studies (Chapel Hill: University of North Carolina Press, 1987), 167; and Solomon, *In the Company of Educated Women*, 53; see also Marion Talbot and Lois Kimball Mathews Rosenberry, *The History of the American Association of University Women, 1881-1931* (Boston: Houghton Mifflin, 1931); Elene Wilson Farello, *A History of the Education of Women in the United States* (New York: Vantage Press, 1970); Mary Caroline Crawford, *The College Girl in America* (Boston: L.C. Page, 1904); and Thomas Woody, *A History of Women's Education in the United States*, 2 vols. (New York: Octagon Books, 1966).

105. David E. Whisnant, *All That Is Native and Fine: The Politics of Culture in an American Region* (Chapel Hill: University of North Carolina Press, 1983), 19-101 et passim; Henry D. Shapiro, *Appalachia on Our Mind: The Southern Mountains and Mountaineers in the American Consciousness, 1870-1920* (Chapel Hill: University of North Carolina Press, 1978), passim; and David E. Whisnant, "Second-Level Appalachian History: Another Look at Some Fotched-On Women," *Appalachian Journal* 9 (Winter-Spring 1982): 115-23; see also Willie E. Nelms, "Cora Wilson Stewart and the Crusade against Illiteracy in Kentucky, 1916-1920," *Register of the Kentucky Historical Society* 82

(Spring 1984): 151-69; Nancy K. Forderhase, "'The Clear Call of Thoroughbred Women': The Kentucky Federation of Women's Clubs and the Crusade for Educational Reform, 1903-1909," ibid. 83 (Winter 1985): 19-35; idem, "Eve Returns to the Garden: Women Reformers in Appalachian Kentucky in the Early Twentieth Century," ibid. 85 (Summer 1987): 237-61; Lucy Furman, "Katherine Pettit—Pioneer Mountain Worker," ibid. 35 (January 1937): 75-80; Carol Crowe-Carraco, "Mary Breckinridge and the Frontier Nursing Service," ibid. 79 (July 1978): 179-91; and Anne G. Campbell, "Mary Breckinridge and the American Committee for Devastated France: The Foundations of the Frontier Nursing Service," ibid. 82 (Summer 1984): 257-76.

106. James S. Greene III, "Progressives in the Kentucky Mountains: The Formative Years of the Pine Mountain Settlement School, 1913-1930" (Ph.D. diss., Ohio State University, 1982), 33.

107. Debra Herman, "College and After: The Vassar Experiment in Women's Education, 1861-1929" (Ph.D. diss., Stanford University, 1979), 47. For other studies of women's colleges see Patricia Ann Palmieri, "In Adamless Eden: A Social Portrait of the Academic Community at Wellesley College, 1875-1920" (Ed.D. diss., Harvard University, 1981); Virginia Wolf Briscoe, "Bryn Mawr College Traditions: Women's Rituals as Expressive Behavior" (Ph.D. diss., University of Pennsylvania, 1981); and Sally Schwager, "'Harvard Women': A History of the Founding of Radcliffe College" (Ed.D. diss., Harvard University, 1982).

108. Mary Evans Frederickson, "A Place to Speak Our Minds: The Southern Summer School for Women Workers" (Ph.D. diss., University of North Carolina, Chapel Hill, 1981), 5, 192, 196, 198, 199. The material pertaining to Zilla Hawes is drawn from American Civil Liberties Union release, 27 July 1934, Highlander Research and Education Center Records (microform ed., 1980), reel 2. The Highlander Center, New Market, Tenn., graciously lent me microfilm. The original manuscript collection is with the State Historical Society of Wisconsin, Madison.

109. Roxana Robinson, *Georgia O'Keeffe: A Life* (New York: Harper & Row, 1989), 33-34, 75-76.

110. Benita Eisler, *O'Keeffe and Stieglitz: An American Romance* (New York: Doubleday, 1991), 3, 71-72, 116, 117, 119, 120, 122, 127, 135-37.

111. Kate Chopin, *The Awakening: An Authoritative Text, Contexts, Criticism*, ed. Margaret Culley (New York: W.W. Norton, 1976); Ellen Glasgow, *Virginia* (originally published in 1913; reprint, Garden City, N.Y.: Doubleday, Doran, 1929); and Mary Johnston, *Hagar* (Boston: Houghton Mifflin, 1913); see also Jones, *Tomorrow Is Another Day*, 154, 225-26, et passim; Anna Shannon Elfenbein, *Women on the Color Line: Evolving Stereotypes and the Writings of George Washington Cable, Grace King, Kate Chopin* (Charlottesville: University Press of Virginia, 1989); Lynda S. Boren and Sara deSaussure Davis, eds., *Kate Chopin Reconsidered: Beyond the Bayou* (Baton Rouge: Louisiana State University Press, 1992); and Taylor, *Gender, Race, and Region in the Writings of Grace King, Ruth McEnery Stuart, and Kate Chopin*.

112. Gerda Lerner, *The Majority Finds Its Past: Placing Women in History* (New York: Oxford University Press, 1979; paperback ed., 1981), 108-9; see also Ralph E. Luker, *The Social Gospel in Black and White: American Racial Reform, 1885-1912* (Chapel Hill: University of North Carolina Press, 1991).

113. Jacquelyn Dowd Hall, *Revolt against Chivalry: Jessie Daniel Ames and the Women's Campaign against Lynching* (New York: Columbia University Press, 1979), 65-106, quotations on 66, 101.

114. Scott, *Southern Lady*, 180-84.

115. Wheeler, *New Women of the New South*, xv, 21.

116. Ibid.; Grantham, *Southern Progressivism*, 217.

117. Laura Clay to editor of the *Herald*, 16 February 1919, Laura Clay Papers, box 11, 46M4, Margaret I. King Library, University of Kentucky, Lexington; see also Paul E. Fuller, *Laura Clay and the Woman's Rights Movement* (Lexington: University Press of Kentucky, 1975).

118. Wheeler, *New Women of the New South*, 158-59; Sidney R. Bland, "Fighting the Odds: Militant Suffragists in South Carolina," a paper presented at the Citadel Conference on the New South, Charleston, S.C., 19 April 1979, copy in my possession; Melba Dean Porter (Hay), "Madeline McDowell Breckinridge: Her Role in the Kentucky Woman Suffrage Movement, 1908-1920," *Register of the Kentucky Historical Society* 72 (October 1974): 342-63; see also Fuller, *Laura Clay and the Woman's Rights Movement*.

119. Wheeler, *New Women of the New South*, 39, 40-45; see Mary Martha Thomas, *New Women in Alabama: Social Reform and Suffrage, 1890-1920* (Tuscaloosa: University of Alabama Press, 1992); see also Virginia Bernhard et al., eds., *Hidden Histories of Women in the New South* (Columbia: University of Missouri Press, 1994).

120. Mrs. Dudley's quotation is from an exhibit, Tennessee State Museum, Nashville; the eulogy is from Guilford Dudley, Jr., to Margaret Ripley Wolfe, 27 June 1975; and James A. Hoobler, "Anne Dallas Dudley," *Distinctive Women of Tennessee*, 5.

121. Irvin, *Women in Kentucky*, 92, 94, 95; and Porter (Hay), "Madeline McDowell Breckinridge," 343, 358, 363. For a sound discussion of Desha Breckinridge, Madeline's husband, who was editor of the *Lexington Herald*, and his sister, the educator and social worker Sophonisba Preston Breckinridge, see Klotter, *Breckinridges of Kentucky*, 189-243.

122. Scott, *Southern Lady*, 184; Folmsbee, Corlew, and Mitchell, *Tennessee: A Short History*, 452-53. The ratification struggle damaged Governor Roberts's popularity. This was one of several factors that divided the Democratic party in the state in the 1920 gubernatorial election, resulting in the victory of the Republican candidate, Alfred Taylor: see Gary W. Reichard, "The Defeat of Governor Roberts," *Tennessee Historical Quarterly* 30 (Spring 1971): 94-109. For a general history of the suffrage crusade see Flexner, *Century of Struggle*. The standard work on Tennessee is Taylor, *Woman Suffrage Movement in Tennessee*; see also Anastatia Sims, "'Powers that Pray' and 'Powers that Prey': Tennessee and the Fight for Women Suffrage," *Tennessee Historical Quarterly* 50 (Winter 1991): 203-25; Wheeler, *New Women of the New South*, 31-36, 172, 176, 180-82; and Marjorie Spruill Wheeler, ed., *Votes for Women: The Woman Suffrage Movement in Tennessee, the South, and the Nation*, forthcoming from the University of Tennessee Press.

123. Elizabeth Hayes Turner, "'White-Gloved Ladies' and 'New Women' in the Texas Women Suffrage Movement," in *Southern Women: Histories and Identities*, 129-56, quotation on 156.

124. A. Elizabeth Taylor, "The Woman Suffrage Movement in Arkansas," *Arkansas Historical Quarterly* 15 (Spring 1956): 17-52.

125. Nancy F. Cott, *The Grounding of Modern Feminism* (New Haven, Conn.: Yale University Press, 1987), 3-5; see also Elizabeth Fox-Genovese, *Feminism without Illusions: A Critique of Individualism* (Chapel Hill: University of North Carolina Press, 1991); and Rosalind Rosenberg, *Beyond Separate Spheres: Intellectual Roots of Modern Feminism* (New Haven, Conn.: Yale University Press, 1982).

126. Wheeler took this position as early as 1984 in "Beyond Suffrage: Southern Suffragists and the Campaign for Women's Rights," a paper presented at the Southern Historical Association in Louisville, Ky. At that time she argued: "From the 1890s until the end of the suffrage movement in 1920, their [the suffragists'] prime objective was recognition of woman's status with full rights and privileges." A copy of the paper is in my possession. See also Wheeler, *New Women of the New South*, 184-85.

127. William Faulkner, *Light in August* (originally published in 1932; reprint, New York: Random House, 1959), 9-10; see also Diane Roberts, *Faulkner and Southern Womanhood* (Athens: University of Georgia Press, 1994).

Chapter 6. Looking for New Heavens and a New Earth

1. National Emergency Council, *Report on Economic Conditions in the South* (Washington, D.C.: United States Government Printing Office, 1938), 1 (hereafter cited as NEC Report); see also Steve Davis, "The South as 'the Nation's No. 1 Economic Problem': The NEC Report of 1938," *Georgia Historical Quarterly* 62 (Summer 1978): 119-32.

2. NEC Report, 41-44.

3. Ibid., passim; see also Jo Ann Carrigan, "Public Health," *Encyclopedia of Southern Culture*, 1152-54; and Carole E. Hill, "Rural Health," ibid., 1154-55.

4. NEC Report, 5.

5. Rosalind Rosenberg, *Divided Lives: American Women in the Twentieth Century* (New York: Hill & Wang, 1992), 6.

6. Jack Temple Kirby, *Rural Worlds Lost: The American South, 1920-1960* (Baton Rouge: Louisiana State University Press, 1987), 163. The quotations are from Kirby's sensitively written chapter "Women, Wedlock, Hearth, Health, Death," 166-67; see also Tom E. Terrill and Jerrold Hirsch, eds., *Such as Us: Southern Voices of the Thirties* (Chapel Hill: University of North Carolina Press, 1978).

7. For a general study of American women during the depression era see Susan Ware, *Holding Their Own: American Women in the 1930s* (Boston: Twayne Publishers, 1982).

8. Pauline Tabor, *Pauline's* (Louisville, Ky.: Touchstone Publishing, 1972), n.p. (this book has no page numbers).

9. Campbell, *Celluloid South*, 118-40, quotation from 140.

10. Nancy Milford, *Zelda* (New York: Avon Books, 1971), 38-39.

11. Ibid., 19, 36-37, 42. The advent of the automobile rather dramatically affected the patterns of courtship during the 1920s: see Beth L. Bailey, *From Front Porch to Back Seat: Courtship in Twentieth-Century America*, paperback ed. (Baltimore: Johns Hopkins University Press, 1989); see also Virginia Scharff, *Taking the Wheel: Women and the Coming of the Motor Age* (New York and Toronto: Free Press and Collier Macmillan Canada, 1991).

12. Milford, *Zelda*, xi; see also William Wiser, *The Great Good Place: American Expatriate Women in Paris* (New York: W.W. Norton, 1991), 212-63.

13. Quoted in Pyron, *Southern Daughter*, 117; see also Marianne Walker, *Margaret Mitchell and John Marsh: The Love Story behind "Gone with the Wind"* (Atlanta: Peachtree Publishers, 1993).

14. Pyron, *Southern Daughter*, 118.

15. Ibid.; Mitchell is quoted on 117.

16. Quoted in ibid., 137.

17. "Tallulah Bankhead," *Current Biography, 1941*, ed. Maxine Block (New York: H.W. Wilson, 1941), 36-39.

18. "Lillian Hellman," *Contemporary Authors*, ed. Hal May (Detroit: Gale Research Co., 1985), 112:239; see also William Wright, *Lillian Hellman: The Image, the Woman* (New York: Simon & Schuster, 1986), 15-33 et passim.

19. June Carter Cash, *From the Heart* (New York: Prentice Hall Press, 1987), 89.

20. Bill C. Malone, "Country Music," *Encyclopedia of Southern Culture*, 1004; see also Chet Hagan, *Grand Ole Opry: The Complete Story of a Great American Institution and Its Stars* (New York: Henry Holt, 1989), 147.

21. Recollections of James Marion Ripley, Church Hill, Tenn., 1987, tapes in my possession.

22. Ibid.

23. From my memories of my father, Clarence Estill Ripley.

24. Carol Ruth Berkin, "Women's Lives," *Encyclopedia of Southern Culture*, 1519.

25. Flexner, *Century of Struggle*, 342; see also Stanley J. Lemons, *The Woman Citizen: Social Feminism in the 1920s* (Charlottesville: University Press of Virginia, 1990).

26. Wheeler, *New Women of the New South*, 192; and Martha H. Swain, "The Public Role of Southern Women," in *Sex, Race, and the Role of Women in the South*, 38-39; see also Joanne V. Hawks, M. Carolyn Ellis, and J. Byron Morris, "Women in the Mississippi Legislature (1924-1981)," *Journal of Mississippi History* 43 (November 1981): 266-93; and Joanne V. Hawks and Mary Carolyn Ellis, "Heirs of the Southern Progressive Tradition: Women in Southern Legislatures in the 1920s," in *Southern Women*, ed. Carolina Matheny Dillman (New York: Hemisphere Publishing, 1988), 85.

27. Hawks and Ellis, "Heirs of the Southern Progressive Tradition," 82-83.

28. Joanne Varner Hawks, "A Select Few: Alabama's Women Legislators, 1922-1983," *Alabama Review* 38 (July 1985): 177.

29. M. Carolyn Ellis and Joanne V. Hawks, "Ladies in the Gentlemen's Club: South Carolina Women Legislators, 1928-1984," *Proceedings of the South Carolina Historical Association*, 1986, 17; and idem, "Creating a Different Pattern: Florida's Women Legislators, 1928-1986," *Florida Historical Quarterly* 66 (July 1987): 71.

30. Hawks and Ellis, "Heirs of the Southern Progressive Tradition," 88-89.

31. Blanche Wiesen Cook, *Eleanor Roosevelt, 1884-1933* (New York: Viking, 1992), 28-29.

32. Ibid., 349-50.

33. Hoff, *Law, Gender, and Injustice*, 202.

34. Ibid., 342; and Wheeler, *New Women of the New South*, 195-96; see also Robert S. Gallagher, "The Fight for Women's Suffrage: An Interview with Alice Paul," in *Historical Viewpoints*, 151-69. I also benefited from reading Bland, "Fighting the Odds."

35. Swain, "Organized Women in Mississippi," 91-92.

36. Stanley Coben, *Rebellion against Victorianism: The Impetus for Cultural Change in 1920s America* (New York: Oxford University Press, 1991), 102, 108; see also Judith Sealander, *As Minority Becomes Majority: Federal Reaction to the Phenomenon of Women in the Work Force, 1920-1963*, Contributions in Women's Studies no. 40 (Westport, Conn.: Greenwood Press, 1983).

37. Swain, "Organized Women in Mississippi," 101-2, quotation on 101. Among the elective positions to which southern women gained access during the early twentieth century was that of county superintendent of schools. This was true in Tennessee during the interwar period as well as in some other southern states: see Debbie Mauldin

Cottrell, *Pioneer Woman Educator: The Progressive Spirit of Annie Webb Blanton* (College Station: Texas A & M University Press, 1993); Blanton had been elected state superintendent of public instruction in Texas in 1918; see also Joseph F. Kett, "Women and the Progressive Impulse in Southern Education," in *Web of Southern Social Relations*, 166-80.

38. Robert E. Corlew, *Tennessee: A Short History Updated through 1989*, 2d ed. (Knoxville: University of Tennessee Press, 1990), 444.

39. Riley, *Divorce*, 124-26, 159.

40. Ibid., 127.

41. Kirby, *Rural Worlds Lost*, 173.

42. Swain, "Public Role of Southern Women," 38-41.

43. Martha H. Swain, "A New Deal for Mississippi Women, 1933-1943," *Journal of Mississippi History* 46 (August 1984): 191-212; idem, "'The Forgotten Woman': Ellen S. Woodward and Women's Relief in the New Deal," *Prologue: Journal of the National Archives* 15 (Winter 1983): 201-13; and Susan Ware, *Beyond Suffrage: Women in the New Deal* (Cambridge, Mass.: Harvard University Press, 1981). Swain's book *Ellen S. Woodward: New Deal Advocate for Women's Work Relief and Security* (Jackson: University Press of Mississippi, c. 1995) is forthcoming.

44. Baker, "Domestication of Politics," 625, 644.

45. Eula Mae Stockman, Greenville, S.C., interview by Margaret Ripley Wolfe, 22 May 1993, tape in my possession; Mrs. Stockman was graduated from Greenville Woman's College. Gladys Holleman Barlow, Smithfield, Va., interview by Margaret Ripley Wolfe, 18 August 1993, notes in my possession; Mrs. Barlow was graduated from Westhampton College in Richmond. Thomas W. West, *Marion College, 1873-1967* (Strasburg, Va.: Shenandoah Publishing House, 1970), 1, 7-33; Reuben E. Alley, *History of the University of Richmond, 1830-1971* (Charlottesville: University Press of Virginia, 1977), 112-52 (Westhampton College, which is now a division of the University of Richmond, originated as a women's college); Ashmore, *Greenville*, 32, 58, 60, 72, 81, 110, 120, 121, 123, 136, 268, 270.

46. Quoted in Virginia Foster (Durr), "The Emancipation of Pure, White, Southern Womanhood," *New South*, Winter 1971, 48-49.

47. For an excellent example of a long-lived local YWCA in the South see Ethel Simpson, *The First Fifty Years of the Young Women's Christian Association* [of Greenville, South Carolina] (Greenville, S.C.: privately printed, c. 1967); see also Jodi Vandenberg-Daves, "The Manly Pursuit of a Partnership between the Sexes: The Debate over YMCA Programs for Women and Girls, 1914-1933," *Journal of American History* 78 (March 1992): 1324-46.

48. From my experience as a consultant to the Tennessee Extension Homemakers Council, October 1988; see Kate Adele Hill, *Home Demonstration Work in Texas* (San Antonio, Tex.: Naylor, 1958).

49. Hilbert Campbell and Charles Modlin, Blacksburg, Va., interview by Margaret Ripley Wolfe, 21 May 1992, tape and transcript in my possession. Campbell and Modlin, who are professors of English at Virginia Polytechnic Institute and State University, are authorities on Sherwood Anderson and are personal friends of the late Eleanor Copenhaver Anderson; see also Margaret Ripley Wolfe, "Eleanor Copenhaver Anderson of the National Board of the YWCA: Appalachian Feminist and Author's Wife," *Winesburg Eagle: The Official Publication of the Sherwood Anderson Society* 38 (Summer 1993): 2-9.

50. Liselotte Bendix Stern to Margaret Ripley Wolfe, undated letter from 1992, in my possession. Mrs. Stern was a close personal friend of Lucy Carner, who at one time headed the Industrial Department of the National Board of the YWCA. Through this connection Mrs. Stern also became an acquaintance of Eleanor Copenhaver Anderson and other Y staffers.

51. Kay Mills, *This Little Light of Mine: The Life of Fannie Lou Hamer* (New York: Dutton, 1993), 1, 7, 9; Fannie's statement appears on 9. See also Sarah Rice, *He Included Me: The Autobiography of Sarah Rice*, ed. Louise Westling (Athens: University of Georgia Press, 1989); and Ellen Tarry, *The Third Door: The Autobiography of an American Negro Woman*, introduction by Nellie Y. McKay (paperback ed., Tuscaloosa: University of Alabama Press, 1992).

52. Foster Durr, "Emancipation of Pure, White, Southern Womanhood," 46-54, quotations from 54; see also Hollinger F. Barnard, ed., *Outside the Magic Circle: The Autobiography of Virginia Foster Durr*, foreword by Studs Terkel (University: University of Alabama Press, 1986).

53. Kathleen M. Blee, *Women of the Klan: Racism and Gender in the 1920s* (Berkeley: University of California Press, 1991), 2, 25; see also Nancy MacLean, *Behind the Mask of Chivalry: The Making of the Second Ku Klux Klan* (New York: Oxford University Press, 1994).

54. Hall, *Revolt against Chivalry*, passim; Morton Sosna, *In Search of the Silent South: Southern Liberals and the Race Issue*, Contemporary American History Series, ed. William E. Leuchtenburg (New York: Columbia University Press, 1977), 172-97; see also W. Fitzhugh Brundage, *Lynching in the New South: Georgia and Virginia, 1880-1930*, Blacks in the New World, ed. August Meier and John H. Bracey (Urbana: University of Illinois Press, 1993).

55. Nancy MacLean, "The Leo Frank Case Reconsidered: Gender and Sexual Politics in the Making of Reactionary Populism," *Journal of American History* 78 (December 1991): 917-48.

56. Randall Patton, "Lillian Smith and the Transformation of American Liberalism, 1945-1950," *Georgia Historical Quarterly* 76 (Summer 1992): 375, 383; see also Roseanne V. Comacho, "Race, Region, and Gender in a Reassessment of Lillian Smith," *Southern Women: Histories and Identities*, 157-76.

57. Sosna, *In Search of the Silent South*, 179; and Anne C. Loveland, *Lillian Smith: A Southerner Confronting the South* (Baton Rouge: Louisiana State University Press, 1986); see also W.J. Stuckey, *Caroline Gordon* (New York: Twayne Publishers, 1972); Caroline Gordon, *None Shall Look Back* (New York: Charles Scribner's Sons, 1937; reprint ed., New York: Cooper Square Publishers, 1971), 11-16 et passim; and Walter Sullivan, "Strange Children: Caroline Gordon and Allen Tate," in *Home Ground: Southern Autobiography*, ed. J. Bill Berry (Columbia: University of Missouri Press, 1991), 123-30.

58. Louise Leonard to Minnie Fisher, 16 October 1929, SSS Papers. At the time when I studied this letter and the response to it cited below, they were contained in a box of loose materials set aside for use by students at Cornell University.

59. Fisher to Leonard, 23 October 1929, SSS Papers.

60. Sherwood Anderson, "Southern Women in Industry," a speech delivered on 3 February 1931 at Richmond, Va., Sherwood Anderson Manuscripts, Newberry Library, Chicago, Ill.

61. Margaret Ripley Wolfe, "Redesigning Dixie: Toward a Humanistic Society," a

paper presented at the seventy-sixth meeting of the American Historical Association, Pacific Coast Branch, San Diego, Calif., 12 August 1983.

62. Wolfe, "Feminizing Dixie," 196-97; and idem, "Eleanor Copenhaver Anderson of the National Board of the YWCA," 2-9. See Daniel J. Walkowitz, "The Making of a Feminine Professional Identity: Social Workers in the 1920s," *American Historical Review* 95 (October 1990): 1051-75; see also John Glen, *Highlander: No Ordinary School, 1932-1962* (Lexington: University Press of Kentucky, 1988); and Robert F. Martin, *Howard Kester and the Struggle for Social Justice in the South, 1904-1977* (Charlottesville: University Press of Virginia, 1991).

63. Hall et al., *Like a Family*, 214-15.

64. John A. Salmond, *Miss Lucy of the CIO: The Life and Times of Lucy Randolph Mason, 1882-1959* (Athens: University of Georgia Press, 1988); see also Frank T. Adams, *James A. Dombrowski: An American Heretic, 1897-1983* (Knoxville: University of Tennessee Press, 1992), 117, 134, 140, 175-76, 182-83, 187, 280-81.

65. Diary of Hilda Hulbert (February 1935), Highlander Research and Education Center records (microform ed., 1980), reel 10.

66. "Relations with Henderson County, North Carolina, in Regard to the Southern Industrial Conference, June 1946, from the Viewpoint of Brooks S. Creedy" (mimeographed), National Board YWCA records, New York City, box 20, Sophia Smith Collection, Smith College, Northampton, Mass.

67. The material involved in this discussion is drawn from my careful study of the records of the National Board of the YWCA in the organization's headquarters in New York City and at Smith College and the papers of the SSS at Cornell University. Doris Cohen Brody, "American Labor Education Service, 1927-1962: An Organization in Workers' Education" (Ph.D. diss., Cornell University, 1973) is useful for understanding the general national context within which the SSS developed.

68. Eleanor Copenhaver, Biennial Report, 1928-29, National Board YWCA records, New York City.

69. Frederickson, "A Place to Speak Our Minds," 94. The SSS papers indicate that Edens was a student in 1929, 1934, 1935, and 1938, a member of the household staff in 1936, 1937, and 1939; from files of SSS students, faculty, and household staff, boxes 7, 112.

70. These dissertations are very helpful in understanding the SSS and the YWCA activities with respect to class: Frederickson, "A Place to Speak Our Minds"; Marion Winifred Roydhouse, "The 'Universal Sisterhood of Women': Women and Labor Reform in North Carolina, 1900-1932" (Ph.D. diss., Duke University, 1980); and Dolores Elizabeth Janiewski, "From Field to Factory: Race, Class, Sex, and the Woman Worker in Durham, 1880-1940" (Ph.D. diss., Duke University, 1979).

71. Report of executive (unidentified) of Business Girls Conference, 1934, National Board YWCA records, box 6, Smith College.

72. Brownie Lee Jones interview by Mary Frederickson, 5 August 1976, Southern Oral History Program in cooperation with the Twentieth Century Trade Union Woman: Vehicle for Social Change Oral History Project (Ann Arbor: University of Michigan, 1978), 27. For a brief discussion of abortion in the rural South see Kirby, *Rural Worlds Lost*, 166; see also Linda Gordon, *Woman's Body Woman's Right: Birth Control in America*, rev. ed. (New York: Penguin Books, 1990); Angus McLaren, *A History of Contraception: From Antiquity to the Present Day*, Family: Sexuality and Social Relations in Past Times, ed. Peter Laslett, Michael Anderson, and Keith Wrightson (Oxford:

Basil Blackwell, 1990); and Ellen Chesler, *Woman of Valor: Margaret Sanger and the Birth Control Movement in America* (New York: Summit Books, 1992).

73. This account was related to me with the stipulation that the family's anonymity be preserved. I have no reason to doubt the accuracy of the story. See Carole R. McCann, *Birth Control Politics in the United States, 1916-1945* (Ithaca, N.Y.: Cornell University Press, 1994).

74. Kirby, *Rural Worlds Lost*, 166.

75. Frederickson, "A Place to Speak Our Minds," 3.

76. Wolfe, "Eleanor Copenhaver Anderson of the National Board of the YWCA," 5; and diary of Eleanor Copenhaver Anderson, 4-5 January 1936, copy in my possession—the original is the property of Professor Hilbert Campbell, Department of English, Virginia Polytechnic Institute and State University, Blacksburg, Va., who graciously lent me all of Eleanor's surviving diaries from the 1930s and allowed me to copy them.

77. David W. Hacker, "Dreamers and the Betrayal," *Arkansas Gazette Sunday Magazine*, 21 November 1954, from the papers of Commonwealth College contained in Highlander's manuscripts.

78. Ibid., 28 November 1954.

79. "Tupelo Law: City Limits Union Organizers; NLRB Has a New Problem," *Newsweek*, 22 November 1937, 17-18.

80. NEC Report, 21-22.

81. Quoted in Jensen, *With These Hands*, 183-84.

82. Kirby, *Rural Worlds Lost*, 172.

83. Anderson, "Southern Women in Industry."

84. Robert A. Caro, *The Years of Lyndon Johnson: The Path to Power* (New York: Alfred A. Knopf, 1983), 502-15, particularly 505.

85. Ibid., 511; see also Margaret Jarman Hagood, *Mothers in the South: Portraiture of the White Tenant Farm Woman*, Family in America, ed. David J. Rothman and Sheila M. Rothman (New York: Arno Press and the *New York Times*, 1972).

86. From an essay written by one of my students, Ruth A. Street, Kingsport, Tenn.

87. "Glimpses of the Elizabethton Strikes: Low Wages Force Workers to Protest—Girl Striker Tells Her Story," *Brotherhood of Locomotive Firemen and Enginemen's Magazine*, undated clipping [ca. 1929], 423-25, copy in my possession; see also James A. Hodges, "Challenge to the New South: The Great Textile Strike in Elizabethton, Tennessee, 1929," *Tennessee Historical Quarterly* 23 (December 1964): 343-57; and Jacquelyn Dowd Hall, "Disorderly Women: Gender and Labor Militancy in the Appalachian South," *Journal of American History* 73 (September 1986): 354-82. Another useful source that deals with southern female factory workers is Victoria Byerly, *Hard Times Cotton Mill Girls: Personal Histories of Womanhood and Poverty in the South*, introduction by Cletus E. Daniel (Ithaca, N.Y.: ILR Press, 1986).

88. Material drawn from all of the sources in no. 87, particularly Hall, "Disorderly Women," 364, as well as my study of strikers' reminiscences contained in the SSS papers; see also Jacquelyn Dowd Hall, "Disorderly Women," *Helicon Nine: The Journal of Women's Arts and Letters* no. 17-18 (Spring 1987): 100-111; and Hall et al., "Cotton Mill People," 245-86.

89. William Lundy (retired miner), interview by Margaret Ripley Wolfe, 1 February 1976, Kingsport, Tenn., notes in my possession. The physician whom Lundy spoke about was Dr. Hugh W. Clement: recollections of Hugh W. Clement, 1975, in my possession.

90. The Reverend Clarence Meyer to Margaret Ripley Wolfe, 25 September 1974.

91. Quoted in Thomas H. Coode and John F. Bauman, "'Dear Mr. Hopkins': A New Dealer Reports from Eastern Kentucky," *Register of the Kentucky Historical Society* 78 (Winter 1980): 59. Eleanor Roosevelt's most recent biographer, Blanche Wiesen Cook, writes: "For all the deletions and restraint, the thousands of letters [between Eleanor Roosevelt and Lorena Hickok] that remain are amorous and specific. . . . There are few ambiguities in this correspondence, and a letter that was defined as 'particularly susceptible to misinterpretation' reads: 'I wish I could lie down beside you tonight & take you in my arms'"; see Cook, *Eleanor Roosevelt*, 477-500, specifically 478. In all probability Eleanor and Lorena were lovers.

92. James Still, *River of Earth* (New York: Viking Press, 1940; reprint ed., New York: Popular Library, 1968). Another novel that relates to women's experience in coal camps is Myra Page, *Daughter of the Hills: A Woman's Part in the Coal Miners' Struggle*, introduction by Alice Kessler-Harris and Paul Lauter, afterword by Deborah S. Rosenfelt (New York: Citadel Press, 1950; reprint, New York: Feminist Press, 1977); see also May Cravath Wharton, *Doctor Woman of the Cumberlands: The Autobiography of May Cravath Wharton, M.D.* (originally published in 1953; reprint, Nashville: Parthenon Press for Uplands Cumberland Mountain Sanatorium, Pleasant Hill, Tenn., 1972); and W.B. Barton, *An Appalachian Doctor and His Patients* (New York: Vantage Press, 1977).

93. Julia Kirk Blackwelder, *Women of the Depression: Caste and Culture in San Antonio, 1929-1939* (College Station: Texas A & M Press, 1984) 1, 9, 10; see also Douglas L. Smith, *The New Deal in the Urban South* (Baton Rouge: Louisiana State University Press, 1988); and Roger Biles, *The South and the New Deal* (Lexington: University Press of Kentucky, 1994).

94. For a study of this relationship from the perspective of both black and white women, see Susan Tucker, *Telling Memories Among Southern Women: Domestic Workers and Their Employers in the Segregated South* (Baton Rouge: Louisiana State University Press, 1988); see also John B. Kirby, *Black Americans of the Roosevelt Era: Liberalism and Race*, Twentieth-Century America, ed. Dewey W. Grantham (Knoxville: University of Tennessee Press, 1980).

95. "Maya Angelou," *Current Biography Yearbook, 1974* (New York: H.W. Wilson, 1975), 12-15, quotation on 13; see also Maya Angelou, *I Know Why the Caged Bird Sings* (New York: Random House, c. 1970) and "Why I Moved Back [to the South]," *Ebony*, February 1982, 130-34.

96. Ruth A. Banes, "Blues-Singing Women," *Encyclopedia of Southern Culture*, 1531.

97. Bill C. Malone, "Protest," *Encyclopedia of Southern Culture*, 1023; and Warren French, "Film, Musical," ibid., 921.

98. *World Book Encyclopedia*, 1992 ed., s.v. "Josephine Baker," by Gerald Bordman; and "Josephine Baker," *Current Biography Yearbook*, ed. Charles Moritz (New York: H.W. Wilson, 1965), 19-22; see also Phyllis Rose, *Jazz Cleopatra: Josephine Baker in Her Time* (New York: Doubleday, 1989); and Wiser, *Great Good Place*, 264-314.

99. Rosetta Reitz, "Sweethearts on Parade," *Helicon Nine: The Journal of Women's Arts and Letters* no. 17-18 (Spring 1987): 135-44, quotations on 135.

100. Grace Paysinger Roland, *Walking down Memory's Lane* (n.p.: privately printed, n.d.), 150-51. Dr. Charles P. Roland graciously shared with me a copy of his mother's memoirs.

101. Quoted in *Bristol Herald Courier*, 2 January 1942, clipping in a scrapbook from the Marion Collection.

102. Ibid., 11 October 1940.

103. "Confederate General Enjoys 102nd Birthday," 128-29.

104. For general treatments of American women during World War II see Susan M. Hartmann, *The Home Front and Beyond: American Women in the 1940s* (Boston: Twayne, 1982); and D'Ann Campbell, *Women at War with America: Private Lives in a Patriotric Era* (Cambridge, Mass.: Harvard University Press, 1984).

105. Jane Weaver Poulton, *A Better Legend: From the World War II Letters of Jack and Jane Poulton* (Charlottesville: University Press of Virginia, 1993); and Judy Barrett Litoff and David C. Smith, eds., *Dear Boys: World War II Letters from a Woman Back Home*, with a biographical essay by Martha H. Swain (Jackson: University Press of Mississippi, 1991). The latter book deals with a bimonthly column written by Keith Frazier Somerville, a woman with a unisex name, that appeared from January 1943 through August 1945 in the *Bolivar Commercial*, a weekly Cleveland, Mississippi, newspaper; see also Judy Barrett Litoff and David C. Smith, "'Writing Is Fighting, Too': The World War II Correspondence of Southern Women," *Georgia Historical Quarterly* 76 (Summer 1992): 436-57.

106. Roland, *Walking down Memory's Lane*, 152-53.

107. From my memories of family stories.

108. Ibid.

109. As told to me by Helen Davidson at Murfreesboro, Tenn., October 1988.

110. Margaret Ripley Wolfe, *Kingsport, Tennessee: A Planned American City* (Lexington: University Press of Kentucky, 1987), 139-48.

111. Mary Martha Thomas, *Riveting and Rationing in Dixie: Alabama Women and the Second World War* (Tuscaloosa: University of Alabama Press, 1987); and photographs from Records of the Social Security Administration, RG 47G, National Archives and Records Administration (NARA), Washington, D.C.; see also "Agnes E. Meyer on Wartime Conditions in the Urban South," in *Major Problems in the History of the American South*, vol. 2: *The New South*, ed. Paul D. Escott and David R. Goldfield (Lexington, Mass.: D.C. Heath, 1990), 419-23.

112. Photographs contained in RG 111 SC (this is the extraordinary collection of military photographs filed in card-catalog arrangements), NARA. Many of these images have identifications with the names, ranks, and home addresses of those pictured.

113. Annie Leibovitz, "The Unshakable Janet Reno," *Vogue*, August 1993, 261-62; and Winifred Wood, *We Were WASPS*, with drawings by Dorothy Swain (n.p.: privately printed, 1978).

114. Marianne Verges, *On Silver Wings: The Women Airforce Service Pilots of World War II*, foreword by Senator Barry Goldwater (New York: Ballantine Books, 1991), 11-12; see also Sally Van Wagenen Keil, *Those Wonderful Women in Their Flying Machines: The Unknown Heroines of World War II* (New York: Rawson, Wade Publishers, 1979), 40-44.

115. Verges, *On Silver Wings*, 12-13.

116. "Girl Pilots," *Life*, 19 July 1943, 73-81.

117. Verges, *On Silver Wings*, 220-21 et passim.

118. Doris Brinker Tanner, "Cornelia Fort: A WASP in World War II, Part I," *Tennessee Historical Quarterly* 40 (Winter 1981): 381-94; and idem, "Cornelia Fort: Pioneer Woman Military Aviator, Part II," ibid. 41 (Spring 1982): 67-80; see also Janene Leonhirth, "Tennessee's Experiment: Women as Military Flight Instructors," ibid. 51 (Fall 1992): 170-78.

119. Liz Strohous, "The WASPS in WWII," tape, Forum Recordings, Marion, Iowa.

120. Elizabeth Fox-Genovese, "Mixed Messages: Women and the Impact of World War II," *Southern Humanities Review* 27 (Summer 1993): 235-45.

Chapter 7. A Time to Get and a Time to Lose

1. Charles P. Roland, *The Improbable Era: The South since World War II* (Lexington: University Press of Kentucky, 1975); and David R. Goldfield, *Promised Land: The South since 1945*, American History Series, ed. John Hope Franklin and Abraham S. Eisenstadt (Arlington Heights, Ill.: Harlan Davidson, 1987).

2. Roland, *Improbable Era*, 185-93.

3. Hagan, *Grand Ole Opry*, 157-62.

4. See Loretta Lynn with George Vecsey, *Loretta Lynn: Coal Miner's Daughter* (Chicago: Henry Regnery, 1976); and Ellis Nassour, *Honky Tonk Angel: The Intimate Story of Patsy Cline* (New York: St. Martin's Press, 1993).

5. *Johnson City* (Tenn.) *Press*, 31 October 1987.

6. James Brady, "In Step With: Jean MacArthur," *Parade Magazine*, 15 March 1987, 16; the particulars of General MacArthur's birth are from *World Book Encyclopedia*, 1982 ed., s.v. "Douglas MacArthur," Jules Archer.

7. Kyoko Inoue, *MacArthur's Japanese Constitution: A Linguistic and Cultural Study of Its Making* (Chicago: University of Chicago Press, 1991), 221-65, 279.

8. Arthur White, "Overpaid, Oversexed, Over Here: The Yanks Came with Chocolate and Left with British Brides," *Time*, 28 May 1984, 33.

9. The quotations are from a research paper prepared by one of my students, Penny Hagy, for History of Tennessee, Spring 1984.

10. Hodding Carter, "The Shrinking South," *Look*, 4 March 1958, 21-25.

11. Margaret Ripley Wolfe, "Appalachians in Muncie: A Case Study of an American Exodus," *Locus: An Historical Journal of Regional Perspectives* 4 (Spring 1992): 169-89, particularly 170; this article contains extensive bibliographical listings; see also Jack Temple Kirby, "The Southern Exodus, 1910-1960: A Primer for Historians," *Journal of Southern History* 49 (November 1983): 585-600; Joe William Trotter, Jr., ed., *The Great Migration in Historical Perspective: New Dimensions of Race, Class, and Gender* (Bloomington: Indiana University Press, 1991); and Nicholas Lemann, *The Promised land: The Great Black Migration and How It Changed America* (New York: Vintage Books, 1992).

12. Harriette Arnow, *The Dollmaker*, with afterword by Joyce Carol Oates (New York: Macmillan, 1954; reprint, New York: Avon Books, 1974).

13. Joanne Meyerowitz, "Beyond the Feminine Mystique: A Reassessment of Postwar Mass Culture, 1946-1958," *Journal of American History* 79 (March 1993): 1455-82, particularly 1455. See Jackie Byars, *All that Hollywood Allows: Re-reading Gender in 1950s Melodrama*, Gender and American Culture, ed. Linda K. Kerber and Nell Irvin Painter (Chapel Hill: University of North Carolina Press, 1991); see also Betty Friedan, *The Feminine Mystique* (New York: W.W. Norton, 1963; paperback ed., New York: Dell, 1970); idem, *The Second Stage* (New York: Summit Books, 1981); and idem, *The Fountain of Age* (New York: Simon & Schuster, 1993).

14. Meyerowitz, "Beyond the Feminine Mystique," 1458.

15. Marcia Cohen, *The Sisterhood: The True Story of the Women Who Changed the World* (New York: Simon & Schuster, 1988), 13-20, 266-69.

16. David W. Noble, David A. Horowitz, and Peter N. Carroll, *Twentieth Century*

Limited: A History of Recent America (Boston: Houghton Mifflin, 1980), 313-44; James T. Patterson, *America in the Twentieth Century: A History* (New York: Harcourt Brace Jovanovich, 1976), 371-409; and Walter T.K. Nugent, *Modern America* (Boston: Houghton Mifflin, 1973), 285-317.

17. Walker Percy, *The Moviegoer* (New York: Alfred A. Knopf, 1961), 65.

18. Mark Steadman, "Humor [in Literature]," *Encyclopedia of Southern Culture*, 856; quotation from McKern, *Redneck Mothers, Good Ol' Girls, and Other Southern Belles*, 36; see Robert H. Brinkmeyer, Jr., *The Art and Vision of Flannery O'Connor* (Baton Rouge: Louisiana State University Press, 1993); Carol S. Manning, *With Ears Opening Like Morning Glories: Eudora Welty and the Love of Storytelling*, Contributions in Women's Studies vol. 58 (Westport, Conn.: Greenwood Press, 1985); Albert J. Devlin, ed., *Welty: A Life in Literature* (Jackson: University Press of Mississippi, 1987); and Joseph R. Millichap, "Carson McCullers," and Warren Akin IV and Suzanne Marrs, "Eudora Welty," in *Encyclopedia of Southern Culture*, 889 and 899-900 respectively; see also Gordon E. Bigelow, *Frontier Eden: The Literary Career of Marjorie Kinnan Rawlings* (Gainesville: University Press of Florida, 1966).

19. Gail Godwin, *A Mother and Two Daughters* (New York: Viking Press, 1982); idem, *A Southern Family* (New York: William Morrow, 1987); idem, *Father Melancholy's Daughter* (New York: William Morrow, 1991); Lee Smith, *Oral History* (New York: Putnam, 1983); idem, *Family Linen* (New York: Putnam, 1985); idem, *Fair and Tender Ladies* (New York: Putnam, 1988); idem, *The Devil's Dream* (New York: Putnam, 1992); see also "Alumni Scholarship Winner Writes Best Sellers," *Kentucky Open Door* 1 (1994): 9; and Bobbie Ann Mason, *Feather Crowns: A Novel* (New York: HarperCollins, 1993).

20. Quotation from Anne Moody, *Coming of Age in Mississippi: An Autobiography* (New York: Dell, 1968), 186. Alice Walker won the Pulitzer Prize for fiction in 1983 for her novel *The Color Purple*. The story, told through the letters of two sisters, hardly reflects well on black men; it generated some controversy first as a book and then as a film; see also Alice Walker, *In Search of Our Mothers' Gardens: Womanist Prose* (New York: Harcourt Brace Jovanovich, 1984), 15-21.

21. For general studies of the post-World War II-era South see Roland, *Improbable Era*; Goldfield, *Promised Land* and *Black, White, and Southern: Race Relations and Southern Culture, 1940 to the Present* (Baton Rouge: Louisiana State University Press, 1990); see also Bruce J. Schulman, *From Cotton Belt to Sunbelt: Federal Policy, Economic Development, and the Transformation of the South, 1938-1980* (New York: Oxford University Press, 1991).

22. Elaine Brown, *A Taste of Power: A Black Woman's Story* (New York: Pantheon Books, 1992), 272.

23. "Angela (Yvonne) Davis," *Current Biography Yearbook, 1972*, ed. Charles Moritz (New York: H.W. Wilson, 1973), 97-101. Davis had turned down the offer of a scholarship in nursing at Fisk University, a black institution in Nashville. She probably had already become disenchanted with educational approaches in the South. Still, if she had spent her college years in the South, she might have followed an entirely different course in life: see, e.g., Amy Thompson McCandless, "The Higher Education of Black Women in the Contemporary South," *Mississippi Quarterly: The Journal of Southern Culture* 55 (Fall 1992): 453-65.

24. "Wilma (Glodean) Rudolph," *Current Biography, 1961*, ed. Charles Moritz (New York: H.W. Wilson, 1962), 399-401. Southern women have been counted among

what may be the toughest professional athletes going, the competitors on the rodeo circuit: see Mary Lou LeCompte, *Cowgirls of the Rodeo: Pioneer Professional Athletes, Sports and Society,* ed. Benjamin G. Rader and Randy Roberts (Urbana: University of Illinois Press, 1993), passim.

25. James Brady, "In Step With: Tina Turner," *Parade Magazine,* 1 November 1987, 10; see also "The Lady Has Legs!" *Vanity Fair,* May 1993, 114-21, 166, 171-75, 177.

26. *World Book Encyclopedia,* 1982 ed., s.v. "Nikki Giovanni," by Clark Griffith; see also Virginia C. Fowler, *Nikki Giovanni,* Twayne's United States Authors Series, ed. Frank Day (New York: Twayne Publishers, 1992).

27. Wolfe, "Twentieth Century Feminism, Southern Style," 149; and Banner, *American Beauty,* 249-91; see also Beverly Lowry, "Born to Preen: Why Southern Girls Dominate Beauty Contests," *Southern Magazine,* September 1987, 29.

28. Lowry, "Born to Preen," 29-31.

29. Associated Press story in *Kingsport* (Tenn.) *Times-News,* 22 September 1993.

30. Don E. Carleton, *Red Scare! Right-Wing Hysteria, Fifties Fanaticism, and Their Legacy in Texas* (Austin: Texas Monthly Press, 1985), 111-34.

31. From my study of National Board YWCA records in New York City and SSS papers.

32. Hallie Farmer's comments were contained in correspondence of Sarah Harder, president of the AAUW, to Margaret Ripley Wolfe, 22 February 1988; see "Prof. Hallie Farmer," *Leaders in Education: A Biographical Directory,* ed. J. McKeen Cattell, Jaques Cattell, and E.E. Ross, 2d ed. (New York: Science Press, 1941), 322; and Carolyn Hinshaw Edwards, *Hallie Farmer: Crusader for Legislative Reform in Alabama* (Huntsville, Ala.: Strode Publishers, Inc., 1979); see also Talbot, *History of the American Association of University Women,* 48-62.

33. Hilda Hulbert diary, Highlander papers.

34. Durr, *Outside the Magic Circle,* 254-57; quotation from 255.

35. John Salmond, *A Southern Rebel: The Life and Times of Aubrey Willis Williams, 1890-1965* (Chapel Hill: University of North Carolina Press, 1983), 231, 235-36.

36. Irwin Klibaner, "The Travail of Southern Radicals: The Southern Conference Educational Fund, 1946-1976," *Journal of Southern History* 49 (May 1983): 179-202, particularly 191; see also Anne Braden, *The Wall Between* (New York: Monthly Review Press, 1958), 252-53.

37. *Encyclopedia Americana,* 1982 ed., s.v. "Mary McLeod Bethune."

38. *Woman's Journal* (published at Radcliffe College), October 1984, n.p. Brown's papers are at Radcliffe; Karen Kennelly, "Charlotte Hawkins Brown," *Dictionary of American Biography: Supplement Seven, 1961-1965,* ed. John A. Garraty (New York: Charles Scribner's Sons, 1981), 82-84; and Wilhelmena S. Robinson, *International Library of Negro Life and History* (New York: Publishers Co., Inc., 1968), 167-68.

39. For a discussion of the Montgomery black community and black leadership during the 1950s, particularly E.D. Nixon, see Milton Viorst, *Fire in the Streets: America in the 1960s* (New York: Simon & Schuster, 1979), 17-51; see also Merl E. Reed, *Seedtime for the Modern Civil Rights Movement: The President's Committee on Fair Employment Practice, 1941-1946* (Baton Rouge: Louisiana State University Press, 1991); Juan Williams, *Eyes on the Prize: America's Civil Rights Years, 1954-1965* (New York: Viking Penguin, 1988); and David Chalmers, *And the Crooked Places Made Straight: The Struggle for Social Change in the 1960s* (Baltimore: Johns Hopkins University Press, 1991); see also Henry Hampton and Steve Fayer with Sarah Flynn, *Voices of Freedom: An Oral*

History of the Civil Rights Movement from the 1950s through the 1980s (New York: Bantam Books, 1990).

40. Highlander papers contain references to Rosa Parks's connections with the school; see also Rosa Parks with Jim Haskins, *Rosa Parks: My Story* (New York: Dial Books, 1992).

41. The political scientist Jo Freeman identifies the conditions that must exist for a movement to originate: a preexisting communications network or infrastructure (one that is cooptable to new ideas), a situation of strain, and finally a crisis that serves as a catalyst for action: see Jo Freeman, *The Politics of Women's Liberation: A Case Study of an Emerging Social Movement and Its Relation to the Policy Process* (New York: David McKay, 1975), passim; see also Howell Raines, *My Soul Is Rested: Movement Days in the Deep South* (New York: Penguin Books, 1983); Robin D.G. Kelley, "'We Are Not What We Seem': Rethinking Black Working-Class Opposition in the Jim Crow South," *Journal of American History* 80 (June 1993): 75-112; and August Meier and John H. Bracey, Jr., "The NAACP as a Reform Movement, 1909-1963: 'To reach the Conscience of America,'" *Journal of Southern History* 59 (February 1993): 3-30.

42. Wolfe, "Redesigning Dixie," passim.

43. Jo Ann Gibson Robinson, *The Montgomery Bus Boycott and the Women Who Started It: The Memoir of Jo Ann Gibson Robinson*, ed. with a foreword by David J. Garrow (Knoxville: University of Tennessee Press, 1987), ix-x et passim.

44. Quoted in Wendall A. Parris, "Highlander Folk School, an Adult Education School with a Purpose," *Negro History Bulletin* 21 (May 1958): 185; see also Cynthia Stokes Brown, ed., *Ready from Within: Septima Clark and the Civil Rights Movement*, introduction by Cynthia Stokes Brown (Navarro, Calif.: Wild Trees Press, 1986); and Septima Poinsette Clark, *Echo in My Soul* (New York: E.P. Dutton, 1962).

45. Frank Adams, "Highlander Folk School: Getting Information, Going Back and Teaching It," *Harvard Educational Review* 42 (November 1972): 497-520, especially 511-13.

46. Dan Wakefield, "The Siege at Highlander," *Nation*, 7 November 1959, 323-25.

47. Myles Horton to Maxwell Hahn of the Field Foundation, 19 June 1961, Highlander papers, reel 7.

48. Ibid.

49. Septima Clark to Dorothy Cotton, 19 May 1961, Highlander papers, reel 7.

50. Bernice V. Robinson, Mississippi Voter-Education Report, 19 July 1962, Highlander papers, reel 7.

51. Bernice V. Robinson to Myles Horton, 15 June 1963, Highlander papers, reel 7.

52. Mills, *This Little Light of Mine*, 1-5, particularly 1 and 3.

53. Sara Evans, *Personal Politics: The Roots of Women's Liberation in the Civil Rights Movement and the New Left* (New York: Alfred A. Knopf, 1979), 29-37; and Mary King, *Freedom Song: A Personal Story of the 1960s Civil Rights Movement*, foreword by Andrew J. Young (New York: William Morrow, 1987), 33-78 et passim; see also Katharine Du Pre Lumpkin, *The Making of a Southerner*, foreword by Darlene Clark Hine (Athens: University of Georgia Press, 1991).

54. Evans, *Personal Politics*, 45-53.

55. Ibid., 83-89; Evans follows the Robin Morgan version. See King, *Freedom Song*, 443-54, 464-65; see also Nancie Caraway, *Segregated Sisterhood: Racism and the Politics of American Feminism* (Knoxville: University of Tennessee Press, 1991).

56. King, *Freedom Song*, 136.

57. For insight into the treatment that the Black Panthers accorded their women see Brown, *A Taste of Power*, passim.

58. Mills, *This Little Light of Mine*, 274.

59. Clark, *Ready from Within*, 77-83, quotation on 77.

60. Parks, *Rosa Parks*, 81-82.

61. Ibid., 165-66.

62. Evans, *Personal Politics*, 217; Freeman, *Politics of Women's Liberation*, 44-70; see also Abbott, *Womenfolks*, 197-208.

63. Lynda Van Devanter with Christopher Morgan, *Home before Morning: The Story of an Army Nurse in Vietnam* (New York: Warner Books, 1983); see also Elizabeth M. Norman, *Women at War: The Story of Fifty Military Nurses Who Served in Vietnam* (Philadelphia: University of Pennsylvania Press, 1990); and Winnie Smith, *American Daughter Gone to War: On the Front Lines with an Army Nurse in Vietnam* (New York: William Morrow, 1992).

64. Freeman, *Politics of Women's Liberation*, 53-54.

65. "Facts on Affirmative Action" and "Facts on Legal Rights for Women," NOW Legal Defense and Education Fund, June 1988; *National Times* (NOW), October-December 1988.

66. Martha H. Swain, "The Political Dyanamics of Women's Organizations in Mississippi since 1920," 7-8, an unpublished manuscript from "Ideals and Realities: A Public Forum on the History of Women in Politics in Mississippi," Mississippi University for Women, 17-18 April 1986, copy in my possession.

67. *Washington Post*, 7 October 1978; "Countdown on the ERA," *Time*, 14 June 1982, 25; see also Edith Mayo and Jerry Frye, "ERA: Postmortem of a Failure in Political Communication," *OAH Newsletter* 11 (August 1993): 21-24; Joan Hoff-Wilson, ed., *Rights of Passage: The Past and Future of the ERA* (Bloomington: Indiana University Press, 1986); Mary Frances Berry, *Why ERA Failed: Politics, Women's Rights, and the Amending Process of the Constitution*, Everywoman: Studies in History, Literature, and Culture, ed. Susan Gubar and Joan Hoff-Wilson, First Midland Book ed. (Bloomington: Indiana University Press, 1988); and Donald G. Mathews and Jane De Hart, *Sex, Gender, and the Politics of ERA: A State and the Nation* (New York: Oxford University Press, 1991).

68. Rosalynn Carter, *First Lady from Plains* (New York: Fawcett Gold Medal Book published by Ballantine Books, 1984), 95-96.

69. Michael Winerip, "Kentucky's Godmother to the Poor" (Eula Hall), *People*, Fall 1991, 100-103; see also Tilda Kemplen, *From Roots to Roses: The Autobiography of Tilda Kemplen*, ed. Nancy Herzberg (Athens: University of Georgia Press, 1992). Kemplen is the founder and director of Mountain Communities Childcare and Development Centers, Inc., in Campbell and Claiborne counties of Tennessee.

70. Friedan's *Second Stage* is cited in note 13 above; see Sylvia Ann Hewlett, *A Lesser Life: The Myth of Women's Liberation in America* (New York: William Morrow, 1986); Susan Faludi, *Backlash: The Undeclared War against American Women* (New York: Crown Publishers, 1991); and Nicholas Davidson, *The Failure of Feminism* (Buffalo, N.Y.: Prometheus Books, 1988); see also Susan M. Hartmann, *From Margin to Mainstream: American Women and Politics since 1960* (Philadelphia: Temple University Press, 1989); and Christine Hoff Sommers, *Who Stole Feminism? How Women Have Betrayed Women* (New York: Simon & Schuster, 1994).

71. From my notes on the Women and the Constitution: A Bicentennial Perspec-

tive Symposium, 10-12 February 1988, Atlanta, Ga.; which I attended as a delegate from Tennessee.

72. McLaren, *History of Contraception*, 240-41; and Judith D. Schwartz, "How Birth Control Has Changed Women's Sexuality," *Glamour*, March 1993, 236-37, 270, 272.

73. Sarah Weddington, *A Question of Choice* (New York: G.P. Putnam's Sons, 1992), 11 et passim.

74. Ira Glasser, "Reagan's Legacy: Supreme Court Threatens to Turn Back the Clock on Civil Rights," *Civil Liberties*, Spring-Summer 1988, 1, 6; "High Court Asked to Review *Roe v. Wade*, *National Times*, October-December 1988, 1, 3; and "Facts on Reproductive Rights," NOW Legal Defense and Education Fund, June 1988.

75. "Facts on Reproductive Rights." On 20 July 1990 President Bush learned that Justice William J. Brennan was going to retire from the U.S. Supreme Court. This gave Bush the opportunity to nominate a replacement; his choice was David Souter: see Richard Lacayo, "A Blank Slate," *Time*, 6 August 1990, 16-18; and Margaret Carlson, "An Eighteenth Century Man," ibid., 19-22.

76. *Landmark Briefs and Arguments of the Supreme Court of the United States: Constitutional law*, vol. dealing with *Webster v. Reproductive Health Services, Inc.*, 1989, Documents for Landmark Abortion Cases, University Publications of America, Bethesda, Md.

77. *New York Times*, 10 November 1993.

78. National Organization for Women, express wire, n.d (February 1994); and Associated Press story, *Kingsport* (Tenn.) *Times-News*, 25 January 1994.

79. Anne Gibson and Timothy Fast, *The Women's Atlas of the United States* (New York: Facts on File Publications, 1986), 14, 26, 32, 35, 58-61, 70, 78, 168, 172, et passim.

80. Women journalists have also made their mark: see, e.g., Maria Braden, *She Said What? Interviews with Women Newspaper Columnists* (Lexington: University Press of Kentucky, 1993); and Sallie Bingham, *Passion and Prejudice: A Family Memoir* (New York: Alfred A. Knopf, 1989); see also Susan E. Tifft and Alex S. Jones, *The Patriarch: The Rise and Fall of the Bingham Dynasty* (New York: Summit Books, 1991).

81. See Lise Vogel, *Mothers on the Job: Maternity Policy in the U.S. Workforce* (Newark, N.J.: Rutgers University Press, 1993); and Arlene Skolnick, *Embattled Paradise: The American Family in an Age of Uncertainty* (New York: Basic Books, 1991); see also Eileen Boris, *Home to Work: Motherhood and the Politics of Industrial Homework in the United States* (Philadelphia: Temple University Press, 1994).

82. Data in *Hope Healthletter*, October 1988, 7; see also Arlie Hochschild and Anne Machung, *The Second Shift* (New York: Avon, 1990).

83. Quoted in Associated Press story in *Kingsport* (Tenn.) *Times-News*, 12 January 1989.

84. David Van Biema and Michael Wallis, "Activist Wilma Mankiller Is Set to Become the First Female Chief of the Cherokee Nation," *People*, 2 December 1985, 91-92, quotation on 92; see also Wilma Mankiller and Michael Wallis, *A Chief and Her People: An Autobiography of the Principal Chief of the Cherokee Nation* (New York: St. Martin's Press, 1993).

85. "A Woman for Lear's: Maria Elena Torano of Miami, Florida," *Lear's*, September 1993, 101-2, 116; see also Ronald H. Bayor, "Models of Ethnic and Racial Politics in the Urban Sunbelt South," in *Searching for the Sunbelt: Historical Perspectives on a Region*, ed. Raymond A. Mohl (Knoxville: University of Tennessee Press, 1990), 104-23;

and Elliott Barkan, "New Origins, New Homeland, New Region: American Immigration and the Emergence of the Sunbelt, 1955-1985," in ibid., 124-48; and Raymond A. Mohl, "Miami: New Immigrant City," in ibid., 149-75.

86. Quoted in Dougan, "Arkansas Married Woman's Property Law," 3.

87. Goldfield, *Promised Land*, 224.

Epilogue

1. *Kingsport* (Tenn.) *Times-News*, 26 September 1989.

2. Ibid., 30 April 1993.

3. Margaret Atwood, *The Handmaid's Tale* (New York: Fawcett Crest, 1985), passim; "About the Author" appears at the end of the book.

4. From my notes on the Women and the Constitution symposium.

Index